DEVELOPING WITH L   ...
Object-Oriented Techniques

DEVELOPING WITH DELPHI
Object-Oriented Techniques

Edward C. Weber
J. Neal Ford
Christopher R. Weber

For book and bookstore information

http://www.prenhall.com

Prentice Hall PTR
Upper Saddle River, NJ 07458

Library of Congress Cataloging–in–Publication Data

Weber, Edward C.
    Developing with Delphi : object-oriented techniques / Edward C.
  Weber, Christopher R. Weber, J. Neal Ford.
        p.   cm.
    Includes index.
    ISBN 0–13–378118–6
    1. Object-oriented programming (Computer science)   2. Delphi
  (Computer file)   3. Computer software—Development.   I. Weber,
  Christopher R.   II. Ford, J. Neal.   III. Title.
  QA76.64.W42 1996
  005.265—dc20   95–41344
                                                              CIP

Acquisitions editor: Mark Taub
Cover designer: Anthony Gemmellaro
Cover director: Jerry Votta
Manufacturing buyer: Alexis R. Heydt
Compositor/Production services: Pine Tree Composition, Inc.

The publisher offers discounts on this book when ordered in
bulk quantities.

For more information contact:
  Corporate Sales Department
  Prentice Hall PTR
  One Lake Street
  Upper Saddle River, New Jersey 07458

  Phone: 800–382–3419
  Fax: 201–236–7141
  email: corpsales@prenhall.com

Printed in the United States of America
10 9 8 7 6 5 4 3 2

ISBN: 0-13-378118-6

Prentice Hall International (UK) Limited, *London*
Prentice Hall of Australia Pty. Limited, *Sydney*
Prentice Hall Canada, Inc., *Toronto*
Prentice Hall Hispanoamericana, S.A., *Mexico*
Prentice Hall of India Private Limited, *New Delhi*
Prentice Hall of Japan, Inc., *Tokyo*
Simon & Schuster Asia Pte. Ltd., *Singapore*
Editora Prentice Hall do Brasil, Ltda., *Rio de Janeiro*

*To Diana, Candy, and Diane—who reflect our
love brighter than it is cast*

CONTENTS

ACKNOWLEDGMENTS

The authors would like to collectively thank the following for their support in this effort: the folks and Borland International who created a development tool which inspired us to start this process; Mark Taub and the folks at Prentice-Hall, who took on this project and made it a reality; The DSW Group, for allowing us to be creative while providing our livelihoods; Kathryn Alderman, who helped us out of many a jam; Jim Needham who helped us over some technical humps in the road; and finally, to all the friends and family who serve as our support systems in like. Also . . .

Ed would like to thank the people who gave him the inspiration, friendship, and love without which, this book would not exist: First and fittingly to my mother and father who gave me the determination to overcome obstacles; my brothers and sister who always have given me someone to look up to; Chris and Neal, for making this book a reality in spite of me; Sue Udall, who has always been there when I need her; Sharon Sherman, whose reliability serves to keep my workdays sane; Tom Janney, whose advice and willing ear are more than any accountant should provide; Terry Dietzler, my partner in business (and occasionally on the tennis court) for understanding and support through all of the difficult times in the past nine years; finally and most importantly, to the woman I love, Diana. She has filled my life with more joy than I deserve.

Neal would like to thank the following: Borland International generally and Anders Hejlsberg specifically for such a fabulous technical feat; The DSW Group, for providing the atmosphere that made this book possible; my mother Hazel Campbell, who made this possible in multiple and myriad ways; Sharon Sherman for generally keeping the world organized; Dr. James Head and Dr. K.N. King, for excellent and enduring instruction on the craft of programming; Chuck Huggins, for continuing friendship and support; Maggie and Blanche, who helped in every way that they could; and finally, my wife Candy, whom I love more than anything else in the world. Ultimately, she made this book possible by her continuing support and perseverance for a husband whos career and hobby have merged.

Chris would like to express special gratitude to his family without whose support his contribution to this book would have been impossible; most of all to my wife Diane who showed far more patience with me during the writing of this book than I deserved, and to my two boys, Douglas and Nicholas, who often made due without their dad for undue lengths of time. Also, special thanks to Neal who kept our team abreast of Delphi developments, and to Ed for asking me to join in the authorship of this tome. OK, Honey-bear, now we have time to go for a walk.

CHAPTER 1

OVERVIEW: WHY DELPHI?

In setting out to write a book on PC-based software engineering, we were troubled with the choice of what development product to incorporate into our effort. Having a firm knowledge of the concepts of structured, modular, and object-oriented programming made cataloguing our requirements easier, but finding our candidate quite difficult. Few off-the-shelf products embodied even the majority of our prerequisites in these areas—until Delphi. It fulfills them all. Delphi has emerged as one of the rare development tools that allows for the creation of truly well-crafted software applications while at the same time offers the ease of use and toolset required by today's development professionals.

Our story really begins in the summer of 1994. We had attended the Borland International Conference in Orlando, FL in order to make some business contacts and improve our knowledge base for a seminar series we were about to embark on—teaching dBASE for Windows. During the conference, we saw and read several tidbits about a new product coming from Borland code named "Delphi", a Pascal-based tool for creating applications under Windows. We, like so many of you, were familiar with Pascal as our first programming language back in college, so we decided to attend a short session on the product. Well, none of us had done much with Pascal since our university days, and the shock we received was profound.

Most other development products and languages face a trade-off between a quality code base and an appealing user friendly interface. Products like Dataease, Access, and Visual Basic provide a robust user interface, but they lack the strong language base needed to create truly large and robust applications. Products like C++, Smalltalk, and Ada provide excellent language support but lack a flexible and easy to use set of tools. Delphi promised the power and reusability of Object Pascal with an easy to use and robust toolset.

1

Delphi is now a reality. In the text that follows, we will outline the significant features that set Delphi apart from other application development tools. In subsequent chapters, we will detail our strategies for its use.

FULLY OBJECT-ORIENTED DEVELOPMENT

With the increase in the availability of software development tools, selecting a tool that provides the best language features becomes critical for both productivity and product durability. Most development experts agree that object-oriented languages provide the most flexible and stable environment for creating large mission-critical applications.

There are several languages that support object-oriented software development on the market today. C++ is the most commonly used. Because C++ is so widely used, why not use it for our purposes? Until recently, most C++ language products had very little tool support. Although the situation has improved, limited support for database access and the complexity of the C++ language present a barrier to all but the most hearty of developers.

Delphi's Object Pascal is a much simpler object-oriented language and, as a result, easier for most developers to learn. It also has inherent support for database manipulation and an extremely diverse set of components making novice development in the product easy. Delphi supports all of the major constructs of an object-oriented language including *abstraction, encapsulation, polymorphism,* and *inheritance.* Additionally, it provides several layers of information hiding that makes the creation and use of components (Window objects) easier and safer. As part of our design approach, we will review the basic tenets of object-oriented languages and why they are so important to development today and in the future.

VISUAL TOOLS

Delphi is one of the first Windows-based development tools designed to run under a single document interface (SDI). This feature has been requested by many users of Windows applications and is a large part of the Windows95 interface. By creating Delphi to meet this standard, Borland has prepared the product for integration into this new operating system.

Delphi also provides a two-way tools environment. This unique product feature provides developers the ability to build an application both graphically with visual tools and directly in source code. Two-way tools are an important feature of language-based development tools. Because tool information is stored directly in your source code, the risk of lost intermediate design files is eliminated.

In other development packages, programmers change their generated source code in order to "tweak" the application. This can render later use of these customized tools impossible. Borland, on the other hand, has pioneered the ability to have Windows design tools that directly read and manipulate source code. Should you desire to tweak a Delphi

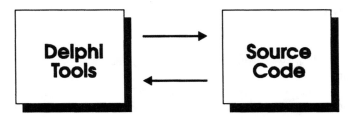

FIGURE 1.1   Two-way Tools

source code file, you can still reuse the tool later, and your code enhancements will be reflected in the tool (see Figure 1.1). Other software tools generate source code for objects from tool data-storage files or behind the scenes. User modifications made after object instantiation are not reflected in the tool itself (see Figure 1.2).

Delphi also smooths the learning curve necessary to understand tool usage and storage. Authors of articles and books on other products go to special pains to explain the data storage mechanism of tools in those environments. This information is necessary for their readers to truly master application development. Yet all too often, the tools generated in these products are inflexible and cannot easily accommodate common functions needed by the developer. In fact, most developers establish their own design standards a priori and are then forced to find ways to make their tools behave in a manner appropriate to that standard. Conversely, Delphi tool development has been engineered so that a user can configure and even redefine the entire interface. This promotes form and application creation with the application's functional abstraction in mind.

It is also a pleasant surprise to learn that Delphi is actually written in Delphi. Because of this, you can view the source code for all of the components in the Delphi Visual Component Library (VCL). These facts point out even more about this product. It tells us that Delphi is completely configurable and that we can even change the behavior of the default object classes (though, as we shall later see, this is a dangerous and bad idea). Delphi's open architecture not only provides us the opportunity to customize the environment, but it also shows us the true capabilities of the language base.

FIGURE 1.2   Traditional One-way Development Tools

COMPILED EXECUTABLES

While a few other application languages provide both graphical and programmatic tools, most are limited to using a run-time engine that interprets the code. Once again, Delphi departs from the standard. Because of the efficiency of the Pascal compiler, Delphi can parse and compile source code into machine code very quickly. While interpreted language products like Visual Basic for Applications and Powerbuilder provide flexible tools, they do not allow for the compilation of integrated executable files (see Figure 1.3).

It is easy to see how much smaller and faster machine code is when compared to interpreted code. Machine code level compilation also provides us with the ability to create Windows compliant DLLs (Dynamic Link Libraries). Developers in other environments need to use outside tools to create these highly reuseable sets of source code. Delphi provides you with this feature as an inherent part of the development environment.

There is an idea floating around that other products will "catch-up" with this technology. This is incorrect. In order to create this type of compiled code, a language requires strong data-typing. While some languages provide this (notably C, C++, and ASM), it is very difficult for them to make tools that operate as efficiently. Without venturing far afield into a lengthy discussion about compiler technology, suffice it to say that the speed at which the Pascal compiler works is not possible in languages that are not designed around creating fast compilers. This is attributable to the unique "grammar" structure of the Pascal language.

LANGUAGE STANDARD

Nicholas Wirth created the Pascal language in the late 1960s. Designed as a teaching language, Pascal quickly developed a strong following among computer science students and professionals. The history of software languages has played a large role in the longevity

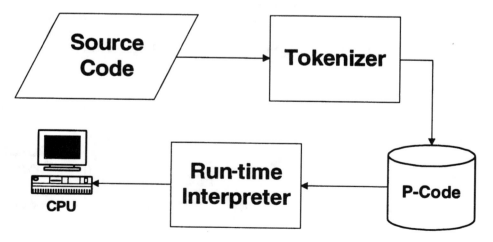

FIGURE 1.3   Traditional P-Code Language Processing

of the Pascal language. Earlier languages were designed around the role that they would play in the workplace. Pascal was designed around the concept of simplicity. This is critical in understanding why Delphi is so usable.

Wirth originally envisioned Pascal as a follow-on language to Algol 60. As Wirth worked with the team that designed Algol 68, he came to believe that the language being designed was overly complex and tried to incorporate too much into the language definition. He developed Pascal in an effort to reduce the symbol set associated with a language. As a result, Pascal has very few reserved words and is designed with the idea that additions to the language should be written in the language itself. This same concept was later used by Kernnigan and Ritchie to develop the C language.

Delphi takes this concept to the next logical level. With an object-oriented language base, Delphi relies on the developer to create reusable components in order to extend the product's basic features. (Borland ships a library of components with Delphi in order to give the developer a "leg up" on this task.) Because the compiler can parse source code so quickly, it is possible to use components created in Delphi as if they were native to the language.

Nearly all computer science departments now teach programming in Pascal. This gives many computer professionals a familiarity with the language. Pascal's simplicity continues to provide an easy learning curve for those new to the language.

CONCLUSION

We have designed this book to teach you the fundamental aspects of quality application design and implementation. We first cover the basics of application design through a review of design methodologies available to developers. We then review the basic tenets of object-oriented programming and discuss why it has emerged as the archetype for new language development. We couple this paradigm with our design techniques and show you how to apply them to the development of Delphi components and applications. Lastly, we demonstrate the methodologies needed to create large client/server applications using various database server platforms.

CHAPTER 2

SOFTWARE ENGINEERING CONCEPTS

Many Delphi95 developers are new to the object-oriented programming environment. As new "OOP-philes", they are unaware of the reasons for and capabilities of an object-oriented language. This chapter is designed to teach the basic concepts of software engineering with OOP. We will begin with a brief review of software development and the strides that have been made to improve the software creation process. We will see that the need for better tools has resulted in the coming of age of object-oriented languages.

SOFTWARE HISTORY

When man first started to construct dwellings, the task was a somewhat haphazard process. Small buildings were created easily and problems that cropped up later could quickly be fixed. The techniques used to create small buildings were soon abandoned as shelter requirements became more complex. The old methods just wouldn't work anymore as larger structures began to collapse upon themselves, much to the chagrin of the occupants. Out of these calamities architectural engineering was born. The creation of modular construction components as a result of standardized measurements, is at least as old as organized civilization.

Early construction tools were limited to stone and mud, but even with these limitations fantastic creations were possible. One needs to only look at the great pyramids of Khafra and Cyops at Giza to see the accomplishments of ancient civilizations. Craftsmanship, time, and patience were the key. Over time, as materials began to be prefabricated, more flexible and less labor-intensive techniques were introduced. Now, the modern skyscraper with its prefab steel girders and premeasured components serves as a lesson for what can be achieved with standardized materials and improved engineering techniques. The Sears Tower took far less people and time to construct than the pyramids. Admittedly, it won't last as long, but then again, it was never meant to.

What does all of this have to do with software? Everything! The history of software development is analogous to that of construction. Early software projects were small, requiring only a few developers, customized code, and little time. These programs served their users well. However, as system requirements increased, the old development methods used were no longer sufficient. Applications became too complex and began to collapse upon themselves, leaving developers scratching their collective heads. Larger and larger software development projects have brought about the need for more robust development tools and techniques in software engineering.

The art of software development began with the first computer, the ENIAC, just as knowledge about building began with man's first structures. However, the theory of software development started as an idea before the first machines were created. The EDVAC Report written by von Neumann in 1954, outlined the first interface between hardware and software. Most modern hardware and its underlying software has been based on Von Neuman's basic design. Like the stones of the pyramids, once machine code became too cumbersome to use, higher level languages began to flourish. FORTRAN, COBOL, and ALGOL were among the early standouts in the area of language development. We will see that these languages, while useful and powerful in their time, now appear as the split trees of log cabin construction when compared to the modular and object-oriented languages of today.

PROGRAMMING IN THE LARGE

Consider the typical software PC development project of the 1980s. It was probably very small and used by, at best, a handful of users. It manipulated department level data and produced a small group of reports. Due to the limitations of the hardware and software, most large applications resided on a mainframe or minicomputer. Any interoffice connectivity or data-handling capabilities rested with programmers in the MIS Department who were required to use tools and write applications that had lifespans of up to 15 years. COBOL emerged as the language of choice for most business software development projects.

As PC hardware and connectivity improved, more software decision makers opted to move development to desktop platforms. Unfortunately, the tools and techniques that had been used on host platforms proved difficult to migrate. Software developed with those tools required a great deal of maintenance. If you examine the goals of most development professionals, you'll find a great deal of commonality, regardless of the platform or tools used. These goals typically include maintainability and quick development as priorities. Other goals might be extensibility, documentation, cost, and reusability. Each are closely related, and effect one another. Faster development naturally leads to lower costs. Reuse typically results in less maintenance and faster development.

As you can see from Figure 2.1, the more time spent by a programmer in a develop-

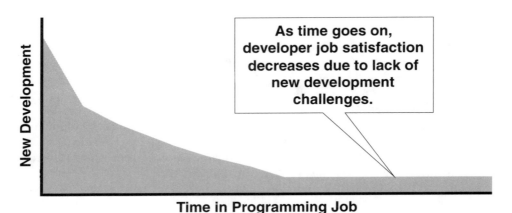

FIGURE 2.1   Job Satisfaction vs. Time in a Development Shop

ment shop, the less likely he or she will spend working on new development. This is due to the need to maintain existing applications produced by the shop. Once a programmer writes one application, they are required to maintain it. Because most PC-based applications are coupled to the individual programmer's own abstraction, it is difficult for others to maintain these applications. This cycle leads to an established developer getting bored and frustrated with his job and moving on. New maintenance programmers, hired as replacements, invariably come to the conclusion that the previous job holder didn't know what they were doing, because the application doesn't measure up to the new developer's abstraction of how the application should work. An endless cycle begins.

If you were to magnify this problem as it applies to large-scale application development, you would see why these significant issues must be addressed. Programming in the large presents issues not normally addressed in small development projects. As you add programmers to a project, you begin to realize just how many problems exist in traditional development methodologies. In the following sections, we will address a few different development methodologies and discuss their strengths and weaknesses.

STRUCTURED PROGRAMMING

Most application developers start their development career by learning structured programming. Structured programming relies on a process known as "top-down" design. Within this process, developers identify the task at hand and break it down into small pieces that can be easily understood. This process is known as *decomposition* (Figure 2.2).

Decomposition provides the developer with a list of tasks that must be completed in order to finish the project. The decomposition must begin with an *abstraction* of the sys-

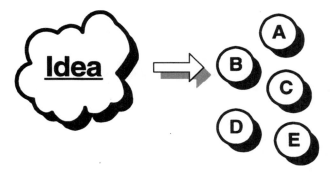

FIGURE 2.2 Decomposition

tem to be created. The abstraction is a perspective of what needs to be accomplished in order for the system to be complete. This perspective is generally system specific and provides the developer with a way to approach the application. A typical decomposition leads to the development of a system that has a top-down architecture. This type of system has a main routine that branches off functionality into smaller and smaller subroutines.

A top-down structure is a natural extension to the decomposition of the system. Generally the decomposition is based on functional aspects of the job to be done. Each of the circles in Figure 2.3 can be considered a functional piece of the system to be created.

Once the design process is complete, the implementation phase of the software development cycle can begin. From the original system abstraction, the system architecture is determined. For this reason, the system abstraction is critical. A great deal of time and learning must take place in the initial phase of system design to ensure a proper and useable abstraction.

Applications written using the decomposition model can be broken up into modules, each of which perform a specified task as defined in the abstraction. As these modules become too complex, developers break them down further into smaller modules in order to simplify the development process by isolating subtasks. Much of the application writing process and modularization is dependent on the language chosen to create the system. In fact, the choice of language can significantly change the final configuration of the system's modules. Because no software development process is started without a mind as to the tools to be used, care should be taken early in the design process to ensure a sensi-

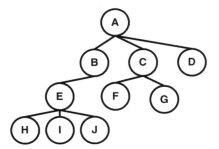

FIGURE 2.3 Top-Down System Architecture

ble abstraction and module configuration that is realizable within the bounds of the selected tools.

Once an application has been written by a developer or development team, a methodology is usually established for later development. This methodology is used in subsequent system development effort and slowly improved. In future projects, the development team will typically copy sections of source code from earlier applications in order to use them for the new one. This type of approach is generally referred to as a *template system.* Figure 2.4 elucidates the application of a template system on the development process.

The template approach offers many advantages over virgin coding. First, it enforces an application architecture across different systems. This adds to maintainability and typically provides a consistent user interface among a suite of applications. Template programming also provides a systematic approach for new team members ensuring a consistent standard across future applications. Learning by new team members is also reduced due to the lessened software surface area that must be mastered before an application can be delivered. This can be likened to learning to drive a car. The new driver does not need to learn how the car works. He or she only needs to learn how to apply driving techniques.

Template software development techniques are also useful because they create more stable applications. Once a template is perfected, developers no longer need to worry about the possible errors that might crop up in the architecture of the template code. Finally, template programs tend to be very flexible. Using an existing template does not limit the scope or complexity of a new application. It just provides a launching point to avoid the redundancies of creating new application techniques. The structured programming approach to software development using templates has served the needs of many software teams for years.

Unfortunately, large-scale development and constant reuse reveals cracks in the template methodology.

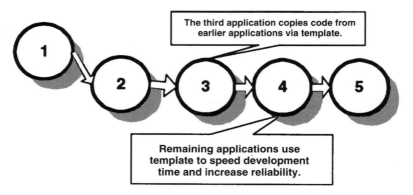

FIGURE 2.4   Template Approach for New Systems

LIMITS OF STRUCTURED PROGRAMMING

The abstraction used in creating a software system designed with structured programming in mind does not focus its attention on maintainability or code reuse. The focus is instead placed on the application at hand. With users and management teams breathing down the software professional's neck, it is easy to lose focus on the long-term needs of the developers, users, and management alike. If the developer instead focuses on the long-term view, he or she will be more likely to achieve professional goals and meet the user's needs now and in the future.

By focusing on the application at hand, the abstraction used to create the initial templates for software development are flawed if viewed in the light of reuseability. This abstraction leads to later modification of the template for other applications. While at first these modifications seem minor, one must realize that each change to a template creates a new version of the code. This *versioning* leads to a larger and larger volume of source code to maintain which, in turn, increases long-term software costs. If we again use the analogy of programming to construction, the pyramids of Egypt typify the limits of structured programming. Each pyramid created taught the Egyptians something about construction. This being the case, each pyramid was slightly different. Even those built around the same time period have their slopes set to different angles. What is the likelihood that stones cut for one pyramid could be used in another? Slim indeed.

Template-based development also can prove to be inflexible. As templates are improved, existing systems based on older versions are not easily updated. It is extremely unlikely that a software professional would have the time to revisit older applications in order to add improvements developed for newer systems. The prevailing attitude says, "If it ain't broke, don't fix it." This is wise given the constraints of the methodology. The Egyptians never went back to improve older pyramid designs, they just built them bigger and better the next time.

Another limit imposed by template programming is a lack of composability (see Figure 2.5). Abstractions used to create a new software application are decomposed to identify the modules needed to complete the project. Typically, these elements are not composable, that is they cannot be used in different combinations to achieve a different goal.

Since software written to a specific abstraction is not originally designed for reuse,

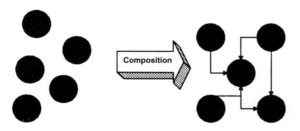

FIGURE 2.5 Composability Implies the Ability to Reconfigure Component Parts

composability is generally not a goal of the developer. This limitation provides the basis for the current paradigm in software production, *modular programming.*

MODULAR PROGRAMMING

The need to create truly reuseable software components is the basis of modular software construction. By realizing that software creation is as much a tools building process as it is an applications development process, software professionals can greatly reduce the time spent on new development and maintenance. Software developers are some of the last few professionals that create their own tools. Independent application developers should realize that this includes them. Each application should be thought of as an opportunity to learn new skills and create new tools that can be used in later development.

There are rules that should be followed before setting off in creating new tools. It would probably be a bad idea to create a new power saw before evaluating the safety issues involved. Software development is no different. Imagine a routine that performs unexpected activities when used by an unsuspecting developer. The likely consequences would be the abandonment of the routine in favor of writing something new. This is all too often the situation in software development. Each developer uses his or her own tools mainly because no one else's will do the job due to their tools' modular limitations.

Abstraction

The first step to creating truly reuseable modularized systems is to learn to identify a *generalized abstraction.* As we mentioned earlier, most applications are built from a specific abstraction. As such, these abstractions are not very portable to other applications. Creating a generalized abstraction requires experience. Try to imagine a builder attempting to fashion tools for construction without ever having built something before. The tools would likely not meet the builder's needs and would be discarded.

Software professionals must have some experience creating applications before they attempt to fashion tools for the process. Working with experienced developers certainly helps in this process. Once a sufficient amount of experience is brought to bear on a development problem, tools can be designed to handle future occurrences. By recognizing the general pattern of the problem domain, the tools can be fashioned in such a way as to cover the common manifestations of that problem.

We no longer write applications in assembler. The reason for this is simple. Assembly language requires a great deal of code surface area to write and maintain. Assembly code is not easily grouped together into logical pieces. This is a requirement for the human brain to comprehend a complex set of items. Humans perform an operation called "chunking" in order to grasp a large set of individual items. Without a clear delineation for categorizing the source code, the chunking of assembly code is difficult. If we were to unravel the surface area of assembly code for an application into a line, it would be very long.

Other languages provide a more digestible surface area. The Fortran language exists at a higher level of abstraction. Its surface area is smaller than assembler. Fortran is designed around an abstraction that also exists at a higher level than assembler and it is designed for a more specific purpose. However, it does not have all of the capabilities of assembly language. Access to low-level hardware has been sacrificed for development speed and maintainability.

Delphi's Object-Pascal, like Fortran, also exists at a higher level than assembler, but its abstraction is different. It is designed around application development in the Windows environment. Figure 2.6 depicts the breadth of the different abstractions.

With less surface area, Delphi applications are easier to develop and maintain under the Windows environment. A fourth language has also been added to the figure. The *My Delphi* language is not currently selling on the market. This is because, as its name implies, it is a customized version of the Delphi language. Because of the facets of modular programming, developers can create language versions that are based on their own abstractions.

Object-Pascal is a very simple language. Delphi has merely added functions and object classes that make the development environment easier to work in by reducing the surface area. Delphi's Visual Component Library (VCL) is written in Object-Pascal and provides the initial starting point for creating the *My Delphi*.

In order to create your own language base, you must establish an abstraction that is useable. This requires knowledge of what your typical applications will need to do. We will demonstrate how easy it is to extend the Delphi language and component base to create a language abstraction that meets your needs.

Semantic Abstraction

The trick to creating a usable abstraction for any given language also relies on the developer's ability to establish a *semantic abstraction*. Most discussions of object-oriented programming use a language as a basis for the discussion. The language used also serves to

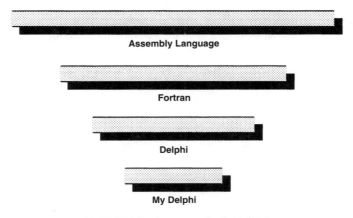

FIGURE 2.6   Language Surface Area

drive an abstract's implementation. A semantic abstraction is critical to the creation of reusable tools. Each language has a unique architecture. This architecture leads to application design being structured in a particular way. As water flows on a path of least resistance, so does application development. By understanding the way in which applications are most easily and efficiently created in a given language, you can most easily create tools for that language. This process serves to mold the abstraction creation and point to a "best" way of creating application development tools.

Published Interface

In order for later developers to understand how an asset you've created should be used or to know whether the asset even exists, a *published interface* is necessary. A published interface documents how your routine or component should be used. It should contain any information the user of the asset will need. In fact, the interface should be established even before any work is done to create the asset. This ensures that the concept used has been completely thought through prior to implementation. It is the equivalent of storyboarding a user interface design before writing an application.

Information Hiding

Another aspect of creating a set of quality reusable code is *information hiding*. The user of a set of routines should need no knowledge of the inner workings of the routines. This allows for a more flexible design and provides a level of safety in case of future modifications. By hiding the implementation details of a routine or component, a developer can have the freedom to change it later to improve performance.

An automobile provides a useful example of information hiding. Most drivers have no real knowledge of the inner workings of the car. They merely have a knowledge of the user's manual which provides them the means through which they can drive the car. Should a manufacturer decide to change some aspect of the car's inner workings, it will not generally affect the way the car works. Suppose the car manufacturer changes the way the float mechanism works within the gas tank to make it more accurate. The float is designed to give the driver feedback as to how much fuel is left in the tank. The meter on the dashboard reflects this information, though unbeknownst to the driver, in a more accurate fashion. The red light still tells the driver that the car is about to run out of gas.

This change does not affect the use of the car as long as the driver is working within the published interface. The published interface says, "when the red light comes on, fill the tank with gas." Should the user of a subsystem decide to utilize internal information about the subsystem to get greater performance, he or she will run the danger of losing the advantages of information hiding. Suppose the driver of the car learned that when the light comes on, there are really two gallons of gas left before the tank is empty. If the driver uses this information, he or she can keep driving for another 30 or 40 miles after the light goes on before *really* running out of gas. This information might suit the driver well until a new float is installed in the tank. The new, more accurate float may signal that gas

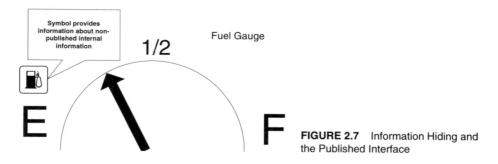

Symbol provides information about non-published internal information

1/2   Fuel Gauge

E   F

FIGURE 2.7   Information Hiding and the Published Interface

is low with only one half of a gallon left. The driver, operating under the knowledge of the old float's accuracy, could be left stranded (see Figure 2.7).

The concept of information hiding and its limits provide an important barrier between a modularized subsystem and the surrounding application. If a subsystem does not provide a needed functionality, then it is incumbent upon the subsystem's designer to implement that aspect. A user of a subsystem should never peek past the published interface, less they be stranded when the internal workings of the subsystem are modified.

If a subsystem cannot be modified, careful documentation of any "barrier crossings" must be made, and those crossings must be tested each time the subsystem is modified. The need for constant retesting and intimate knowledge of a subsystem should be deterrent enough to keep users of modular subsystems from crossing the published interface barrier that separates the subsystem from the implementing application.

Encapsulation

Information hiding provides only a knowledge barrier between modular code and a using application. *Encapsulation* is a technique that provides a "physical" barrier between a subsystem and the application that uses it. Delphi, with its Object-Pascal basis, has a huge amount of encapsulation support. Most routines are designed to perform a task that has been identified in the application abstraction. Unfortunately, an abstraction generally does not specify the means by which a routine is to be linked into the application.

Routines written for applications are often not protected from external factors as they should be. Each routine (or object) should be created in such a way as to not interfere with or be interfered by any external routines. Encapsulation is critical to the creation of reusable assets. Without encapsulation, function code may not affect an application adversely the first time it is used. Later uses of the same code can lead to unexpected side effects unintended by the designer of the routine. Consider the appliances you use around the home. Imagine the frustration of plugging in your new popcorn popper only to find out when you turn it on that it changes your TV's channel setting. These are wholly unrelated functions. Without encapsulation, routines can similarly affect the outlying application just as unexpectedly.

Pascal blocks (BEGIN . . . END) provide a built-in level of encapsulation by preventing variables created in the block from being visible outside of the block. Variables can be seen within nested blocks. While handy to be able to access, the common use of variables created in "outer" blocks by "inner" blocks can lead to less reusability. This concept of variable *coupling* will be discussed further on. Pascal *units* also provide a built-in mechanism for encapsulating internal operations. The *interface* section of a unit identifies those items with scope extending beyond the unit. These exposed items are available to any routine that uses the unit. Consider the following unit.PAS file.

```
unit Heartcal;

interface
Function TargetHeartRate(Age, SittingHeartRate: Integer): ↵
          Integer;

implementation

Function MaxRate(Age: Integer): Integer;
begin
  Result := 220 - Age;
end;

Function TargetHeartRate(Age, SittingHeartRate: Integer): ↵
          Integer;
var
   HeartRateReserve: Integer;
begin
  HeartRateReserve := MaxRate(Age)-SittingHeartRate;
  Result := ROUND(HeartRateReserve*0.75) + SittingHeartRate;
end;
end.
```

This simple unit demonstrates a readily available encapsulation technique that can be used in Delphi. Excluding the MaxRate function declaration from the interface portion of the unit prevents it from being called by other programs that use this unit. This technique prevents scoping errors for applications that might have a MaxRate calculation of their own that has nothing to do with physical training heart rate calculations.

Suppose a unit in an application attempted to contain a uses clause that appeared like the one below and the MaxRate function in our HeartCal unit was identified in the interface section in the unit.

```
uses
   SysUtils, WinTypes, WinProcs, Messages, Classes, Graphics,
   Controls, Forms, Dialogs, StdCtrls, Finance, HeartCal;
```

If the `Finance` unit contained a `MaxRate` function needed by the new unit it would be unable to call it without the unit identifier prefix: `Finance.MaxRate`. While this solution may work, it places an undue burden on the developer to remember where all of his needed functions reside. All of this is due to the fact that Delphi resolves identifier references within units from right to left. The `HeartCal` interface functions would be used before any others in the uses statement. By encapsulating the MaxRate function inside of the unit we can eliminate a possible unintended external use of the function.

Delphi supports additional levels of encapsulation when using units. According to the *Delphi Users Guide,* it is possible for units to access functions stored in other units not included within the uses statement. This is possible via a type of "uses chaining" technique. Suppose unit A uses unit B. If within unit B's interface section, the uses clause contains unit C, then unit A will have access to all routines declared within unit C's interface section (Figure 2.8).

Unit A can call the functions defined within unit C only through the use of the unit identifier. For example, if in unit A you wanted to call the MaxRate function, you could do so with the `C.MaxRate` syntax. The unit identifier allows you access to all items declared within the interface portion of the unit. This is not clearly spelled out in the Delphi documentation. Unit A cannot call C's MaxRate function without the unit identifier. While it is possible to call routines declared in units not identified in the uses clause of a unit in this way, we do not recommend it.

By placing calls to functions within units not identified within the uses clause of a unit, a great deal of confusion can arise as to how unit A has access to unit C's functions. This "knowledge" that B uses C, violates the information hiding of unit B and relies on the fact that unit B will always use unit C in the future. Suppose that unit B is changed at a later date and no longer needs to use a function in unit C, and unit C is removed from the interface uses statement in B. Unit A would no longer work because knowledge of B was used in its creation.

While on the subject of unit function access, it is important to point out another aspect that can cause confusion. Suppose unit A needs some of the functionality found in unit B. Unit A would merely include unit B in its uses clause. What if unit B needed something in unit A? Adding unit A to unit B's interface uses clause would cause a recursive compiler reference and prevent the application from being compiled. To get around this problem, it is possible to have unit B place the reference to unit A in its implementation section uses statement. This prevents the recursive problem. Units referenced within

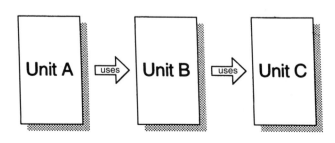

FIGURE 2.8 Cascading Uses between Units in Delphi

the uses statement found in the implementation section of a unit are not available to units that use that unit. To support information hiding, we recommend that unless there is a pressing need for the exporting of units being used in a unit, that all units used be listed in the uses clause within the implementation section.

We will elaborate more about encapsulation as it relates to Delphi as we progress. Suffice it to say that, where possible, it is generally a good idea to isolate functions and variables as much as possible to prevent them from interfering with and being interfered by other units. You should move as many of the function and variable declarations as possible into the implementation section of your units where they will be hidden from the outlying application.

Coupling

Coupling between and within modules in an application is an important issue in development. Any connection, whether direct or indirect, between a module and another portion of the application is considered a **coupling point.** A real world example of coupling is train cars. Each car has a single couple between it and the next car. Why? Wouldn't it be safer to have several coupling points between the cars? The reason that train cars have only one coupling point between them has to do with reusability and portability. Train engines generally do not take the same cars from their starting point to their final destination. Instead, the engine hauls a set of cars to an intermediate point along the route where other trains will meet it. Cars are uncoupled and reattached to other engines to allow them to reach their final destination. This attaching and reattaching of cars would be significantly more difficult if cars had more than one coupling point.

You can think of application functions as train cars. The more coupling points that exist between an application and the routine, the harder it will be to reuse the function in a subsequent application. Coupling points can take on many forms. Every function has at least one coupling point. Without the call to the routine itself, it could not be used in the application. This coupling point is a necessity. Any other coupling points between the function and the application serve to reduce the reusability of the routine. The most common of these are references to external variables not declared in the routine.

Variables declared in the interface portion of a unit can be seen by other units using the unit. This lends to the tendency of developers using these variables within the other units. This use constitutes unnecessary coupling between the units. Consider the following units:

```
unit Fcouple;

interface

uses
    SysUtils, WinTypes, WinProcs, Messages, Classes, Graphics,
    Controls, Forms, Dialogs, StdCtrls;
```

```
type
  TForm1 = class(TForm)
    OK: TButton;
    procedure OKClick(Sender: TObject);
  private
    { Private declarations }
  public
    { Public declarations }
  end;

var
  Form1: TForm1;

implementation

{$R *.DFM}
uses
  UChange;

procedure TForm1.OKClick(Sender: TObject);
begin
  self.Caption := NewCaption;
end;
end.
```

This form unit uses the following UChange unit.

```
unit UChange;

interface
uses
  SysUtils, WinTypes, WinProcs, Messages, Classes, Graphics,
  Controls, Forms, Dialogs;

function NewCaption: string;

implementation
uses
  FCouple;

function NewCaption: string;
begin
  Result := Form1.Caption + '1';
end;
end.
```

As you can see, the FCouple unit uses the UChange unit in its implementation section. This is good encapsulation practice. Unfortunately, there is a higher degree of coupling between these two units than there should be. How could the UChange unit be used again in another application? It cannot unless the new application happened to name a form variable Form1. This is highly unlikely and very restrictive.

You will also notice that the UChange unit uses the FCouple unit within its implementation section. This is another coupling point between the two modules. Again, the likelihood of another application using the same unit name is very low. The best method for removing these unwanted coupling points is through the use of parameters. Parameters can give functions information not known to them at compile time. These units can be modified to utilize Delphi's parameter passing abilities in order to decouple these routines. A newer version of these units follows:

```
unit FCouple;

interface

uses
   SysUtils, WinTypes, WinProcs, Messages, Classes, Graphics,
   Controls, Forms, Dialogs, StdCtrls;

type
   TForm1 = class(TForm)
     OK: TButton;
     procedure OKClick(Sender: TObject);
   private
     { Private declarations }
   public
     { Public declarations }
   end;

var
   Form1: TForm1;

implementation

{$R *.DFM}
uses
   UChange;

procedure TForm1.OKClick(Sender: TObject);
begin
   self.Caption := NewCaption(self);
                     {note the added parameter}
end;
end.
```

The new loosely coupled UChange unit looks like this:

```
function NewCaption(FormRef: TFORM): string;

implementation

function NewCaption(FormRef: TFORM): string;
{the parameter is received}
begin
    Result := FormRef.Caption + '1';
end;
```

A few points need to be explained to understand this new version. The reference to self used in the OKClick event of the form's button can cause confusion. Since the OKClick method is a method of the TForm1 class, self is a reference to the form. So, in the OKClick routine, the parameter being passed to the NewCaption routine in the UChange unit is a TForm1 object.

The NewCaption routine now accepts a parameter called TFormRef. This is typed as a TForm class object. This seems strange since our calling OKClick routine is passing a reference to a TForm1 object. This does not cause a type conflict in the compiler because the TForm1 object is itself a subclass of the TForm class. This use of *type-casting* is readily handled by the compiler and is extremely useful in creating reuseable modules. We will discuss the concept of run-time type identification (RTTI) and typecasting in detail later on.

Notice that there is now no longer a uses clause referencing the FCouple unit in the UChange unit. This uses clause is unnecessary as there are no longer any references to the Form object variable in the Form unit. Once this coupling point is removed, the unit becomes a completely reusable module that can be utilized by any form in any application.

There are other types of coupling points besides variable references. Any unit that uses another unit in order to accomplish its task adds coupling points to the unit. For example, it is common practice to include a uses clause in the interface section of units used to create forms. It is automatically included in any form unit by the Delphi tools. The standard form unit uses clause is shown here.

```
uses
    SysUtils, WinTypes, WinProcs, Messages, Classes, Graphics,
    Controls, Forms, Dialogs, StdCtrls;
```

These units contain all of the units needed to add the components installed in the component palette. Unfortunately, it has often become common practice within the development community to include this uses clause in any unit that needs to reference one of the stock classes (VCL) that come with Delphi. While including all of the units listed above allows you to safely reference any object class in the VCL, it is almost guaranteed to be overkill for most nonform units. You add overhead and a higher degree of coupling between your unit and the units listed in the uses clause. Suppose two of these VCL units are merged into a single unit in a later implementation of Delphi. This would require you to edit each unit that used the now missing unit in order to recompile.

A better practice is to include only those units that are needed within a unit in the uses clause. This lessens the degree of coupling between the unit and the outlying environment and makes the code more maintainable. The uses clause for the `UChange` unit used in our example only needs to access the `TForm` class definition. This means that the unit only needs the `Forms` unit to be included in the interface section of unit.

```
uses Forms;
```

It is generally a good idea to reduce as much as possible the number of items declared or references in the interface section of a unit. This will increase the encapsulation of the unit as well as potentially reduce the number of coupling points needed to use it.

Cohesion

Without a high degree of *cohesion,* module reusability is reduced. Cohesion can be considered the "single-mindedness" of a routine or module. When creating a new application module it is common for developers to write functions that do too much. By this, we mean that the function is designed to perform a set of tasks that may not necessarily need always be executed together. Consider the form in Figure 2.9.

This form is designed to calculate the sales tax on a given sale value. The Click event for the button is designed to calculate the tax and store the string value of it to one of the Label objects on the form. Here is the code that can be used for this task.

```
procedure TSalesCalc.CalcTaxClick(Sender: TObject);
var
    SaleAmount,TaxAmount : single;
const
    StateTax = 0.04;
    LocalTax = 0.01;
begin
    SaleAmount := StrToFloat(self.SaleValue.Text);
    TaxAmount := (StateTax + LocalTax)* SaleAmount;
    self.TotalTax.Caption := FloatToStr(TaxAmount);
end;
```

Notice that the procedure creates constant values for the sales tax rates in order to encapsulate them from possible accidental changes within the procedure. Unfortunately, this routine is not very cohesive. While fairly simple, it actually is performing several different tasks. First, it calculates the state tax and the local tax. These may be needed later in

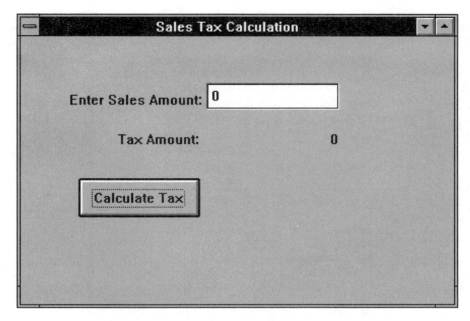

FIGURE 2.9   Sales Tax Calculation Form

the application as separate items. What if you later needed a summation of the local taxes collected on all of the sales for a government filing? The calculation for local tax amounts would have to be rewritten in another routine. Using this type of development technique, it is possible that the same calculation would be performed in several routines throughout the application. The same is true for the state tax calculation. The real purpose of the push-button on the form is to force the display of the total tax amount on the form. The actual calculations needed for this process should be placed in another routine or even another unit. This example, in its current implementation, is an example of *logical cohesion*. Because the sales tax information is related together logically, it has been incorrectly incorporated into a single routine.

The source code listing below shows a better, more cohesive version of the sales tax calculation button's OnClick event. This version uses another unit called USalesTx that contains the two functions CalculateStateTax() and CalculateLocalTax(). Here is the new form unit code encompassing all of the implementation section of the unit:

```
implementation
uses USalesTx; {note the use of the external procedure}

{$R *.DFM}

procedure TSalesCalc.CalcTaxClick(Sender: TObject);
```

```
var
    SaleAmount,TaxAmount : single;
begin
    SaleAmount := StrToFloat(self.SaleValue.Text);
    TaxAmount := CalculateStateTax(SaleAmount)+ ⏎
        CalculateLocalTax(SaleAmount);
    self.TotalTax.Caption := FloatToStr(TaxAmount);
end;
end.
```

Here is the source listing for the USalesTax unit:

```
unit Usalestx;

interface
const
    StateSalesTaxRate = 0.04;
    LocalSalesTaxRate = 0.01;

function CalculateStateTax(const SaleAmount: single): ⏎
        single;

function CalculateLocalTax(const SaleAmount: single): ⏎
        single;

implementation
{ calculates state tax amount given sales amount }
function CalculateStateTax(const SaleAmount: single): ⏎
        single;
begin
    Result := SaleAmount * StateSalesTaxRate
end;
{ calculates local tax amount given sales amount }
function CalculateLocalTax(const SaleAmount: single): ⏎
        single;
begin
    Result := SaleAmount * LocalSalesTaxRate
end;
end.
```

There are a few things to take note of within these new units. First, the uses clause containing the USalesTx reference is within the implementation section of the FSalesTx form's unit. This provides a level of encapsulation and information hiding for any form or routine that might launch this form. The calling form will not have to know anything about the USalesTx unit and will not have any accidental access to it. Also, the *const* declaration for the sales tax amounts has been placed in the interface section of the

`USalesTx` unit. This allows other units to see what the sales tax calculations are based on and so they can have access to them. The form could display the value of the sales tax percentage rates by merely referencing these constants.

You will also note that the calculations have been separated into two distinct functions. They can now be called individually. This is only a very simple example of cohesion. Each time you write a unit or function, you must consider whether or not it is cohesive enough to encourage reuse. A function that performs ten actions is not very reusable if you only want to perform one of them.

A common mistake in attempting to create cohesive routines is to place items that have a similar time dependency in the same routine. A classic example of this is an initialization routine. A typical initialization routine might set any number of variables default values and/or open several files. This type of cohesion is known as *temporal cohesion* and should generally be avoided. You can never be sure when one of these initializations will need to be performed again in the application and be inaccessible due to the temporal cohesion of the routine.

Procedural cohesion occurs when a routine contains several activities that must be performed in a particular order but are otherwise unrelated. These types of routines suffer from a lack of forethought regarding the future of the application. You can never be sure when the order of events in a particular routine will need to be changed or substantially increased. Functions organized with procedural cohesion can become unmanageably large and difficult to reuse.

Communicational cohesion exists in routines that are designed to access a common data structure but perform several unrelated operations. An example of this type of poor cohesion usually centers on a Pascal record or object's internal structure. The routine would be written to originally require some access to the structure. Later, having already written the code to access the structure, the programmer decides to add functionality not originally intended in the routine. This avoids having to redesign the routine to make it more cohesive but leaves it less modular.

Finally, the arbitrary limiting of routine length or scope can result in another type of poor cohesion, *coincidental cohesion*. Creating application routines based not on some specific functionality but, instead, by some arbitrary organizational rule results in this type of cohesion. This type of cohesion is generally referred to as "spaghetti coding" and is commonly avoided by most developers.

It is important to keep cohesion in mind when writing any routine. By not breaking the functionality you want down into several reusable activities, you will most likely have to rewrite or significantly modify your existing work. Cohesion is a critical part of creating modular systems and is too often overlooked.

LIMITS OF MODULAR PROGRAMMING

Given all of the great aspects of modular programming, you might assume it is the best design choice available. Unfortunately, modular design has some flaws. Modular systems are based on the idea that activity is at the core of most applications. By this, we mean that modular systems are always centered around some functionality. This tends to ignore the role that data plays within an application. Data represents the application's reason for existence. Indeed, without the need to track and manipulate data, the application would never be written in the first place.

The real world is a collection of data. Each item in the real world has some characteristics that we can refer to as data. As these items become more complex, the need to track them in some way can become critical enough to warrant the creation of an application. Only then does the focus typically shift the activity that needs to be performed. The activity always remains centered around the data.

Consider an order entry application that needs to track orders that contain customer information. In the real world, you would only need to look at the order to find the customer's name. In a modular application you would typically have some type of data structure that represents the order and passes that structure to a function. The function would traverse the structure and return the customer's name. If the real world worked like a modular application development environment, you would have to take the order over to the customer name machine and feed it the order (hopefully a copy of the order). The machine would then tell you the customer name.

This seems a little silly but it demonstrates an important point. Modular systems do not model the real world very well. They are centered on the activity surrounding the data being tracked and not the data itself. The goal of application development is to successfully model the real world for the user. This way, the application will be more useable and understandable to the user. By modeling the application around the real world, developers can better relate the activities and data being recreated to the user.

Modular applications also suffer some limitations that restrict the reusability of the routines being written. Each exported routine and variable uses up the name space available in the application. This resource problem can manifest itself in application by limiting a future development's ability to use a particular variable name or function name. Modular subsystems can interfere with one and other through name space conflicts. Delphi relieves some of this problem through the encapsulating abilities of units. Because programmers can define routines and variables within the implementation section of a unit, these elements can be protected from accidental usage by other units. Also, this encapsulation prevents the unit from interfering with other units that may have exposed variables or functions of the same name.

Unit encapsulation can only take you so far. Each exposed item (those defined in the interface section of the unit) reduces the amount of free name space in the application and results in a much more restricted development environment.

There is often a need to create and use variations on previously created routines. If the programmer was careful enough, new routines can be written to substitute for cohesive routines written earlier. By practicing good cohesion, developers can give themselves a limited ability to replace the functionality of one routine with a new one. Unfortunately, this capability is very limited and always requires a complete rewrite of the function that must be replaced. There are no facilities to force the new version of a routine to match up with the functionality or even the parameters required of the old version. Additionally, the old version would not be able to coexist with the new version. This means that a unit would not be able to call both the old and modified version of routines with the same name.

Suppose you had an existing SalesTax routine. It might calculate the state sales tax based on given sales amount. This type of routine could serve you well through many applications. Listed here is a sample unit that contains this function:

```
unit Utax2;

interface

function SalesTax(SaleAmount: single): single;

implementation
function SalesTax(SaleAmount: single): single;
const
  Rate = 0.04;

begin
   Result := SaleAmount * Rate;
end;
end.
```

This routine could be used by many other units within an application. It could also be used by more generic routines designed to be used in other applications. Figure 2.10 shows a potential relationship between the SalesTax routine and a few application spe-

FIGURE 2.10 Use of Modular SalesTax Function

cific and generic routines. The shaded modules indicate those that are capable of being used in many applications.

You may want to replace the SalesTax function with a version that adds the local tax as well. This would need to be written using the same routine name with the same unit name. Otherwise the generic routines would not use the new calculation. Writing a new unit of the same name would automatically cause the other units to use this new calculation. Unfortunately, the new unit's calculation is dependent on the earlier version. What would happen if the state sales tax rate changes in the future? Both the older version of the SalesTax routine and the new version would have to be modified. You cannot alleviate this problem by having the new routine call the old routine as part of its functionality. This would only result in a recursive call by the new SalesTax routine of itself. There is no solution in modular programming techniques for this type of problem.

In Chapter 3 we will introduce you to the concepts contained in object-oriented design and the ways in which it allows us to overcome the limitations of structured and modular programming techniques.

CHAPTER **3**

OBJECT-ORIENTED PROGRAMMING

A HISTORY OF OOP

Due to the limits of modular programming, language developers and computer science researchers have looked for ways to make the application development process more closely model the real world. The real world has proven to be a very complex problem to model. The sheer scope of the items and processes that need to be tracked has lead language experts to the concept of object-oriented programming. This type of development environment, while powerful and complex, requires a significant amount of processor speed in order to perform up to the expectations of software developers. Until recently, true object-oriented languages were restricted to the classroom, as computer processor speeds caught up to the language technology.

Simula 67 was the first object-oriented language developed. Created between 1965 and 1967, Simula 67 was the first language to introduce the concept of a *class*. Similar to the block structures found in other languages like Algol, classes allowed for the grouping of both data and activity together. The difference between Simula's class structure and other existing mechanisms was that the class structure served only as a recipe for creating multiple structures with the same organization. This reusability provided a leap in potential productivity.

By creating classes, you, the developer, can take real world items and quantify them more accurately. A class serves as a formula for creating program implementation of the items needed for the application. For example, if you were writing an application to track and maintain orders, you could design an order class to have all of the characteristics and activities that an order can perform. Once your class was established, your application could then be programmed to create other class members, known as *objects*, which would provide necessary application functionality.

This capability of object-oriented languages was carried forward into the languages most commonly used today. These include C++, Eiffel, Smalltalk, Ada, and Object-Pascal. Each of these languages have incorporated various charateristics of object orientation, and each is a different implementation of the object-oriented paradigm. C++ is the object-oriented extension to C. It has object features such as operator overloading, templates, automatic object construction and destruction, and multiple inheritance. Smalltalk is an interpreted language that supports multiple inheritance, and all data types exist as objects. Ada while object-based, not object-oriented, supports activity threading and has generic packages. Popular xBASE languages are also moving toward object-oriented programming. These include Computer Associates Visual Objects, Borland's dBASE for Windows, and Microsoft's Visual FoxPro.

Due to the large design and implementation paradigm shift between object-oriented languages and traditional structured and modular languages, object-oriented languages have only slowly come to be accepted. Much of the knowledge required to design applications written for non-object-oriented languages is not useful in object-oriented design. Traditional language implementation centers the design process on the activity to be performed by the application, while object-oriented languages center the implementation on the data being represented. It is our experience that nonprogrammers have an easier time learning and adopting the OOP concept. Because traditional programmers have worked so hard at writing applications that are unlike the real world, they now have a difficult time with this implementation shift.

We will look at the basic tenets of object-oriented languages in this chapter and see how they solve some of the problems associated with writing applications in modular programming languages. Before looking at the functional aspects of object-oriented languages, we will discuss the concepts of objects and classes.

OBJECTS VS. CLASSES

An object class is simply the collection of attributes and activities that an object within the classification can have or perform. For example, *human* is a real world classification. We identify humans as those individuals that have the attributes associated with the human class. Those attributes might include eye color, height, weight, gender, hair color, etc. Innate activities are also part of all animate object classes. Human objects can breathe, walk, eat, sleep, think, etc. By defining a class in an object-oriented language, you can then create *instances* of object classes you have defined. Each of us is an instance of the human class. Imagine a class as a recipe, and objects as cakes made with the recipe.

Figure 3.1 demonstrates the relationship between objects and classes. The box on the left side of the diagram is the class definition of a PC. The definition only contains attributes of the object in this example. The definition itself cannot be used to process any information. It merely defines what a PC will be. The right hand side of the figure shows PCs created from the class definition. Each is similar but has attributes that can be modi-

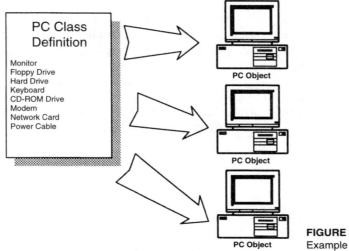

FIGURE 3.1 Classes vs. Objects Example

fied to customize the equipment. Objects themselves are generally not static and can be modified. You cannot change their number of available attributes but you can change the values of those attributes. For example, the PC class definition in Figure 3.1 shows that each PC would have a hard drive. The size of this hard drive can be modifiable, but each PC will have one as its inclusion in part of the class definition.

MESSAGING

One of the aspects of object-oriented programming is the concept of *messaging*. Messaging is the way in which the application can get or set information about an object or tell an object to do something. In a modular programming environment, in order to have a particular order processed you would need to have a ProcessOrders routine that acted on some type of data structure that represented the order. In an object-oriented environment, the order object would be sent a message telling it to process itself. This code might take on a form like this:

```
Order.Name := 'The DSW Group, Ltd.'
Order.Address := '1775 The Exchange'
Order.Phone := '404-953-0393'
Order.Process;
```

This example shows the use of the send message operator ('.') used in Delphi. Following the send operator is the specific attribute that is to be modified. In this example, the Name, Address, and Phone attributes, or *properties,* of Order object are modified before the Order is told to process. Messages associated with objects must all be defined with the object class definition. An Order must have one or more of the properties modified in this example or the program would not work properly. Activities in Delphi are known as *methods*. The Order object class used in the preceding figure must have a Process method defined in order for the example to work. Delphi object classes can also have events defined for them. We will talk about these special attributes later.

To create an object class in Delphi you will need to determine what properties and methods you would like the object to have. The source code below creates a simple class called THuman. This class has no methods, but does have a few properties, or fields, that can be assigned and referenced by code that creates objects of that class.

```
unit UHuman;

interface

type
THuman = CLASS
   Name, Address, City, State, Zip : string;
   Age : Integer;
   Salary : single;
end;          { end of class declaration }

implementation
end.
```

To utilize this object class we have created a CRT application. The source code for creating the object and assigning its fields is shown below.

```
program Crtapp1;

uses WinCrt,SysUtils,UHuman;

var
    Bob : THuman; {we've declared a variable of type THuman}
begin
    writeln('Creating Bob . . . ');
    Bob := THuman.Create; {Bob is now an object}
    Bob.Name := 'Bob Smith';
    Bob.Address := '111 Main Street';
    Bob.City := 'Buffalo';
    Bob.State := 'NY';
    Bob.Salary := 335.66;
    Bob.Age := 10;
    writeln('Bob is this old: ' + IntToStr(Bob.Age));
    Bob.Free;
end.
```

In addition to assigning property values, this example shows the basic method of creating objects based on a class definition. By creating the Bob variable as the type THuman, we tell the compiler that variable Bob is going to be a human. The declaration alone does not *instantiate,* or create, Bob. In order to instantiate the object we must call the Create method. Each object class has a Create method, known as a *constructor,* which is used to allocate a memory block that holds the object. Once the object is instantiated, the properties can be assigned. After the object is no longer needed, it is important to call the object class's Free method, sometimes called a *destructor.* Once again, we do not have to write this method ourselves as each class created in Delphi has inherited it from one of its ancestors. The Free method allows the memory space utilized by the object to be reclaimed by Windows. Without the Free method call, the application would leave this memory tied up resulting in resource leakage. If enough unused objects are left lying about, your Windows environment could run out of useable memory.

You are not limited to creating objects that have only properties. You can also define your own methods to perform some needed activity. Let us say that humans need to be able to get older. This would require us to build in some functionality that would increment the Age field. The code below shows the new class definition for the THuman class. There are two new methods defined as procedures.

```
unit UHuman;

interface

type
THuman = CLASS
    Name, Address, City, State, Zip : string;
    Age : Integer;
    Salary : single;
    procedure GrowOlder;
    procedure Talk;
end;          { end of class declaration }

implementation
procedure THuman.GrowOlder;
begin
    Age := Age + 1;
end;
procedure THuman.Talk;
begin
    writeln('Blah, blah, blah');
end;
end.
```

Once the new procedures are defined in the type section, the actual code for these is placed in the implementation section of the unit. The routine names are prefaced with the

THuman. identifier that associates them with the THuman class. The incrementation of the Age field looks fairly simple. Hidden within the code is the concept of *self*. Why does incrementing a variable called Age reference the field in the object? This is a built in behavior of Delphi objects and serves to simplify the writing of methods. Any variable referenced within a method is automatically first assumed to be a field in the object. These fields can be referenced explicitly through the use of the self keyword. You could write the GrowOlder method as shown below:

```
procedure THuman.GrowOlder;
begin
    self.Age := self.Age + 1;
end;
```

Messaging allows for the tying of properties and methods to specific object classes. This provides a great deal of encapsulation. When you modify the properties of an object, you cannot affect other objects in the same or other classes. Only by changing the class definition (or recipe) can you affect more than an individual object. For example, changing the monitor on a computer has no effect on other computers in your office. For greater power, you also have the ability to change the definition of classes. You could define the PC object class to have each computer equipped with a 486 processor. By changing the class definition, all objects within the class incorporate the change. Once again, this does not affect objects in other classes (in most cases—see the section on Inheritance).

When working with the form tool in Delphi, you are actually creating source code that uses objects to implement the functionality you want. Each interface component is really an object of a particular class (buttons, labels, entry fields, etc.). The form itself is also an object. Each of the components on the form have attributes and methods available to them. When you are in the Design mode, you have access to some of the component properties through the Object Inspector. You can also change component properties at run-time through the use of messaging and property assignment. As you add components to a form, you are actually defining a new form class that has properties for each of the components.

INHERITANCE

In the previous chapter we saw the limitations associated with traditional modular programming. One of these limitations surrounds the use of modified routines. We looked at replacing a generic sales tax calculation routine with an application-specific version and saw that this required a complete rewrite of the existing routine in order to incorporate the needed changes. Object-oriented languages provide a facility known as *inheritance* to allow for greater reuse of source code.

Consider the human class we created earlier. Humans have a specific set of properties and methods. Defining all of these for an application would be exhausting but possible. Suppose you decided that you also needed to create dogs for the application. You could go through the process of defining the dog class and meticulously setting up all of its properties and methods. Once finished (or probably before), you would realize that dogs and humans have a lot in common. In fact, you might figure out that they are both members of a common classification, *mammals.*

Rather than creating both from scratch, you can use inheritance to create a base class called mammals and then create subclasses called humans and dogs from it. This technique provides great flexibility because we only need to do the brunt of the work once and reuse it again later for different object classes. Figure 3.2 shows the relationship between these three classes.

The diagramming technique used in this figure was introduced by Grady Booch and will be discussed later in greater detail. Because the human and dog classes descend from the mammal class, they have all of the properties and methods defined within the mammal class. They are free to have additional properties and methods defined within themselves to "flesh out" their class definitions. The mammal class in this example can be referred to as the *superclass* of the human and dog classes. The human and dog classes exist as *subclasses.*

If we recreate our human class as a descendant of the mammal class, our unit file that contains the human class definition looks like the following:

```
unit UHuman;

interface
{ Need the UMammal unit file for inheritance }
uses UMammal;

type
THuman = CLASS(TMammal) { inherits from TMammal }
   Name, Address, City, State, Zip : string;
   Salary : single;
   procedure Talk;
end;        { end of class declaration }
```

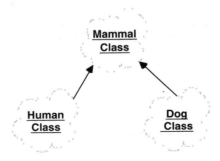

FIGURE 3.2 Inheritance Relationship Diagram

```
implementation
procedure THuman.Talk;
begin
    writeln('Blah, blah, blah');
end;
end.
```

Notice that the unit now uses the UMammal unit. This allows inheritance to take place. Because the TMammal class is visible to the THuman class definition, the new class can inherit from it. The Age field and the GrowOlder procedure have been removed from the THuman class. Because all mammals have an age and can grow older, both the property and method have been moved to the TMammal class definition. The unit containing the TMammal class definition:

```
unit UMammal;

interface
type
{ create enumerated types for eye color and fur }
TEyeColor = (BLUE,BROWN,BLACK,YELLOW);
TFur = (THICK, THIN, NONE);
TMammal = CLASS
    BodyTemp : single;
    EyeColor : TEyeColor;
    Fur      : TFur;
    Age      : Integer;
    procedure GrowOlder;
end;          { end of class declaration }

implementation
procedure TMammal.GrowOlder;
begin
    Age := Age + 1;
end;
end.
```

By moving Age and GrowOlder to the superclass, we can have access to them in new subclasses. The dog class we outlined earlier can be used for an example. This code below defines a new dog class:

```
unit Udog;

interface
{ Need the UMammal unit file for inheritance }
uses UMammal;
```

```
type
TBreed = (GoldenRetriever, CockerSpaniel,
              BorderCollie, Beagle);
TDog = CLASS(TMammal) { inherits from TMammal }
  Name : string;
  Breed : TBreed;
  procedure Bark;
end;          { end of class declaration }

implementation
procedure TDog.Bark;
begin
  writeln('Woof, Woof, Woof');
end;
end.
```

Just like the human we created earlier, we can create a dog and use it in our code.

```
var
  Rover : TDog;
begin
  { Create the dog }
  Rover := TDog.Create;
  Rover.Name := 'Blitzen';
  Rover.Breed := Beagle;
  Rover.Age := 9;
  Rover.GrowOlder;
  writeln('Rover is this old: ' + IntToStr(Rover.Age));
  Rover.Bark;
  Rover.Free;
end;
```

As you can see from this example, the use of inheritance can greatly reduce the amount of code you need to write to create new, reusable assets. This object-oriented feature also allows routines written with existing classes to continue to work without your needing to worry about backward compatibility. Consider the human class that was outlined above. Let us say we decide later that the human class we have been using will not work in a particular software project. We need some more capabilities for our human class and need to change the way a few of the methods work. This is the type of functionality particularly suited to inheritance.

Instead of changing the existing human class, we should consider creating a new class. Any changes to the human class may adversely affect our existing applications. We must decide where in the inheritance tree this new class to be designed should be placed. This is a significant decision and should be thoroughly thought out based on the information we can ascertain about the utility of the new class. We could create a class very similar to the human class that descends from the mammal class. All of the aspects of the new class that are like the human class would have to be rewritten. The alternative is to create a class that descends from the human class. This would be a better choice if our new class is substantially similar to the human class.

To simplify this example, we will assume that our new class is much like a human with a few extra attributes and methods. Figure 3.3 shows the inheritance tree for our new class. We needed a class to simulate the activities of someone in our client's legal department so the new lawyer class exists as a subclass to the human class.

Once again, the work required to create the new useful class was greatly reduced through the use of inheritance. By using a thorough plan for developing your object classes, you can achieve a degree of flexibility and reusability not available in traditional programming languages.

Some object-oriented programming languages support the concept of *multiple inheritance.* This language feature allows you to create classes that are directly descended from more than one superclass. This feature provides a greater degree of flexibility than that found with single inheritance. The concept of multiple inheritance can be summed up with a phrase used to start many bad jokes: "What do you get when you cross a . . . with a . . . ". Real world examples of multiple inheritance can be found in nature. Many species allow for cross breeding with other species that produce a discernible subspecies. Horses and donkeys can be bred to produce mules. Some popular dog breeds are really combinations of separate breeds. Domestic Himalayan cats are a mix of Persian and Siamese breeds. These examples serve to demonstrate the usefulness of multiple inheritance.

The trouble with multiple inheritance is the decisions that must be made about the manifestation of the new class. The answer to the question, "What happens when you cross . . ." has important consequences to any development project. With single inheritance it is easy to see what the results of the inheritance will be. If you never saw a mule, how would you know what the cross between a horse and a donkey would look like? The possibilities are numerous. Would it have four legs or eight? Would it be short or tall? Be-

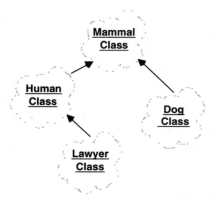

FIGURE 3.3 Subclasses of Subclasses

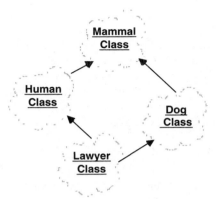

FIGURE 3.4   Multiple Inheritance

cause nature's gene selection process is currently beyond our understanding, we cannot predict the results of the combination of two species. We must test it first.

This has important ramifications in object-oriented programming. When crossing two object classes together, the results must be predictable and definable. Unless the combination of classes results in a superset class that contains all of the properties and methods of the two (or more) superclasses, the complexity of the class relationships can cause confusion. Consider the combination of the classes we have already diagrammed. Different interpretations of how a new class is defined using multiple inheritance could result in some very strange and difficult to relate to class relationships. Figure 3.4 demonstrates what could result with multiple inheritance.

What parts of a dog would the lawyer class inherit? This is the key problem with using and supporting multiple inheritance. The debate within the object-oriented programming community has done little to settle the argument. Delphi does not support multiple inheritance at this time.

All form component objects in the Delphi language are inherited from the base class called TComponent. This provides the foundation for all aspects of Delphi's object-oriented programming user interface extensions. In fact, all classes, whether denoted or not, inherit from a *base class* called TObject. The `class` keyword has an implied inheritance and can be written using TObject or not. The examples used earlier in this chapter did not reference TObject but could have. The line of code below shows the use of the TObject class as a superclass.

```
type
  { All classes inherit from TObject whether denoted as
    below or not }
  TMammal = class(TObject);
```

POLYMORPHISM

In an effort to support the practices of the real world, object-oriented languages support *polymorphism*. Polymorphism allows for objects of different classes to recognize and process the same messages. This is the same concept behind the use of verbs in the English language. Let's look at the verb "run". What types of things can run? People, animals, cars, computers, and different types of equipment can run. Your nose can run. You can even run a fever when you are sick. Each of these uses of the verb *run* is an example of polymorphism.

We do not create a different word for each object in the real world that might run. To do this would make our lives significantly more complicated. Think of the number of new words that would have to be added to our language if we had to create a new verb for each activity that each object could perform. The average vocabulary for someone in the United States is less than 500 words. The sheer volume of new words needed to remove polymorphism from our language boggles the mind.

We use verbs in context and derive their meanings from the object of the verb in the sentence. When you say "my nose is running", no one pictures legs sprouting from your nostrils and your proboscis scampering across the floor. By providing polymorphism, object-oriented languages once again allow us to model the real world more effectively. Fields and methods can be assigned names that reflect the real world names for those object properties without the need to come up with some type of naming convention. There are three different types of polymorphism that can be utilized within your object class designs.

Inherited polymorphism occurs when objects of different classes process the same message because they inherit it from a common ancestor. In our human and dog example, both had an Age field and could grow older because they were descendants of the TMammal class. Our lawyer class could also talk because it was a descendant of the human class. In comparing a lawyer to a human, we could characterize their polymorphic use of the talk method as inherited.

Independent polymorphism is used when different classes use the same field or method name for different values or activities. We could write a class method for dogs called "run". The Run method could outline the mechanics involved in a dog's running. We could also write a Run method for humans. Because humans use two legs to run and dogs use four, it would not benefit us to move the dog's Run method into the mammal class definition. We are allowed to create a run class for humans that is independent of the Run method in dogs. Both classes will recognize the run message but process it differently. This allows us to utilize a similar concept across classes and isolate its implementation inside of the different classes.

Coincidental polymorphism occurs when two classes have the same method or field name but have unrelated implementation. Noses can run. Conceptually, this is fundamentally different from an animal running. We only use the term "running" because of real world terminology. The stock market can "jump" and so can a kangaroo. These are unrelated and would not typically be used together in context. We recommend that coincidental polymorphism be avoided unless it assists in the real world modeling of your object classes.

CONTAINERSHIP

Objects can contain other objects. In order to model this real world occurrence, objects in Delphi can contain other objects. This is usually accomplished through the use of object fields. For example, we could create a Car object class and also an Engine object class. The Car object class could have an engine property. The source code listings below demonstrates this technique:

```pascal
unit Ucar;

interface
type
  { Block type for engine }
  TBlock = (STRAIGHT, VEE);
  { engine type definition }
  TEngine = class(TObject)
    Block : TBlock;
    Cylinders : Integer;
    EFI : Boolean;
    Manufacturer : string;
  end;
  { Upholstery type for interior }
  TUpholstery = (CLOTH,LEATHER,VINYL);
  { Car class definition }
  TCar = class(TObject)
    Engine : TEngine; { can contain an engine object }
    Color : string;
    Upholstery : TUpholstery;
    GasTankGallons : Integer;
    procedure Go;
  end;

implementation
procedure TCar.Go;
begin
  if self.engine.cylinders = 8 then
    writeln('vroom, vroom, guzzle, guzzle')
  else
    writeln('vroom');
end;
end.
```

It is important when using this technique to remember that all objects need to be instantiated before their fields can be accessed. This is often forgotten for objects contained within other objects. The resources utilized by contained objects also must be freed up before the container object variable goes out of scope. The following source code listing demonstrates the creation of both contained and container objects and their creation and destruction.

```pascal
program PContain;

uses WinCrt, Ucar in 'UCAR.PAS';

var
  MyCar : TCar;
  MyEngine : TEngine;
begin
  { instantiate the car object }
  MyCar := TCar.Create;
  { instantiate the engine object }
  MyEngine := TEngine.Create;
  MyEngine.Cylinders := 8;
  MyEngine.Block := VEE;
  MyEngine.EFI := TRUE;
  MyEngine.Manufacturer := 'Ford';

  { Put the engine in the car }
  MyCar.Engine := MyEngine;

  { set other fields in the car object }
  MyCar.Color := 'Black';
  MyCar.Upholstery := LEATHER;
  MyCar.Go;

  { Change the engine's manufacturer }
  MyCar.Engine.Manufacturer := 'Chevy';

  { print out the new manufacturer's name }
  writeln(MyEngine.Manufacturer);

  { release the memory resources allocated
    for these objects }
  writeln('Freeing MyCar.Engine');
  MyCar.Engine.Free;
  writeln('Freeing MyCar');
  MyCar.Free;
end.
```

There are a few items to note in this example. First, we have created a separate variable to hold the Engine object before it is placed in the car. The `MyEngine` variable holds a reference to the engine object in memory. The assignment of `MyCar.Engine` to this variable sets the `.Engine` property to point to the same memory space as the `Engine` variable. Any changes made to the variable MyEngine's properties will also affect the Engine object stored in the car. The code which changes the engine's manufacturer demonstrates this technique. Changing the manufacturer of `MyCar.Engine` also changes the MyEngine object's manufacturer property.

The order in which the different objects are freed is important. We first free the car's Engine object and then the Car object. The `MyEngine` variable does not have to be freed. This is due to the fact that it references the same memory location as the Engine field in the Car object. Anytime you have containership, release the memory associated with the contained objects first and then that of the container. This will prevent the possibility of orphaned memory.

Objects can contain more than just one other object. Forms created with the form tool in Delphi are containers that contain all of the components on the form. Panels also act as containers. The concept of containership serves to place real world abstractions into a useable object framework. We will be discussing more about containership and object relationships in later chapters.

CHAPTER 4

DELPHI'S OBJECT-ORIENTED IMPLEMENTATION

OVERVIEW

We have already reviewed the theory behind object-oriented programming. In this chapter we will be examining in detail how Delphi implements class creation. We have seen the basics of creating a simple class. The source code below demonstrates this technique.

```
unit UMammal;

interface
type
TEyeColor = (BLUE,BROWN,BLACK,YELLOW);
TFur = (THICK, THIN, NONE);
TMammal = class
  BodyTemp : single;
  EyeColor : TEyeColor;
  Fur      : TFur;
  Age      : Integer;
  procedure GrowOlder;
end;          { end of class declaration }

implementation
procedure TMammal.GrowOlder;
  begin
    Age := Age + 1;
  end;
end.
```

TMammal is a fairly simple class and can be used as the base class for other classes. These subclasses might include humans, dogs, cats, etc. While powerful, this class definition lacks some important safeguards that would make it more useable as a superclass. The TMammal class shown provides very little protection against assigning unreasonable values to the different fields. Some of the fields (EyeColor and Fur) are enumerated types. The compiler will trap any errors in assigning incorrect values to these fields. However, there is nothing preventing the programmer from assigning a nonsensical age to some mammal or mammal subclass object. You could assign the human object we created in the last chapter an outrageous age of 1001 years.

The TMammal class definition also does not aid us much in the creation of subclasses. For example, when creating the human subclass we might want to have the person's taste in music automatically change once their age reaches a certain value. In order to accomplish this, we would have to rewrite the existing TMammal.GrowOlder method in the new human subclass and add the features we wanted. This violates many of the rules of encapsulation and coupling that we outlined earlier.

Fortunately, Delphi includes a robust and very powerful set of statements and keywords that can be used in defining classes. These statements and keywords provide the layers of encapsulation we need for creating large applications. They also provide us with a way to enforce *ancestral compatibility*. This chapter will discuss these features found in Delphi's object definition syntax. They provide the capabilities required to create truly reusable object classes.

CONSTRUCTORS AND DESTRUCTORS

In the last chapter, we used the Create and Free methods available to all TObject subclasses. The Create method is known as a Constructor method. Its purpose is to allocate memory for the instantiation of new objects. When declared, variables of any object type do not point to a location in memory that contains an object. Once the instantiation occurs, the variable acts as a reference pointer to the newly created object.

The Free method is known as a Destructor method. It deallocates memory for objects that are no longer needed in the application. As we mentioned in the last chapter, it is critical that you remember to call an object destructor before allowing a variable object reference to go out of scope. Once the destructor is called, the memory previously used to contain the object is released for later usage by any active Windows application. It is sometimes possible to continue to reference the fields of an object after its destructor is called. This is due to the fact that the object variable reference is still pointing to the location in memory where the object data is stored. This is an extremely dangerous practice, as any future Windows memory allocation within your application or another application could claim that memory space and cause a general protection fault.

It is possible to create your own constructors and destructors for any class. Constructors are beneficial because they allow you to assign field values to default values and perform other object setup-type operations. In the TMammal class we would like to have a few of the fields be preset to particular values. This would allow us to reduce the amount of code needed to instantiate a THuman object in a useable state. The code example below demonstrates how we can accomplish this task with the Constructor method.

```
TMammal = class
  BodyTemp : single;
  EyeColor : TEyeColor;
  Fur      : TFur;
  Age      : Integer;
  procedure GrowOlder;
  { Add the constructor method }
  constructor Create;
end;            { end of class declaration }

implementation
{ constructor inits a few field values }
constructor TMammal.Create;
begin
  self.Fur := THICK;
  self.EyeColor := BROWN;
  self.Age := 1
end;
```

Constructors do not have to be named Create. Some programmers prefer Init or other names. It is important to use some sort of standard name to keep your code consistent. Because Delphi uses Create in all of its object classes, we suggest you do the same. Destructors also are not required to have a specific name. Free is the name given to the TObject class's destructor. Again, the name is not required to be Free. Destroy is used by some of the components in Delphi's Visual Component Library (VCL), but they also support the Free destructor. It is advisable to use the Free naming convention for consistency.

Constructors/Destructors and Container Objects

Constructors can be used to make instantiation of container objects less code intensive. In the last chapter, we demonstrated the need to instantiate the container object as well as any contained objects before fields could be assigned to them. The instantiation of the contained objects could be placed in the container object's constructor code. Recall our example of a car containing an Engine object. The code below demonstrates how a constructor could be written for the car class to automatically instantiate the contained Engine object.

```
unit Ucar;

interface
type
```

```
{ Block type for engine }
TBlock = (STRAIGHT, VEE);
{ engine bdefinition }
TEngine = class(TObject)
  Block : TBlock;
  Manufacturer : string;
  Cylinders : Integer;
  EFI : Boolean;
  constructor Create;
end;
{ Upholstery type for interior }
TUpholstery = (CLOTH,LEATHER,VINYL);
{ Body Styling Types }
TBodyStyle = (COUPE, SEDAN, WAGON);
{ Car class definition }
TCar = class(TObject)
  Engine : TEngine; { contains an engine object }
  Color : string;
  BodyStyle : TBodyStyle;
  Upholstery : TUpholstery;
  GasTankGallons : Integer;
  constructor Create;
  destructor Free;
  procedure Go;
end;

implementation

constructor TCar.Create;
begin
  self.Color := 'Blue';
  self.BodyStyle := SEDAN;
  self.Upholstery := CLOTH;
  self.GasTankGallons := 12;
  self.Engine := TEngine.Create;
end;

destructor TCar.Free;
begin
  self.Engine.Free;
end;

procedure TCar.Go;
begin
  if self.engine.cylinders = 8 then
    writeln('vroom, vroom, guzzle')
  else
```

```
      writeln('vroom');
end;

constructor TEngine.Create;
begin
   self.Block := STRAIGHT;
   self.Manufacturer := 'Ford';
   self.Cylinders := 6;
   self.EFI := TRUE;
end;
end.
```

Notice that both the TCar and TEngine object classes have defined their own constructors. The engine constructor merely sets some default field values. The car constructor instantiates the Engine object along with its other fields. Instantiating a TCar object results in a blue sedan with a straight-6 Ford engine, electronic fuel injection and a twelve gallon gas tank. These will be our factory default settings. If, in a particular case, we needed some options changed, we would simply modify the necessary fields after issuing the Create call. The code below demonstrates the small amount of code that needs to be written to create a new car object and set a few options.

```
var
   MyCar : TCar;
begin
   { instantiate the car object }
   MyCar := TCar.Create;        { also creates the engine }

   { set other fields in the car object }
   MyCar.Color := 'Black';
   MyCar.Engine.Cylinders := 8;
   MyCar.Engine.Block := VEE;

   MyCar.Go;

   writeln('Freeing MyCar');
   MyCar.Free;        { Also frees the Engine object }
end.
```

Notice in this code example that the constructor and destructor for the TEngine object is never explicitly called. This is because the TCar object's Create constructor and Free destructor are handling them for us. This technique does have some drawbacks. It is now impossible to create a Car object without also creating an engine for it. It is also difficult to use an independently created engine and place it in the car as was done in the last chapter. The following code demonstrates how you would designate a car's engine to be different from the default Engine, object.

```
program Pcont2;

uses WinCrt, Ucar in 'UCAR.PAS';

var
   MyCar : TCar;
   MyEngine : TEngine;
begin
   { instantiate the car object and its engine }
   MyCar := TCar.Create;
   { set other fields in the car object }
   MyCar.Color := 'Black';

   { create a seperate engine object }
   MyEngine := TEngine.Create;
   MyEngine.Cylinders := 8;
   MyEngine.Block := VEE;

   { free the existing car engine and
     replace it with the new one }
   MyCar.Engine.Free;
   MyCar.Engine := MyEngine;

   MyCar.Go;

   writeln('Freeing MyCar');
   MyCar.Free; { frees both car and engine }
end.
```

Constructors/Destructors and Inheritance

The TCar and TEngine classes used in the previous examples are descendants of the TObject class. As descendants, these object classes could create their own constructors and destructors and substitute them for the default methods. This technique is useful because the TObject methods are extremely limited. If we attempt to go a level deeper in our inheritance structure, we will experience some difficulties in attempting to initialize fields within constructors. We may decide to create a subclass of our TCar class called TSportsCar. This new class will have a few more fields and some additional methods. The source code for this new class is listed below.

```
unit Usports;

interface
uses UCar;
type
  TSportsCar = class(TCar)
    TopSpeed : Integer;
    Seats : Integer;
    Convertable : Boolean;
    constructor Create;
    destructor Free;
    procedure Go;
  end;


implementation
constructor TSportsCar.Create;
begin
  { Repeated init code }
  self.Color := 'Blue';
  self.BodyStyle := SEDAN;
  self.Upholstery := CLOTH;
  self.GasTankGallons := 12;
  self.Engine := TEngine.Create;
  { new init code }
  self.TopSpeed := 200;
  self.Seats := 2;
  self.Convertable := TRUE;
end;

destructor TSportsCar.Free;
begin
  self.engine.Free;
end;

procedure TSportsCar.Go;
begin
  writeln('vroom, vroom, vroom . . . screeeeech . . . crash')
end;
end.
```

You can see from this example that we had to rewrite a good deal of the code in the constructor and destructor from our ancestor TCar class. This is due to the way we originally defined our constructors and destructors in both classes. In order for you to avoid the need to constantly rewrite code found in parent class methods, you need to understand the various ways Delphi allows you to dispatch methods.

METHOD DISPATCHING

When defining the TSportsCar class we will undoubtedly want to have access to its ancestor class's constructor. Without this access, we have to repeat all of the constructor field initializations over again. However, by understanding the different types of methods that can be written in Delphi, we can greatly reduce the amount of coding that is necessary in creating new classes.

Method dispatching is a term applied to the technique that determines the way Delphi uses source code at run-time and how methods can be used (or not used) by descendant classes. There are three types of method dispatching that can be invoked within a class definition: *static*, *virtual*, and *dynamic*.

Static Methods

The default method declaration causes the creation of *static methods.* Static methods reside in a fixed location in memory. Each object created as a member of a class uses this fixed memory location to execute the method. Having a fixed location provides the fastest possible message processing as no redirection is needed to find the needed routine in memory.

Static methods are used not only by the class which defines the method, but also by members of descendant classes. Both use the methods at the same fixed memory location. Should a subclass redefine a method having the same name, objects in the subclass will use the new static method and be unable to access the method of the superclass. The definition of the subclass's static method breaks the ties that bind it to its parent class's method having the same name. Though quickly processed, you can see the disadvantages of static methods. It is impossible for our TSportsCar class to invoke static methods from the TCar superclass. Because all of the methods defined in the superclass are static, the creation of a new constructor or destructor function will replace the pointer to the location of the superclass's static method with one from the new subclass. Figure 4.1 shows how these pointers are arranged. As you can see, now that a new Create constructor has been written, the TSportsCar object can no longer access its parent's constructor.

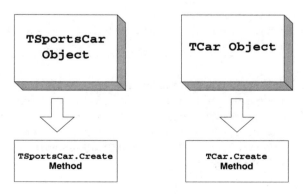

FIGURE 4.1 Static Method Dispatching Pointers

There is a temptation to attempt to directly access the `TCar.Create` method from within the constructor of the subclass. The code *might* look something like the listing below.

```
constructor TSportsCar.Create;
begin
  { call the superclass's constructor }
  TCar.Create;
  { new init code }
  self.TopSpeed := 200;
  self.Seats := 2;
  self.Convertable := TRUE;
end;
```

This solution proves problematic. The constructor can still access the superclass's constructor. This is due to the fact that, until the object is fully instantiated, it still does not have its methods pointers changed from the superclass. Unfortunately, this technique will not work outside of the constructor. Other methods that would need to call a superclass method will not be able to do so after the constructor has been executed. This technique also lends itself to a high degree of maintenance. Should any changes be required of the superclass's name, our subclass will need to be modified in multiple places. We must look at another method of dispatching to accomplish the task of calling a superclass's methods.

Because static methods are completely redefined for each new subclass, there are no limitations as to how they will work, what type they will return, or the types and number of parameters. This provides a great deal of freedom when creating new subclasses. We could write a new `Go` method for our `TSportsCar` class that accepts a parameter. The ancestor class has no parameter for this same method name. The source code below might be used to accomplish this.

```
procedure TSportsCar.Go(Where : string);
begin
  writeln('Going to '+Where);
  writeln('vroom, vroom, vroom . . . screech . . . crash')
end;
```

The freedom to completely change the way a descendant class processes a message is a double-edged sword. While providing flexibility, it removes a great deal of consistency between a class and its superclass. A programmer using a `TSportsCar` object would naturally assume that telling the car to `Go` would take the same form as that of a regular car. The change to the subclass message processing leads to difficult to understand interfaces and more difficulty in the use of subclasses.

Virtual Methods

Static methods provide speed in message processing at the expense of consistency and useability. *Virtual methods* are the counterparts to static methods. Virtual methods can be defined using the `virtual` keyword at the end of a method declaration. This keyword forces objects in the class to look in the *virtual method table* (VMT) in memory to resolve any references to the method. The VMT contains pointers to all virtual methods defined for the class and any superclasses. Through the use of virtual methods, you can promote consistency and code reuse within your class definitions.

Declaring a method as virtual requires any subclasses that declare a method of the same name to return the same type and take on the same number and types of parameters. Due to the indirection used in dispatching virtual method calls, they operate somewhat more slowly than static methods. Figure 4.2 shows the pointer references present in an object that utilizes a virtual method.

You can see from Figure 4.2 that it is possible to have two methods of the same name within the VMT. In the figure, the object shown has two methods called `Create` within its VMT. One is defined within its class definition and the other is inherited from its ancestor class's definition. Because both methods are accessible to objects in this class, it is possible to have the class's `Create` method call its superclass's `Create` method.

To define any method as virtual, you need to use the `virtual` keyword at the end of the method declaration line. The source code listing below shows a redefinition of our `TCar` class with all of the methods defined as `virtual`.

```
TCar = class(TObject)
    Engine : TEngine; { contains an engine object }
    Color : string;
    BodyStyle : TBodyStyle;
    Upholstery : TUpholstery;
```

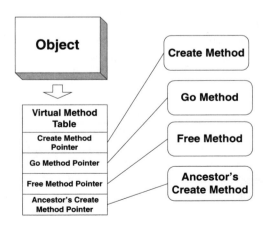

FIGURE 4.2 Virtual Method Table

```
GasTankGallons : Integer;
{ define all methods as virtual so they can be
  overridden by subclasses }
constructor Create; virtual;
destructor Free; virtual;
procedure Go; virtual;
end;
```

Using virtual methods will reduce the speed of the method dispatching within your application. We can test the speed differences between static and virtual methods by creating 'stub' methods of each type. By calling these methods numerous times within some type of program control loop, we can see how much faster static methods are. The source code below has been added to our TSportsCar class.

```
{ Stub methods for speed tests on
  method dispatching }
procedure TSportsCar.StatDo;
var x,y : integer;
begin
end;
procedure TSportsCar.VirtDo;
var x,y : integer;
begin
end;
```

We can use the code below to test the speed differences between the two methods. In conducting this small test we discover that static methods are called twice as fast as virtual methods. (Note that all performance measurements cited are relative to our testing machine.)

```
writeln(TimeToStr(Time));
for i:=1 To 5000000 do
  Corvette.StatDo;
writeln(TimeToStr(Time));
for i:=1 To 5000000 do
  Corvette.VirtDo;
writeln(TimeToStr(Time));
```

Testing code like this is misleading. The test unrealistically uses two methods, neither of which have any code statements within them. The test also uses a loop of 5 million iterations. The duration of these loops were 5 and 11 seconds respectively on our test machine. While being twice as fast in raw message processing, static methods quickly lose their speed advantage as code is added to the methods. With just four lines of simple math operations added to each method, our simple test showed that static methods ended up being only about 30% faster. The speed advantage continued to decrease as more statements were added to each loop.

On our machine, Delphi dispatched virtual methods at approximately 500,000 per second. This incredibly fast performance compares to method dispatch times of 2,500 per second for some interpretive languages now on the market. You can see that virtual methods perform at perfectly acceptable speeds.

Overriding Virtual Methods

You have seen that creating methods of the same names as those in their superclasses results in the inability to access the superclass's method. The use of virtual methods eliminates this problem. The *inherited* statement can be used within a method of a descendant class to call methods in the superclass. The source code below demonstrates a call by the TSportsCar Create method to its superclass's Create method.

```
type
  TSportsCar = class(TCar)
    TopSpeed : Integer;
    Seats : Integer;
    Convertable : Boolean;
    constructor Create;
    destructor Free;
    procedure Go(Where : string);
end;

implementation
constructor TSportsCar.Create;
begin
  { call the virtual method from the superclass }
  inherited Create;
  { new init code }
  self.TopSpeed := 200;
  self.Seats := 2;
  self.Convertable := TRUE;
end;
```

In this example, the Create constructor is defined as a static method. Even as a static method, this constructor can call its ancestor's constructor method. Unfortunately, any subclass to the TSportsCar class will not be able to access the TSportsCar.Create method.

In order to make this constructor accessible to its descendants, we need to make it virtual as well. If we add the virtual keyword to its declaration, the descendants of the TSportsCar class will be able to call its constructor. This type of *method chaining* can help reduce the amount of source code needed to implement a new class. Unfortunately, by declaring a new class's method as virtual, you do not guarantee that its declaration is

compatible with its superclass's method declaration. The code below shows how the
TSportsCar.Go method can be written in a way that is incompatible with its superclass's method.

```
type
  TSportsCar = class(TCar)
    TopSpeed : Integer;
    Seats : Integer;
    Convertable : Boolean;
    constructor Create; virtual;
    destructor Free; virtual;
    procedure Go(Where : string); virtual;
    { Stub methods to test speed of method
      dispatching }
    procedure StatDo;
    procedure VirtDo; virtual;
  end;

implementation
constructor TSportsCar.Create;
begin
  { call inherited method }
  inherited Create;
  { new init code }
  self.TopSpeed := 200;
  self.Seats := 2;
  self.Convertable := TRUE;
end;

destructor TSportsCar.Free;
begin
  inherited Free;
end;

{ incompatable syntax with superclass's method }
procedure TSportsCar.Go(Where : string);
begin
  writeln('Going to '+Where);
  writeln('vroom, vroom, vroom . . . screeeeech . . . crash')
end;
```

The Go method in the TSportscar class accepts a parameter not used in its parent's
class definition. This syntax incompatibility makes it difficult to chain methods between
methods in an inheritance tree. Suppose a later subclass dropped the requirement for the
parameter to the Go method. There would be no way for the subclass to call the
TSportsCar.Go method without a syntax error unless it forced a string parameter to be

passed. This type of inconsistency makes the creation of complex class structures very difficult.

In order to alleviate this problem, Delphi has included the `override` keyword. Override allows for the creation of virtual methods that the compiler checks for syntax compatibility with ancestor classes. By using the override keyword in place of the virtual keyword, any incompatibilities between superclasses and subclasses will generate Error 131:

```
Error 131: Header does not match previous definition.
```

By making the calling syntax compatible, the new class will not generate this error. This syntax checking makes the use of the virtual and override keywords an integral part of consistent object class design. We recommend that you use the override indicator for any class that creates a method with the same name as one of its superclass's virtual methods. If you attempt to override a static method, you will receive the following error message:

```
Error 188: Cannot override a static method.
```

The override indicator will not allow you to substitute a new virtual method for an existing static one. The need to override methods usually includes a call to the ancestor class's method having the same name. The need to add functionality to a class method is best served using this technique. It is not a generally a good idea to override a method with a new routine that performs an unrelated task to the superclass's method. This will cause confusion for anyone trying to read and understand your class hierarchy. Only those interested in 'job security' should consider making a class hierarchy that is both confusing and difficult to use.

The source listing below shows our new `TSportsCar` class definition with the override methods.

```
type
  TSportsCar = class(TCar)
    TopSpeed : Integer;
    Seats : Integer;
    Convertable : Boolean;
    constructor Create; virtual;
    destructor Free; virtual;
    procedure Go; override;
    { Stub methods to test speed of method dispatching }
    procedure StatDo;
    procedure VirtDo; virtual;
  end;

implementation
constructor TSportsCar.Create;
```

```
begin
  { call inherited method }
  inherited Create;
  { new init code }
  self.TopSpeed := 200;
  self.Seats := 2;
  self.Convertable := TRUE;
end;

destructor TSportsCar.Free;
begin
  inherited Free;
end;

{ incompatable syntax with superclass's method }
procedure TSportsCar.Go(Where : string);
begin
  writeln('Going to '+Where);
  writeln('vroom, vroom, vroom . . . screeeeech . . . crash')
end;
{ Stub methods for speed tests on
  method dispatching }
procedure TSportsCar.StatDo;
var x,y : integer;
begin
end;
procedure TSportsCar.VirtDo;
var x,y : integer;
begin
end;
end.
```

Special attention should be given to overriding constructors and destructors. As in the example above, always call the inherited constructor *first* in any new class constructor. Also, always call any inherited destructor *last* in any new class destructor. This will ensure the proper instantiation and memory release for objects created as members of the new class.

Dynamic Methods

Delphi also supports the creation of Dynamic methods. Dynamic methods are another form of virtual method. There is not a reference to the dynamic method in the VMT. Instead, the method pointer is stored in a dynamic method table (DMT). This table contains only those methods defined within the object's class. References to dynamic methods created in superclasses are looked up in the dynamic method reference tables created for those classes. A method number is stored in the DMT which addresses a specific place in memory where the method is located.

Calls to inherited dynamic methods are dispatched by searching the inheritance tree for the method name in each antecedent superclass. This recursive process is repeated until the method reference can be resolved. Because pointers to each inherited method are not stored with the objects, the objects take up less memory. Unfortunately, this technique for dispatching also can result in slower code execution. For this reason, dynamic methods should not be used for methods that are called often within a class or class hierarchy. Because memory size is not critical to most Delphi applications, we recommend that virtual methods be used as a default method dispatching practice.

FIELD AND METHOD SCOPING

Objects in the real world often have attributes that cannot be seen or accessed outside of the object itself. As human beings, we have a group of internal organs that are not visible or modifiable to those looking at us. These include the heart, stomach, kidneys, lungs, etc. Protection is offered with this type of attribute hiding. Being critical to our survival, it is a good thing someone cannot come along and easily change or remove our hearts.

Delphi provides several layers of encapsulation through the use of field scoping within an object class. Scoping directives can be used to identify a list of fields and methods that cannot be seen and/or modified outside of the class. These directives include *private, protected, public,* and *published.* By declaring your object class fields with these statements, you can determine where the fields can be seen and modified by those using and inheriting from your classes.

Published

Fields are considered published unless otherwise denoted within a class definition. The published declaration of a field denotes that it can be seen and modified by any user or inheritor of the class. Published fields can also be seen at design time by objects used as components in the form designer. The creation of components is beyond the scope of this chapter and will be covered in a later chapter. The `published` directive has no effect on the disposition of methods. They are not modifiable at any time.

Public

Publicly scoped fields have the same run-time scoping as published fields. They can be seen and modified by users of objects within the class and within descendant classes. To specify that a field should have this scope, the public statement should be used before declaring the fields. The example below shows the creation of our `TSportsCar` class with all of its fields declared public.

```
type
  TSportsCar = class(TCar)
  { public declaration allows all users and descendent
```

```
      classes to see/modify the fields }
public
   TopSpeed : Integer;
   Seats : Integer;
   Convertable : Boolean;
   constructor Create; virtual;
   destructor Free; virtual;
   procedure Go; override;
   { Stub methods to test speed of method dispatching }
   procedure StatDo;
   procedure VirtDo; virtual;
end;
```

The methods defined within this class definition are also public in scope. Once the `public` statement is issued, all subsequent methods and fields are scoped accordingly. In order to modify any of the subsequent declarations, another scoping statement must be issued.

Because the public statement is designed for the creation and design time modification of component fields and properties, we recommend that it not be used unless you are creating components. The need to encapsulate the access to certain fields and methods makes the use of other, more restrictive, directives in the definition of a class necessary.

Private

The `private` directive restricts the access to fields and methods to the class being defined. This directive is useful for adding functionality or data that is only needed by the class internally. For example, the number of times the car has been started affects the lifetime of the car's battery. After a specific number of starts, the battery will need to be replaced.

The number of starts is not something that is readily tracked outside of the object by the user. Instead, this piece of information will need to be tracked internally and only show up as a factor to the user when the battery needs replacement. The source listing below shows the new `NumberOfStarts` property added to our car class. The `Go` method has also been modified to use this field in determining whether it can actually start the car.

```
{ Car class definition }
TCar = class(TObject)
{ declare fields only available inside methods }
private
   { counter field to track number of starts for car }
   NumberOfStarts : Integer;
public
   Engine : TEngine; { contains an engine object }
```

```
      Color : string;
      BodyStyle : TBodyStyle;
      Upholstery : TUpholstery;
      GasTankGallons : Integer;
      NeedNewBattery : Boolean;
      { define all methods as virtual so they can be
        overridden by subclasses }
      constructor Create; virtual;
      destructor Free; virtual;
      procedure Go; virtual;
      { Method designed to reset battery indicator and
        number of starts counter }
      procedure InstallNewBattery; virtual;
   end;

implementation

constructor TCar.Create;
begin
   self.Color := 'Blue';
   self.BodyStyle := SEDAN;
   self.Upholstery := CLOTH;
   self.GasTankGallons := 12;
   self.Engine := TEngine.Create;
end;

destructor TCar.Free;
begin
   self.Engine.Free;
end;

procedure TCar.Go;
begin
   if self.NumberOfStarts > 1000 then
     self.NeedNewBattery := TRUE
   else
   begin
     self.NumberOfStarts := self.NumberOfStarts + 1;
     if self.engine.cylinders = 8 then
       writeln('vroom, vroom, guzzle')
     else
       writeln('vroom');
   end;
end;
{ routine designed to reset internal counter and
  status flag for new battery requirement }
procedure TCar.InstallNewBattery;
```

```
begin
  self.NumberOfStarts := 0;
  self.NeedNewBattery := FALSE;
end;
```

There are a few important points to note in this example. First, the `private` declaration has been added near the top of the class definition with the `NumberOfStarts` field beneath it. Following this declaration, the `public` directive is issued to ensure the remaining fields and methods are available to the users of the class. It is best to list your fields and methods with the most restrictive scope first, followed by less restrictive declarations after. This makes the reading of class definition easier and follows a standard set forth within the Delphi documentation.

In addition to the `NumberOfStarts` field, the `NeedsNewBattery` field has also been added. This field will serve as a flag to indicate to users of the class when a new battery is needed. The `InstallNewBattery` method has been added for this purpose. This method resets the battery indicator along with the `NumberOfStarts` counter. It was not necessary to initialize either of the new fields within the constructor. Fields automatically initialize to their "zero" state when an object is instantiated. Because integers are initialized to zero and Boolean fields are initialized to FALSE, we did not need to add this code to our constructor.

The Go method has been modified to take the new properties into account. Each time the car is told to 'Go', it increments the `NumberOfStarts` field. If the value exceeds 1000, a message is displayed indicating that the car will not start. The source code below can be used to test this new aspect of our `TCar` class. You will note in the example that we are using a `TSportsCar`. Since it is a descendent of the TCar class, any changes made to the parent class will be reflected in it.

```
program Inhercon;

uses WinCrt,SysUtils,Ucar in 'UCAR.PAS',
  Usports in USPORTS.PAS';

var
  Corvette : TSportsCar;
  i : longint;
begin
  Corvette := TSportsCar.Create;
  Writeln('The color is '+Corvette.Color);
  Writeln('The top speed is '+IntToStr(Corvette.TopSpeed));
  for i:=1 to 10 do
  begin
    Corvette.Go;
    if Corvette.NeedNewBattery then
    begin
      writeln('Can't Start. Replacing Battery.');
      Corvette.InstallNewBattery
```

```
       end;
     end;
   end.
```

This code uses the new `InstallNewBattery` method to reset the internal counters and indicators to keep the car going. The code listing above has no access to the private field within the object but, it can measure the effects of this field's values through the use of the `NeedNewBattery` field. In addition to changing the performance of the `TCar.Go` method, we have also changed the way the override method in its descendent works. This step is often necessary when modifying the basic workings of a method in a class from which one or several subclasses is based. The `TSportsCar.Go` method is shown below.

```
{ compatable syntax with superclass's method }
procedure TSportsCar.Go;
begin
  inherited Go;
  if not self.NeedNewBattery then
    writeln('vroom, vroom, vroom . . . screeeeech . . . crash')
end;
```

It is important to note that the `TSportsCar` class does not have access to the `NumberOfStarts` field contained within its own structure. This is the nature of private fields. In order for the `TSportsCar` class to have access to this field it would have to be declared as `public` or `protected`.

Protected

The `protected` directive makes access to fields and methods available only to object classes defined within the same unit or descendant classes. This restrictive denotation provides us with the ability to more closely model the real world. There are certain aspects of cars that are not typically modified outside of the factory. These attributes might not be seen or modified by the user of a car.

This field scoping is useful for setting and manipulating values that are needed within both the originating class and its subclasses. For example, the top speed of a car might be determined by the size of the engine and the car's aerodynamics. While the engine may be able to be modified by the user of the object, the aerodynamics cannot. In the source listing below, we have introduced a protected aerodynamic field into the `TCar` class. This factor, combined with the engine cylinder count, will be used to calculate the top speed of the vehicle.

```
TCar = class(TObject)
  { declare fields only available inside methods }
  private
    { counter field to track number of starts for car }
```

```
      NumberOfStarts : Integer;
    { declare fields available to class and subclasses }
  protected
      AeroFactor : single;
  public
      Engine : TEngine; { contains an engine object }
      Color : string;
      BodyStyle : TBodyStyle;
      Upholstery : TUpholstery;
      GasTankGallons : Integer;
      NeedNewBattery : Boolean;
      { define all methods as virtual so they can be
        overridden by subclasses }
      constructor Create; virtual;
      destructor Free; virtual;
      procedure Go; virtual;
      { Method designed to reset battery indicator and
        number of starts counter }
      procedure InstallNewBattery; virtual;
      { Top Speed Calculation }
      function TopSpeed : single; virtual;
    end;

implementation

constructor TCar.Create;
begin
    self.Color := 'Blue';
    self.BodyStyle := SEDAN;
    self.Upholstery := CLOTH;
    self.GasTankGallons := 12;
    { assign aero dynamic factor initial value }
    self.AeroFactor := 1.0;
    self.Engine := TEngine.Create;
end;

destructor TCar.Free;
begin
    self.Engine.Free;
end;

{ Function designed to calculate top speed of car based
  on engine size and aerodynamic factor }
function TCar.TopSpeed : single;
begin
    Result := 120*self.Engine.Cylinders/8*self.AeroFactor;
end;
```

The TopSpeed method has been added. It is a calculation based on the number of cylinders in the engine and the aerodynamic factor. The users of the car object do not have any way to change the AeroFactor. It is critical that subclasses have access to this value. Our sports car subclass would definitely have a need to modify the aerodynamics of the cars produced. The source listing below shows the constructor code for the TSortsCar class and its effect on the new protected field's value. You will notice that the TCar constructor is called before the value is changed. Again, it is best to always call parent class constructors before executing subclass constructor code.

```
constructor TSportsCar.Create;
begin
  { call inherited method }
  inherited Create;
  { new init code }
  self.Seats := 2;
  self.Convertable := TRUE;
  { reset the aerodynamic factor }
  self.AeroFactor := 1.25
end;
```

You can see from this example that a new sports car will achieve a top speed 25% higher than a simple car object with the same options. Any other subclasses would also have access to the AeroFactor property.

In addition to subclasses, classes defined within the same unit or a class that defines a protected field or method can access the protected aspect. In our UCAR.PAS unit, we have defined both the TCar and TEngine classes. Any protected fields or methods defined within either class can be accessed by the other. Let's add two new protected aspects to our engine class. These will be used to track spark plug efficiency and allow us to replace the plugs. Both the TCar and TEngine classes will have access to both the field and the method. Descendants of the TEngine class will also be able to access them. Below is the new class definition for TEngine.

```
type
  { Block type for engine }
  TBlock = (STRAIGHT, VEE);
  { engine type definition }
  TEngine = class(TObject)
  protected
    PlugEfficiency : single;
    procedure ReplacePlugs; virtual;
  public
    Block : TBlock;
    Manufacturer : string;
    Cylinders : Integer;
    EFI : Boolean;
```

```
       constructor Create;
     end;
  .
  .
  .

  constructor TEngine.Create;
  begin
    self.Block := STRAIGHT;
    self.Manufacturer := 'Ford';
    self.Cylinders := 6;
    self.EFI := TRUE;
    self.PlugEfficiency := 1.0
  end;

  procedure TEngine.ReplacePlugs;
  begin
    self.PlugEfficiency := 1.0
  end;
```

The TCar class can access the new method and field in its methods. The Go method has been modified to reduce spark plug efficiency by .1% each time it is called. A new TuneUp method has been added to replace the spark plugs when desired. Finally, the TopSpeed method has also been modified to lower the top speed as spark plug efficiency lowers. The listing for these methods in the TCar class are shown below.

```
{ Tune-up method which accesses protected method in the
  TEngine class }
procedure TCar.TuneUp;
begin
  self.Engine.ReplacePlugs;
end;

{ Function designed to calculate top speed of car based
  on engine size and aerodynamic factor }
function TCar.TopSpeed : single;
begin
  Result := 120*self.Engine.Cylinders/8*self.AeroFactor*
            self.Engine.PlugEfficiency;
end;

procedure TCar.Go;
begin
  if self.NumberOfStarts > 3 then
    self.NeedNewBattery := TRUE
  else
  begin
```

```
      self.NumberOfStarts := self.NumberOfStarts + 1;
      self.Engine.PlugEfficiency :=
self.Engine.PlugEfficiency*0.999;
      if self.engine.cylinders = 8 then
        writeln('vroom, vroom, guzzle')
      else
        writeln('vroom');
  end;
end;
```

PROPERTIES

Aside from the ability to assign enumerated types as fields to objects, we have not seen a way to provide any validation to field assignment. A process of validating field assignments using methods could be used for this task. Currently our sports car class has a field designed to identify the number of seats in the car. It is defined as an integer in the type definition. Integers can have a wide range of values beyond what might typically be found in your average sports car. Can you imagine a sports car with 233 seats?

In order to prevent this type of misassignment, we could develop a standard approach to creating and assigning field values. First, all fields would need to be delcared as private in scope. This would prevent their assignment outside of the class definition. Next, we would need to write methods for each field that would handle the validation and assignment of values to the fields. Finally, we would need a way to find out the current value of the field. The following source code listing demonstrates the use of this technique.

```
type
  TSportsCar = class(TCar)
  private
    FSeats : Integer; { hidden field holds seat count }
  public
    Convertible : Boolean;
    constructor Create; virtual;
    destructor Free; virtual;
    procedure Go; override;
    { Stub methods to test speed of method
      dispatching }
    procedure StatDo;
    procedure VirtDo; virtual;
    { Get and Set routines for FSeats Field }
    function GetSeats : integer; virtual;
    procedure SetSeats(NumberOfSeats : integer); virtual;
  end;
```

```
.
.
.
{ GetSeats results in current seat count }
function TSportsCar.GetSeats : Integer;
begin
  Result := self.FSeats;
end;
{ SetSeats validates the assignment of seat count }
procedure TSportsCar.SetSeats(NumberOfSeats : Integer);
begin
  if (NumberOfSeats = 4) or (NumberOfSeats = 2) then
    self.FSeats := NumberOfSeats
  else
    writeln('Error assigning seat count')
end;
```

You can see from this example that the creation of Get and Set methods can aid in forcing the correct assignment of fields. Unfortunately, this process has some drawbacks. We have to create two messages (GetXXX and SetXXX) for each field for which we want validation. This makes the interface between our applications and our object classes more difficult to understand. It also does not model the real world very well. What we really need is a way to assign field values and read their current values with a single message. This functionality is provided with the use of the property declaration.

Properties are the conduit through which we can read and write values to fields. By creating a property, we can validate the assignment of a field without cluttering our interface with difficult to use methods. Additionally, we can use properties to cause fields to manifest themselves as read-only, or provide additional functionality in the assignment of fields.

Read/Write Methods

The simplest property type is a *direct access property.* Direct access properties simply provide an interface to private fields within an object class. The source code listing below shows the declaration of a property to read and write a field within the TSportsCar class.

```
type
  TSportsCar = class(TCar)
  private
    FSeats : Integer;
    FConvertible : Boolean;
  public
    property Convertible : boolean read FConvertible
                                    write FConvertible;
    constructor Create; virtual;
```

```
  destructor Free; virtual;
  procedure Go; override;
  { Stub methods to test speed of method
    dispatching }
  procedure StatDo;
  procedure VirtDo; virtual;
  { Get and Set routines for FSeats Field }
  function GetSeats : integer; virtual;
  procedure SetSeats(NumberOfSeats : integer); virtual;
end;
```

Like fields, properties must be defined as being a certain type. In this example, the Convertible property is declared as boolean. The Convertible property has both a read and a write section. These are directly mapped to the private FConvertible field. This particular property does not serve any assignment validation purpose since there are only two values for any Boolean type anyway. The property creation provides users of the class the ability to assign the property in the same way as a field assignment. The source listing below demonstrates the use of the new Convertible property.

```
Corvette := TSportsCar.Create;
Corvette.Convertible := FALSE;
```

As you can see from this example, the creation of the property has done little at this time to improve our object class. We will see later how creating seemingly unneeded properties like this one will serve us in the future. We can see from this example the typical syntax and field setup needed to use properties. The field is declared as private to prevent users of the class from directly accessing it. The property declaration provides the access to the field.

Properties can be used to validate the assignment of fields within object classes. Our earlier example of creating 'Get' and 'Set' methods can be used to demonstrate this technique. The following listing shows the declaration of a property that utilizes the methods we wrote earlier to control the assignment of the FSeats field.

```
type
  TSportsCar = class(TCar)
  private
    FSeats : Integer;
    FConvertible : Boolean;
    { Get and Set routines for FSeats Field }
    procedure SetSeats(NumberOfSeats : integer); virtual;
  public
    property Convertible : boolean  read FConvertible
                                    write FConvertible;
    property Seats : integer read FSeats write SetSeats;
```

Instead of merely passing assigned values directly to the field, this property calls the SetSeats method depending on whether the source code is attempting to retrieve or assign the seat count. You should note that the field assignment method is declared as a private method so as to ensure that it not be called by programs using the class. This example demonstrates the typical use of properties. They provide access and use of fields while protecting them from invalid assignment. We no longer needed the 'Get' method. If we wanted the retrieval of the seat count to perform some other action we could have used it.

Default Values and Properties

Properties provide the ability to set default values for them. This is critical for properties of objects derived from the TComponent class. We will talk about the creation of default values when we discuss component creation in a later chapter. It is important that fields referenced by a property have a reasonable default value assigned to them in the constructor. This default value assignment was covered earlier in this chapter.

Read-only Properties

Occasionally, there is a need to have a property that can be read by the user of the class but not written to. The use of properties is ideal for this situation. You are permitted to create properties with only a read keyword. Let's add a field to our TSportsCar class to contain the current odometer reading. Because the odometer tracks the number of miles driven, we will change the Go method to increment the odometer each time it is called. The source listing below shows the TSportsCar class as it is modified with the new Odometer property.

```
type
  TSportsCar = class(TCar)
  private
    FSeats : Integer;
    FConvertible : Boolean;
    FOdometer : integer;
    { Set routine for FSeats Field }
    procedure SetSeats(NumberOfSeats : integer); virtual;
public
    property Convertible : boolean  read FConvertible
                                    write FConvertible;
    property Seats : integer read FSeats write SetSeats;
    property Odometer : integer read FOdometer;
 . . .
```

Here we have added a private FOdometer field to contain the current reading. The Odometer property declaration contains only a read section and no write section.

This will allow users of the class to read the odometer value but not be able to change it. Should the user of the class attempt to write to the Odometer property, the following error message will result.

```
Error 174 : Cannot assign to read-only property
```

Property Side Effects

The Delphi manuals discuss the implementation of side effects when working with properties. The term *side effect* has traditionally had bad connotations when used in the discussion of software engineering. A side effect is an action taken by a routine not intended by the caller of the routine. You could encounter side effects in procedures, functions, methods, and even properties. However, the careful creation of side effects can serve to improve your class definitions and make them more useable.

Earlier we saw the assignment of the FConvertible field in our sports car object class being handled by a property. At the time we created it, it seemed like an unnecessary step because our field could only contain one of two values: TRUE or FALSE. You will see in the following code listing that the creation of a property for something as simple as a Boolean field can add functionality to an object class.

```
type
  TSportsCar = class(TCar)
  private
    FSeats : Integer;
    FConvertible : Boolean;
    { Get and Set routines for FSeats Field }
    procedure SetSeats(NumberOfSeats : integer); virtual;
    procedure SetConvertible(RagTop : boolean); virtual;
  public
    property Convertible : boolean   read FConvertible
                                     write SetConvertible;
    .
    .
    .
procedure TSportsCar.SetConvertible(RagTop : boolean);
begin
  self.FConvertible := RagTop;
  if RagTop then
    self.AeroFactor := self.AeroFactor*0.95;
end;
```

Again, the Set routine for the field is declared as a private method. In addition to merely assigning the field value, the SetConvertible method changes the aerodynamic factor of the car to a lower value if it is a rag top convertible. This helps the

TSportsCar class model the real world better. If you change a sports car from a hard top to a rag top, it becomes less aerodynamic.

The use of side effects in the creation of Get/Set methods should be done with great care. Side effects can often be the sign of poor class design. If there is not a real world equivalent to the side effect, it probably doesn't belong in the assignment of a property.

When to Use Properties

We recommend the use of properties for every field within an object class. By making all fields private and adding properties, you build in room to grow and change. Consider our earlier example of the Convertible property on a sports car. Initially, there seemed little reason to hide the field from users of the class. Later, as more information came to light about the performance of sports cars, we could take advantage of the property to implement the needed side effect of changing the type of roof on the car.

There is little chance that you will know for certain all of the possible side effects and validations that will ever be needed within a class. Accepting this fact, you should define all fields as private first. Add the needed properties to access these fields as either protected or public. This will ensure the needed access to the stored values without sacrificing the flexibility that is needed with changing requirements and understanding of the system being modeled.

We will make extensive use of properties in our discussions about creating components in Delphi. You will see a more extensive use of properties and the common ways in which they can help make components more useable.

CHAPTER 5

OBJECT-ORIENTED DESIGN

OVERVIEW

Now that we have discussed the implementation of object-oriented programming in Delphi, we will turn our attention to the way in which these facilities can be used to create applications. The first step in creating an application is to focus on the real-world problem that the new system is attempting to model. User interviews and paper documentation examinations can be used to familiarize yourself with the environment in which the application will reside. Typically, this process is formalized in order to document the activities involved in the design and to remove ambiguities that often surround the process of creating applications for end-users. Developers have a choice as to what type of design process to use in creating applications. In this chapter we will discuss the basic method currently used to design and write applications. We will look at its shortfalls and introduce a new methodology more suited to object-oriented programming. However, before we delve into the intricacies of object-oriented design, we should introduce some diagramming techniques that make it easier to visualize class relationships.

OBJECT-ORIENTED DESIGN DIAGRAMMING TECHNIQUES

All types of object-oriented programming methodologies have their own diagramming technique, and not surprisingly all proponents of one technique believe that all others are deficient. We are going to show the bare basics of two techniques that are widely used: Booch and Rumbaugh.

Each of these diagramming techniques have a representative for classes and objects, and a well defined way with which to attach them together. These diagrams are useful in creating a visual design of the hierarchy of your classes, which is vital as they grow larger. These diagrams can also be used as specifications for a project. They are general enough so that users can understand the basic relationships, and comment on how well the design models the real world.

Class Relationships

Class relationships are inheritance relationships. The simple test for a class relationship is the "is-a" test. If you can say that one class "is-a" variety of another class, then there is an inheritance relationship. For example, you can say a TButton "is-a" TComponent, thus there is an inheritance relationship. You could not however say that Form_main "is-a" Button_close. This is not an inheritance relationship.

Diagramatically, Booch represents classes as "amorphous blobs", trying to indicate that they are abstract. Figure 5.1 shows the Booch representation of a class.

The labels inside the blob represent the name of the class, its attributes, operations, and constraints. For simplicity, it is not always required to put all attributes and operations within the diagram, only those that are relevant to the current part of the system that is being diagrammed.

Figure 5.2 displays a Booch diagram of two classes, the second inherited from the first. Rumbaugh's diagramming technique is a little more straightforward, but is based in principle on Booch's work (as are many of the OOP models in existence today). In the Rumbaugh model, classes are represented as blocks as depicted in Figure 5.3. Rumbaugh also uses lines to show inheritance relationships. Figure 5.4 shows an example of two related classes, both inherited from the same parent.

Object Relationships

Both Booch and Rumbaugh make the important distinction between classes and objects. An object relationship is typically a containing relationship. The simple test for containership is the "has-a" test. If an object "has-a" some other object, then the second object is contained in the first. For example, a form "has-a" button, so the button is contained by the form.

Figure 5.5 shows the object notations for both Booch and Rumbaugh. Notice that

FIGURE 5.1   Booch Diagram of a Class

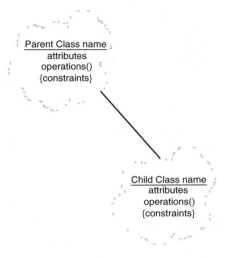

FIGURE 5.2 Booch Diagram of a Class Relationship

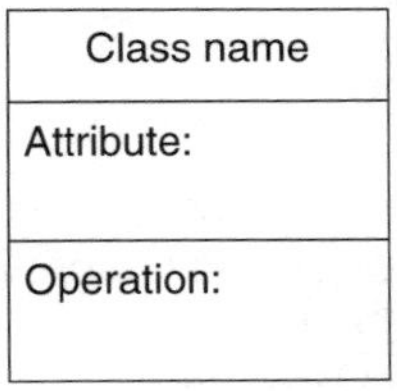

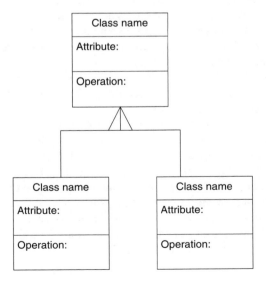

FIGURE 5.3 Rumbaugh's Representation of a Class

FIGURE 5.4 Rumbaugh's Inheritance Diagramming Technique

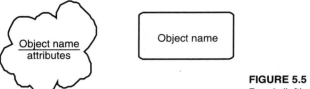

FIGURE 5.5   Object Notations for
Booch (left) and Rumbaugh (right)

Booch's objects are solid versions of the amorphous cloud, whereas Rumbaugh's objects
are rectangles with rounded edges.

DESIGN MODELS

The design of software applications continues to evolve. There are several different
schools of thought as to the best models. Each has its own advantages and disadvantages.
We are going to look at the prototyping model, the traditional waterfall, and the round-trip
gestalt waterfall approach.

Prototyping Model

By far, the most popular of all microcomputer based design methodologies is a prototyping model. This involves creating a small working model of the eventual application, usually just the user interface and not even minimal functionality. The prototype is shown to
the end-users as soon as possible to elicit responses about the way it functions. This allows the designers to discover flaws quickly, rather than spend a lot of time implementing
some functionality that was not needed or was incorrectly designed.

The obvious advantages of the prototyping model are early responses from the users
and quick feasibility verification. However, there are some distinct disadvantages to this
model. First, no matter how much you inform them, the prototype looks like the finished
application to the users. A frequent comment heard at the demonstration of a prototype is,
"It looks great. Can we have it now?" Users sometimes don't understand the underlying
complexity, and therefore can't understand why a seemingly functional piece of software
still has to be worked on for months.

Secondly, and more seriously, most prototypes don't scale very well. If you are
going to build a complex system (that is, a large software application), it is hard to create
a smaller version of it that encompasses all of its functionality. Indeed, if you could build
a smaller version that didn't sacrifice anything, why not build it that way in the first
place? Thus, a prototype is not a very good representation of the finished application. In
fact, it is very rare to even be able to salvage any of the prototype's code for the working
application. The only thing in which prototypes excel is user interface design. It is useful
to let the eventual users of the system try it and make suggestions. The closer the system
is to the way they want it to work, the happier they will be.

Because of the scalability problem, the prototype model is usually only used for very small projects. A more used approach for large application development is the waterfall model.

The Traditional Waterfall Model

Traditional software development has used the *Waterfall Design* model for creating applications. Figure 5.6 shows the steps generally used in this methodology. As you can see, there is a clear distinction between each phase of development and a one-way path from start to finish.

The steps involved in this methodology are familiar to most application developers. The limitations associated with this model can prevent applications from meeting user needs due to the distance between analysis and integration. In other words, once you have finished a particular stage, you cannot go back to it, just as water cannot flow back up a waterfall.

The problem with this approach is the reluctance or refusal to address design problems from an earlier stage. For example, if you discover a design flaw while you are in the coding stage, you shouldn't go back to redesign, you should make it work as best as possible. Of course, the problem tends to grow, and even if you can create a working application, it is very hard to maintain and modify. A better approach allows changes to any stage of the project at any time. This is the recursive model.

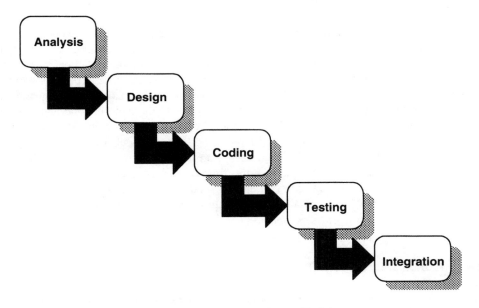

FIGURE 5.6   Waterfall Design Model

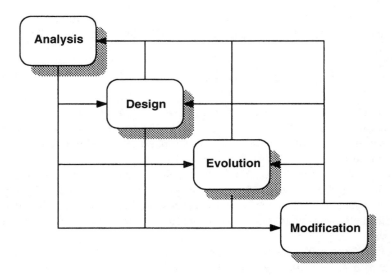

FIGURE 5.7   Recursive Object-oriented Design Model

The Recursive Model

Booch developed a recursive design process that can make the task of object-oriented programming easier and more effective. The steps involved in this process are shown in Figure 5.7.

You can see from this diagram that the model allows for a great deal of backtracking within the design process. This may mean revising working code to accommodate the new design. However, in the long run, the better the design models the real world, the easier it will be to extend its functionality to match another characteristic of the real world object you are modeling. Each step is designed to tie the application back to its real-world abstraction. This forces the application to model the real world more closely and allows for the incremental process of changing the design to take place as late as the modification stage.

The recursive model is the preferred design model. Like many things in object-oriented design, the initial stages are more time consuming, because more effort is put into creating the abstraction. But, this time is returned as soon as you must modify or add new features to the system. If it closely models the real world, it should extend easily to match its real world counterpart. This process of modeling the real world as objects is known as *real-world decomposition.*

REAL-WORLD DECOMPOSITION

When you design a computer program, you are creating a model of something in the real world using a programming language. You are creating an *abstract* version of a real world object. However, there are several different types of abstraction. These types are not mutually exclusive. Indeed, the best models incorporate all of these types of abstraction.

Semantic Abstraction

Each language has a *semantic abstraction* associated with the creation of objects. This abstraction is rooted in the capabilities and features available to the developer in attempting to take a process and model it programatically. The semantic abstraction for Delphi is defined by the object-oriented design features of Object-Pascal and the way Delphi models applications. For example, applications (except CRT applications) have an application object, which creates the forms used by the application. This application object is part of the semantic abstraction provided by Delphi.

Delphi's object model is very robust and provides a great many features that allow us to implement our designs so that they closely correspond to their real-world counterparts. Semantic abstraction involves the creation of object classes that can be used as base classes for specific applications.

Domain Abstraction

Abstraction involving the specific objects needed to create an application is referred to as *domain abstraction* (Figure 5.8). Each application has a specific set of entities that it is attempting to model. As such, it is important to create object classes that match up closely with these entities.

How can this be done without recreating needed classes from scratch? The answer lies in using existing semantic class designs and descending their capabilities into the domain abstracts needed for the application. The form tool within Delphi is an excellent example of domain abstraction.

Delphi applications do not use the TForm class directly in their implementation. In-

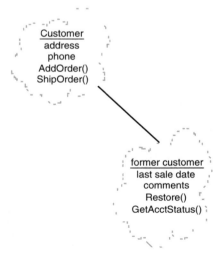

FIGURE 5.8 Example of a Domain Abstraction Relationship Between Customers and Former Customers

stead, you create TForm subclasses that match up with the domain specific features needed by your application. This process is not limited to form design. Any existing or invented semantic class can be used to create a new class that closely models the real world entities needed for the application at hand.

Toolset Abstraction

Toolset abstraction is the process of taking data structures and operating system features and creating classes and objects to represent them (Figure 5.9). Delphi comes with many different object classes that can be used in the application development process. The components that we use to create forms provide a toolset of features needed in most applications. Without these basic classes, we would be left to develop our own tools from scratch.

Unfortunately, as good as these tools are, they do not model the specific requirements of most applications. That is left to domain abstraction. They do, however, provide a sort of additional language, which exists on top of Object-Pascal, which subsequently provides high level functionality with very little code.

Incidentally, most work in object-oriented languages so far has been at this toolset abstraction level. For example, the Windows API is a perfect candidate to objectize. While OOP is certainly excellent for performing this sort of abstraction, the real power of OOP extends to the problem domain as well, into domain abstraction. The best use of OOP is to model not just the tools used to create applications, but to model the solutions to problems in object-oriented terms as well. We feel that too much emphasis has been placed on toolset abstraction at the expense of the more powerful domain abstraction.

VCL

Delphi has a superb toolset abstraction, which provides a metalanguage for controlling aspects of a Delphi application. This additional language that Delphi provides is the Visual

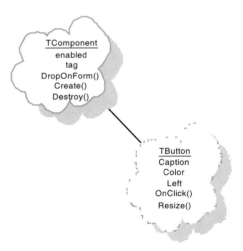

FIGURE 5.9 Toolset Abstraction Relationship between Class TComponent and Descendant TButton

Component Library (VCL). A great deal of useful work can be performed by Delphi by using only the properties and methods implemented in VCL. So, VCL is like a fourth generation language that sits atop the third generation Object-Pascal. In fact, you can drop to a second generation language (assembler) if you need to. Very few language products give you that much flexibility.

The aspect of Delphi that is the most powerful is this VCL application framework. If the Delphi environment featured a less useful toolset abstraction, it wouldn't be nearly as powerful. Part of the strength of VCL lies in its object oriented nature. The class hierarchy of VCL components was designed with extensibility in mind, so that programmers can completely extend the environment in an invisible, seamless way.

LIST PROPERTIES VS. INHERITANCE

We will visit one more topic of interest that pertains to object-oriented design, and that is the question of list properties vs. inheritance. The question here is a bit philosophic, but it sheds some light on the kind of decisions that occur over and over again as you design classes.

There are essentially two different ways to add properties (either variables or methods) to a class: either inherit from the class and add the new properties in the descendant, or provide each class with a list property which can contain a series of objects. For example, when you create a new form using the form designer, you are actually creating a descendant of TForm, to which you add components (Figure 5.10). The alternative is to create a list of components that is part of TForm, and place all the form components in the list (Figure 5.11). In fact, the form class already provides this functionality, but only at run-time, in the components array property of the form.

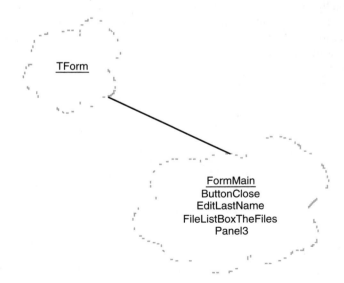

FIGURE 5.10 Class Relationship
Between TForm and its Descendants

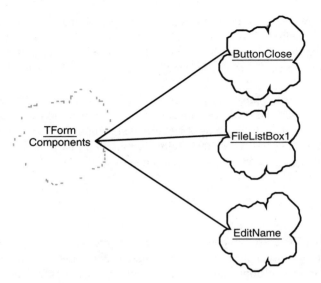

FIGURE 5.11   Form Components as a List, Rather than New Properties in an Inherited Class

So which is better? In fact, inheritance is a better mechanism, because it encapsulates common characteristics. For example, any time you find that you have two classes that have the same code in them, you should move the common code out to a new class, which is the parent of the original two. Then, that code is only written once, but used in all the descendants of the class.

CONCLUSION

In this chapter we touched on the subject of object-oriented application design. This is obviously a large topic, of which we have only scratched the surface. If you are interested in reading further on this topic, there are many books available. Object-oriented design for applications requires an investment of time to fully understand it, but the benefits far outweigh the learning curve. Once you have become accustomed to object-oriented programming, it's very difficult to go back to old habits!

CHAPTER 6

FORM DESIGNER

Delphi's form designer is extremely powerful. Forms are the primary interface between your users and your application, so forms and the form designer are the focus of application development in Delphi. As you will find, Delphi's form designer is both easy to use yet capable of accomodating almost any interface task. In this chapter, we will examine this remarkable tool.

When visual design tools first became available, they were usually programs that read-in what the user had laid out on the screen and generated an intermediate file. This file was either in the source language of the product or in some specialized scripting language. These tools were nice because they allowed the programmer to visually design their interface, which was typically the most time consuming task in product development.

The problem with tools from this generation is that you could not change the generated code and see your changes in the design view. So, you could use the designer up to a point, but then if you wanted to do anything that had to be done by manipulating the generated code, you had to decide if you were ready to maintain your form only in code without the use of the designer. If you had made changes to the generated code, the designer would refuse to open the form.

TWO-WAY TOOLS DEFINED

Two-way tools are the next generation of design tools. With two-way tools, you never have to make the decision to abandon the graphical design tool. Within Delphi, you can use the designer for a while, switch to directly manipulating the generated source code, and then switch back into the designer. As long as your changes to the source code are syntactically correct, you can reopen the modified form in the design view and continue to work graphically.

This aspect makes the Delphi tools the best of both worlds. Some programmers prefer to do some of their work in code and a little through designers, while other programmers would prefer to just use the designer. No matter which type you are, Delphi lets you work the way you want to.

Delphi's two-way tools ability brings up an interesting point. Before Delphi, all the other two-way tool products have been built atop languages that are based on an interpreter instead of a compiler. For example, dBASE for Windows also has two-way tools, but the dBASE language must have the interpreter running, both at design time and at run-time. However, Delphi has no interpreter—it is a native compiler for Intel processors. How does Delphi "know" what code has been typed into the program editor, either by the design tool or by the programmer?

The answer embodies the reason why Object-Pascal was picked as the language base for Delphi. Because of the grammar structure of the Object-Pascal language and the 10 years of experience that Borland has with Pascal compilers, Object-Pascal can be compiled faster than any other language. The Delphi environment looks at the code that is typed into the editor and updates what is seen on the form in real-time. This means that Delphi is constantly scanning the editor, looking for changes, and incorporating the changes in the form designer so quickly that the form appears to change instantaneously.

A Fairly Useless but Spectacular Example

Just like the title says, this is not something that you would do often, but is a spectacular demonstration of the symbiosis of the designer and the editor. Create a blank form and lay a button on it as shown in Figure 6.1.

Now, using the Edit menu, **Cut** the button off the form (or use the Ctrl-X shortcut). Now, click on the editor tab and go to the bottom of the source file. Now, select **Paste** (or Ctrl-V) and paste the button into the editor as shown in Figure 6.2.

The code that was pasted into the editor is the same as the code for a button that would reside in the DFM file, which is the file that keeps property values for a form. You can now make changes to this code. For example, let's change the caption to say, "Two-way button", change the location to be on the left side of the form rather than the right, and make the button wider (Figure 6.3).

Now, highlight all of the button code and cut it from the editor, using **Edit | Cut** (or Ctrl-X), go back to the Form designer, and paste the button back on the form (with **Edit | Paste** or Ctrl-V). Notice that the button is in the new location, the caption is changed, and it is wider as shown in Figure 6.4.

This simple example shows how well synchronized the editor and the designer are. This is clearly not the most efficient way to modify properties but it does show the power behind the interface. The two-way tools concept runs deeply throughout Delphi.

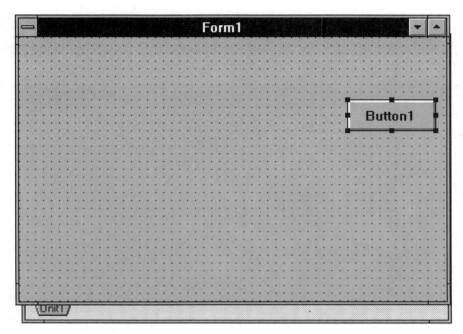

FIGURE 6.1 A Simple Form with a Single Button Component

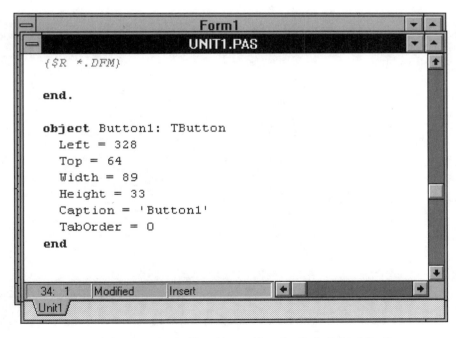

FIGURE 6.2 Two-Way Tools Allow You to View the Code Behind the Component

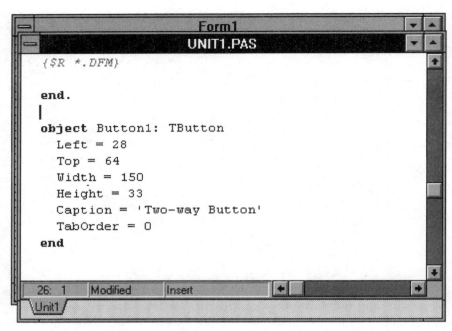

```
{$R *.DFM}


end.

object Button1: TButton
  Left = 28
  Top = 64
  Width = 150
  Height = 33
  Caption = 'Two-way Button'
  TabOrder = 0
end
```

FIGURE 6.3 Code Behind the Component Can be Changed in the Code Editor

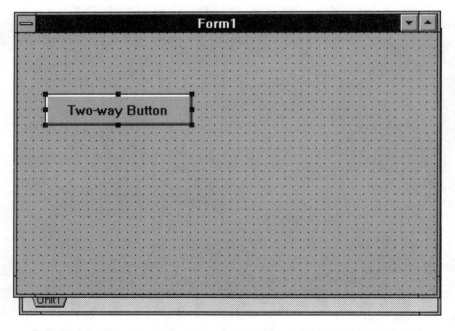

FIGURE 6.4 Changes to the Underlying Code are Reflected in the Component's Visual Representation

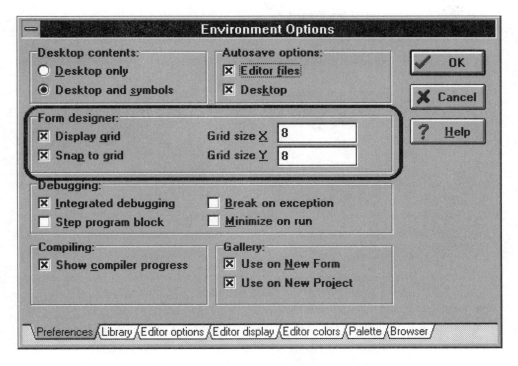

FIGURE 6.5 Envrionment Options with the Form Design Parameters Circled

Form Designer Configuration

Like so many of the elements of the Delphi environment, the Form designer is user-configurable as well. Within the **Options | Environment** dialog, there is a section devoted to the Form designer (Figure 6.5).

You can specify the grid size along either axis, or you can optionally not display the grid at all. The Snap to Grid setting determines whether or not components that are dropped on the form always line up to the closest grid points. If this feature is enabled, components will "snap" to the nearest grid axis when they are laid on the form. This generally makes it easier to line up multiple components.

COMPONENT TYPES

Forms aren't very interesting if they don't have anything on them. All the controls that you can drop on a form are called components. The component palette contains all of your currently available component types. The components are broken up by type onto separate pages. Use the page tabs to choose which type of component you want to view.

Placing Components on Forms

There are a couple of ways to drop components on a form. The easiest way is to mouse-click the desired component and then click on the Form Designer; your component's upper left hand corner will appear where you clicked. The component will appear in its default size. You can drop a component and resize it at the same time. After selecting the desired component, click on the form and drag a box that's the size that you want the component to be. When you release the mouse button, the component will be the size you've drawn (with a few exceptions, which we will cover shortly).

If you need more than one component of a certain type, you can double click on the component in the palette, and Delphi will place as many components of that type as you like. When Delphi pastes multiple components on your form, it offsets the additional controls so that they won't hide one another.

Another way to place multiple components on the form is to hold down the shift key as you select a component. Then, every time you click on the form, a new component of that type will be placed. When you have as many of the desired controls as you want, click on the pointer symbol to the far left of the component palette.

There are two basic types of components in Delphi—visible and nonvisible. They are both placed on the form in the same way, and their properties are set in the same way, but they behave differently at run-time.

Visible

Visible components are controls that are visible at run-time. Examples of visible components are editboxes, labels, buttons, etc. Visible components are the obvious form controls that the user of the application will see when it is running, and they generally will accept focus, meaning that the user can select them and interact with them.

NonVisible

Nonvisible components appear on the form at design time, but are completely invisible to the user at run-time. You usually place nonvisible components on a form to provide a service of some kind to other components or the entire application. The placement of nonvisible components is not important, and they can overlap other items.

A good example of an invisible component is the timer control. The timer component allows the programmer to perform some action at regular time intervals, such as updating a database or simulating a clock.

CREATING A SIMPLE FORM

Let's create a simple form that has a just few components on it. This is not meant to be a particularly useful form, but it will illustrate the basic concepts of the Form Designer.

Adding Components to the Form

We are going to add a few components, both visible and invisible, to a form and have them interact with one another. First, we are going to create a new project, consisting of one form. Because Delphi is project centric, you should always have a project active to design forms. You can create forms without having a project open, but there is no way to run a form unless it's included in a project.

We are going to add the following components to the blank form:

- 2 text labels (from the Standard page)
- 1 timer control (from the System page)
- 2 pushbuttons (from the Standard page)
- 1 gauge (from the Samples page)
- 1 group box (from the Standard page)
- 1 edit component (from the Standard page)

Figure 6.6 is the outcome of our work.

Manipulating Components

The location of these controls is not important and, as you will see, very easy to change. The Delphi Form Designer allows you to visually lay out and manipulate all the controls on the form, either individually or in groups.

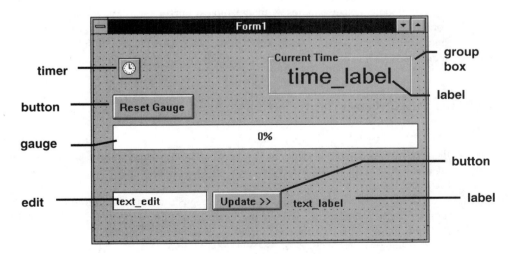

FIGURE 6.6   A Simple Form

FIGURE 6.7   A Selected Component in Design View Showing its Resize Handles

Moving components.   Once the components are on the form, you can easily move them into new positions. By clicking on any component, visible or nonvisible, you can drag it to a new location. Normally, only one component on the form has focus, meaning that it is the control that is ready to be manipulated. The focus control has a re-size border, which is dark and has handles on the corners and sides (Figure 6.7). The focus control is also the control whose properties are currently shown in the Object Inspector.

You can move more than one component at a time if you want. There are several ways to do this. First, you can click on a component, then hold down the shift key and click on additional components. You can select as many components as you like this way, and they will all move together when you drag any one of them. You will also notice that the focus indicator changes into a group selection highlight, denoting that you have multiple components selected (Figure 6.8).

The other easy way to move multiple components is to "rubber band" them. To rubber band components, click on the form surface away from any components and hold down the left mouse button. Now as you drag the mouse cursor, you will see an expanding selection rectangle. Any component that is touched by the rectangle will be selected when you release the mouse button. Notice the group selection highlighting for all the encompassed components. When you are finished moving the controls, click somewhere away from the marked components and they will unhighlight.

Resizing components.   You can resize visible components by grabbing one of the component resize handles with the mouse cursor and expanding or contracting the component. For invisible components, you can try to resize them, but they will always snap back to their default size. Of course, because the invisible components will never be seen in the running application, the inability to resize them is not a problem.

USING THE OBJECT INSPECTOR TO SET PROPERTIES

The Object Inspector in Delphi is a simple yet powerful way to control the attributes of all the elements of an application. Basically, the Object Inspector allows the programmer to change characteristics, such as color, alignment, help text, etc., of any form component or the Form itself.

The combobox at the top of the object inspector contains a reference to the component whose properties you are currently setting. In Figure 6.9 the properties listed are for the form named Form1, of type TForm1. The properties are alphabetized and the properties that have "+" signs by them are expandable, like an outline. To change the properties on another component, you can either select the component on the form, or select it from

FIGURE 6.8   Multiple Components Selected in Design View

the combobox at the top of the Object Inspector. The component names are alphabetized within the Object Inspector.

Of course, one of the problems with this type of interface is determining the purpose of each of the properties. Fortunately, Delphi has extremely good context sensitive help. If you don't know what a particular property is for, just hit the F1 key while your cursor is on the property, and you will get help on that property.

Delphi also makes it easy to set the same property for a group of components. In the previous section, we saw a couple of ways to select more than one component so that we could move them as a group. While multiple components are selected, the Object Inspector shows a list of all the properties that all the components have in common. You can change the same property for multiple components in this one place. For example, in Figure 6.10 the gauge and the Reset Gauge button on our sample form are both selected.

The Object Inspector displays all the properties that the gauge and the button have in common. Notice that, because the gauge and button's left sides are aligned, the left property above is the same for both. If we wanted to move both components to the left by

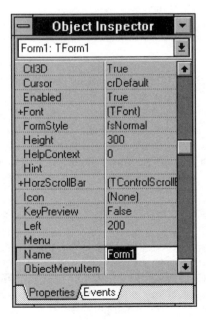

FIGURE 6.9   The Object Inspector with the Form Object Selected

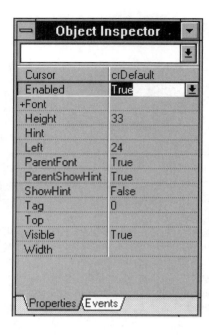

FIGURE 6.10 The Object Inspector Shows Common Properties for a Selection of Multiple Components

5, we could change the left property in the Object Inspector instead of dragging the components in the Form Designer. This is an easy way to set properties like "enabled" or "visible" for a group of properties with just one step.

Types of Properties

There are essentially three types of properties within the object inspector: simple, enumerated, and property editor types.

Simple types.   Simple types are properties into which you can just type a value. For example, the name property takes a string, and the left property takes a number. These simple property types take a single value, usually of a native Delphi type (that is, string, integer, etc.).

Enumerated types.   Enumerated types include the Boolean values (true or false), and also any properties where you must pick a value from a list of possible values. The Align property has a list of possible values, and you must pick an item from the list. If you click on the down arrow to the right of that field, you will get a drop down list of all of the acceptable values (Figure 6.11). You can directly type these values into the field if you want, but you are guaranteed not to misspell them if you pick them from the list! You can also toggle through all of the possible enumerated types for a component

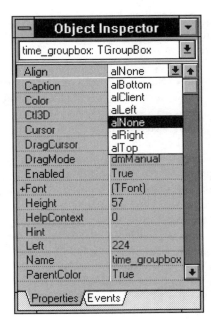

FIGURE 6.11 Enumerated Properties Reveal their Possible Values in a Drop-Down List

by double clicking within the field. Every time you double click, it shows you the next value on the list, and will roll over to the top of the list when you reach the bottom.

Property editor types.   A property editor type will display a small button with an ellipsis (" . . . ") in the entry field for the property. When you click on the ellipsis, a property editor will appear. For example, the font picker dialog box opens in response to clicking on the property edit button in the Font property. Delphi comes stocked with a wide variety of property editors. They allow setting relatively complicated properties through dialog boxes.

Component Name

You modify most component properties to change the behavior or appearance of the component. The Name property doesn't have to be changed—if you leave the naming to Delphi, it will make sure that you don't have two components with the same name. As you may have noticed, Delphi names components the same as their type name (without the initial "T") along with a serialized number. For example, the first component of type TPanel will be named panel1. The second TPanel component will be named panel2, etc.

Although you aren't forced to, we recommend that you always give your components meaningful names. In general, the first thing you should do after you have laid all your components on a form is go through and change their name properties. Delphi makes it easy to do this; every time you switch components in the object inspector, the same property selected for the previously selected component will be highlighted (if it is available). For example, to change the name properties, pick the first component on the list and select its Name property. When you select the next component, you will be sitting on its Name property in the object inspector.

We recommend changing component names because it makes your code much more readable. This is the same reasoning behind creating meaningful variable names. Software engineering studies have shown that program code is read three times as often as it's written. In other words, code is usually written once, but has to be read (for documentation, maintenance, modifications, etc.) on an average of three times. If you take the extra time to make your code lucid when it's written, you will be saving yourself interpretation time later. For example, the assignment `LabelFName.enabled := true` makes much more sense than `label1.enabled := true`. In the first case, it's clear which label is being enabled, while in the second case, you would have to refer somewhere else to find out which label was being enabled.

We also recommend that you prefix your component names with the type of component. For example, all label components would begin with "Label". This makes it easier to ascertain the type of the component when you're writing event handler code. This naming convention also makes it easy to determine component types in the drop-down list of the object inspector, and they all appear in alphabetical order.

PROGRAMMING EVENTS

The Event tab on the Object Inspector shows the events that are associated with a particular component.

The panel in Figure 6.12 lists all of the events that are available for buttons. Notice that almost all events start with "On". This makes it easy to spot events, and it also implies some action has occurred.

Event Handlers

Events in Delphi can be broken down into two types: *system* initiated and *user* initiated. System events are events that Windows takes care of, such as OnEnter and OnExit. The OnEnter event is automatically fired when the component becomes active, and the OnExit event is automatically fired when the component becomes inactive. User events are fired when the user takes the specified action, such as clicking on a button. When the user clicks a button, the button's OnClick event fires.

For both types of events, if you want something specific to happen, you can attach code to that event. For example, if you want a particular routine to execute when the user clicks on a button, you would write code and attach it to the button's OnClick event. This code is called an *event handler*. You will often use an event handler to change some of the properties of your form's components at run-time.

To actually write an event handler, choose the component that you want to associate the event with, choose the event page of the Object Inspector, and double click in the entry field for the event you want to handle. This will bring up the program editor with the

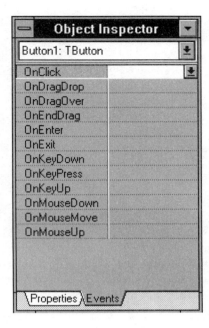

FIGURE 6.12 The Object Inspector Events Page for a Button

event header already defined, along with the Object-Pascal code that is necessary for every event handler. You can also invoke the program editor by double clicking on a component in the Form Designer. This assumes that you want to write an event handler for the default event for that component. The default event is different for every component type, but it is always the event that will probably be handled the most. For example, the default event handler for buttons is the OnClick event.

A Simple Example

Let's make our sample form do something. We are going to put a clock in the box in the upper right and make the gauge and buttons work.

First, we are going to look at the event handler for the Reset Gauge button. The Gauge component has a progress property that indicates how much of the gauge is filled up. When the user clicks on the Reset Gauge button, we want the progress indicator to be zero:

```
procedure TForm1. ButtonResetGaugeClick ( Sender : TObject);
 begin
   Gauge1.progress := 0
end;
```

The next event handler we are going to create is for the Update button. When the user clicks on the button, we want to change the caption property of the LabelText component to be the same as the current contents of the EditText editbox. In this event handler, we'll assign the value of the LabelText's Caption property to the Text property of the EditText box.

```
procedure TForm1.ButtonUpdateClick(Sender: TObject);
begin
  LabelText.caption := EditText.text
end;
```

The above two procedures show handlers for *user events,* namely button clicks. Our last event handler is an example of a *system event.* There is no difference in the way that the event handler is written, just when the event occurs. It is the event handler that is attached to the only event a timer control has, the OnTimer event. This event is fired every time the timer "ticks", and how often it ticks is one of its properties. This event handler also demonstrates setting the properties for several different components within one event handler.

```
procedure TForm1.TimerTimeTimer(Sender: TObject);
begin
  { set the current time }
  LabelTime.caption := TimeToStr( time );
  {if the gauge isn't at it's maximum value,
   add 1 to it's progress }
  if Gauge1.progress <= Gauge1.MaxValue then
    Gauge1.progress := Gauge1.progress + 1;
end;
```

First, this event handler sets the caption of the LabelTime component to the current time. Since this happens every time the timer ticks, the caption of that label will keep up with the time. The second responsibility of this event handler is to make the gauge fill up. The event handler checks to see if the gauge's Progress property is still less than the gauge's MaxValue property. If it is, one is added to the gauge's progress, causing the gauge to fill up. Remember that the Reset Gauge button resets the gauge's Progress property to zero, which changes how much of the gauge is filled up.

RUNNING A FORM

To run a form and test it, you must compile and link the project that the form is part of (Figure 6.13). In this case, the project is named Sample1.dpr, and the form is named fSamp1.pas. The easiest way to run the project is to click on the "run" button on the main

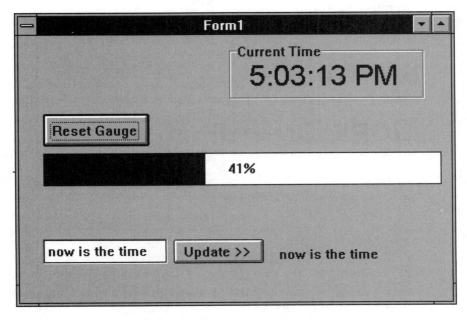

FIGURE 6.13   The Time Form in Run Mode

speedbar. If the project needs compiling, Delphi will take care of it and start the program running.

The user has typed "now is the time" in the edit box and pressed the Update button. The gauge is 41% full, meaning that the gauge's Progress property value is 41. The time shows 5:03:13 PM, and it is updated every second, so it is in effect a real-time clock.

For this project, the programmer only had to write four lines of code—the program editor automatically created all the rest. Creating simple applications like this in Delphi is often just a matter of setting a few component properties and writing code for the selected events within Delphi's predefined code skeletons. What could be easier?

CHAPTER 7

MORE ON FORMS

SETTING TAB ORDER

As you navigate through a form in Delphi, you are changing the *focus* from one control to the next. At any given time, some component on the form must have focus, and only one component at a time can have focus. Some of the components in Delphi can accept focus, and others can't. The controls that can accept focus usually show that they have focus: buttons have a slightly darker border and a rectangle around the button text, edit fields have the cursor in them, etc. As the user presses the tab key or the shift-tab key, focus will move to the next or previous control.

For example, in the sample form shown in Figure 7.1, focus moves from the Disable button to the Radio buttons to the Edit field to the Close button. Every component in Delphi that can accept focus has a TabOrder property. The number you set in a control's TabOrder property determines when, in turn, that control will receive the focus as you tab through the form. Because these tab order numbers are just component properties, you could set them yourself, individually. However, like so much in Delphi, there's a much easier way. Right click on the form and choose Tab Order. You'll be presented with the Edit Tab Order dialog (Figure 7.2).

This dialog provides you with an easy way to set the TabOrder numbers. Just arrange the components in the order that you want the cursor to go to them, and Delphi sets the TabOrder properties for you.

And remember, TabOrder is just another property. It is perfectly acceptable to change it at run-time if you need to.

Some components, notably the ScrollBox component, have a TabStop property. For

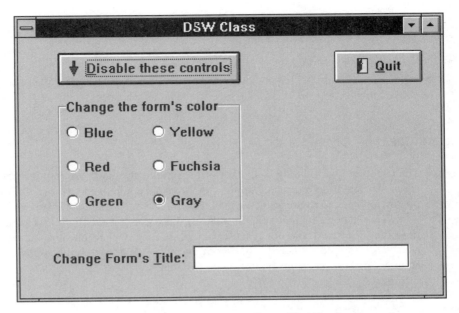

FIGURE 7.1   A Typical Form with a Button That Has the Focus

FIGURE 7.2   The TabOrder Dialog

these components, you can specify whether you want the component to be in the tab order or not. This gives you a greater amount of flexibility with these controls.

If label components can't receive focus, how does the hotkey feature work in conjunction with Edit components? Labels can't receive focus, but they have a special property called FocusControl which points to another component on the form. The component that is pointed to in the FocusControl will receive the focus whenever the label's hotkey is pressed.

SETTING CREATION ORDER

The Creation Order dialog is another of the options available through the editor's speed-menu. The creation order only applies to nonvisual components. Notice in Figure 7.3 that the three components are all nonvisual: TDataSource, TTable, and TTimer.

This dialog sets the creation order of these components both at design time and at run-time. Because some nonvisual components may depend on other nonvisual components (for example, related database components), you need to be able to control their creation order. This mechanism lets you do just that.

ALIGNMENT OF CONTROLS

It often seems that the most time consuming task of working in a visual design environment like Delphi's is the constant tweaking of where your components appear on the form. It sometimes seems like you have traded the time that it takes to create these pro-

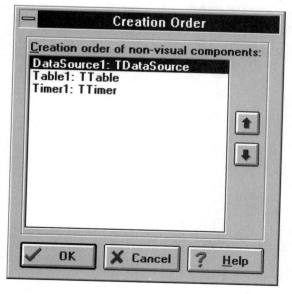

FIGURE 7.3   The Creation Order Dialog

gram interfaces by hand with the time it takes to get them all lined up! Fortunately, the
Delphi design environment once again comes to the rescue.

Align

It is always tough to visually line components up on a form. You can use the grid in the
Form Designer, but, no matter how small you have the grid set, it never seems small
enough to help with minute changes.

If you right click on the form and choose **Align . . .** from the speedmenu, you are
presented with the Alignment dialog (Figure 7.4). This is the easy way to align a group of
controls. If you have a group of controls selected when you bring up this dialog, whatever
changes you make here affect all of the selected components. Not only will this dialog let
you align the sides and tops together, but it will also center the controls in the window
(both horizontally and vertically) and space the components equally within a given space.

There is another alignment palette that appears as a floating toolbar rather than a di-
alog box. You can access it by choosing **View | Alignment Palette** (Figure 7.5). This
palette will stay on the screen until you close it, and it contains the same options that the
Alignment dialog does. In case you can't discern what the icons mean, you can place the
cursor over them and get standard "tool tip" help.

Locking Controls

Another problem that rears its head in visual design tools is keeping your controls where
you want them. It is too easy to click on a component to give it focus so that you can modify its property only to accidentally move the component at the same time. This is particu-

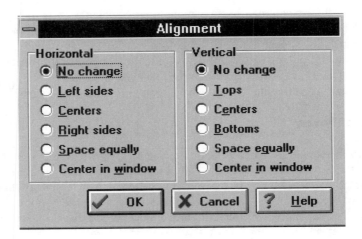

FIGURE 7.4   The Alignment Dialog

FIGURE 7.5 The Alignment Palette

larly annoying when you've spent a lot of time getting something lined up in a particular location.

Delphi will allow you to "lock" Form components in place once you have the layout you want. Once you have the controls in the location that you want, choose the **Edit |
Lock Controls** toggle. Once it is toggled on, you will not be able to move the controls on the form until you unlock them.

GROUPING CONTROLS

It is often convenient to create groups of controls that can act in some ways like a single control. For example, if you move a speedbar from the top of the form to the bottom, you will want all the controls on it to move with it. Delphi provides several ways to group components: Panels, GroupBoxes, and Bevels.

Panels and GroupBoxes

Both Panels and GroupBoxes are *container classes,* like the form. That means that these components can contain other components. This is handy because often you want the controls that are on the Panel or GroupBox to move with it. If you move one of these controls at design time or at run-time, all of their controls move with them.

All form controls have a Parent property, which is set to the component that "owns" it. Notice that the form is also a container class; so the Parent property for Panels and Groupboxes is the form that they belong to. The Parent property, for all of the components within a Panel or GroupBox, is set to the component that contains them.

Panels are usually used for speedbars and status bars. See the upcoming section on creating Speedbars and Status bars for more information on Panels.

ScrollBoxes

ScrollBoxes are also a container component. They are usually used for the main body of the form. A ScrollBox is a panel within a larger form that can grow scrollbars just like a form, but independently of the form. For example, it is common to have a Panel along the top of the form for a speedbar and another Panel along the bottom of the form for a status bar. You can place a Scrollbox in the middle area, so that if the user scrolls the form, the speedbar and status bar don't scroll off the screen. A Scrollbox is really just a self-contained scrollable region.

Bevels

Unlike Panels, GroupBoxes, and ScrollBoxes, Bevels are not containers! They are primarily just for decoration—to create a beveled "3D" look for forms. When you move a Bevel component, none of the components that happen to lie within it move.

CREATING SPEEDBARS AND STATUS LINES

The Panel component is ideal for creating both speedbars and status lines. One of the properties that make Panels so good for these tasks is the Align property. If you set its Align property to alTop, the panel will always "stick" to the top of the form, right under the title bar. By the same token, setting the Align property to alBottom causes the panel to line up along the bottom of the form. The advantage of these Alignment properties is that their components will continue to remain in the same relative position even if the form is moved or resized.

By using these components in conjunction with ScrollBoxes, it is easy to create a form whose middle portion can scroll to accommodate more data while the speedbar and the status bar maintain the correct positions.

Speedbars

To create a speedbar, just place a panel component on the form, set it's Align property to alTop, and start placing speedbuttons on it. Speedbuttons are specialized types of buttons that won't accept focus. Notice that you can't tab to a speedbutton. You can create specialized versions of speedbar buttons, such as two speedbuttons that act together as toggles—when one is up, the other is down and vice versa. This is accomplished through the AllowAllUp property and the GroupIndex property. Any buttons that have the same GroupIndex property will act as a group, just like radio buttons. When one is clicked, all the others within that group will become unselected, and the button that is clicked will stay down. If AllowAllUp is true, then all of the buttons with the same GroupIndex property can appear in the up state at the same time.

Of course, you aren't restricted to just placing speedbuttons on the speedbar. You can place any Delphi component on a speedbar—just set the component's TabStop property to false (so that the user can't tab up to your speedbar) and you have a Speedbar component. Of course, you could place the component on the speedbar and not disable the ability to tab to it, but that would be fairly nonstandard Windows, which generally should be avoided. See the chapter about user interface design for more details.

Status Lines

A status line is just another panel component with it's Align property set to alBottom. You can use either the Caption property for the panel to place status information (includ-

FIGURE 7.6   The Delphi Editor Status Line

ing the ability to left, center, or right justify the message with the Align property) or place a text field on top of the status bar.

Frequently, in a Windows program, the status bar is broken up into several sections, each with its own status information. A good example of this is the Delphi editor status line. Notice that this status line in Figure 7.6 has line number information, save status of the file, whether the editor is in Insert or Overtype mode, and the scrollbar. You can create these sorts of "multiple" status lines by taking several panel components and placing them inside one another.

In Figure 7.7, the Status 1 panel's Alignment property is set to taLeftJustify, Status 2 is taCenterJustify, and Status 3 is taRightJustify. By placing several Panel components together and modifying their BevelInner and BevelOuter properties, you can create the same sort of "nested" status bars. Obviously, you can also put a Scrollbar component on a status bar if you wanted to recreate the same type of scrollbar that the Delphi editor uses. Just as with the speedbars, you aren't restricted as to what types of components that you can place on a status bar—anything that you can place on a regular Panel can be placed on a status bar as well. However, you should probably set the TabStop property for all of the status bar components to false just as you would for a speedbar.

DIALOG BOX COMPONENTS

Dialog box components illustrate the perfect use of Delphi's component architecture. First, almost every Windows program needs to use these standard dialogs. Indeed, these components just call built-in Windows dialog boxes. Secondly, this can save you a great deal of time, because this common thing that you must do in almost every application is already created for you. Lastly, they give your programs a consistent look and feel with your other programs and with other Windows programs as well.

In this section, we are going to look at a couple of the Dialog box components—the Open and Save dialogs. Once you are familiar with how one works, you can use any of the others in much the same manner.

Open Dialog

The Open Dialog component implements a standard Windows File Open dialog box. To invoke this dialog from a form, just drop the FileOpen component on the form and send it the message to execute itself:

FIGURE 7.7   Several Nested Panel Components Acting as a Status Line

```
OpenDialog1.execute;
```

Your execute statement will suspend execution of your code and open the dialog box into which the user can enter information. Once the dialog box has been closed, you can view and assign the OpenDialog properties that you need. For example, to find out what file the user specified, use the OpenDialog's FileName property.

You can also change some of the characteristics of the dialog box before you execute it. For example, you can set the file specification that appears in the File Name entry field (Figure 7.8) by entering a default file name in the OpenDialog's FileName property. You can also use the Filter Editor to create entries in the combobox which appears beneath **List Files of Type.** Access the Filter Editor by clicking on the Filter property.

This dialog (Figure 7.9) lets you specify both a name for the filter (which will appear in the drop-down list under **List Files of Type**) and the file specification (which will appear under **File Name**). In this manner, you can allow your user to restrict the files that are shown in the list window. There is also a HistoryList property, which you can set to provide a history list combobox rather than a regular edit field under File Name. To use the combobox and history list, you must set the combobox type to fsComboBox.

Save Dialog

The Save dialog is very similar to the Open dialog (Figure 7.10). It has most of the same options as the Open dialog, and is invoked the same way. You can also provide file types (with their corresponding filters) and history comboboxes.

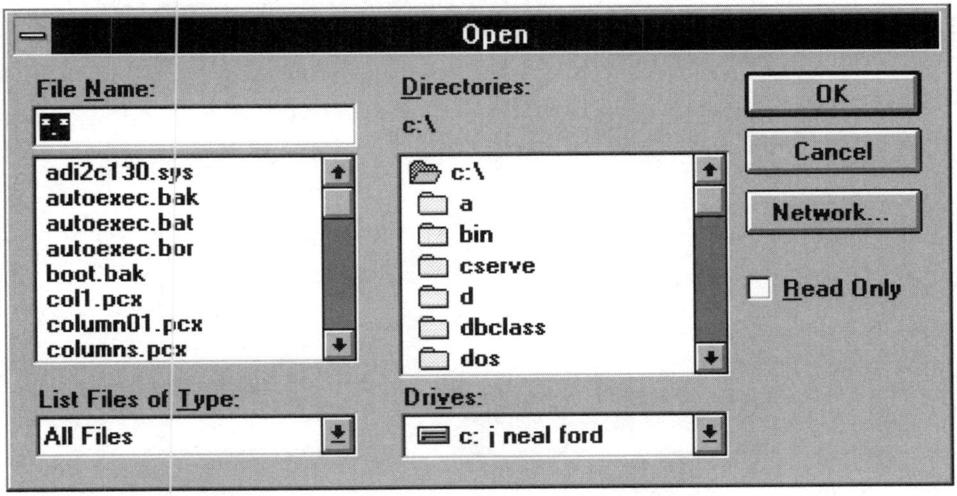

FIGURE 7.8   The File Open Dialog Generated by a FileOpen Component

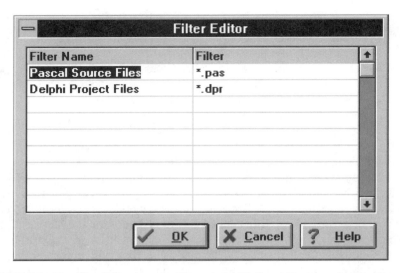

FIGURE 7.9   The Filter Editor Accessed through the FileOpen Component's Filter Property

Dialog Box Example

To demonstrate dialog boxes, examine Figure 7.11. It consists of three speedbutttons: **File Open, File Save,** and **Exit**; it also has OpenDialog and SaveDialog components, and two group boxes with embedded edit fields. When this form is run, the choices the user makes

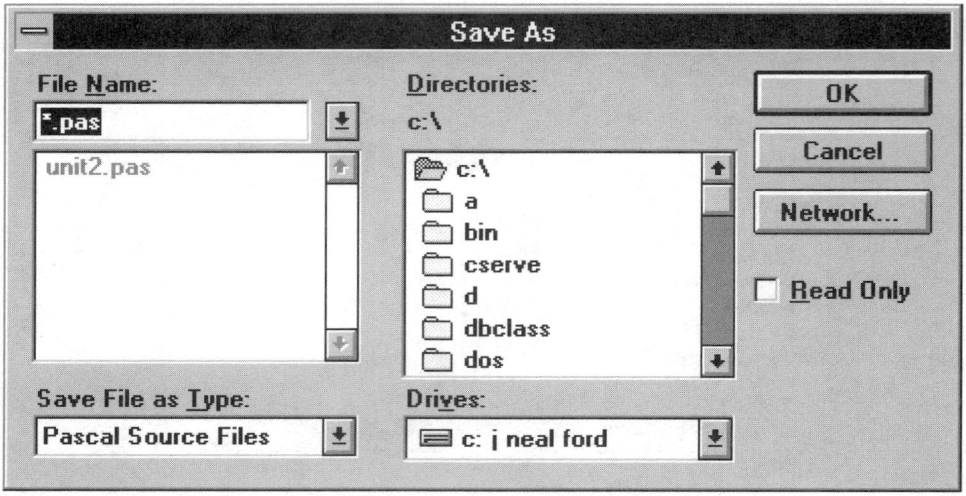

FIGURE 7.10   The Save Dialog Generated by a SaveDialog Component

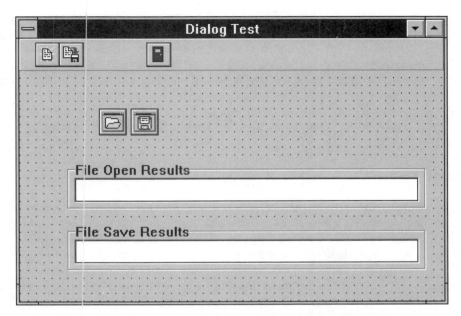

FIGURE 7.11 The Dialog Test Form with Both Save Dialog and Open Dialog Components

through the Open and Save dialogs will appear in the corresponding edit boxes at the bottom of the form.

Here is the source code for the relevant events:

```
procedure TFormDialogTest.SpeedButtonFileOpenClick(Sender:
TObject);
begin
  OpenDialog1.execute;
  EditFileOpen.text := OpenDialog1.fileName
end;

procedure TForm_dialogTest.SpeedButtonFileSaveClick(Sender:
TObject);
begin
  SaveDialog1.execute;
  EditFileSave.text := SaveDialog1.fileName
end;

procedure TForm_dialogTest.SpeedButton3Click(Sender: TObject);
begin
  close
end;
```

The code for `SpeedButton_fileOpen` tells the dialog box to execute itself, then, when the code resumes, sets the `Edit_fileOpen` component's Text property to the filename that the user selected. Similarly, the `SpeedButton_fileSave` button's event retrieves the user's choice and saves it to `Edit_fileSave.text`.

You should use these Dialog box components whenever you need Open and Save interfaces. They make your application more consistent within itself, and it makes your application more consistent with Windows. And, this is all code that you'll never have to write again! Just drop these components on the form and let them take care of the work.

TABBED FORMS

Tabbed forms have become an extremely popular interface in Windows recently. A tabbed form is a form that has index tabs either along the top or bottom which change the appearance of the form whenever they are clicked. Tabbed forms provide a way to create multipage dialogs, without having a series of buttons to take you from one form to the next. Indeed, the Delphi environment is rife with tabbed forms and controls.

You will see two different types of tabbed forms. The first, notebook tabs, places the tabs at the top of the form. The second, using the TabSet component, places the tabs along the bottom of the form.

Notebook Tabs

Notebook tabs are commonly used for dialog boxes that have just a few options. The form has a notebook tab control with three tabs in Figure 7.12. The advantage of the tabbed notebook control is that you can place independent controls on each of the tab pages, then switch to that page to work on them. When you have a given page selected, you cannot see any of the controls on other pages.

To create new tabs, you need to set the Pages property, which is of type TStrings. However, the Pages property has a special property editor for setting tab names. The property editor in Figure 7.13 allows you to add, edit, delete, or change the order of the tabs that exist for your form.

There are two ways to change from page to page on the form at design time or at run-time. The first is to change the PageIndex property. It is a zero-based index for the tab pages. So, for example, to change to the Page 3 tab within a program:

```
TabbedNotebook1.PageIndex := 2; {2 because the list is 0
based}
```

The other way to change tab pages is by using the ActivePage property, which chooses a tab page by name rather than by number. Either of these techniques will work in Design mode or Run mode. Choose whichever is most convenient for the task at hand.

You can also used TabbedNotebook components to create tabs several levels deep.

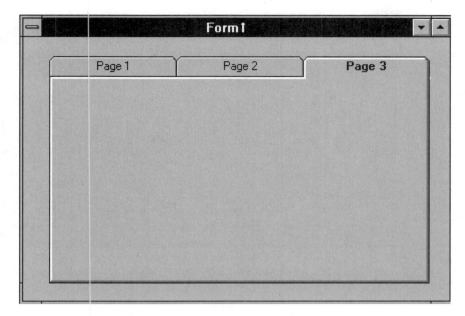

FIGURE 7.12   A Form with a TabbedNotebook Component

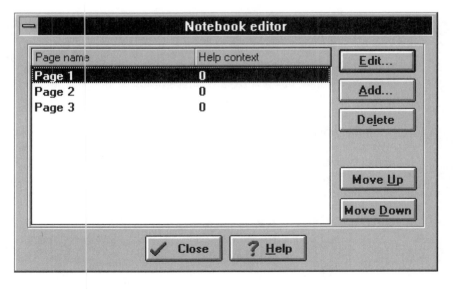

FIGURE 7.13   The Notebook Editor Accessed through the Pages Property

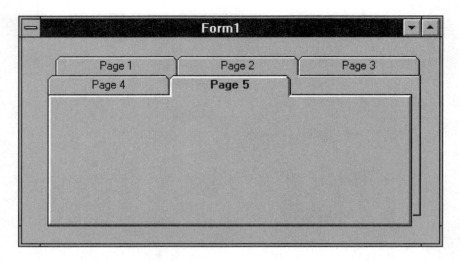

FIGURE 7.14   A TabbedNotebook on a Form with Its TabsPerRow Property Set to 3

To specify the number of tab rows that you want, use the TabsPerRow property. In Figure 7.14 the PageIndex property is set to 4, and the ActivePage is set to "Page 5". So, any controls that are now dropped on the TabbedNotebook will reside on this page.

Notebook Pages and Tabs

The other type of tabbed forms in Delphi are implemented using two components in tandem: the Notebook Pages component and the TabSet component. Either of these components are perfectly useful in other contexts without the other, but they are commonly used together to create bottom tabbed forms.

The dark border that you see around the inside of the window frame in Figure 7.15 is the Notebook Page in design view. Its Align property is set to alTop. The TabSet, which has 5 tabs defined, has its Align property set to alBottom, so it will always be at the bottom of the form, even if it's resized or maximized.

Both the TabSet and the Notebook Pages have an Index property: either PageIndex or TabIndex. Because both of these index types are zero-based, you can create a form that changes notebook pages whenever you click on the appropriate tab by placing the following line of code in the TabSet's OnClick event:

```
Notebook1.PageIndex := TabSet1.TabIndex
```

When the TabSet's `TabIndex` is changed by clicking on it, it also changes the `PageIndex` of the Notebook, changing the form to that Notebook Page.

If the AutoScroll property of the Tabset is true, the Tabset will automatically be-

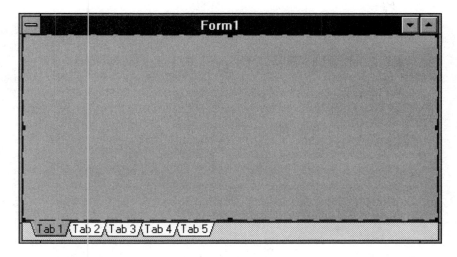

FIGURE 7.15   A Form with a Notebook and a TabSet Component Working in Tandem

come scrollable if the form is resized. Figure 7.16 is an example of the form in Figure
7.15 squeezed so that all the tabs won't fit. The scroll arrows on the right appeared automatically when the form was resized to be smaller.

FORMS THAT CALL OTHER FORMS

A common task that you'll want to add to your applications is the ability of having one
form call another form. We saw in an earlier chapter an example of how to set the main

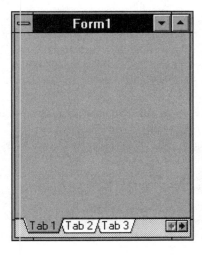

FIGURE 7.16 An Undersized Form
Resulting in the Appearance of a Scroll
Arrow to Indicate the Presence of Addi-
tional Tabs

form for the project using the Project Options dialog. However, that implies that there are at least two forms in the project, and one will probably have to call the other.

The first thing you have to do to call another form is include that form's unit file in the uses clause of the calling form's unit file. You must do this so that the calling form's unit can "see" the class definition of the called form. Once you have included the unit name in the uses clause, you can proceed to create objects based on that form class.

We've already noted that, like everything in Delphi, forms are just objects. So, to call a form from another form, you must create an instance of the target Form object and send it the message to open itself. There are several ways to create an instance of a form in Delphi. The easiest way is to let Delphi do it for you. If you look in the interface unit of every form unit, you can see that Delphi has created the class type of the form for you, but it has also created a variable of that type, which is the class name minus the prefix "T". For example, if you have a class `TFormCalledForm`, Delphi automatically places the following declaration in the unit's interface section:

```
var
    FormCalledForm: TFormCalledForm;
```

This creates a Form object variable (which hasn't been initialized yet) of the type `TFormCalledForm`. Because this variable declaration is in the unit's interface section, this variable is visible to the entire unit and any other units or programs that use this unit. Note that this is just a variable, it has not been instantiated into an object yet. To do that you must run its constructor code.

Delphi actually makes it easy to take care of the detail of running the constructor for the form for you as well. Within the **Options | Projects . . .** dialog, choose the Forms page (Figure 7.17). This dialog lets you specify which forms you want created automatically when your application starts. All forms on the left side will be created, and can be called with no further action on your part, whereas the forms on the right are not automatically created. You have to instantiate them as they are needed.

You must decide which forms you want auto-created. This presents one of those speed/resources vs. ease of use conditions. If you auto-create all of your forms, it will take a little longer for your program to become active—there is more code that it must execute to start up. One problem, but probably a bigger problem in Windows 3.x, is that all the resources for the forms are allocated when the forms are constructed. This means that you will have fewer resources to work with. On the other hand, you can create all of your forms yourself. They will appear a little more slowly (because they are being constructed on the fly), but they will only consume resources while they are active, rather than throughout the entire lifetime of the application.

Which method should you choose? This is probably best answered on a case by case basis. As a rule of thumb, if there are any forms that you are sure that the user is going to access every time he or she starts the application, go ahead and let Delphi auto-create them—you will get the very best performance with those forms. If, on the other hand, there are forms that are used infrequently (like configuration forms), manually con-

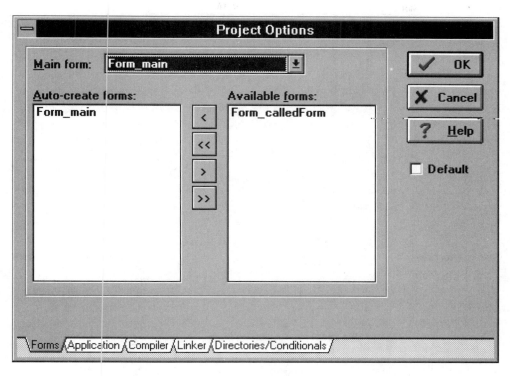

FIGURE 7.17 The Forms Page of the Project I Options Dialog Showing the Creation Order of the Project's Forms

struct them just as they are needed. This means that the forms that aren't likely to get called every time the program is run won't continually take up precious resources, and your application will start as quickly as possible.

Here is an example of a form that calls another form, and the easiest (least code) to accomplish the call. The form in Figure 7.18 has a button that invokes the second form. Figure 7.19 shows the form that is called. When the user types some text into the edit field on the second form and clicks the OK button, the second form closes and the calling form gets focus again. The edit field on the calling form now contains the text that the user typed into the called form. Thus, you can pass information from one form to another.

Among the various ways to accomplish opening another form, this is the easiest. Study the following code, which is in the OnClick event for the button:

```
procedure TFormMain.ButtonCallFormClick(Sender: TObject);
begin
  FormCalledForm.showmodal;
  EditCalledText.text := FormCalledForm.EditString.text;
end;
```

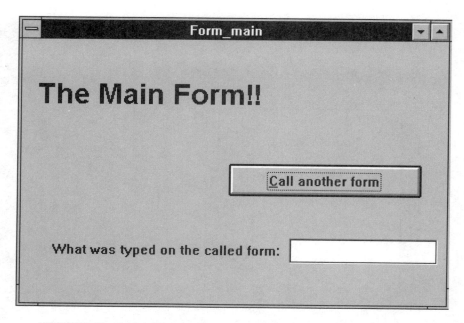

FIGURE 7.18   A Main Form can act as a Switchboard to Open Other Forms (see Figure 7.19)

The ShowModal method of the form opens it as a modal dialog box. This suspends execution of the remainder of the code until the dialog form closes. (The definition and implications of modal vs. nonmodal dialogs will be covered in the Event Driven Programming chapter.) Our example assumes that the form has been included in the auto-create list. If it wasn't, this code would cause a general protection fault! We would be trying to call a

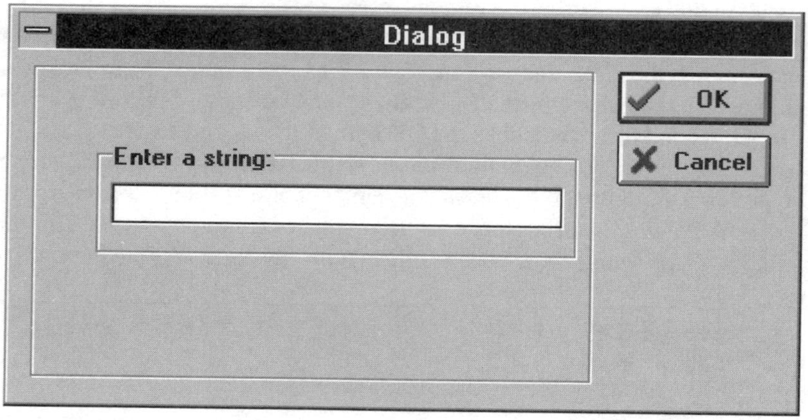

FIGURE 7.19   A Dialog Form Opened by the Main Form (in Figure 17.8)

method of an object that hasn't been instantiated. However, if the form is in the auto-create list, the ShowModal method will be successful.

If the form isn't in the auto-create list, you must instantiate it yourself. Here is an example of the necessary code:

```
procedure TForm_main.ButtonCallFormClick(Sender: TObject);
begin
  FormCalledForm := TFormCalledForm.create( self );
  FormCalledForm.showmodal;
  EditCalledText.text :=
      FormCalledForm.EditString.text;
  FormCalledForm.destroy
end;
```

Notice that the "guts" of this routine are the same as the one above. The only difference is that the Form object is explicitly instantiated within the routine. Notice that, if we create the object, we should take it upon ourselves to destroy it as well (so that its resources will be reclaimed properly).

Lastly, you aren't forced to use the variable that the unit declares as the object instance variable—you can create your own variable to represent it. Thus, you can create a local variable within the routine that calls the form, instantiate the form, show it, get your information from it, and then destroy (or destruct) the form's instance. Here is an example:

```
procedure TForm_main.Button_callFormClick(Sender: TObject);
var
  f : TForm_calledForm;
begin
  f := TForm_calledForm.create( self );
  f.showmodal;
  Edit_calledText.text := f.edit_string.text;
  f.destroy
end;
```

In the button's OnClick routine, a variable f was created. Then, f was instantiated to be a TForm_calledForm object. The Create method requires a parameter to indicate who will "own" the object. In this case, you should pass "self", which indicates that the current form will own the new one.

After f is instantiated, you can treat it the same way that you treated the instance variable that Delphi created for the form (form_calledForm). After the form is shown, and the user has responded and closed the called form, Edit_calledText. text is assigned to the text that the user typed in on the called form.

CHAPTER 8

MENUS

COMMON MENU CHARACTERISTICS

Menus are obviously another basic characteristic of Windows programs, and you must be able to create them to create Windows programs. This chapter deals with how to make the two kinds of menus that are available: main menus and popup menus.

Even though each of these menus are different, they are still standard Windows controls, and as such have many common characteristics. First, we will look at the common characteristics of both types of menus, then we will look at the differences.

Insertion Point

The *insertion point* is the location where the next menu command will be placed when you type it in (Figure 8.1). Since your menu currently doesn't have any entries, the insertion point is at the first entry location. As you type menu items into the Menu Designer, you are actually filling in the Caption property for that item in the Object Inspector, and you can change the characteristics for that menu item by using the Object Inspector. When you fill in the Caption property, Delphi will massage that name to create a valid component name and fill that name in.

As you add items, the insertion point will move to the right or down. To add an item below the current item, click on the item and the insertion point will move down to the next available location.

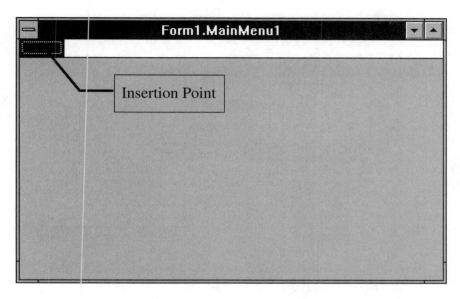

FIGURE 8.1 Editing a Menu on a Form

Breaks

You have probably noticed that most Windows menus have horizontal lines within the menu to break the menu into logical groups. These are known as *breaks*. There are several different varieties of breaks in Delphi. The most common type is just a horizontal line. That type of break can be created by creating a menu item whose caption is a single dash ("-"). At run-time, the dash will become an unbroken line.

Delphi also allows you to create some more sophisticated types of breaks in order to turn a menu into a multicolumn menu. That is what the Break property is for. There are three different possible entries for the Break property: mbNone, mbBreak, and mbBar-Break. mbNone specifies no break at all. mbBreak specifies a multicolumn break with no vertical dividing line, while mbBarBreak also adds a vertical line between columns. The menu item that has the Break property set is the first item in the new column.

Cascading Submenus

Another common feature of Windows menus are cascading submenus (Figure 8.2). To create cascading menus from either of the menu types in Delphi, right click on the item that will lead to the menu and choose Create Submenu. That will create a new insertion point to the right of the current menu.

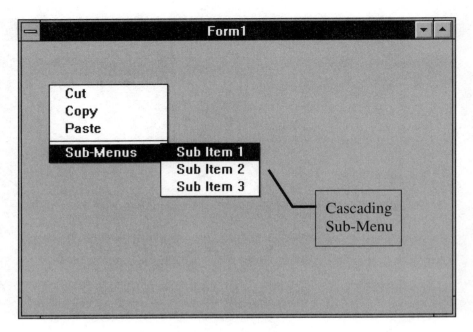

FIGURE 8.2   Cascading Popup Menus

Delphi handles the chore of placing the triangle on the menu item at run-time indicating that a submenu exists.

Menu Toggles

It is common in Windows menus to have menu items that have checkmarks beside them, indicating that the control toggles some behavior and that currently it is toggled on. This is easily implemented in Delphi via the Checked property. If Checked is true, the menu item appears with a checkmark next to it; if Checked is false, it does not.

Shortcut Keys

Shortcut keys are the key combinations that appear next to menu items that indicate what keyboard key combination will produce the same action. Within Delphi, set the ShortCut property from the pull-down list in the object inspector at design time. If you need to set the property at run-time, Delphi provides functions that allow you to accomplish this.

DESIGNERS

Once you are familiar with the Form Designer, you will find that the Menu Designers work similarly. Both the Form Designer and the Menu Designers use the Object Inspector to set the characteristics of the items they contain.

Main Menus

To invoke the Menu Designer, first drop a MainMenu component on the form. Then, you can get to the designer by either choosing the Items property for the Main Menu in the Object Inspector, or you can right click on the component itself and choose Menu Designer from the popup menu. Either activity leads you to the Menu Designer as seen in Figure 8.3.

Just dropping the menu on the form does not automatically associate that menu with the form. To create that association, set the form's MainMenu property to point to the Menu component.

Popup Menus

To create popup menus, drop a PopupMenu component on the form, and invoke the designer either by clicking on its Menu property or by right clicking on the Menu component and choosing Design Menu. That will lead you to the Popup Menu Designer, shown in Figure 8.4 with several options.

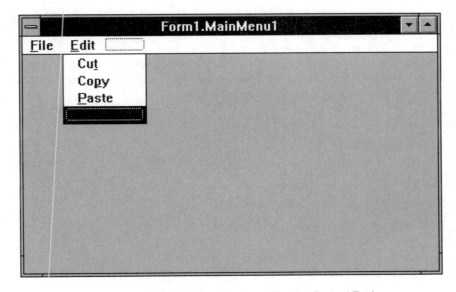

FIGURE 8.3   A Form's Menu Designer Showing Several Entries

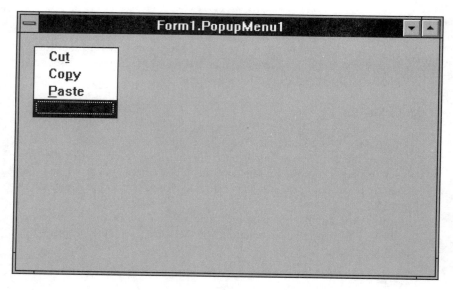

FIGURE 8.4   A Form's Popup Menu

Normally, popup menus are only one column, with occasional cascading submenus. However, both menu designers allow you to create multicolumn menus by using the Break property previously discussed.

Just like the Main Menu, dropping a PopupMenu component on the form does not automatically associate it with any other component. Every component has a PopupMenu property; set that property to associate a popup menu with that component. For example, the form can have a popup menu by setting its PopupMenu property, and other components (buttons, edit fields, etc.) can have their own popup menus by dropping other Popup Menu components on the form and setting the PopupMenu property of these components to the appropriate Popup Menu components.

CHAPTER 9

DELPHI TEMPLATES

CREATING TEMPLATES

A template is a saved format of some item that you want to use over and over again. A simple example would be a cookie cutter or a stencil. Probably a better example are the dies that are used to make CPU processor chips. Once the design of the chip is finalized, a very tiny stencil is made and chips are stamped out of silicon and placed in computers.

Delphi has a collection of predefined templates for forms, menus, and projects. Delphi keeps these templates in "galleries" and presents them to you as if they were pictures hanging on a wall. Whenever you start to create a new project, form, or menu, you can choose one of the templates from the appropriate gallery.

One of the options available to you in the **Options | Environment | Preferences** dialog (Figure 9.1) is whether or not to invoke the template gallery every time you create a new form or project.

If these options are set, you will be presented with the appropriate gallery for that item and you can choose which template will be used as the stencil for your new form or project.

Delphi is customizable in the way that it will let you use templates. You can manage Delphi galleries by using the **Options | Gallery** menu item, which presents the dialog in Figure 9.2.

This dialog allows you to add, edit, delete, and set defaults for any of the items that you have in your gallery. Delphi allows you to create templates for forms, projects, and menus. First, we will look at the mechanics of template creation, then we will look at the advantages and disadvantages of software templates.

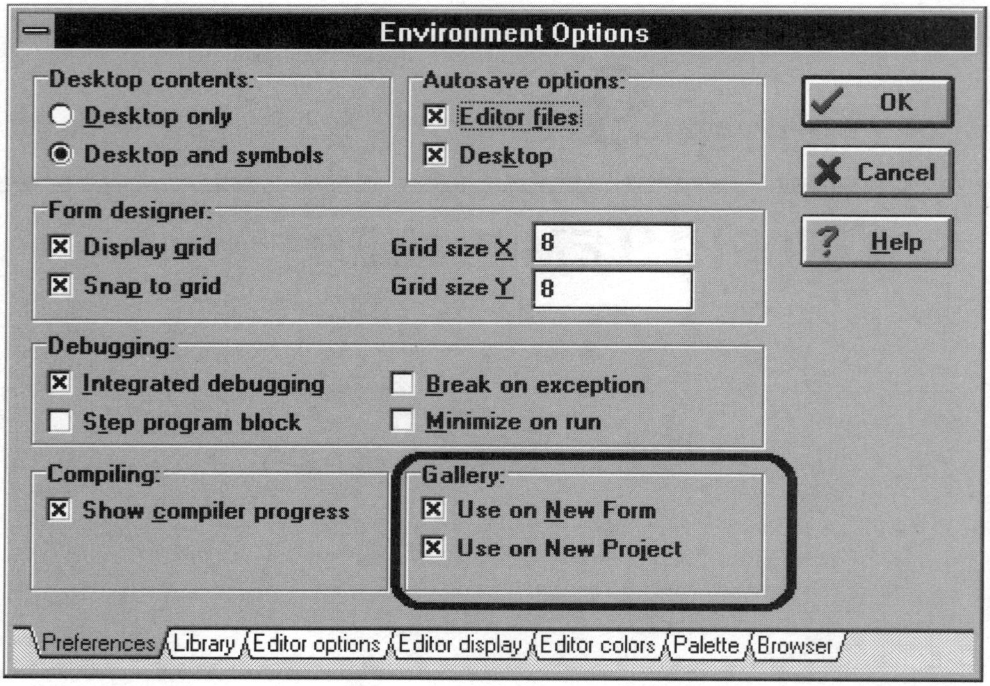

FIGURE 9.1   Gallery Options on the Options I Environment I Preferences Dialog

Form Templates

A form template is a predefined form that you can use as a starting point when you want to create a new form. For example, if you find that you are repeatedly creating a dialog box with the same options and the same general layout, that dialog is probably a good candidate for templatization. Then, when you need to create another version of the dialog box, you can start with the template and customize it for its particular use.

Any form that you create in Delphi can be saved as a template. In fact, one of the speedmenu options available in the Form Designer is **Save as Template.** If you choose this option, you will be presented with the **Save Form Template** dialog (Figure 9.3).

On the left, appears a list of the Forms in your current project. On the right, you can specify the File name, the Title, the Description, and the Bitmap for your template. Many templates are included with Delphi. The Title, Bitmap, and Description appear in the gallery as denoted in Figure 9.4.

Project Templates

Just as you can save forms as templates, you can save entire projects as templates. Just create the project that you want to save, then pull up the gallery manager via the **Options I Gallery** menu, select the Project Gallery page, and click on Add. It's that easy!

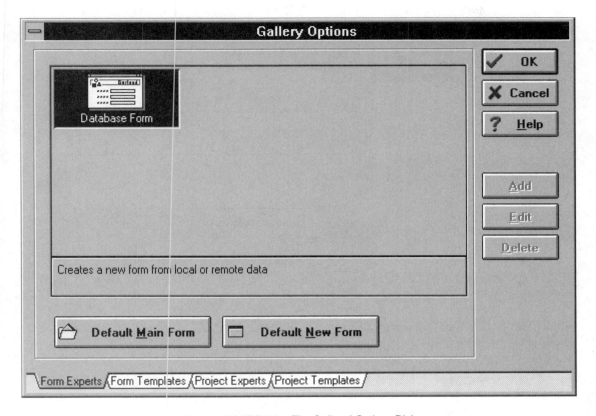

FIGURE 9.2   The Gallery I Options Dialog

Notice that Delphi comes with some built-in project templates, including MDI (Multiple Document Interface) and SDI (Single Document Interface) project templates. These are both handy for creating each of their respective types of applications without having to set up the window relationships manually during development.

Menu Templates

Just like projects and forms, you can save useful menu layouts as templates, too. Again, it's a speedmenu option from within the Menu Designer, along with the option to insert a menu template into the menu being edited (Figure 9.5).

ADVANTAGES AND DISADVANTAGES OF TEMPLATES

Some software developers are sold on the idea of templates. In fact, some development environments use templates heavily to try to create reuseable code. Like so many similar techniques, there are advantages and disadvantages to using templates.

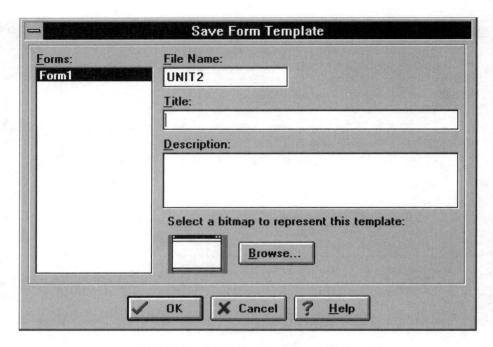

FIGURE 9.3   The Save Form Template Dialog

Advantages

Speed of development.   One obvious advantage of templates is decreased development time. If you already have many of the features that you are going to include in your application in a template, you can create the application in relatively little time. This is also true of form templates. For example, the dual list box form, which allows you to copy items from one list into another list, is so common that it is included with Delphi as one of the form templates.

Pseudo-reuse of code.   Using templates allows you to reuse code that you have written. However, we call this *pseudo-reuse* of code because it does not give you the flexibility of code reuse that true object-oriented programming does. While you may think that using templates is making good use of reusable code, there are some problems with this approach which we will discuss in the disadvantages section.

Consistency in code and interface.   Another advantage that template utilization has is that it enforces consistency for projects, forms, and menus for which they are the basis. For example, most companies like to have a standard look and feel. By using templates, you can be assured that all the developers are starting from the same basic design. Along with strict application standards, teams of programmers can work on a project simultaneously and still be confident of a similar appearance.

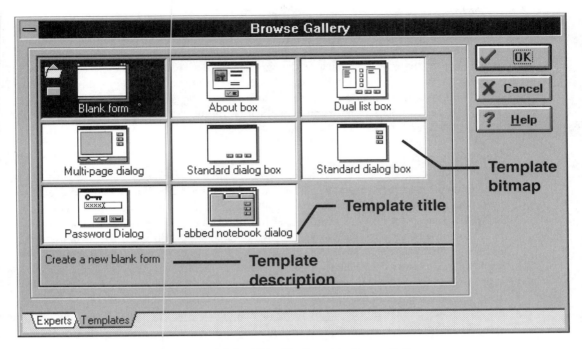

FIGURE 9.4   The Template Browse Gallery

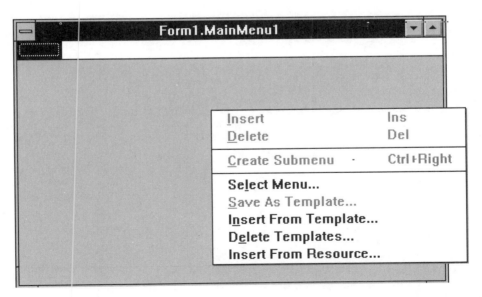

FIGURE 9.5   Speed Menu Access for Saving a Menu as a Menu Template

Lower maintenance cost than building from scratch.   It just makes sense that if you can write some of your most common code once and reuse it many times, you are cutting down on the cost of subsequent development. One of the things that you should always strive for in application development is to make the code that you create as generic as possible. If you create a reusable asset every time you write a program, you can start to build programs more quickly, since much of the code is already completed. And of course, quicker completion means more application for the money (or is that more money for the application?).

Disadvantages

Creeping inconsistency.   The first and most serious problem with templates is the problem of creeping inconsistency. To illustrate, let's say you've created a template that you are using for all your forms. After having used it for several forms, you realize that it could be better designed, so you change the template. You use it for several more forms, and then you realize several more ways that it could be improved upon. Figure 9.6 graphically displays what is happening.

As time goes on, your applications will be less and less consistent, because you are changing the template. Nevermind that you are improving it, you are still compromising the consistency that you aimed for by using the template in the first place. As you will see later, object-oriented techniques do not suffer from this problem.

Delusion of code reuse.   Ostensibly, you are reusing the code that makes up the template. However, this type of code reuse doesn't *scale* well. Like the consistency prob-

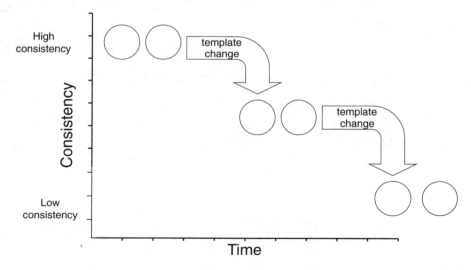

FIGURE 9.6   Consistency in the Use of Form Templates Over Time

lem, as you improve the template, none of the applications that previously used the template are improved. To make them consistent with the improved applications, you have to go back and do some redesign work, which defeats the purpose of generic, reusable code.

No cascading bug fixes.   Cascading bug fixes is perhaps the biggest problem with templates. If you use a template to create some reusable items (projects, forms, or menus) and later discover that there are bugs in the template, you can fix the template, which takes care of all future development, but that doesn't fix the items that were created previously. The original template that was used for the initial construction still has the bug, and usually extensive remedial programming is required to fix it. By the way, this is not the case for object-oriented programming. With OOP, if you discover a bug in one of the ancestors of an object, you can fix the ancestor and just recompile the parts of the application that depend on it, and they will reflect your fixes.

Higher maintenance cost than OOP.   For all of the reasons presented above, using templates translates to higher maintenance cost than with object-oriented programming. True, templates are cheaper then recoding from scratch every time, yet not as efficient for creating generic code as OOP.

WHY USE TEMPLATES IN DELPHI?

Because Delphi is an object-oriented language, you may wonder why Borland even included templates. However, there are some good reasons for their inclusion.

The main reason that templates are used in Delphi is because of the basic design of Delphi's tools. The Form Designer can only work with direct descendants (children) of the predefined parent type TForm. In other words, if you create a new form (descendant of TForm) called TChildForm, you cannot then create a further subclass of TMyForm (TGrandchildForm) and still work in the graphical form designer. Delphi is a completely object-oriented language, thus you can create arbitrarily complex class relationships (parent/child/etc. relationships). There is no Object-Pascal limitation within the inheritance mechanism. If you have no need to bring TGrandchildForm into the Form Designer, you could create the described class relationships. Nonetheless, it is the inherent design of the form tool, not the underlying language, that prevents graphical editing of the type of subclass discussed here.

Thus, because you can't use object-oriented techniques and still use the visual design tools (which few people will be willing to give up), there remains a compelling reason to use templates.

Template Design Guidelines

Because templates provide the best way to create reusable project, form, and menu elements, there are some design guidelines you should follow to help offset some of the disadvantages discussed above.

Static templates.   When you create your templates, try to anticipate all of the features that it needs to include. You want to avoid modifying it, even to make improvements, as long as possible in order to keep your level of consistency high. Also, you should rigorously test your code to make sure that as few bugs as possible are present. No one plans to write buggy code, but it is vital in templates that you don't have to perform numerous bug fixes.

In general, you should make your templates as *static* as possible. In other words, you don't want to make changes to it once you've started using it. Every change you make exacerbates the potential problems with template usage.

Feature overabundance.   Another good idea with template design is to add every possible feature that you think you might ever want. For example, it's easier to make superfluous controls inactive and invisible on a form than to constantly have to add controls that should have been included in the first place. If there is some future use that you anticipate for the template, but that you don't want to implement initially, it is wise to go ahead and put as much of the feature in place as possible. It will make actually implementing that feature easier when it is time for its appearance.

The items most conducive to templates are generic dialog box forms (like the form templates that are included with Delphi) and standard menu structures, which Delphi also includes. For example, most Windows programs have the File menu first, and the Window and Help menus last. This structure is a good candidate for a template, as most of the Windows applications you write will include this type of menu. In fact, this is already one of the built-in menu templates; yet another example of the Delphi development team giving us what we need and want.

CHAPTER 10

EVENT DRIVEN PROGRAMMING

THE ESSENCE OF EDP

Event driven programming (EDP) means just that—programming by responding to events. This is a different style of programming for many programmers because their DOS programs were usually not very event driven. However, if you've ever written a program that executes some set-up code, puts a menu on the screen, and then goes into an endless loop that takes menu requests, processes them, and returns to the menu until the user quits, you have written an event driven program. What you accomplished was to restrict the events that were possible through the menu. The only events you were interested in were the menu choices that the user made.

One of the problems with writing event driven programs in DOS is that you have to write all of the code to create the event loop yourself. In fact, that is why most languages in the DOS heyday provided a framework to make it easier to write in an EDP manner. The framework that Pascal used (and still uses in DOS) is called Turbo Vision.

However, EDP is much easier and more natural in the Windows environment, because Windows is already event driven. In essence, event driven means that the program doesn't restrict the user as to what they can do next. The programmer has no way of knowing what action the user is going to perform next. They may pick a menu item, click a button, mark some text, etc. So, EDP means that you write code to handle whatever events occur that you're interested in, rather than write code that always executes in the same restricted order.

If you've used Delphi at all, the EDP model should start to look familiar to you by now. Delphi is a completely event driven programming environment. Notice that when you attach code to event handlers in Delphi, you have no idea when that code will be executed except that it will execute whenever the event that it is tied to occurs. While this is a big change from non-EDP, it is well worth the effort, because it is clearly easier for your users to work with an event driven program than with a nonevent driven program.

Types of Events

The kinds of events that can occur can be roughly broken down into two types: *user events* and *system events*.

User events. User events are actions that are initiated by the user. Examples of user events are OnClick (the user clicked the mouse), OnKeyDown, OnDragOver, OnDblClick. These events are always tied to a user's actions.

System events. The other type of events that can occur are system events. System events are events that the operating system fires for you. For example, the OnTimer (the Timer component issues one of these events every Interval seconds), the OnCreate event, the OnPaint event, etc. Usually, these system events are not directly initiated by a user action.

Regardless of how the event was called, Delphi looks to see if you have assigned any code to the event handler. If you have, then that code is executed, otherwise, the event is passed over and your program continues.

EXAMPLE: THE IQ TEST

EDP definitely takes a different mind set, and it does take some getting used to if you've never worked in it before. Let's look at an example that is both good at illustrating how much easier it is to do some things using EDP (Figure 10.1), and it's a great practical joke to play on someone around the office!

As you can see, this form is designed to look a lot like the error messages generated by Delphi. The difference is when you try to click on the OK button with the mouse, the button runs away from the mouse! It is impossible to click on the button with the mouse—it will keep eluding the mouse forever. Also notice that this dialog doesn't have a window system menu (which would also let you close this dialog). It was created by setting the form's BorderIcons property to an empty set.

So, how to you close the dialog box? Hit the Enter key. The reason this is called IQ Test is because so many people have become so "mouse centric" after they've been using Windows for a while that they forget that you can click buttons that have the focus with the Enter key as well. Because there is only one component on the form that can receive the focus, hitting the Enter key presses that button.

The important event that makes this little demonstration possible is the OnMouse-Move event for the button. Here is the code:

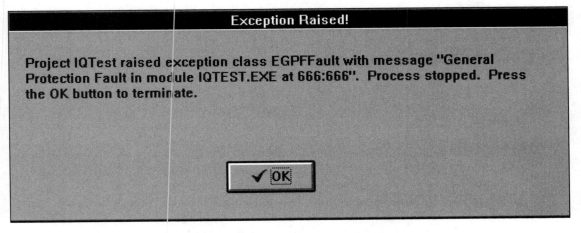

FIGURE 10.1   Our Exception Raised Form

```
procedure TForm1.okbuttonMouseMove(Sender: TObject; Shift:
        TShiftState; X, Y: Integer);
begin
  if okbutton.top < 5 then
      okbutton.top := 125
    else
      okButton.top := okbutton.top -10;
    if okbutton.left < 3 then
      okbutton.left := 300
    else
      okbutton.left := okbutton.left -10;
end;
```

This is all the code for the button. Notice that the event mechanism in Delphi is what is actually doing all the work here. Delphi is doing the job of firing the event every time the mouse moves over the button; each firing of the event causes the code to execute, and all this code is doing is making the button move up and left. Delphi also handles the case when the button doesn't move enough to get the mouse pointer off of the button— Delphi just fires the event again as soon as the mouse moves, making the button move again.

This is a simple but useful demonstration of the different mind set that is required to carry out event driven programming. Once you get used to it, you will find that Delphi's implementation of EDP is outstanding. That's what makes Delphi a better product for creating Windows programs.

OPENING FORMS

The last aspect of EDP that needs to be discussed deals with opening forms, especially from other forms. There are two different methods for opening forms in Delphi: Show and Showmodal; let's see how we can utilize ShowModal to control the flow of our EDP applications.

Show

Show and ShowModal do essentially the same job: Both of them open an already instantiated form, which really just unhides the form. Once the form object has been instantiated, the form is ready to do anything it's capable of, including showing itself.

The real distinction between these two methods is this: When you open a form using Show, the program that called the form doesn't stop executing. In other words, when you open a form using Show, whatever code called the Show method (whether from a menu, a button, etc.) will continue executing. There is nothing inherent about opening a form that causes program execution to pause. Thus, if you open a form with Show, don't expect your program to come to a halt waiting for input from the new form—whatever code called it will continue executing. This allows you to create multiform applications where the user can open as many forms as they like, and freely click back and forth between them.

Show works just fine for multiform situations. However, what if you need to place a dialog box on the screen to prompt your user to place a disk in the floppy drive. In this case, you don't want your code to keep executing until you're sure your user has responded—you don't want your program trying to write to the floppy drive before the disk is there. That's what ShowModal was designed for.

ShowModal

When a form is opened with ShowModal, all program execution from the calling form stops until the modal form is closed. This is exactly what you would want when asking your user to insert a floppy disk.

In fact, you have probably noticed the two distinct types of windows that Windows provides. One type has minimize and maximize buttons, a system menu, and is resizeable. Also, you can click away from these windows to another window and then back again—there are no restrictions upon which form you can place the focus. These types of windows are known as modeless. The other type of window is usually used for dialog boxes. They have no resize handles, and you can't click away from them. These windows are referred to as modal, because they force the user into a mode of operation. The only way to get rid of a modal window is to click on the close button or press the Windows closure hotkeys (alt-F4).

Delphi doesn't actually restrict the border types of ShowModal windows. There is a BorderStyle property for all forms that determines what type of border the window will have. So, you can make resizeable windows that are actually modal (opened by using

ShowModal), and create dialog-box-like forms that are actually nonmodal. However, unless you have a compelling reason for this, it's not a good idea. It will make your program behave differently from the Windows default behavior, which is bad news in an environment that is supposed to be largely consistent from application to application.

CHAPTER 11

EXCEPTION HANDLING

You may wonder why exception handling deserves an entire chapter to itself. First of all, it is a new feature to Object-Pascal—none of the previous versions have had structured exception handling. Secondly, it is one of the secrets to creating robust, production quality software that handles errors gracefully and doesn't lead to resource leakage (which can be a serious problem in Windows development). Lastly, it is a feature that has previously only been available to languages that have a strong software engineering influence (notably Ada and C++). Of course, as we have said several times already, Object-Pascal is now a language that *has* a strong software engineering flavor. The wise and consistent use of exception handling has great benefits. We are going to talk about all of these benefits in this chapter.

Exception handling is really just an extension of several other error handling techniques that have been available in many languages for quite some time. In fact, rudimentary exception handling is available in any language that supports conditional branching to a label (the dreaded spaghetti code feature of GOTO). The C language used just such a variation for exception handling through the use of the SETJMP and LONGJMP facilities (which allowed the programmer to jump from the current block of code to a block of code that may or may not be within the same source file). Likewise, Visual Basic for Applications uses a GoTo statement to jump to error handling within the current procedure or further back along the call stack. What distinguishes structured exception handling (ala Object-Pascal, Ada, and C++) are language provisions that allow for greater control of how exceptions are handled both at a local (procedural) level and a global (application) level.

Object-Pascal has two different but related uses for exception handling: resource protection and error handling. We are going to discuss both, but first, some definitions are in order.

TRADITIONAL ERROR HANDLING

Errors are a fact of life in Windows programs. No one has yet (nor are we close to) a computing environment or user that doesn't cause error conditions of some kind. In the absence of any language feature to help handle errors, programmers have in the past relied on the return values from functions to indicate errors, building each function to return an error indicator. This obviously has some problems associated with it. The function either just returns false on failure and true on success, or it returns some sort of error code. It is the programmer's responsibility to check the error code and take appropriate action. This leads to code that looks like this:

```
procedure DoSomething;
const
    ERROR1 = 1
    ERROR2 = 2
    ERROR3 = 3
begin
    if not Function1 then { Function1 returned false }
        { take some action here };
    case Function2 of
        ERROR1 : { take some action here }
        ERROR2 : { take some action here }
        ERROR3 : { take some action here }
    end; {case}
end; {procedure}
```

The problem with this approach is that it makes for very cluttered code, and that cuts down on the readability and ease of maintenance of the code. As we have stated before, code is read more often than it is written, so readable code is important. Also, with this approach, you must decide how much error handling you want to provide.

Optimistic Error Handling

Optimistic error handling can be thought of as seeing the glass half full—you don't anticipate many errors. This means that you only return error codes from the routines that you think are most likely to generate errors, and hope that the routines that don't return error codes don't encounter many errors. Obviously, this does not lead to the most robust type of application. You can almost bet your life that your users will find those routines and single them out as the place to create error conditions!

Exhaustive Error Handling

The polar alternative to optimistic error handling is *exhaustive error handling*. This type of error handling assumes that the worst will always happen, and you create every routine with error conditions in mind. This type of error handling leads directly to the type of code that is shown above, where the readability of the code is compromised by the great lengths that are taken to avoid errors.

Another factor to consider when deciding how much error handling code to provide is performance. If you clutter your code with too many error handling provisions, you will degrade the performance of your application. This performance vs. robustness problem is a common one in application development. Fortunately, there is a good solution to this problem in the form of exceptions.

Exceptions

Exceptions differ from the above approaches by providing an easy, convenient way to handle error conditions without compromising your code's readability, performance, or robustness. We will talk about the types and syntax of exceptions shortly. In a broad sense, exception handling is a way to group code together that might lead to an error condition, and trap an error in a controlled way if it occurs. You get the robustness of exhaustive error handling without the degradation of code quality, but, at the same time, you get the code readability and performance of optimistic error handling. Enough advertisement! Let us now turn to the definition and usage of exceptions and exception handlers.

EXCEPTION HANDLING

The American Heritage dictionary defines an *exception* as "a case that does not conform to the normal rules." In software engineering parlance, an exception is an event or condition that is not part of the normal execution of program code. Most exceptions are considered error conditions that must be taken into account by the programmer, although exceptions don't have to be associated with errors. An exception is anything that must be accounted for that is not part of the domain logic of the program. In other words, exceptions are unusual conditions that the programmer must take into account that don't necessarily get him closer to solving the problem at hand. On the other hand, unhandled exceptions can cause the program to completely fail, which obviously doesn't address the purpose for which the program was written.

A common example is in order. If you tried to allocate some memory for part of your program's execution and the memory was completely exhausted, your program could not continue executing. Or if you were trying to write some data to the disk and the disk was full, your program would not be able to continue. These are both exceptions. They are both conditions that don't have any real bearing on solving the domain problem, yet they can prevent the program from executing to its conclusion. Another example of an exception is when you have asked your user to input a file name, and the user has entered an invalid one (too long, or contains invalid characters, etc.). Your program cannot continue solving its problem until this is resolved, which usually entails asking the user to try again.

Of course, as a programmer, you are all too familiar with similar conditions. A large part of robust application development is anticipating and handling these sorts of potential errors. Structured exception handling is a fairly painless way to create robust applications.

To give you an idea of how powerful this mechanism is, another example is in order. One of the most dreaded sights in Windows is the General Protection Fault dialog box. A general protection fault means that a program has written into a region of memory that it doesn't own, and therefore has corrupted whatever was supposed to be there. This corrupted memory might belong to the operating system itself, so it has always been necessary to exit Windows entirely and restart it to ensure that the operating system wasn't corrupted. Notice our use of the past tense. Because Delphi is written in Object-Pascal, the software engineers had access to Object-Pascal's robust exception handling, and they used it to a good end. Figure 11.1 shows what you will see when you generate a general protection fault from within Delphi.

Just click on the OK button and continue working! Because Delphi's programmers used exception handling to check for errors and for resource allocation, they were able to stop your application from corrupting any other application's memory, and you don't have to restart Windows!

There are two distinct types of exception handling in Delphi. The first type of exception creates resource protection blocks, and the second type handles explicit errors. We will examine how both types of exceptions can be used simultaneously after we further define and give examples of each.

Resource Protection Blocks—try . . . finally . . . end

The first type of exceptions in Delphi are *resource protection blocks.* Resources in Windows programming are things that you must allocate for use and eventually release. These things include memory, graphics resources, window handles, object instances, and a host of other items. If you create a program that allocates some resources and never releases them, you cause a condition known as *resource leakage.* In other words, if you allocate memory and never deallocate it when you are finished with it, no other programs (including Windows itself) can use that memory. If this happens often enough, Windows will run out of whatever resource that your program is leaking, and Windows does not often react gracefully in these situations. Depending on what resource you aren't reclaiming, Windows may cause a general protection fault, issue an out of memory error, or possibly just lock up your computer and become unresponsive.

FIGURE 11.1   A General Protection Fault Error Message in Delphi Allows You to Continue Working

Resource leakage is obviously undesirable, and programs that exhibit leakage are frequently referred to as misbehaving applications. As you write Windows programs, it is very important that you remember to release any resource that you have allocated. Delphi takes care of releasing the resources that it uses, so you never have to worry about resource leakage through the objects found in the Visual Component Library. However, any resource that you explicitly allocate must be explicitly deallocated by you. For example, if you allocate some memory for a procedure, you must deallocate that memory before the procedure ends, otherwise you will have stranded that memory, meaning that neither your program nor any other programs, including Windows, can use that memory.

```
procedure DoSomething;
var
    p : pointer;
begin
    getmem( p, 1024 );  {allocate resource}

    { perform some actions here, including manipulating the
      memory pointed to by p}

    freemem( p, 1024 );  { free resource }
end;
```

In the example above, memory is allocated for the pointer p, some actions are performed using that memory pointer, and eventually p is released before the procedure ends. If the call to freemem wasn't included at the bottom of the procedure, the 1024 bytes of memory that belonged to p would never be reclaimed, and your application has just "leaked" 1024 bytes of memory.

So, as long as you remember to "clean up after yourself", you shouldn't experience resource leakage. However, consider the following situation:

```
procedure DoSomething;
var
    p : pointer;
    x, y : word;
begin
    getmem( p, 1024 );
    y := 0;
    x := 6 / 0; { this will cause an runtime error! }
    freemem( p, 1024 );
end; {procedure}
```

We will look at ways to handle the divide-by-zero run-time error condition in a moment, so that your application doesn't just terminate. However, assuming that the error doesn't completely halt your application, you still have the problem of resource leakage. The line of code that frees the memory allocated to p never gets executed because of the error, and the memory is lost forever as memory leakage.

Object-Pascal has a special type of exception handling to accomodate just this kind of situation. There is a new type of logical block not found in earlier versions of Pascal. It's called a resource protection block. Its syntax is shown below:

```
getmem( p, 1024 );
try
    { some code }
    { some more code }
finally
    freemem( p, 1024 );
end; {try}
```

All of the code following the `try` reserved word and the `finally` reserved word will execute until an error condition occurs. If no error condition occurs, the code after `finally` will execute normally. However, if an error does occur, the code in the `finally` block will be executed before control passes away from this subroutine. In other words, **the code between** `finally` **and** `end` **will always be executed,** no matter what error conditions may or may not have occurred. This behavior guarantees that the cleanup code to deallocate resources will never be skipped for any reason, and you can prevent resource leakage this way.

This is a powerful mechanism that requires little work on the programmer's part. In general,

YOU SHOULD ALWAYS INCLUDE A RESOURCE PROTECTION BLOCK IN EVERY ROUTINE THAT ALLOCATES SOME RESOURCE,

whether it is memory, graphics controls, or objects that you instantiate yourself.

```
procedure DoSomething;
var
    p : pointer;
begin
    getmem( p, 1024 );
    try
        { some code that manipulates p, which might or might
          not cause an error condition }
    finally
        freemem( p, 1024 );
    end; {try}
end. {procedure}
```

Notice that the syntax for the `try` block doesn't require a `begin . . . end` block. All of the code between `try` and `finally` is protected by the resource protection block. Also notice that you must include an `end` statement to mark the end of the `try` block, even though there isn't a corresponding begin. The `try . . . finally` block resembles a case statement in this way—it requires an `end` without a `begin`.

Resource protection via the `try . . . finally` block is the perfect way to ensure that you never have any resource leakage in your Windows programs. This saves you from having to check for error conditions and provide cleanup code for every possible error contingency. Also notice that the code after `finally` is always executed, so all of the cleanup code to deallocate resources is handled in just one location within the subroutine. This technique can save a lot of redundant coding, which is always difficult to keep synchronized. **No matter what happens, the code after `finally` will always be executed.**

Figure 11.2 is an example form that illustrates how to use resource protection to prevent resource leakage.

This form has two edit components: the first shows the amount of free memory when this form is run; a second shows the current amount of free memory. The button beside the second edit component updates the display of the amount of memory available. The two long buttons do the same naughty thing—try to divide by zero. The difference is that the first button doesn't utilize resource protection and the second button does. Here is the code for the two buttons:

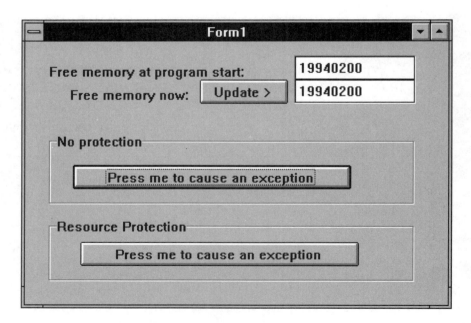

FIGURE 11.2   Resource Protection Example Form

```
procedure TForm1.Button1Click(Sender: TObject);
const
  MemSize = 1024;
var
  P : pointer;
  y : integer;
  x : real;
begin
  GetMem( p, MemSize );
  y := 0;
  { cause an exception }
  x := 1/y;
  FreeMem( p , MemSize );
end;

procedure TForm1.Button2Click(Sender: TObject);
const
  MemSize = 1024;
var
  P : pointer;
  x : real;
  y : integer;
begin
  GetMem( p, MemSize );
  y := 0;
  try
    { cause an exception }
    x := 1/y;
  finally
    FreeMem( p , MemSize );
  end; {try}
end;
```

Notice that in both cases we try to divide by zero. However, the first button doesn't reclaim the memory that is allocated to the pointer variable p. Because the code to deallocate the memory is never reached, this application "leaks" 1024 bytes of memory each time the routine is run. So every time you click the Exception button without resource protection, also click on the Update button and notice how much memory is left over, unstranded. But, if you click on the protected button, no memory is stranded—the call to FreeMem is made no matter what.

What you see if you click either of the two long buttons depends on a couple of factors. One of the environment settings for Delphi is **Break on Exception** (Figure 11.3).

If this option is chosen, when you run your programs within the development environment, Delphi will intercept all exceptions and warn you of them. If you then want to see what the program would do if it were not running in the development environment,

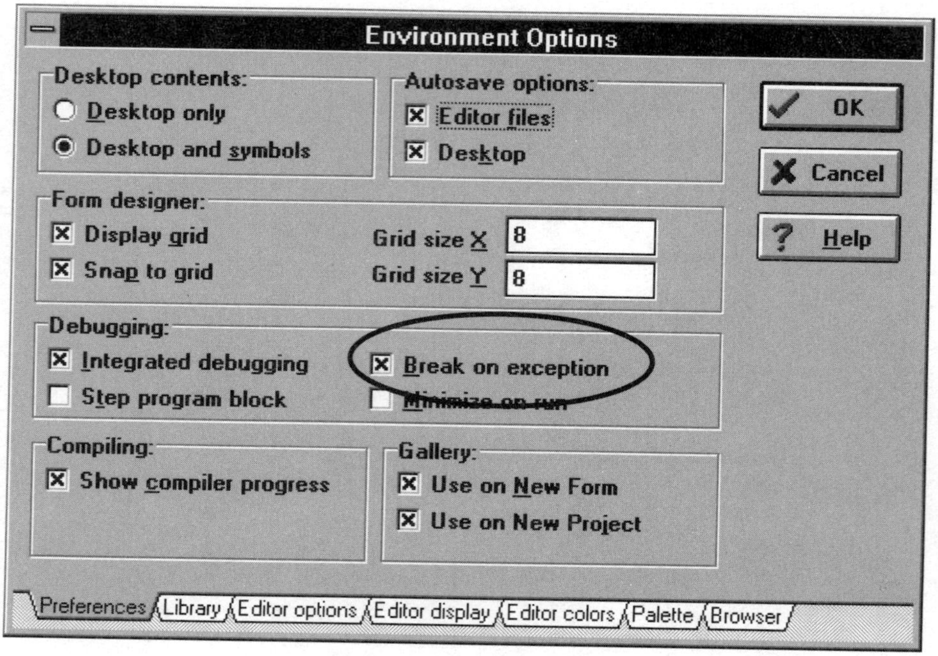

FIGURE 11.3 Delphi Environment Debugging Options

click on the run button again (or chose Run from the Run menu) and your application will then be able to intercept the exception. If you don't want to pass the exception on to your application, you can chose Program Reset from the Run menu to stop program execution. If this option is not checked, then your applications get the first shot at handling whatever exceptions occur.

In the case of Figure 11.4, you will eventually see Delphi's default exception handler for attempted division by zero. Instead of relying on Delphi's default exception handler, we could have written our own. That topic is discussed in an upcoming section.

The only other fragments of code associated with this form are the Update button's OnClick event and the form's `FormActivate` event:

```
procedure TForm1.Button3Click(Sender: TObject);
var
  s : string;
begin
  str( MemAvail, s );
  Current_memory_edit.text := s
end;
```

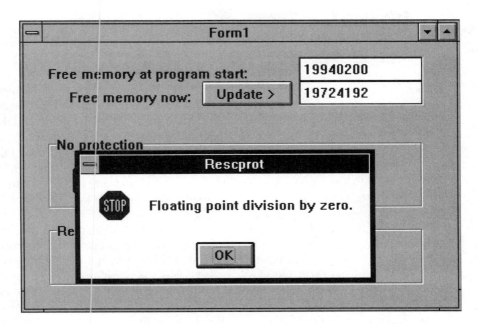

FIGURE 11.4 Delphi's Built-in Exception Handling

```
procedure TForm1.FormActivate(Sender: TObject);
var
  s : string;
begin
  str( MemAvail, s );
  current_memory_edit.text := s;
  start_mem_edit.text := s
end;
```

The next type of exception handling helps you respond gracefully to actual run-time errors, like the division by zero error.

Exception Blocks—try . . . except . . . end

The except clause of the try block actually implements what most people think of as exception handling. The syntax for a try . . . except block is shown below:

```
try
    { some code that might cause an error }
except
    on ExceptionType1 do
        { some error handling code here }
```

```
    on ExceptionType2 do
        { some error handling code here }
end; {try}
```

There is some terminology that is associated with this type of exception handling. When an error occurs, an exception is raised, meaning that the line of code that caused the error is not executed, program flow jumps into the exception part of the block, and the type of the exception is checked against the types specified in the exception block. If one of the types listed matches the type of the raised exception, the code in that portion of the exception block is executed, and then the entire exception block is exited. An exception is said to be handled when its type matches and the corrective code has been executed. The code that caused the error is not automatically tried again. You must have the whole block in a loop to try to execute the code that raised the exception again.

Notice that, unlike the resource protection blocks discussed above, you can handle as many exception types as you like. In other words, you can define exception types and then look for exceptions of that type—you always know what kind of error has occurred by the type of the exception that is raised. Delphi is object-oriented, so the exception types in Delphi are just object instances. When an error occurs, the exception object that is associated with that error is automatically created. Whenever the exception is handled, the object is automatically destroyed. You never have to explicitly issue destructor calls for an exception. If the exception is not handled, the exception is propagated.

This type of exception handling is obviously applicable to many situations. Notice that the try . . . except . . . end scheme for handling errors doesn't suffer from many of the problems of the old "goto" method of error handling. Namely, all of your code within the try block is protected without having to constantly look at function return error values. Also, the code is much more readable, with all of the domain specific code in one place and all of the error handling code in another. This type of exception handling is also superior because exceptions have their own scope. See the upcoming section on the scope of exceptions for more about unhandled exceptions.

Run-time error trapping.   The first and most obvious use for exception blocks is to handle fatal application errors, such as divide by zero. By checking the exception type, you can discover exactly what type of error occurred and take appropriate action. Here's an example:

```
procedure DoSomething;
var
    x, y : real;
begin
    y := 0;
    try
        x := 1/y;
    except
        on EZeroDivide do
            writeln( 'Cannot divide by zero' );
```

```
     on EOverFlow do
        writeln( 'Numbers are too large' );
     on EMathError do
        writeln( 'General math error' );
   end; {try}
end; {procedure}
```

These particular exception types are all built-in exception types in Delphi. Also notice the naming scheme that Delphi assumes about exceptions—all exception types begin with an "E", so that they are easily recognizable as exceptions. Just like the "T" for type naming convention, Delphi doesn't enforce the naming scheme, but it's a good idea to adhere to it to make you code more readable and consistent. Delphi comes with a wide variety of built-in exception types, shown in the object browser in Figure 11.5.

Notice in the code snippet above how we handled math errors in general and the divide by zero error specifically:

```
on EZeroDivide do
   writeln( 'Cannot divide by zero' );
```

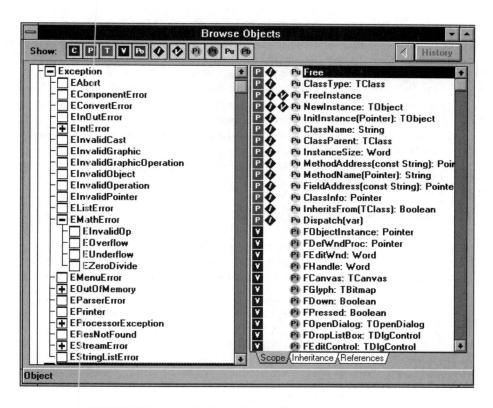

FIGURE 11.5   Delphi's Object Browser Showing Exception Types

```
on EOverFlow do
   writeln( 'Numbers are too large' );
on EMathError do
   writeln( 'General math error' );
```

This is another nice feature of exception handling. In this case, we wanted to handle the divide by zero situation specifically, but handle all the other math errors as a group. Notice in the object browser the EZeroDivide is inherited from EMathError. In other words, EZeroDivide is a specific type of EMathError. Delphi always looks at exception types top to bottom, so if you want to handle a specific exception one way and the rest of its type of exception another, just put the specific exception higher in the list of exception handlers. In our example, we handled EZeroDivide with a special message and the rest of the potential math errors with a generic message. We are able to do that by putting the more specific EZeroDivide exception before the more generic EMath-Error in the case statement.

Application error trapping. Delphi comes with a large collection of prede-fined exception classes. These suffice to handle all of the generic things that can happen during program execution. But what about the error conditions that are specific to a par-ticular application? For example, if you had an application that needed access to a data-base, and the user was required to enter the name of the database, how do you handle the situation when a user has entered an invalid name?

Because exceptions are just objects, you can create your own exceptions by inherit-ing from one of the built-in exception types or inheriting directly from TException, the ancestor of all exeptions. This has a couple of benefits. First, you can move all of the error handling code, both run-time errors and application errors, to one location in the proce-dure or function. Secondly, it means that all exceptions are handled the same way, which leads to more consistent code.

For an example of creating your own exceptions, see the section on user defined ex-ceptions later in this chapter.

Combining Exception Types

So far, we have shown each type of exception handling structure in isolation (either a re-source protection block or an exception block). However, Delphi will allow you to mix and match the two exception types, and that is the most advantageous use. For example:

```
function GetAverage( sum, numItems : integer ) : integer;
var
   p : pointer;
begin
   getmem( p, 1024 );
   try { resource protection block }
      try {exception block }
```

```
          Result := sum div numItems;
      except
          on EDivByZero do
          begin
             Result := 0;
             raise
          end; {on}
      end; {try}
  finally
      freemem( p, 1024 )
  end; {try}
end;
```

In this routine, if zero is passed as the number of items, the function will return 0. However, if we checked for a zero return value in the calling program, we would be defeating the purpose of exception handling. We would then have to check the return value of the function to tell if it encountered any errors. Instead, we are setting Result to zero (so that it won't have an indeterminate value), and we are reraising the exception. Reraising an exception means that we have handled the exception, but we don't want the exception to go away. In this case, we want the EDivByZero to still be raised when we exit this function. That way, the program that called this function could check to see if an exception of that type was raised, and handle it appropriately. So, in the example above, we reraise the EDivByZero exception to tell the calling program that a div by zero was attempted.

Reraising the exception causes this function to terminate, and control to pass back to the calling routine, except that **the finally block is always executed.** Therefore, if you use resource protection blocks in harmony with your exception blocks, you can prevent resource leakage even in extreme error conditions. And that makes your programs far more robust.

BUILT-IN EXCEPTIONS

Delphi comes with a wide assortment of built-in exceptions. Figure 11.6 shows the list displayed in the object browser.

The Exception Class

All of the exceptions in Figure 11.6 are inherited from the Exception class, which is an abstract base class from which all Exception class are derived. The Exception class handles all of the special capabilities of exceptions (such as automatic instantiation and destruction). The Exception class is in the SysUtils unit, which you must include in the uses clause of your unit in order to employ exceptions.

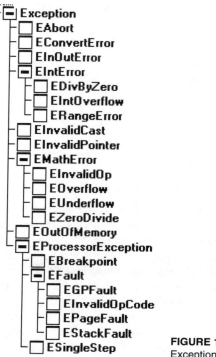

FIGURE 11.6 Delphi's Predefined
Exception Classes

Exceptions and the VCL

Just as you should convert all error handling to exception-based code, the Delphi developers did the same. Delphi's Visual Component Library, which is written in Object-Pascal, makes heavy use of the exception handling mechanism to report errors.

Any time an error occurs in a VCL object, an exception is raised. Therefore, if you have sufficient exception handlers, you can catch these exceptions and take appropriate action. By using exceptions, the Delphi library makes it easy to handle all errors consistently, whether they occur in your own code or while VCL code is running. That makes error handling for the entire application easier, and keeps all of the error handling code together.

USER-DEFINED EXCEPTIONS

As we mentioned earlier, it is possible to create your own exception types within Delphi. Again, you should move all of your error handling to exception based error handling for all of the reasons that we have enumerated earlier:

- better cohesion of application domain code vs. error handling code
- improved readability
- easier maintenance
- consistency in how your application handles errors

Raising Your Own Exceptions

You can create as many exception types as you like by inheriting them initially from the Exception class or one of its descendants. Remember, the Exception type is the abstract base class from which all exceptions are descended. It is this base class that provides all of the built-in functionality of exceptions. For example, to create a new exception called EInvalidBalance:

```
type
    EInvalidBalance = class( Exception );

begin
    try
        { some code that looks at balances }
        { found an invalid balance }
        raise EInvalidBalance.create( 'Invalid Balance' );
    except
        on EInvalidBalance do
            { take some error handling actions here }
    end; {try}
end;
```

Notice in this code that we never actually created a variable for EInvalidBalance, only a type. When we wanted to raise an exception, we instantiated the error object and it was automatically passed on to the error handler, where it was handled and destroyed. In other words, the call to raise EInvalidBalance.create('Invalid Balance') actually created an EInvalidBalance object, which is an instance of the EInvalidBalance class. This error object (which doesn't have an actual name in this case) then gets passed by Delphi to the appropriate exception code, where the exception is handled and the object is destroyed automatically.

Using the Exception Instance Object

There may be cases where you need to get at more of the information contained within this exception object, and Object-Pascal makes that possible. The as..do part of the exception has a special form which lets you name the exception object. For example, in the above code, we could have handled the exception with

```
on E : EInvalidBalance do
   writeln( E.Message );
```

In this case, we have access to the E object instance until the end of this exception handling block. As soon as this exception block (just one line) has executed, Object-Pascal automatically destroys the object by calling its Destroy method. **You never have to explicitly destroy an object instance variable of the exception family, whether you have named it or not.** This is contrary to the way Object-Pascal handles other object references, but exceptions are a special type of object case.

The string that you pass to the exception's Create method is the message that is returned from the Message method used above. The Exception object has other methods associated with it that could be useful in some situations (Figure 11.7).

SCOPE OF EXCEPTIONS

Scoping refers to the visibility and lifetime of a program element, and the scoping of exceptions is unique in some ways.

Exceptions

Essentially, an exception is "alive" until it is handled, which means if it isn't handled in the block in which it is raised, that block will terminate and the exception handlers in the

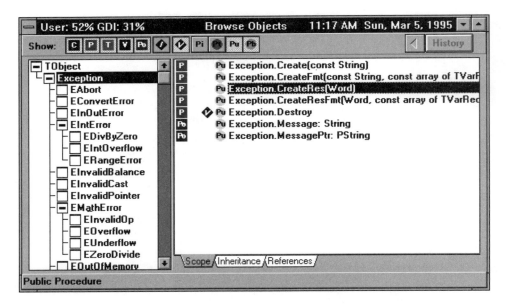

FIGURE 11.7   Public and Published Methods of the Exception Class

calling block will be checked. If the exception isn't handled there, it propagates back up through the call stack until it is handled, or the default Delphi exception handler catches it (which is always at the outermost level). Thus, an exception will be propagated when it is not handled in the current exception block, and it will continue exiting the enclosing blocks until it finds some exception handler to handle it and thus destroy it.

This propagation feature is a benefit to exception handling, because it means that you don't have to handle every kind of exception in every block. This allows you to only handle specific, likely errors within a procedure, but still be assured that if an unlikely error occurs, it will be handled correctly at an outer level.

There is an optional `else` part of the exception handling block, just like the else clause for a case statement:

```
try
    { some code }
except
    on ESomeError do
        { error handling code }
    on EAnotherError do
        { error handling code }
    else
        { handle ALL OTHER exceptions }
end; {try}
```

However, we have not mentioned this possibility until now because

YOU SHOULD NEVER USE AN ELSE BLOCK IN AN EXCEPTION!

The `else` will catch all exceptions that you don't specifically handle, and therefore can hinder the exception scoping mechanism.

Exception Types

The scoping rules discussed above dealt with Exception objects, or instances of the Exception class. Exception types follow the same scoping rules of other class types. Namely, if you want to declare an exception type in a unit and use that type in other units, declare it in the interface section. However, if it is an exception that is only going to be used internally within that unit, declare it in the implementation section, thereby hiding it from other units.

USING EXCEPTIONS FOR ERROR HANDLING

Here's an example that shows the different mind set the exceptions add to the problem of error handling. Below there are two versions of a `GetAverage` function, which returns zero if a division error occurs, but one uses the old style error handling and the other uses exceptions:

```
function GetAverage( sum, numItems : integer ) : integer;
begin
   try
      Result := sum div numItems;
   except
      on EDivByZero do Result := 0;
   end;
end;

function GetAverage( sum, numItems : integer ) : integer;
begin
   if numItems <> 0 then
      Result := sum div numItems
   else
      Result := 0;
end;
```

This code might not look like much of an improvement, but what if you had a routine that had to do a lot of calculations? Instead of checking each and every possible problem with if statements and case statements, you can off-load all of the error checking to the end of the routine, in the exception handler block. Like we've said before, this coding style makes your code much more readable, by separating the application domain code from the error handling code.

Exception handling is definitely a different mind set. However, once you become accustomed to it, you will be amazed at how much more intuitive it seems. You will also immediately notice that the readability of your code increases, and because it's read more than it's written, more readable code translates into more efficient programming. Once you've started using exceptions, you'll never go back.

CHAPTER **12**

BORLAND DATABASE ENGINE OVERVIEW

All of Delphi's access to data is handled by the Borland Database Engine, or BDE. BDE is a proven engine for doing data access not just to local DB and DBF tables, but to client/server systems as well.

Borland, like many companies, reached a crossroads several years ago. They manufactured several products that specialized in database access, and they all performed their data access a little differently. Borland decided to take the common functionality of all their data access products and abstract the functionality into one engine. And they did just that.

Some of you may remember the Paradox engine that Borland sold a few years ago. It was essentially the data access engine from the Paradox DBMS. It could be bought by users of other language products that needed access to Paradox's DB table format. BDE is a superset of the Paradox engine. They took the old engine, added all of the database capabilities of dBASE, and included a method for easy upsizing of databases from a local drive to a full-blown client/server environment. As a matter of fact, BDE can be purchased separately, so if you are developing in a non-Borland language product, you can still take advantage of the proven rapid data access of BDE.

Abstracting the common functionality of the DBMS products into a single engine has several benefits. First and foremost, you only have to write the code to address a database type once, and all of the products that use the engine will have access to that database type. For example, Paradox for Windows and dBASE for Windows can both read and manipulate each of the other's file formats, and that makes both products more flexible. Secondly, by concentrating on a single set of drivers, it is easier to make improvements to the engine's functionality, instead of reinventing the wheel over and over for these different products. This also has the side benefit of upgrading all the database access for the user without having to upgrade the product. For example, if Borland has made any improvements to the database access since dBASE for Windows was released, and you install the improved version of the BDE on your computer during the Delphi installation, dBASE as well as Delphi can immediately use the improved drivers.

Another benefit of a common database engine is that if you have several products on your machine that perform data access through the engine, there is far less redundant code than if they each had an independent database engine. Because Paradox, dBASE, and Delphi share the BDE, combined they take up less disk space than they would if the data access engine was built into each of them. This is a relief to some of us who have gigantic hard disk drives that are nevertheless packed full. Developers are notorious for eating disk space like candy as they typically use such a wide range of products.

What Borland has done by creating BDE is address a growing trend in companies that support multiple development platforms. As you may have heard, Microsoft is also abstracting their data access into a single engine they call the Jet engine (Joint Engine Technology). Access and FoxPro are being modified to use this common engine for all their data access.

This chapter will serve as a general overview of the capabilities of BDE and some of its features. The next chapter will deal specifically with how Delphi performs database access through components.

BDE CONFIGURATION UTILITY

One of the programs that is installed within the Delphi program group during installation is called the Database Engine Configuration; the executable file name is BDECFG.EXE. By default, Delphi puts all BDE related files into a directory named IDAPI, which is the old name for the configuration program. IDAPI is an acronym for Independent Database Application Programmer Interface. As a matter of fact, you can still see lots of remnants of that name floating around in help files and directory names.

Whatever it is named, Figure 12.1 shows what you see when you run the BDECFG program. Actually, depending on which version of Delphi you have, you may not see as many drivers listed initially. If you only have the desktop version, the only two drivers you will see will be DBASE and PARADOX. However, no matter how many drivers you have installed, they are all configured basically the same way.

This BDECFG program is actually the interface to the BDE. You can change many of the characteristics of how BDE works from this utility. This information is kept in a file called IDAPI.CFG (configuration). Whenever you make changes through BDECFG, you must be sure to save the IDAPI.CFG file so that your changes will be committed.

Drivers

The first page of the BDE configuration utility is the list of drivers that are currently installed, along with some of their characteristics. For example, in the screen shot of Figure

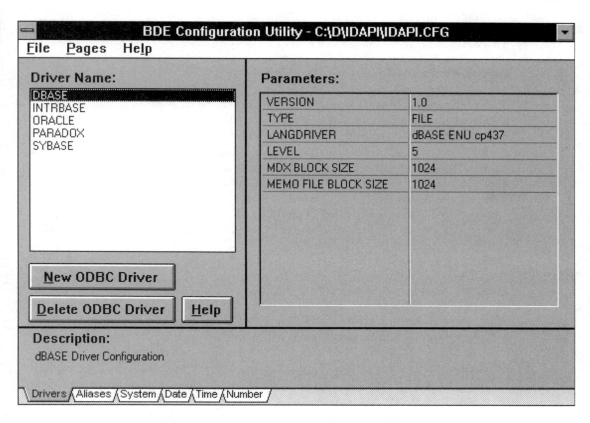

FIGURE 12.1   The Borland Database Engine Configuration Dialog

12.1 you see some of the driver information for dBASE DBF tables. The LEVEL setting allows you to determine what the default type of DBF table you want to work with. For example, if you need to work with dBASE IV type tables, you can set LEVEL to 4 and BDE will create that type of table for you.

DATABASE ALIASES

One of the tasks that you will want to master with BDE is setting database aliases. A common problem when creating applications that need data files is that frequently you have to provide some mechanism to allow the data files to be moved and still allow your program to function. At one time this entailed changing the paths to all the database files that you accessed and recompiling your program. There are obviously better ways to handle this problem, but the point is that you always had to write some code to enable this capability.

BDE removes a great deal of this burden by its use of aliases. Before we define exactly what a BDE alias is, we need to make an important distinction.

Databases vs. Tables

The creator of dBASE made an unfortunate error when he named the file format that was to become the industry standard for many years. When Wayne Radcliff created that file structure, he gave it the extension DBF, which stood for DataBase File.

It is unfortunate because database is a term that has a specific meaning in industry circles. DBF files are actually tables, meaning that it is some ordered collection of data, usually arranged in rows for each record and columns for each field. A database, then, is a *collection* of related tables. When you are creating a database, it is frequently composed of many related tables, each of which are filled with records and columns. However, for now, it is important for you to comprehend the distinction between databases and tables.

Creating Pseudo Databases

In the previous section, we stated that a database is a collection of related tables. Indeed, all client/server database servers have just such a data structure: both a database and the tables that belong to it. However, there is rarely such a mechanism with the types of tables that are usually used in nonserver environments. Yet it would be nice to have such a beast. One option is to create a standard database container, which would hold all your related databases. But the problem with that strategy is that it breaks backwards compatibility: Someone with an older program that didn't know about your special database format would no longer be able to access your data.

Fortunately, there is a simple solution to this problem. Through BDE, you can designate a regular DOS directory as a database name. Because directories already hold a collection of files, you can give a directory a specific identifier and place all your related tables in that directory. Thus, you have a database which is a collection of logically related tables. In BDE parlance, this is called a Pseudo Database. It is not a real database in the database server sense (no referential relationships are defined), but it is a close enough abstraction to provide some advantages. The primary advantage of this scheme is that you can use the database name as a sort of pointer to where your data resides.

To create a Pseudo Database, go to the Alias page of the BDECFG utility (Figure 12.2). To create a new alias, just click on the New Alias button, specify an alias name and a driver type (choose STANDARD for DBF and DB tables), and BDE will create a new alias for you. Then, select the Path property of the new alias and type a directory name into the entry field. Save the configuration file, and that's it. Now, whenever you refer to the table names, you can do so with the alias rather than the directory name.

This may not seem like a great benefit yet. You are trading one name for the other. Where this really becomes handy is when it comes time to move your tables to another location, either out to a network drive when it's time to deploy your application on a server, or when moving them due to hardware space constraints. To move the database files, all

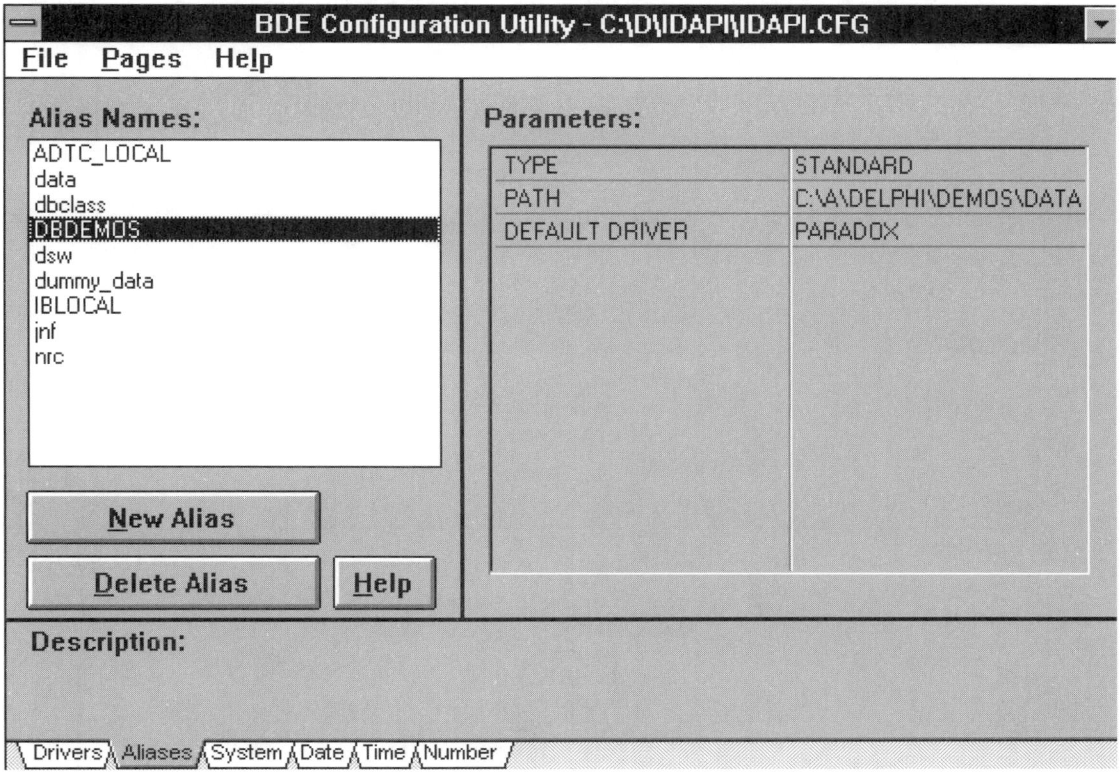

FIGURE 12.2   Creating a Pseudo Database in the BDECFG Utility

you have to do is copy the files to the new directory, then open up BDECFG and change your database alias to point to the new directory. That's all! You don't have to make a single change in your program, and it doesn't need to be recompiled.

Of course, what you are really doing with BDECFG and these aliases is creating a pointer to a pointer. All your data access routines point to the database alias, and you can point the database alias wherever you want. Then, it is a simple matter to change where the database alias points to also change where your data is stored. This is a simple solution to a problem that caused a lot of headaches in the past.

So, whenever you refer to any database table, always refer to it by using the alias name rather than the actual path name. For example, in Database Desktop, when you create a table definition and save it, you are presented with a list of all the disk drives on your system, and a list of database aliases, as well (Figure 12.3). Notice that the database aliases show up exactly like the disk drives. Everywhere in Delphi when you need to refer to a database table, you can specify an alias instead of a directory path.

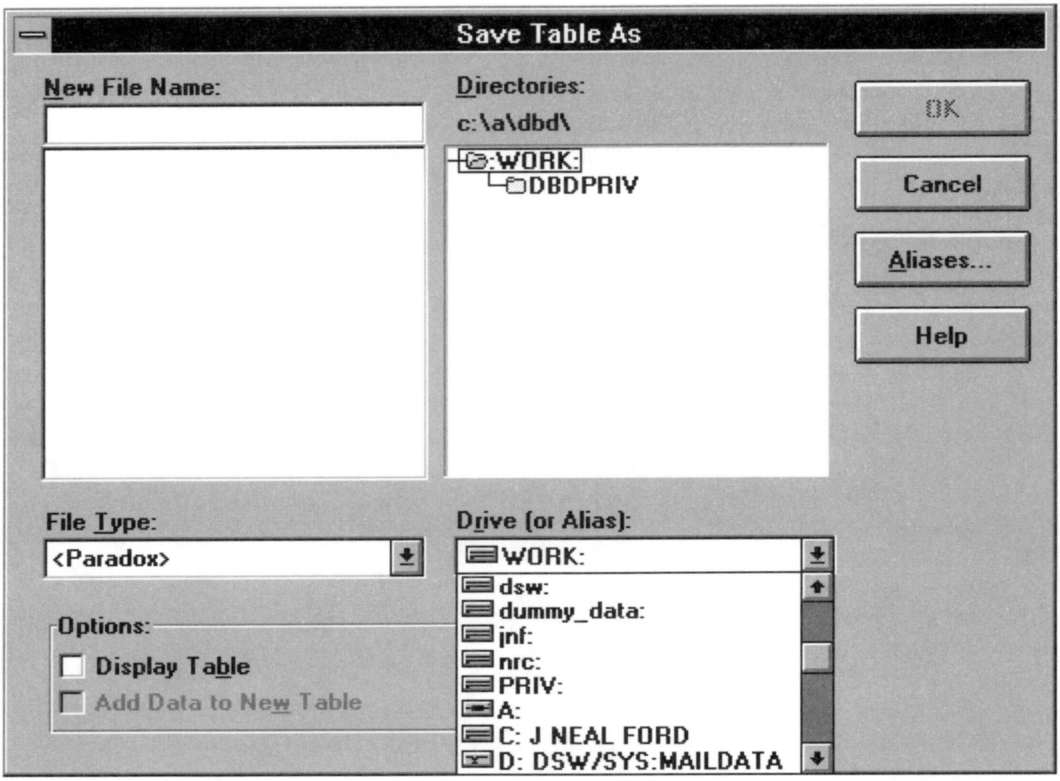

FIGURE 12.3   Saving a Table to a Pseudo Alias Directory

DBs vs. DBFs

The Borland Database Engine gives you equal access to two different database table formats: DBF tables (used by dBASE) and DB tables (used by Paradox). Because BDE is the engine used by these products to access their database files, you get the same database performance in Delphi that these products offer.

dBASE Tables (*.DBF)

The DBF table format is the older of the two, and still the most common. Table 12.1 gives a listing of the field types available in DBF tables.

Note that this is the DBF table type for dBASE 5.0 for Windows, and that this format has some added field types from previous versions of dBASE. If backwards compatibility is a concern, you should stick to the earlier formats that you need to be compatible with. If you want the older type fields to be the default (for example, dBASE IV field types), you can change the LEVEL in the BDE configuration program.

TABLE 12.1 DBF Field Types

Field Type Name	Abbreviation	Description
Character	C	string data
Float	F	real numbers
Numeric	N	integers
Date	D	special date format
Logical	L	Boolean
Memo	M	unlimited text data
OLE	O	OLE container field
Binary	B	BLOB container field (sound, pictures, etc.)

DBF files have some files that accompany the DBF file. One, the DBT file (which has the same name as the DBF file) contains memo, OLE, and binary field information. Also, the MDX file(s) contain indexes for the database. So, anytime you copy the DBF file, you must also copy the corresponding DBT and MDX files.

DBF tables are extremely versatile and easy to work with. However, since this format is a little older, DBF tables don't have some of the more advanced features that DB tables have.

Paradox Tables (*.DB)

Paradox tables have a much wider variety of field types, so it's easier to specify exactly how much storage you need for a particular data field. Table 2.2 lists field types for Paradox tables (LEVEL 5, which corresponds to Paradox 5 for Windows).

Several of these field types need some explanation. DB tables have a date, time, and TimeStamp field. The data holds a date representation in a special Julian internal date format, and the time field is also kept in a special internal format (the number of milliseconds since midnight). The TimeStamp, on the other hand, is a combination of the time of day and the date, and it too is kept in a special format. The user can't edit fields of the TimeStamp type; they are automatically updated every time the record is modified.

The AutoIncrement field is similar to the TimeStamp field in that neither can be edited by the user. They are both automatically generated by the database engine. The AutoIncrement field is used to create primary keys (discussed in the chapter on Database Design). The AutoIncrement field is guaranteed to be unique throughout your entire table.

The Binary field and the Bytes field hold the same type of data (Binary Large ObjectS), but the difference is storage. The Binary type keeps the data in the MB file, which is where a DB table's memo data is kept, whereas the Bytes type keeps its data within the main DB table. This is why the Bytes type is limited to 255 bytes. The advantage of keeping the data (limited data) in the table file is that it can be accessed far more quickly.

Choosing a Database Table Type

This is a tough question, and should probably be decided on a case by case basis. However, there are some capabilities that DB tables have that DBF tables don't. Notice that

TABLE 12.2 DB Field Types

Field Type Name	Abbr	Range	Description
Alpha	A		Character string
Number	N	10E-307 . . . 10E308	Number
Money	$		Decimal number with 2 decimal places
Short	S	-32767 . . . 32767	Short integer
Long Integer	I	-2147483648 . . . 2147483647	Long integer
BCD	#		High precision floating point
Date	Delphi	1/1/9999BC . . . 12/31/9999	Internal Date format
Time	T		Time of day
TimeStamp	@		Combination of date and time
Memo	M		Unlimited text data
Formatted Memo	F		Formatted text (with embedded formatting codes)
Graphic	G		Images
OLE	O		OLE container field
Logical	L		Boolean values
AutoIncrement	+		Automatic counter, guaranteed to be unique table wide
Binary	B		Unknown BLOB data
Bytes	Y		Unformatted BLOB data, stored in DB

these are all features at the *table* level, not at the *form* level. So, for example, you can create minimum and maximum values for data entry by writing validation code for the form entry fields for DBs or DBFs, but DB tables have support for these rules at the table level. The disadvantage of having validation rules at the form level is that if you change the rules, you have to change them on every form that accesses that data. If you forget to change one, you may be putting invalid data into your database. If you can define validation rules at the table level, you can always be sure that the table will refuse to accept data that is invalid.

Default values. You can supply default values for DB table fields, which is a good idea for field values that will almost always be the same. For example, if most of your orders come from the same state, make that state the default value for that field and cut down on the amount of data entry that your users have to perform.

Required fields. You can flag fields as required, which means that the table will refuse to accept a record that has a blank (null) value for that field. This is equivalent to setting a validation rule of "is not null".

Picture clauses. A picture clause determines the formatting for your data. For example, you might have a picture clause that provides a template for entering phone numbers that automatically fills in the parenthesis and the dash. You can create picture clauses at the database level.

Minimum and maximum ranges.   You can specify what minimum and maximum values you want for a particular field.

Referential integrity.   This feature of DB tables is especially powerful. You can define referential integrity between two tables, and the table will take care of maintaining the reference. So, for example, if you have referential integrity (and cascading deletes) defined for customers and their orders and you delete a customer, all of that customer's orders would automatically be deleted as well. However, this is fairly dangerous, especially if you have highly interrelated tables, because you might accidentally delete one record that in turn deletes a large number of related records!

Table lookups.   DB tables also support table lookups, which just insures that the field that you are entering into a table is also in the other table. This is not a formal relationship like the referential integrity link, but is designed to be a convenient way to insure correct data.

Passwords.   DB tables also allow you to create password protection for the tables. When you want to access the table, you must provide a password or you will not be allowed into the table.

DEPLOYING THE BDE

As you know by now, Delphi itself creates true, stand-alone executables. However, the BDE is implemented as a collection of DLLs, which means that if you create an application that uses databases, you must distribute all of the BDE DLL files as well. You can distribute as many copies of BDE with your application as you want—there is no per user licensing fee. However, Borland requires that you distribute the entire BDE package, not just the files that your application uses.

There is a good reason for this requirement. If the person who is installing your application has another BDE based environment on their machine, your program will install the newer BDE engine over their old BDE engine. This won't cause any problems for your user's other software that uses BDE (it's always backwards compatible), but it means that if they are using some of the features of BDE that your program isn't using, they'll need the entire BDE for their programs to continue to function.

Borland has made this distribution process as painless as possible. There is a directory on the Delphi CD-ROM that has two disks worth of compressed BDE, including a set-up utility. You can just copy these two disk images onto floppy disks and either have your users run the separate set-up program or run it yourself during the installation of your application. There is also a text file in the main Delphi set-up directory called

TABLE 12.3   Files Necessary for BDE Distribution

File Name	Description
IDAPI01.DLL	BDE API DLL
IDBAT01.DLL	BDE Batch utilities DLL
IDQRY01.DLL	BDE Query DLL
IDASCI01.DLL	BDE ASCII Driver DLL
IDPDX 01.DLL	BDE Paradox Driver DLL
IDDBAS01.DLL	BDE dBASE Driver DLL
IDR10009.DLL	BDE Resources DLL
ILD01.DLL	Language Reference DLL
IDODBC01.DLL	BDE ODBC Sockets DLL
ODBC.NEW	Microsoft ODBC Driver Manager DLL, version 2.0
ODBCINST.NEW	Microsoft ODBC Driver Installation DLL, version 2.0
TUTILITY.DLL	BDE Tutility DLL
BDECFG.EXE	BDE Configurationn Utility
BDECFG.HLP	BDE Configuration Utility Help
IDAPI.CFG	BDE Configuration File

DEPLOY.TXT that spells out the details required to distribute BDE. For your convenience, Table 12.3 contains a list of the files that you must distribute.

CHAPTER 13

DATABASE DESKTOP

Delphi is not primarily a database development environment. It is a more general purpose tool with strong database capabilities. Because Delphi isn't exclusively a database tool, there are no provisions within the Delphi integrated development environment for dealing with table and query creation, which are jobs that tools like dBASE and Paradox handle within their environments. For Delphi, this is where Database Desktop comes into play.

Database
Desktop

Database Desktop (DBD) is one of the utilities that is installed in the Delphi program group. DBD provides a way for Delphi programmers to create tables and queries, build indexes, and manipulate tables interactively. Of course, you can write Delphi programs to do all of these things (after all, DBD is just making calls to the Borland Database Engine to accomplish all these things, and Delphi can certainly talk to BDE). However, it is nice to have an interactive tool that takes the headache out of setting up tables and working with them.

This chapter is an introduction to the Database Desktop. Those of you who are familiar with Paradox for Windows will recognize some similarities in the way that DBD works. However, you don't have to have any prior knowledge of Borland's database applications to make good use of DBD. Before you see what DBD can do, you need to understand how to configure it.

CONFIGURATION UTILITY

Along with the database desktop utility, Delphi also has a utility named Database Desktop Local Configuration:

Database
Desktop
Local
Configuration

Double clicking on the icon presents you with the Database Desktop Configuration Dialog shown in Figure 13.1.

This separate utility allows you to specify the default Working Directory, the default Private Directory, and where the IDAPI.CFG file resides. Remember, the IDAPI.CFG file is the configuration file that the BDECFG utility saves all of your Borland Database Engine configuration information in.

The Working Directory is the location of the database files that you need to access. The Private Directory is a location where DBD can place temporary files if you are working in a multi-user environment. If your working directory is actually on a network, you must have some storage location for just your temporary files; if they were kept in the same directory as the database files, several users would be trying to write to the same temporary files, with undesirable results. That is why DBD forces you to make this distinction. Typically, the private directory will be a local drive, while the working directory might be a network drive.

```
┌──────────────────────────────────────────────────┐
│ ─ │        Database Desktop Local Settings         │
├──────────────────────────────────────────────────┤
│                                                    │
│   Working Directory:                               │
│   ┌──────────────────────────────────────────┐    │
│   │ C:\A\DBD                                   │    │
│   └──────────────────────────────────────────┘    │
│   Private Directory:                               │
│   ┌──────────────────────────────────────────┐    │
│   │ C:\A\DBD\DBDPRIV                           │    │
│   └──────────────────────────────────────────┘    │
│   IDAPI Configuration File:                        │
│   ┌──────────────────────────────────────────┐    │
│   │ C:\D\IDAPI\IDAPI.CFG                       │    │
│   └──────────────────────────────────────────┘    │
│                                                    │
│    ┌──────────┐   ┌──────────┐   ┌──────────┐     │
│    │    OK    │   │  Cancel  │   │   Help   │     │
│    └──────────┘   └──────────┘   └──────────┘     │
└──────────────────────────────────────────────────┘
```

FIGURE 13.1   The Database Desktop Configuration Dialog

CREATING TABLES

One of the obvious tasks that you will want to use DBD for is to create tables for your Delphi applications. As you have seen in an earlier chapter, BDE can work with two different table types (DBF and DB) and with other table types as well if you have the SQL Links drivers loaded.

When you first start to create a table, DBD asks you what type of table to create (Figure 13.2).

Table formats are slightly different between different versions of software. For example, the dBASE for Windows tables support OLE fields and binary fields, which dBASE IV tables did not. So, DBD allows you to create exactly the type of table that you need. This is particularly important if you are facing backwards compatibility constraints. In fact, if you choose to make a dBASE for Windows table but you don't take advantage of the two new field types, DBD will remind you when you exit table design mode that the table that you have created will work with other versions.

DBF Tables

When you choose to create a DBF table, you are presented with the Table designer, as shown in Figure 13.3.

As we have already reviewed the data types that are possible in a dBASE table, they will not be repeated here. In the figure there is one field defined called NAME that is a character field of up to 20 characters in length.

Notice the Borrow button that is grayed out. If you want to base one table design on another, before you enter any fields into the table, you can "borrow" the structure of another table. This can be a huge time saver if you want a table that is very similar to one you already have.

The other important feature to notice here is how to create indexes. dBASE tables automatically create a production index file for every table you create with indexes. This

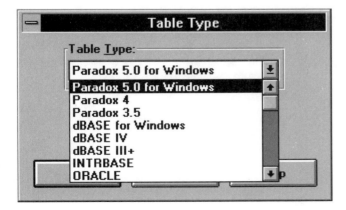

FIGURE 13.2 The Database Desktop Table Type Selection Dialog

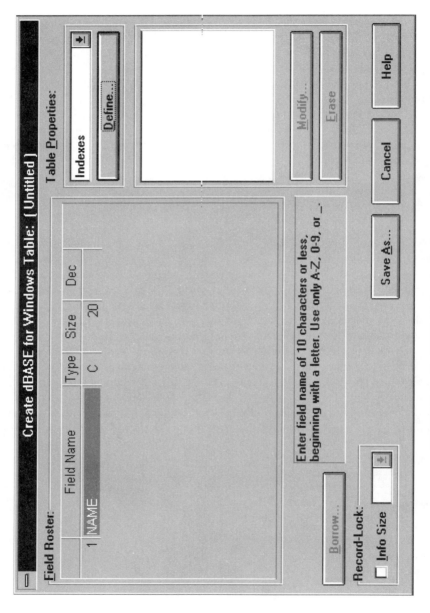

FIGURE 13.3 The DBF Table Creation Dialog

166

Index file (named the same as the Table but with an MDX extension) can contain up to 47 separate indexes. For each field that you want indexed, click on Define (Figure 13.4).

You can base the index on either a single field or an expression, which can contain several fields. For example, if you had fields named Lname and CompName, you could create an index based on the expression "Lname+CompName" which would order the table by last name first, then by company name.

Although DBD will allow you to create indexes and maintains the production index while the table is open, there is no way to view the data in index order within DBD. To do that, you must write the ability to use the index in your Delphi program.

DB Tables

DB tables give you several more options (Figure 13.5).

In this figure, the pull-down list under Table Properties has been selected to show the extra options that the DB Table designer provides. This pull-down list allows you to implement some of the DB Table options that were discussed in our chapter on database design.

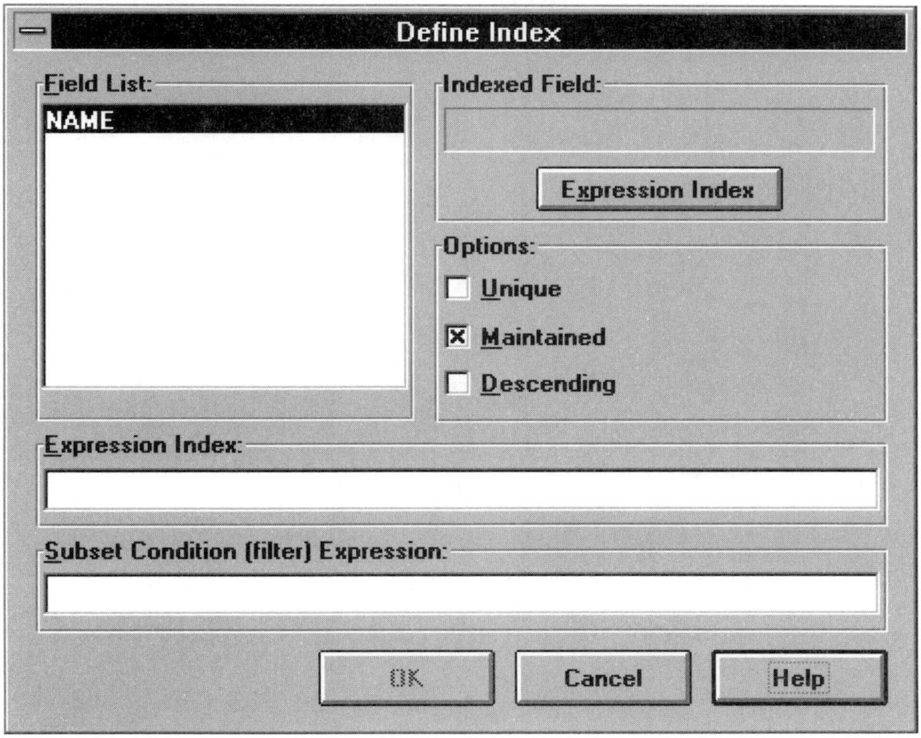

FIGURE 13.4   The Indexes Definition Dialog for dBase Tables

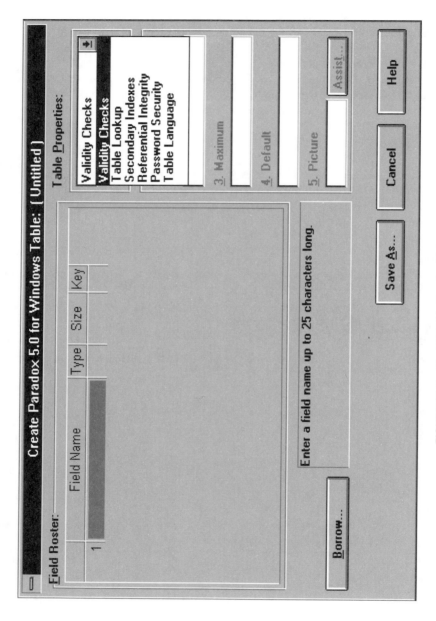

FIGURE 13.5 The DB Table Creation Dialog

   Notice that DB tables have an extra field column called Key. Here you specify which field(s) in the DB table will be the primary key for the table. Once you've designated the primary key field(s), the BDE will automatically enforce entity integrity on that field, ensuring that each entry is unique throughout the table. The engine does this by creating a special index for that key, with a file extension of PX. Just like the production index file for DBF tables, the PX file is automatically maintained. To add additional indexes for other fields, choose Secondary Indexes for that field.

   This Secondary Index dialog (Figure 13.6) displays the fields from a table that has two fields: Name and Address. You can create a secondary index by specifying one or more of these fields; the order that they appear in the Indexed Fields list determines what the sort order for the table will be when this index is active. You can specify with the Change Order arrows whether you want your index to be sorted ascending or descending. Use the Index Options option group to specify whether your index will be automatically maintained (just as the PX index is), and whether or not it should be case sensitive.

   Your secondary indexes are stored in files with the same name as the table but with an extension of .X*nn*, where *nn* is a number. So, if you had three secondary indexes for your table named TEST, they would be named TEST.X00, TEST.X01, and TEST.X02. DB tables also create a .VAL file that contains all of the validation rules for the table.

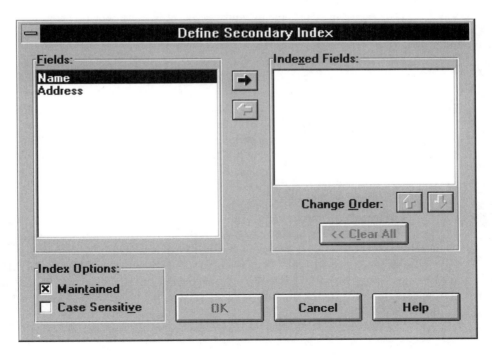

FIGURE 13.6   The Paradox Table Secondary Index Definition Dialog

MANIPULATING DATA

Once you have created a table, you'll need to add data to it. DBD will allow you to add, edit, and delete records in the tables you create.

Adding and Editing Data

When you open a table using either **File | Open** or the open table speedbutton, you are viewing the data in a browse view. This is only a snapshot of the data—you can't actually make changes to the data (including adding records) until you switch to Edit Data view. View Data or Edit Data are available from the View menu. When Edit Data is toggled on, you can make whatever changes you like to the table. Once you have chosen Edit Data, you can choose any of the options on the Record menu, which includes inserting, locking, deleting, table lookups, etc.

Note that you cannot edit memo fields, OLE fields, or binary fields in DBD. These types of fields show up just as a label identifying the type of field. To add or edit data of these types, you must do so through your Delphi program.

Browsing Data

You can always view and change data from a Browse view in DBD (except for the types listed above), and there are some features of the Browse window that you should be aware of.

Rearranging columns.   The Browse in DBD is a very flexible way to view your data. The default order of the columns that it displays is the same order in which the table fields were defined. However, it is sometimes nice to view the data in a different order, perhaps moving two columns side by side to compare values. The DBD Browse makes this easy.

When you move your cursor to one of the column headings, you will notice that the cursor changes shape; into a box. When the cursor changes shape, drag the column to the desired position. This does not change the underlying table definition, only the view that you currently have of the data.

Locking columns.   It is also sometimes convenient to "lock" columns, so that the locked columns stay in the same place while you scroll through the unlocked columns to the right. The Browse in DBD allows you to lock columns from the left margin toward the right. Look in the lower left hand corner of the Browse screen, and you will see the locking control. If you drag it to the right, all the columns to its left will be locked, and all the columns to its right will still be scrollable. When you move the marker, it becomes a double-headed arrow.

In the screen shot of Figure 13.7, the first three columns are locked (CUSTOMER, CUSTKEY, and NAME) and the rest of the columns are free to scroll past, using the scrollbar on the bottom of the window.

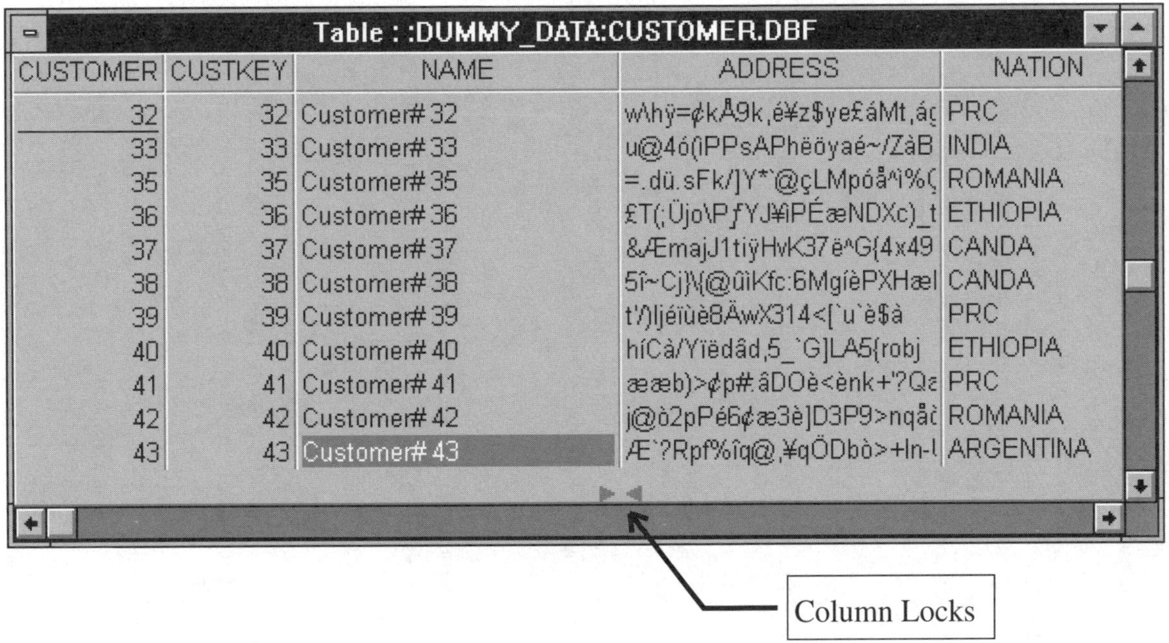

FIGURE 13.7 Locking Columns in the Database Desktop Browser

Saving views.   When you view data in a Browse window, you will sometimes want to save a particular configuration without resorting to changing the underlying table structure. You can accomplish this by saving a view of the Browse. Whenever you make changes to the default view of the data, you will be asked if you want to save the current view under a name when you close the Browse. If you choose to do so, the next time you open that table in a Browse, your settings will be as you left them. To discard a view, go to the Properties menu and choose Delete. This will delete the View file and restore the Browse to the default view. You can have as many views as you like for a particular table; the view settings are saved in a file with a TVF (table view file) extension for DBF files, or a TV extension for DB tables.

CREATING QUERIES

It is fairly common when working with database tables that you need to use only a subset of the fields in the table for a particular purpose: creating a form, creating a report, etc. You may want to view the data from several tables as if it were a single table, for the same purposes. This is particularly true if you have a series of highly interrelated tables (as relational database theory says you should). To derive subsets of data, or to combine fields from several tables, use a *query*. A query can be defined as a view of a subset of data from underlying tables. It is a question that you pose which returns data from fields that you specify. There are two ways to create queries in DBD: QBE or SQL.

SQL

SQL stands for Structured Query Language. This is an ANSI standard language often embedded in a host language for generic data access. That means that most database products can understand some dialect of SQL and return data based on SQL statements. It is a means whereby different software and hardware platforms can exchange information through a common language.

SQL is an extremely complex subject, and it is well beyond the scope of this book. If you are interested in learning more about SQL, there are numerous books on the subject, or you can take a graduate level class at most universities that delves into relational database design and SQL.

However, if you already know SQL, you should be informed that BDE speaks fluent SQL (a subset of ANSI SQL-92), and you can use SQL to define your queries. This is a significant benefit if you eventually plan to upsize your application to use a database server, as you can use basically the same SQL statements that you used for your local data to access your remote data.

To create a SQL query, choose **File | New | SQL Statement** and you will be presented with the SQL Editor shown in Figure 13.8.

This is basically just a text editor where you can type in SQL statements. The SQL statement in the figure requests all the columns from the customer.dbf file in the dummy_data database. To execute this query, click on the lightning bolt speedbutton or

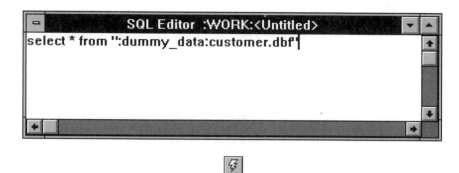

FIGURE 13.8   The DBD SQL Editor and the RunSQL Speedbutton

choose **SQL | Run SQL** from the menu. In either case, the SQL statement will be interpreted by the BDE and the results will be shown in a Browse window.

QBE

The other type of query that you can create in DBD is a QBE query. QBE stands for "Query By Example", and you don't need to know any other languages to use it! A QBE query is created by selecting which fields you want to appear, and how you want them ordered, in a Visual designer. Just like SQL queries, you can specify some conditions and then "run" the query to see the data in a Browse.

To create a QBE query, choose **File | New | QBE** Query. . . . This will request a table to base the query on, and then take you into the Query designer.

The first field you see in Figure 13.9 is the name of the table. If you select the checkbox under its name, you will select all of the fields in the table to be included in your query. After the table name you see a listing of the fields in the table, and you can select (or deselect) those you want to appear in the query.

For example, in Figure 13.10, only the ORDSTAT, TOTPRICE, and ORDDATE fields will appear in the resulting browse.

A Browse is produced when you run the query. As you can see in Figure 13.11, only the fields that were specified appear in the results. Notice that the results of a query are placed in a table named ANSWER.DBF, and the first column in the Browse contains the record numbers for this Answer table.

When you select fields for inclusion by clicking on the checkbox under their name, you actually get a pull-down list that provides several options (Figure 13.12).

Table 13.1 displays the checkmark types and what each represents.

Query conditions.   You can use queries to filter out a subset of records by creating query conditions. Notice that, in the Query designer, you can type values under the field names. These values act as filters for that particular field. So, for example, if you

FIGURE 13.9 The DBD Query By Example Design View

174

Query : <Untitled>
ORDERS.DBF
ORDERKEY
CUSTKEY
ORDSTAT
TOTPRICE
ORDDATE
ORDPRI

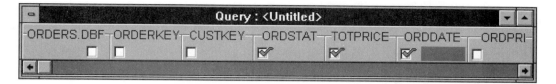

FIGURE 13.10 Projecting Fields Through QBE Design

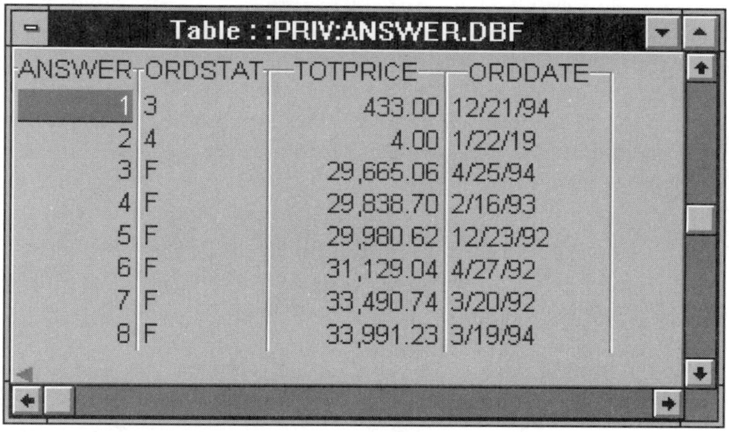

Table : :PRIV:ANSWER.DBF
ANSWER ORDSTAT TOTPRICE ORDDATE
1 3 433.00 12/21/94
2 4 4.00 1/22/19
3 F 29,665.06 4/25/94
4 F 29,838.70 2/16/93
5 F 29,980.62 12/23/92
6 F 31,129.04 4/27/92
7 F 33,490.74 3/20/92
8 F 33,991.23 3/19/94

FIGURE 13.11 The Browse Produced From Figure 13.10

Query : <Untitled>
ORDERS.DBF
ORDERKEY
CUSTKEY
ORDSTAT
TOTPRICE
ORDDATE
ORDPRI
G

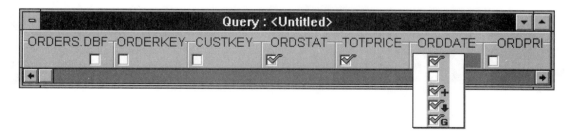

FIGURE 13.12 Inclusion Options in the QBE

TABLE 13.1   The QBE Inclusion Options and Their Meanings

Image	Name	Description
	Check	Check shows all the unique values for the given field. It also sorts the table based on that field.
	Check Plus	Check Plus shows all the records from a field, including duplicates, and does not show the records in sorted order.
	Check Descending	Like Check, Check Descending shows only unique values, but in descending sort order.
	GroupBy	GroupBy is used with query sets, which is beyond the scope of this discussion.

were only interested in the records whose price was over $1090.00, you could place the expression > 1090 under the RETPRICE field and you would only get the values that match this condition (see Figure 13.13 and Figure 13.14)

Any of the relational operators can be used to create an expression, and there are some other operators that allow you to search for strings and substrings. If you need to search for a particular string, you can just enter the value under the field in the Query designer. However, it is common to want to search for just part of a string. For example, find all the part names with blue in them. For these kinds of searches, you can use the wildcard character (".."). It will allow you to find strings that are embedded in other strings. To find all the part names with blue in them, just enter ..blue.. under the Name field (without quotes).

You are not limited to just searching for a single condition—you can also add AND and OR clauses to restrict your view of the data.

AND conditions.   The AND condition in a query acts the same as in Boolean operations. When you join two items with AND, you will get all the items that match both criteria. To create AND conditions in DBD, just place the additional items under the appropriate field names. If you want to search for more than one condition in a particular field, just separate the conditions with a comma. For example, if you were interested in the records returned by the following SQL statement:

```
NAME contains "blue" AND RETPRICE > 1000 AND RETPRICE < 1050
```

Your QBE would look like the Query window in Figure 13.15 and return the records shown in the Table Window below.

FIGURE 13.13   A Selection Criterion for Field RETPRICE in the QBE Design

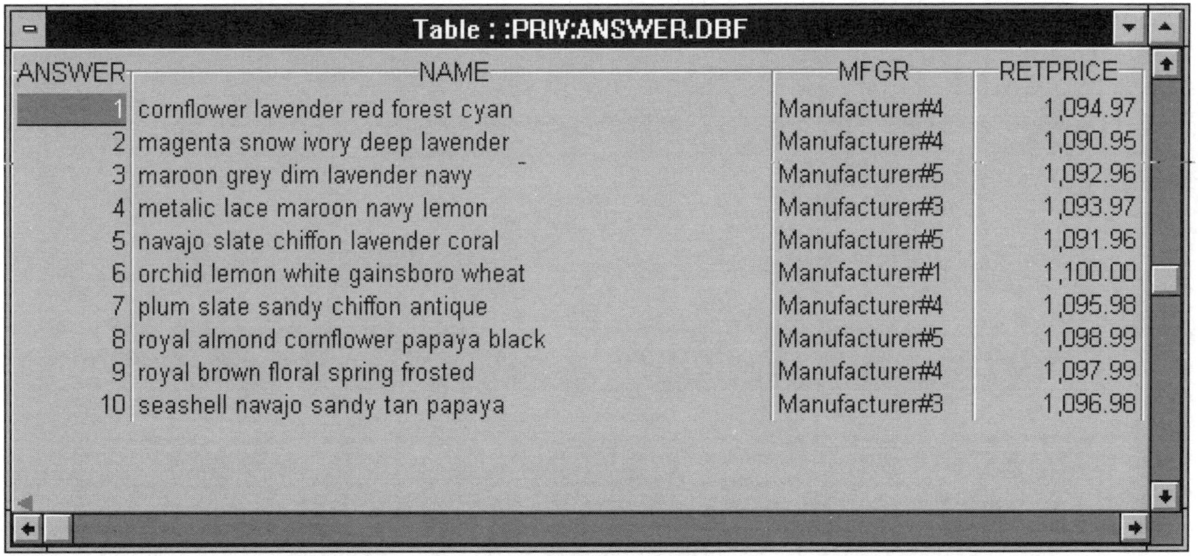

Table : ::PRIV:ANSWER.DBF

ANSWER	NAME	MFGR	RETPRICE
1	cornflower lavender red forest cyan	Manufacturer#4	1,094.97
2	magenta snow ivory deep lavender	Manufacturer#4	1,090.95
3	maroon grey dim lavender navy	Manufacturer#5	1,092.96
4	metalic lace maroon navy lemon	Manufacturer#3	1,093.97
5	navajo slate chiffon lavender coral	Manufacturer#5	1,091.96
6	orchid lemon white gainsboro wheat	Manufacturer#1	1,100.00
7	plum slate sandy chiffon antique	Manufacturer#4	1,095.98
8	royal almond cornflower papaya black	Manufacturer#5	1,098.99
9	royal brown floral spring frosted	Manufacturer#4	1,097.99
10	seashell navajo sandy tan papaya	Manufacturer#3	1,096.98

FIGURE 13.14   The Resulting Browse Filtered by the Selection Criterion in Figure 13.13

FIGURE 13.15 Criteria Entered on the Same Line in the QBE Design are Coupled with the AND Operator

178

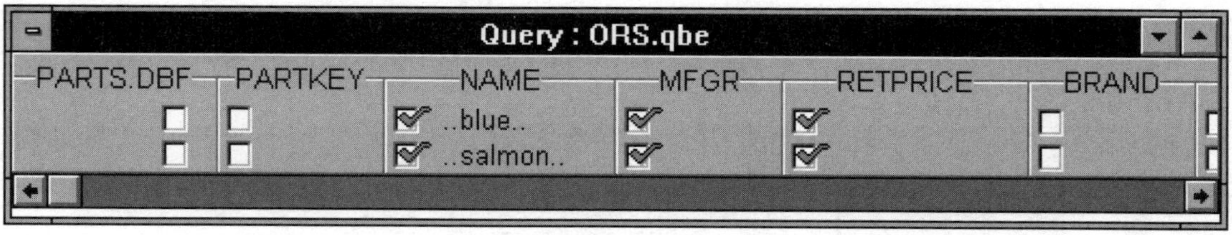

FIGURE 13.16   Criteria Entered on Separate Lines are Coupled with the OR Operator

OR conditions.   You can create OR conditions as well. To create an OR condition, add the OR keyword within the query or create an additional query line. To create an additional query line, either press the INSERT key or go to the bottom line of the query and press the down arrow. You will get another condition line where you can type in values. For example, Figure 13.16 shows the screen that would appear if you wanted all the NAMEs that had blue or salmon in them.

You can also arbitrarily mix AND and OR conditions. Every condition on a single row must be met for a matching record to show in the answers table, and every record that shows up in the answers table has to have matched the conditions on one or more rows. So, if you wanted the following set of records:

```
(NAME contains "blue" AND (RETPRICE >
1000 AND RETPRICE < 1050)) OR (NAME
contains "salmon" AND (MFGR contains "5"
OR "1"))
```

You would enter criteria in the QBE is shown in Figure 13.17. As you can see, these queries can be considerably complex, which means that you can carefully tailor the view of the data that your users are seeing.

Joining tables.   Queries can also be used to join tables together, so that data from separate tables appears to be just one big table. This is a particularly important feature for relational database design, because it encourages you to keep related data in separate tables.

To join two tables in DBD, add the first table and then click on the Add Table button—you will see two database field rows (Figure 13.18).

Each row corresponds to the table whose name is in the first field. Now, to join the tables, click on the Join Tables speedbutton. You will notice that the mouse cursor changes shape when you move it over the query fields. To complete the join, click first in the linking field of the parent table, then in the corresponding linking field of the child table. DBD places a common entry ("join1") which links the tables together (Figure 13.19). The answer table is shown in Figure 13.20.

Notice that the customer information is repeated once for every corresponding order record. Now, even though this data comes from two separate tables, this query makes it

FIGURE 13.17 Mixing AND and OR Operators in the QBE Design

180

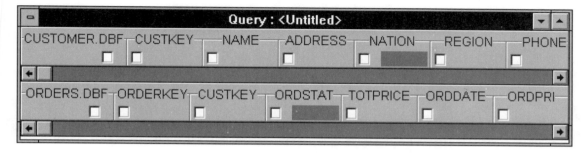

FIGURE 13.18   Adding Tables to the QBE Design

appear as one big (denormalized) table. You aren't restricted to just one join either—you can join as many as 24 tables together.

Back to SQL.   You may have noticed the SQL button on the speedbar. This will show you the SQL code that is the equivalent of the QBE that you are creating. For example, this is the SQL code generated by the above query:

```
SELECT DISTINCT D.NAME, D.NATION, D1.ORDSTAT,D1.TOTPRICE,
D1.ORDDATE FROM ":dummy_data:CUSTOMER.DBF" D,
":dummy_data:ORDERS.DBF" D1
WHERE (D1.CUSTKEY = D.CUSTKEY)
ORDER BY D.NAME, D.NATION, D1.ORDSTAT,
D1.TOTPRICE,
D1.ORDDATE
```

This means that you can use DBD to help you learn or brush up on your SQL. This also means that you can design your queries using the Visual Design tool and use the SQL code generated by it to allow you to make easy changes at run-time to the query conditions. Thus, the QBE, is actually generating SQL behind the scenes for the BDE to interpret.

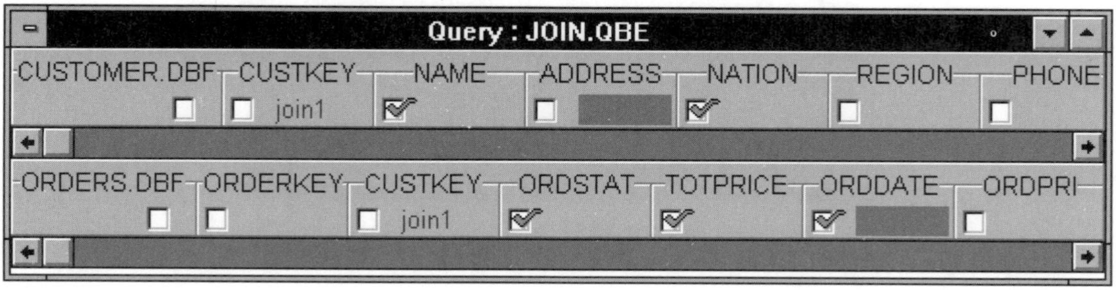

FIGURE 13.19   Joining Tables to the QBE Design

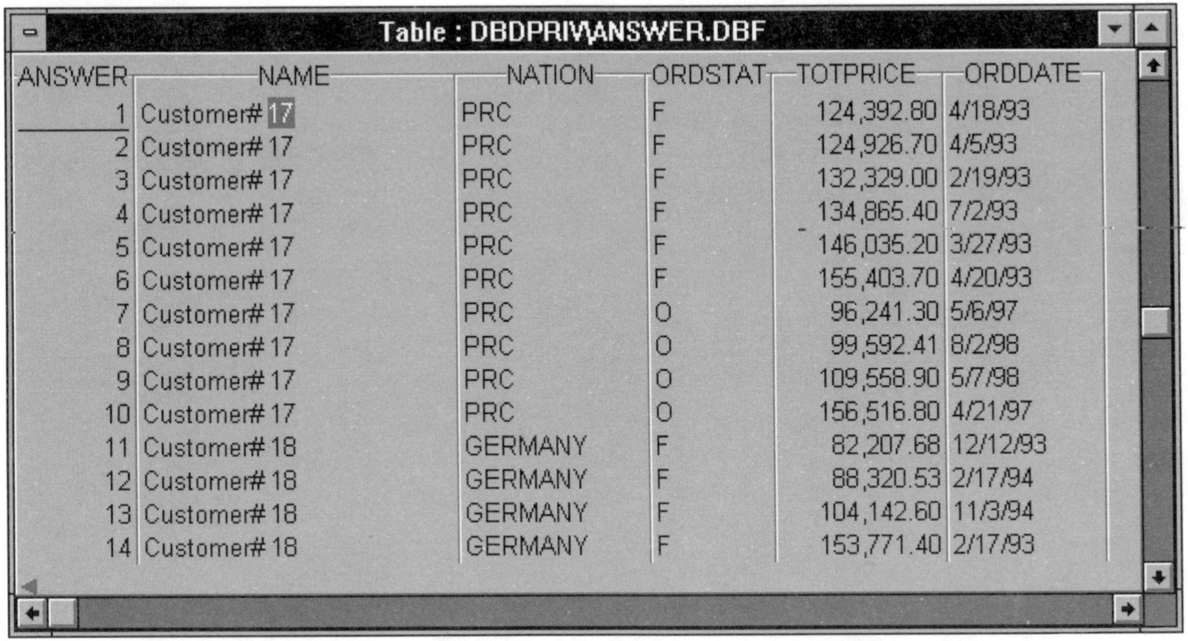

Table : DBDPRIW\ANSWER.DBF

ANSWER	NAME	NATION	ORDSTAT	TOTPRICE	ORDDATE
1	Customer#17	PRC	F	124,392.80	4/18/93
2	Customer#17	PRC	F	124,926.70	4/5/93
3	Customer#17	PRC	F	132,329.00	2/19/93
4	Customer#17	PRC	F	134,865.40	7/2/93
5	Customer#17	PRC	F	146,035.20	3/27/93
6	Customer#17	PRC	F	155,403.70	4/20/93
7	Customer#17	PRC	O	96,241.30	5/6/97
8	Customer#17	PRC	O	99,592.41	8/2/98
9	Customer#17	PRC	O	109,558.90	5/7/98
10	Customer#17	PRC	O	156,516.80	4/21/97
11	Customer#18	GERMANY	F	82,207.68	12/12/93
12	Customer#18	GERMANY	F	88,320.53	2/17/94
13	Customer#18	GERMANY	F	104,142.60	11/3/94
14	Customer#18	GERMANY	F	153,771.40	2/17/93

FIGURE 13.20 Answer Table for Fields Selected in Figure 13.19

182

TABLE 13.2 DBD Tools for Data Definition and Action Queries

Name	Description
Add	Add records to a table, either appending, updating, or both
Copy	Copy records from one table to another
Delete	Delete the table or query, including associated files
Empty	Empties the table, deleting all the records but leaving the structure intact—for dBASE tables, flags all records as deleted but does not pack the table
Passwords	Set a password that will be in effect for the rest of this session, so that you can open a table with this password as many times as you like without presenting the password every time
Rename	Renames tables or queries—for tables, it also renames the associated files (indexes, memo files, etc.), so you should always use this utility to rename your tables
Sort	Sorts a table
Info Structure	Shows the structure of the table, but does not allow changes, however, you can save the structure under another name
Restructure	Changes the structure of a table, even if it already contains data
Subtract	Subtracts the contents of one table from another, will show you what records are unique between two tables

TOOLS AND UTILITIES

Database Desktop also provides some tools to help you manipulate data through batch operations (see Table 13.2). These are sometimes referred to as action or data definition queries in other database products. These are referred to as action queries because they don't just return a subset of the data: they perform some sort of data manipulation (updates, inserts, or deletes) or definition (for example, a domain in an interbase database).

As you can see, Database Desktop serves the needs of a full-blown, database application development environment for Delphi applications. It makes creating and manipulating tables and queries much easier than writing a custom Delphi application to handle these chores. Most of the definition and query work only has to be done once for the application, and that is where Database Desktop's abilities really shine.

chapter opening page

CHAPTER **14**

DataBase Components Review

Data Access Components

The Data Access components give you access to databases and related tools. These are all invisible components at run-time, but provide the underlying functionality of your database based forms.

DataSource

The DataSource component is the conduit through which the data from a DataSet (either a Table or a Query) flows to the data controls (discussed in the next section). In other words, you place a Table or Query component on a form, then place a DataSource component and some data controls (a DBGrid, a DBEdit, etc.) on the form as well. To attach the data controls to the data in the Table or Query, you must set the DataSet property of the DataSource to the Table or Query, then set the DataSource property of the data controls to point to the DataSource (see Figure 14.1).

This may seem a bit abstract at first, but you will come to appreciate this arrangement. It makes it very easy to change the DataSet for the form from the original table to another table or query with the same underlying fields—you only have to change where the DataSource is pointing; you don't have to change any of the DBControls at all. The existence of the DataSource also makes it easier to create forms that represent a special relationship between tables, like the Master-Detail form.

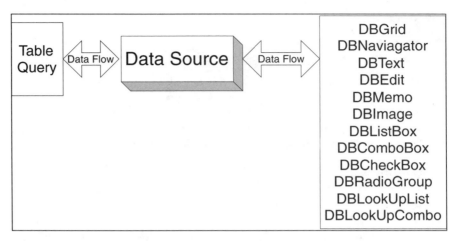

FIGURE 14.1   The DataSource Relationship Between DataSets and DBControls

Table

The Table component is the form representation of a database table. This invisible component gives you access to the database and the table that you specify in its Database and TableName properties. Once you click on the Database property, you will see a pull-down list of all the databases you have defined with BDECFG. Each is a pseudo database (see the chapter entitled Borland Database Engine Overview). Once you pick a database, you can click on the TableName property to view a drop-down list of all the tables that make up that database. Once you have specified these two properties, you can set the Active property toggle to true. You can then see the data from the table in the controls that are attached to this table's DataSource.

Query

The Query component is the form representation of a query, expressed as the underlying SQL command. Like the Table component, Query acts as a DataSet for a DataSource component. The difference between Query and Table components is that the Query component's view of the underlying data is completely governed by the SQL command that is contained in its SQL property. Thus, you could create a query that consists of several tables (and just a few fields from each). To the DataSource, the query looks just like a table that just has the specified fields in it. That means that you can modify the query directly (either at design time or run-time) to easily change the view of the data.

StoredProc

The StoredProc component allows you to call a stored procedure on a database server. Most client/server database systems allow you to create procedures in their own native language (usually based on SQL) to manipulate data. The StoredProc component gives you an easy way to call the server's procedure. The use of this component requires a database server (see the chapter entitled Client Server Applications).

DataBase

The inclusion of a DataBase component on your form is not necessary to perform database access—a Table or Query component is all you need. It is designed to help in client/server environments by allowing you to change certain characteristics of the database. For example, most database servers require users to log onto the database. You can program the DataBase component to just make the user log on once and then maintain a persistent connection to the database between data accesses.

BatchMove

The BatchMove component is a powerful database component. It allows you to operate on groups of data or entire tables. You can use the BatchMove component to move or copy records from one database to another. The Mode property allows you to customize what the component does (for example, batAppend appends records to another table, batDelete deletes records, etc.). You can also take advantage of the error catching events provided by BatchMove. It is the best way to handle append, delete, and update operations on a large group of records.

Report

The Report component is the interface to ReportSmith. It will allow you to set the directory name, the name of the report, etc. This is the interface between Delphi and ReportSmith.

The run-time engine for ReportSmith is called RS_RUN, and it is installed as part of the standard Delphi install. If you include any reports generated by ReportSmith with your applications, you must also distribute the ReportSmith run-time files. Like the Borland DataBase Engine, the files that you must distribute are already compressed into disk images, and can be found on the Delphi CD-ROM.

You can double click on the component in Design mode to run ReportSmith. You can also run reports at run-time using the component. The ReportName property indicates which report will be run.

There are several properties that you can set to affect how ReportSmith runs. For example, you can set the starting and ending page of the report (the StartPage and End-Page properties). You can also specify a directory where the report resides (the ReportDir property). There is also a property which lets you specify the number of copies to print. The Preview property indicates whether you want the report to display on the screen or to print. If Preview is true, output is to the screen (in its own window); if Preview is false then output is to the printer.

The AutoUnLoad property specifies whether or not ReportSmith's run-time engine should remain in memory after the report terminates. If you are going to be running several reports at the same time (or the same report repeatedly), it will save time if you let the report engine stay in memory. If resources are tight, or you probably won't print another report for a while, you can have the run-time engine automatically unload when the report is through. If you have AutoUnLoad set to false, you must explicitly issue the CloseApplication method to unload ReportSmith's run-time engine from memory.

Notice that there are no events associated with the Report component. It actually communicates to ReportSmith and RS_RUN by using Dynamic Data Exchange (DDE).

To run the report, use the run method:

```
Report1.Run;
```

To print a report, use the print method:

```
Report1.Print;
```

DATA CONTROL COMPONENTS

Data Control components are, for the most part, just like their nondata aware counterparts. All of these controls have a DataSource property, and many of them also have a DataField property.

DBGrid

On Component Palette	On Running Form
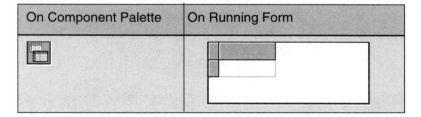	

The DBGrid provides a browse screen for data. Once the DataSource property is set and the DataSet pointed to by the DataSource is active, you can see live data in the grid at design-time. This grid control provides a very versatile way to view data. It has a host of properties that affect how the data looks as well as many functions you may need.

DBNavigator

On Component Palette	On Running Form

DBNavigator provides a way for users to navigate through a database file, and to make changes to it as well. You can control which of the navigator buttons appear, turning them on and off through the component's VisibleButtons property. Here is a guide to each of the buttons:

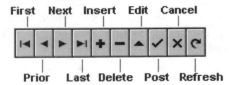

Most of the labels are self explanatory. Edit places the database in Edit mode, meaning that the user can either Cancel to discard changes, or Post to make the changes permanent. This is called buffered editing, because the user can rollback their changes and allow the record to remain in its previous state. The Refresh button ensures that the view on the screen corresponds to the actual records in the database source, including any new records, by requerying that source be it a table or SQL statement. In a multi-user environment, another user may have changed the data since you last updated the on-screen display. The Refresh button ensures that the data in the display is current.

Since you can control which buttons to show, a DBNavigator is an extremely versatile component.

DBText

On Component Paleette	On Running Form
	DBText1

A DBText is just like a regular text label, except it has a DataSource and DataField property. This allows it to automatically change when the user navigates through the database. So, you can have labels on your form that change based on the underlying database.

DBEdit

On Component Paleette	On Running Form
	DBEdit1

A DBEdit is a data aware version of the Edit component. It is used to enter and view data from a database.

DBMemo

On Component Paleette	On Running Form
	DBMemo1

The DBMemo is used to provide an editor so that users can edit memo fields in database tables.

DBImage

On Component Paleette	On Running Form
	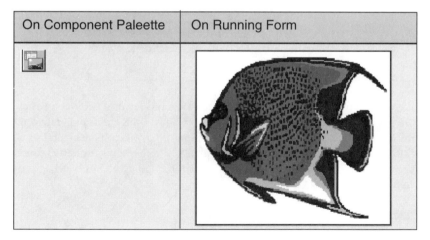

The DBImage component is a data aware graphic display component. It is shown here with its DataSource set to one of the sample tables that ships with Delphi that has graphics stored within it (BIOLIFE.DB). This component could be handy if you created an employee's table that contained everyone's picture as one of the fields. Scan the pictures into bitmaps and insert them into the database, then, use one of these controls to display them.

DBListBox

On Component Palette	On Running Form
	Blue Green Red Purple Black

The DBListBox allows you to restrict what the user can enter into a field in a database. It has a DataSource and DataField property, but it also has an Items property like the regular ListBox. You can specify in the Items property editor the possible allowable values, and the user will be restricted to those values when entering data.

DBComboBox

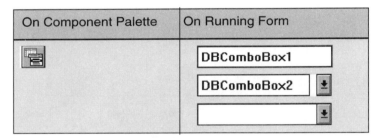

On Component Palette	On Running Form
	DBComboBox1 DBComboBox2 ▼ ▼

Just like a regular ComboBox, the DBComboBox has several different variations, controlled by its Style property. The above graphic shows the csSimple, csDropDown, and csDropDownList variations. Like the DBListBox, this control is designed to allow users to pick from a list of valid values. By placing values in the Items property, you can restrict what the user is allowed to enter. If you need to force the user to only use values from another table, use the DBLookUpCombo instead.

DBCheckBox

On Component Paleette	On Running Form
	☐ DBCheckBox1

The DBCheckBox is the data aware version of a regular checkbox. Once you have set the DataSource for this component, you can use the ValueChecked and ValueUnchecked properties to determine the status of the underlying field. If the field in the table is equal to what you have specified as ValueChecked, the checkbox has a check in it (true), otherwise the value is ValueUnchecked (the checkbox is not checked and is false). Whenever the user changes the check status of the checkbox, the appropriate value is reflected in the underlying table.

DBRadioGroup

On Component Palette	On Running Form
	┌DBRadioGroup1─┐ ◯ Blue ◯ Red ◯ Green ◯ Purple

The DBRadioGroup is like the standard RadioGroup component with an important difference that relates to database manipulation. The DBRadioGroup has an Items property just like the regular RadioGroup, and each value in the Items list can correspond to a field value in a database. For example, if you only want the user to put the values "Blue", "Red", "Green", or "Purple" in the database field, you can place those values in the Items property. When the user selects one of the radio buttons, the value of the Items property for that radio button is placed into the field.

However, there may be situations where you don't want the caption and the field to be the same. For example, you may want the caption to say "Yes" or "No", but actually store the values "1" or "0". For this situation, we employ the Values property. There is a one-to-one correspondence between the Items list and the Values list. If the user selects one of the values in the Items list, its corresponding Value is placed in the table. If you have an Items list that is "Yes" and "No" and a Values list that is "1" or "0", when the user selects the "Yes" radio button, the value "1" will be placed in the database file. This feature is very handy, as it is quite common that your field values may have some internal meaning that is not clear to the end user. This mechanism allows you to base mutually exclusive values in a DBRadioGroup and still have your users pick values that have an intuitive meaning.

DBLookupList

On Component Palette	On Running Form
	Customer# 17
	Customer# 18
	Customer# 19
	Customer# 21
	Customer# 23

The DBLookupList component, along with the DBLookupCombo are extremely powerful components that make a sometimes tedious job a simple matter of changing a few properties. It is a frequent requirement in database related applications to look up a value in another table based on a value in the current table. For instance, you frequently need to retrieve a value out of a lookup table through a foreign key in the current table. You don't want your users to have to know how your primary and foreign keys work in order to be able to enter data. DBLookup components allow you to look up a value in another table based on another field in the current table. And, you don't have to display the lookup field—you can show any field from the associated record.

Here is a simple example. You have an orders form (table_orders and dataSource_orders). You would like to show the customer's name in a list box as you navigate through the records. Add a DBLookupList to the form, along with a Table and DataSource for the customer table (table_customer and DataSource_customer). Now, to create the relationship, first set the DataSource property of the DBLookupList to DataSource_orders, and the DataField property to the customer foreign key. Now, set the LookupSource property to DataSource_customer, set the LookupField property to the Customer primary key, and set the LookupDisplay field to the customer name field in the Customer table. This will cause the DBLookupList to look up the value in the Orders table (the customer foreign key field) and match up the name from the Customer table through its primary key field. Only the customer's name is displayed, as you do not want your users to view key values which only have meaning to the underlying relationships.

Figure 14.2 shows the form we have described. The user has navigated to the orders where the customer foreign key equals 23, and the DBLookupList is showing the related customer's name. And as you navigate through the orders, the lookup list stays in synch with the proper customer name. Note that the names in the Customer table are in the form CUSTOMER# XX, where XX is also the primary key value (kept in the CUSTKEY field). As you can see, the CUSTKEY field in the grid is 23, and so it is showing the corresponding customer name (CUSTOMER #23) from the Customer table.

As you can see, the DBLookupList packs a lot of functionality into a single component. By just setting the appropriate values in properties, we can create fairly sophisticated lookup capabilities. In our example the list box was used for display only. However, this component works perfectly well for data entry as well.

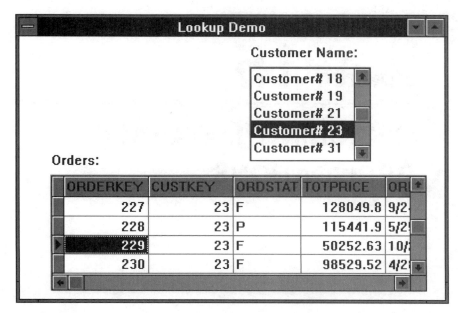

FIGURE 14.2   Looking up the Customer's Name (as "Customer #N") Through Their Foreign Key Field with a DBLookupList Component

DBLookupCombo

On Component Paleette	On Running Form

The DBLookupCombo works just like the DBLookupList, except that it shows the lookup values in a combobox instead of a list. This component also has the LookupSource, LookupField, and LookupDisplay properties discussed, and they work in the same manner. The DBLookupCombo is especially good for data entry: It allows the user to pick from a list of values in another table.

This chapter has been an introduction to the database components that exist in Delphi. As you can see, there is a wide variety and considerable functionality built into Delphi for database application development. We are going to discuss and use these components heavily in the next few chapters, and show you the best techniques for leveraging their power.

CHAPTER **15**

DESIGNING DATABASE APPLICATIONS

Delphi is a powerful application development environment for creating programs that manipulate databases. In this chapter we will use the Data Access and Data Control components that Delphi provides to create forms for manipulating and viewing data from a database.

One of the early decisions you have to make when you are creating a database application is whether to use tables or queries as your datasources. Each has some advantages and disadvantages.

Tables

The Table component is basically a component view of an underlying database.

Advantages

1. The Table component directly interfaces with the Borland Database Engine—there is no intermediate SQL layer. If you don't want to ever have to deal with SQL code, use the Table component.

2. There are some conditions that cause a query to return read-only access to data, meaning that you can view the data but you can't change it. If you need to edit, add, or delete the data, you can't use queries under those particular conditions. In these cases, a Table component is better because it can always provide live access to data.

194

Disadvantages

1. The table can only show you the data from the table that it is based on, whereas a query can display several tables of information as if it were a single table. However, you aren't limited to the number of Table components that you can place on a form, and there are some properties that aid in attaching Table components together.

2. If you plan to eventually move your application and data to a client server environment, it is smarter to go ahead and perform all your data access using SQL. Then, the changes will (hopefully) be minor—just make a few changes to the SQL code to accommodate the new database server and change the database alias driver. Because all database servers use SQL to communicate with the client application, you can do some work now that you can reuse when you upsize your application.

Queries

Queries, whether created directly with SQL statements or through the QBE interface, are actually composed of SQL statements. Thus, the process of creating database applications using queries is more intimately tied to SQL.

Advantages

1. Because you can include more than one table in a query, your application can use the query to view all the data from two or more tables as if it were a single table. You can also filter out records that you don't need, creating a smaller, more efficient data set to begin with.

2. You can change your view of the data at design time or at run-time by changing the SQL code directly. Because the SQL string that determines the view of the data is just a string, you can deactivate the query, modify the SQL string, and reactivate the query at run-time. This has the effect of changing the query, so you will see the new data set in the components that are embedded in your form.

3. All server databases speak some dialect of SQL. If you're planning to eventually upsize your application to a server environment, you can just create the queries once in SQL and use them for both versions of your application. This cuts down on the amount of work it will take to upsize your application.

Disadvantages.   There are some situations that force a query to return a read-only view of your data, meaning that you can read the data but can't edit or add to it. Specifically, for DBF and DB tables, you can ensure a "live" data set if the query:

- involves only a single table
- does not have an ORDER BY clause in the SQL statement
- does not use aggregate commands (like SUM or AVG) in the SQL statement

- does not use calculated fields in the SELECT statement
- uses a WHERE clause that consists only of comparisons of column names to scalar constants (i.e., literal values).

You can use any of the relation operators, including LIKE, and have as many AND and OR clauses as you like.

FORM EXPERT

You can, of course, lay out your database forms by hand, including setting all the properties and data links. However, using the Form Expert is such an easy way to create a form that it's hard to pass up. Even if it won't lay things out just the way you want them, it is a good starting place.

The Form Expert is a utility that walks you through the creation of a database-based form. You supply answers to questions, and it generates the code necessary to create a working form.

Notice that all of the Form Expert's pages have a Next and Prev button, meaning that you can always go back and change one of the previous options.

The first page of the Form Expert dialog (Figure 15.1) asks whether to create a simple form or create a master/detail form. Also, it asks whether you want to use a Table or a Query for the underlying data.

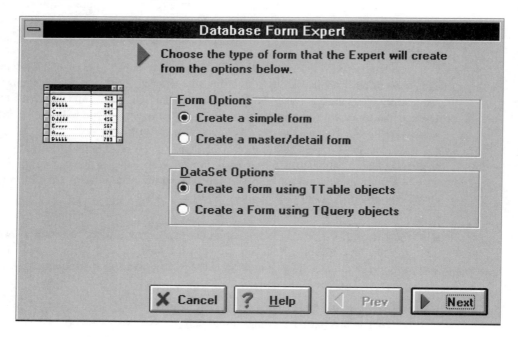

FIGURE 15.1 Choose the Type of Form

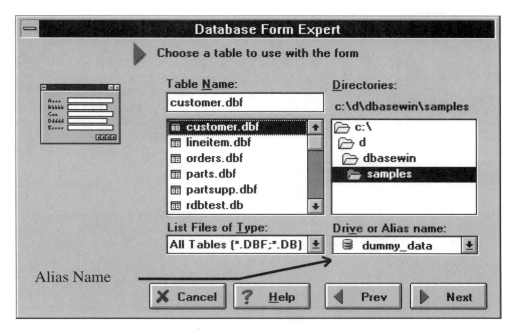

FIGURE 15.2   Choose a Table

The second page (Figure 15.2) asks you to choose a table to base your form on. As you can see, you can provide either a path name or choose your files by their database Alias (which is the preferred method).

Next, the dialog allows you to choose which fields you want on your form (Figure 15.3). The fields on the left are the fields that are available through your data source (either a table or a query), and the fields on the right are the fields that you want on your form. Clicking the single arrows moves one field at a time, and clicking the double arrows moves all of the fields. You can also change the order in which the fields will appear on the form through the up and down arrows.

You then specify what type of layout you would like for the chosen fields (Figure 15.4). Horizontal layout places the fields side by side in tabular fashion. Vertical layout places all the fields in columnar fashion, with one field per row and all the field labels and fields lined up. Grid places a DBGrid component on the form, pointing to the appropriate DataSource.

You will only get this page of the dialog (Figure 15.5) if you pick the Vertical layout option. This dialog asks you to specify whether you want the labels to be to the left of the fields or above the fields.

Figure 15.6 shows the last page of the dialog. Click the checkbox if you want Delphi to make this the main form for the project, or uncheck it if you want another form to call this one. Then, click on the Create button.

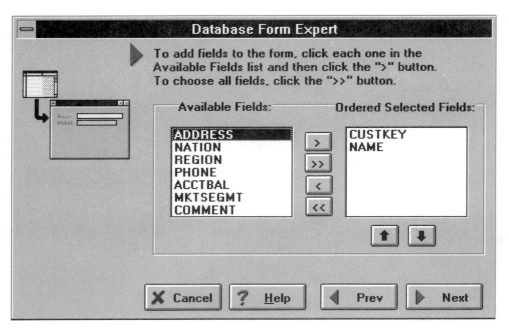

FIGURE 15.3   Choose Fields

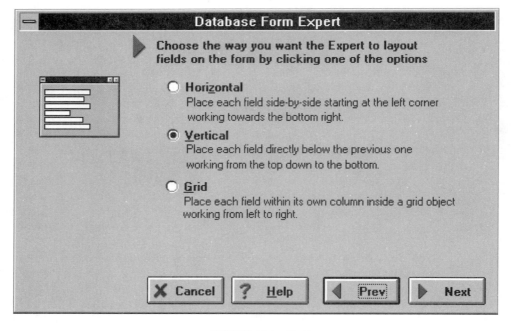

FIGURE 15.4   Field Layout

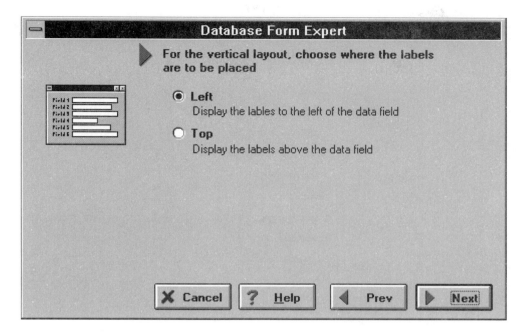

FIGURE 15.5   Label Placement

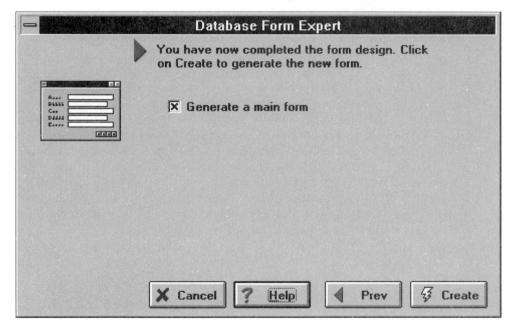

FIGURE 15.6   Create the Form

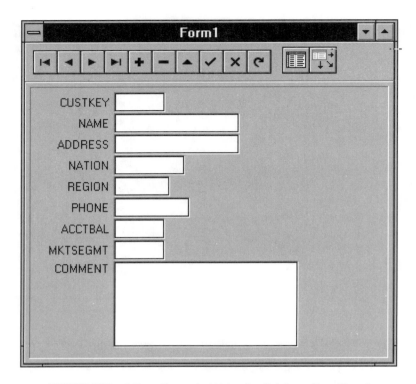

FIGURE 15.7   A Form Generated Using the Database Form Expert

Figure 15.7 shows the form that was generated from our choices. It has all the fields that we chose along with their DataSource and DataField properties already set, the component names set to the names of the fields in the database, and a DBNavigator on a speedbar. This form will run as is, with no writing of code, and, it will allow the user to navigate through the database and make changes. The default for the ToolTip property of the DBNaviagtor is disabled, but you can change that property and automatically provide tool tips for your users.

The Form Expert has also placed the controls on a ScrollBox, so that it will be easy to isolate the data entry parts of the form from the other parts, such as a status bar. It has also set the tab order for the controls to flow from top to bottom.

FIELD PROPERTIES

Every time Delphi creates a form with a DataSet component on it (either a Query or a Table), it creates a Field object for each of the fields in the DataSet automatically. However, you can override this default behavior and create a set of Field objects at design time that are persistent, meaning that they are permanent. The Field objects created by default only exist while the application is running, but persistent Field objects are available when the program is not running. By creating the Field objects at design time, you can change their characteristics from within the Form Designer.

TField Component

Field objects are created from the TField component class. TField itself is an abstract class, meaning that you can't create an instance of it. Instead, it is provided to act as the common ancestor of the Field components that correspond to Field types in a database. Table 15.1 is a list of the actual Field component types.

These are the classes that are actually instantiated, either by Delphi automatically at run-time, or by you in Design mode. The advantage of creating them in Design mode is that you can manipulate their properties through the Object Inspector. You can change the DisplayWidth, whether the data is left, right, or center justified, the Visible property, and a host of others.

Using Field Property Editor

To create Field components while in Design mode, double click on the DataSet (either a Table or a Query) for which you want to add components. This will launch the Field Property Editor (Figure 15.8).

This editor allows you to interact with Field objects. To create the Field objects (Figure 15.9), click on the Add button.

You are presented with a dialog of all the fields in the current DataSet. To create

TABLE 15.1   Actual Field Component Types

Field Component	Corresponds to
TStringField	text data up to 255 characters
TIntegerField	numbers in the range -2147483648..2147483647
TSmallIntField	numbers in the range -32768..32767
TWordField	numbers in the range 0..65535
TFloatField	real numbers with 15-16 digits
TCurrencyField	same as TFloatField
TBCDField	real numbers with a fixed number of digits after the decimal point, accurate to 19 digits
TBooleanField	true or false values
TDateTimeField	date and time values
TDateField	date value
TTimeField	time value
TBlobField	Binary Large OBject field of unlimited size
TBytesField	same as TBlobField
TVarBytesField	binary field of arbitrary size up to 65535 characters
TMemoField	arbitrary length text
TGraphicField	image data (for example, bitmaps) of unlimited size

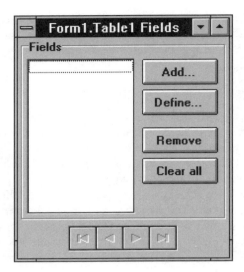

FIGURE 15.8   The Field Property Editor

Field objects for all of them, click OK. If there are some of the fields that you don't want to create Field objects for, leave them unselected.

Now you can begin to see the advantage of creating these Field objects yourself. Notice in Figure 15.10 that the field that is highlighted in the Field Property Editor is also represented in the Object Inspector. Indeed, the object that you are inspecting in the Object Inspector is the Field object. This means that you can change the characteristics of the fields while in Design mode through the Object Inspector, just like all the other objects on your form.

FIGURE 15.9   The Add Fields Dialog

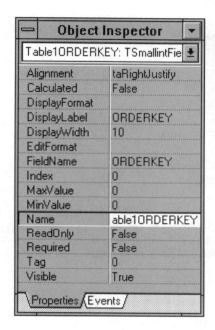

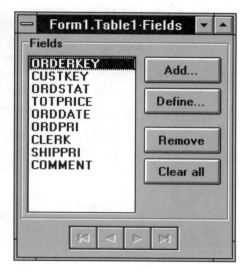

FIGURE 15.10   The Object Inspector and the Field Property Editor

Data Entry and Validation

Two of the best uses for Field objects are data entry help and validations. One of the most common tasks that accompany creating data entry forms is determining how you want your data formatted. To modify how data is displayed upon input, use the EditMask property for string data and the EditFormat property for others, including numeric data. Note that both these methods allow you to embed characters that will become part of the field (for example, dashes and parentheses that are defined as literal characters within the mask will appear as part of the field in the table).

EditMask.   To create an EditMask for a String entry field, choose the String field in the Field Property Editor and click on the tool button in the EditMask field (Figure 15.11).

You are presented with a selection of sample masks, listed on the right. To use one of Delphi's predefined masks, double click on it. You can test the mask in the Test Input window. The Masks button allows you to load mask files for another country's formats.

If you can't use one of the sample masks, you can define your own by typing the special mask characters into the Input Mask entry field. To see a listing of all the possible masks, consult the on-line help under EditMask. For example, the greater than sign (">") forces all characters entered after it to be in upper case, and the less than sign ("<") forces lower case. The letter capital "L" is the mask character to only accept letters, while "A"

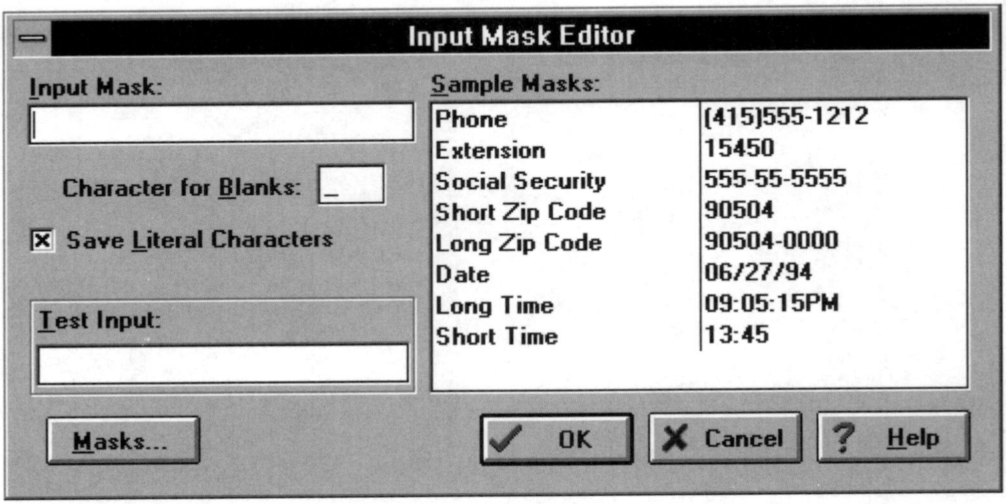

```
┌─────────────────────────────────────────────────────────────┐
│ ⊟                      Input Mask Editor                       │
├─────────────────────────────────────────────────────────────┤
│ Input Mask:                     Sample Masks:                  │
│ ┌─────────────────────────┐   ┌──────────────────────────────┐│
│ │                         │   │ Phone          (415)555-1212 ││
│ └─────────────────────────┘   │ Extension      15450         ││
│                               │ Social Security 555-55-5555  ││
│    Character for Blanks: ┌──┐ │ Short Zip Code  90504        ││
│                         │ _│ │ Long Zip Code   90504-0000   ││
│ ⊠ Save Literal Characters└──┘ │ Date            06/27/94     ││
│                               │ Long Time       09:05:15PM   ││
│ Test Input:                   │ Short Time      13:45        ││
│ ┌─────────────────────────┐   │                              ││
│ │                         │   └──────────────────────────────┘│
│ └─────────────────────────┘                                   │
│ ┌───────────┐        ┌──────────┐ ┌──────────┐ ┌──────────┐   │
│ │ Masks...  │        │ ✓   OK   │ │ ✗ Cancel │ │ ?  Help  │   │
│ └───────────┘        └──────────┘ └──────────┘ └──────────┘   │
└─────────────────────────────────────────────────────────────┘
```

FIGURE 15.11   The Input Mask Editor

will accept letters and numbers, and the "9" will only permit numbers. So, for example, if you needed to create a mask that would force the user to enter 3 uppercase letters followed by 4 numbers, you could create the mask ">LLL-9999". You could then enter the value NCC-1701 (but not NCC-1701D). There are enough mask characters to provide a great deal of control over what your user is allowed to enter.

Validation.   Validation is another compelling reason to create Field objects. Validation is a way for you to ensure that the data in a field conforms to some conditions, either format or value, that you have defined. For example, you may want to make sure that the number entered for price is within a certain range of values. You can use the Validation event for Field objects to attach these validation rules to the Field object.

Because the Validation event is just like any other event, you can place any valid Object Pascal code in it. Here is an example Validation routine:

```
procedure TForm1.Table1TOTPRICEValidate(Sender: TField);
begin
  if table1totprice.AsFloat < 100 then
  begin
    MessageBeep(0);
    editTotprice.SetFocus
  end
end;
```

This example illustrates several features that we haven't yet pointed out. First, on all of the Field objects, you can represent the actual value as another type of value. All of the Field objects have some of the properties AsString, AsInteger, AsFloat, AsBoolean, and AsDateTime. This conversion can't be made in every case, but if it is possible, this provides an additional way to look at your data values. In the example above, the field object `table1totprice.AsFloat` is compared to 100. If the field value is less than 100, the user hears a beep and the cursor jumps back to the Edit field where they entered the incorrect value. Notice the use of the `SetFocus` method to force the focus back to the Edit field that the user just tried to leave (where they were entering the `totprice` that was less than 100).

This is just a simple example of creating data Validation routines. This code could be as elaborate as you need it to be, checking fields against other fields, etc.

MASTER/DETAIL FORMS

Once you are beyond the realm of simple data entry forms, one of the types of forms that programmers always need to create are master/detail forms. The one to many relationship appears frequently in database applications, and users want to be able to view a representation of that relationship.

The typical master/detail form has entry fields for parent records and a browse (grid) for any related child records. For example, if you were creating a customer's orders form, you would have the customer information in regular fields representing the Master record, and the orders for that particular customer in a grid underneath. However, there is no restriction in Delphi about how you must lay out a master/detail form.

The easiest way to create a master/detail form is through the Form Expert. One of the initial options is to create a master/detail form. Most of the dialogs are the same as those we saw earlier, so they won't be repeated here. However, there is one dialog that is unique, where you define the linking relationship between the underlying tables for your form.

This dialog shows you the fields in the Detail table that are indexed (notice that the CUSTKEY index is chosen above it) and all of the fields from the Master table. You must specify how the tables are joined together. In Figure 15.12, both the correct fields are marked. Clicking on the Add button will create an entry down in the Joined Fields entry field, and you will be able to go on to the next dialog.

Figure 15.13 displays a master/detail form to show customer orders, created by the Form Expert.

Notice that the customer information is in the entry fields, and the orders information for that customer is shown in the browse. Also notice that there are two tables and two datasources on the form—one for each table. Even though this form is in Design mode, the Active property for both tables has been toggled true, so you are able to see live data in Design mode reflecting the master/detail relationship.

Keeping the two tables synchronized is obviously the trick here, and Delphi makes it easy with a pair of properties that exist for Table components.

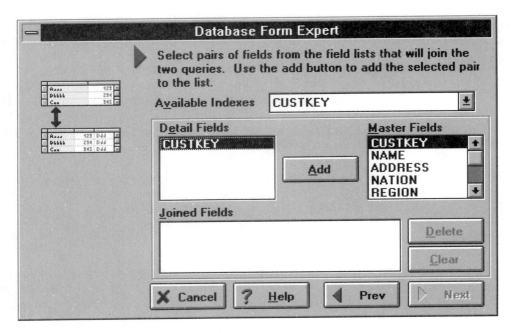

FIGURE 15.12   Setting Master / Detail Relationships in the Database Form Expert

MasterSource	Points from the child table to the DataSource that the master table uses
MasterFields	The field in the parent that controls the access to the children

In our example, the Customer Table component has no special properties set. However, the orders table has its MasterSource property set to DataSource1 (which points to the customer table) and its MasterFields property set to CUSTKEY. This indicates to Delphi that, as you navigate through the Customer table, the form will use the CUSTKEY field in the child table to only show records that match the parent's CUSTKEY.

ADVANCED RELATIONSHIP FORMS

This master/detail relationship for forms is not restricted to just a single master and a single detail. Numerous one to many relationships are common in real world applications. For example, our data has a one to many relationship between customers and orders, as well as a master/detail relationship between orders and lineitems—each order consists of one or many lineitems. It would be nice to show all those relationships on a single form.

Figure 15.14 shows an example of that 2-levels-deep relationship. The form has three grids on it: one for customers, one for orders, and one for lineitems. It also has three tables and three data sources for each of the grids.

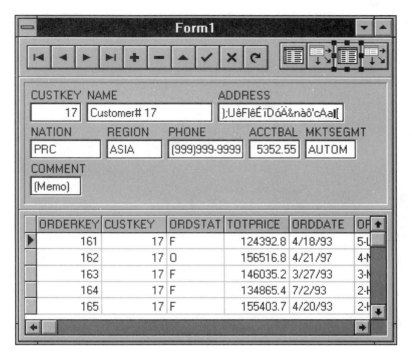

FIGURE 15.13 A Master / Detail Form Created Through the Database Form Expert

To make this form perform its magic, the MasterSource property of the Order table is set to DataSource_customer and the MasterFields property is set to CUSTKEY. Also, the MasterSource property of the lineitem table is set to DataSource_orders, and the MasterFields property is set to ORDERKEY. Now, as you navigate through the customer records, the form shows only the appropriate order records. When you navigate through the order records, you only see the appropriate lineitems for that order. Of course, both detail tables are continuously updated as you move through the master table.

Notice in the screen in Figure 15.15 that the Customer number is 19 and the CUSTKEY value in the orders table is also 19. Also, the ORDERKEY number in the order table is 182; likewise, the ORDERKEY number in the lineitems table is 182.

As you can see, Delphi makes the construction of forms that reflect complex database relationships very easy. Once again, Delphi is doing all the work making sure that the detail tables remain in synchronization with the master table(s).

One thing you should notice about all master/detail forms is that there must be an index defined in the Detail table for the foreign key that points back to the Master table. As we saw above in the Form Expert when creating master/detail forms, you must have an index before you can proceed. The index must exist because the database engine must seek into the Detail table and show just the records that match the Master record's key. If

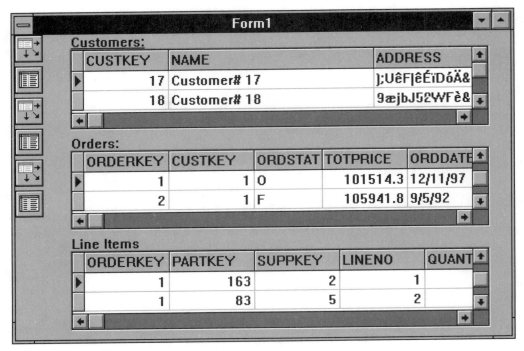

FIGURE 15.14 A Master/Detail Form in Design View for a 2-levels-deep Relationship, Customers, Their Orders, and the Associated Order Details

an index doesn't exist on the foriegn key, this process will be too slow. In general, you should ALWAYS index foriegn keys, otherwise the BDE cannot perform its work efficiently.

BUFFERED EDITING

One of the most common tasks that database applications have to perform is buffered editing. You may have noticed that the default in Delphi when you build forms with Database components is to allow the user to immediately start entering data into the Edit fields. There is no obvious "buffering" occurring. When the user starts typing, the table automatically goes into Edit mode, and so the user can cancel whatever changes have been made by pressing the "Cancel" button on the navigator, but it is still not a good idea to let the user start making changes haphazardly. Often, users don't realize that pressing the Cancel button on the navigator will solve the problem of errant data entry. A better approach is to force the user to specifically enter Editing mode, which can only be exited by explicitly saving the changes or discarding them.

This section will demonstrate how to perfrom buffered editing. When the form

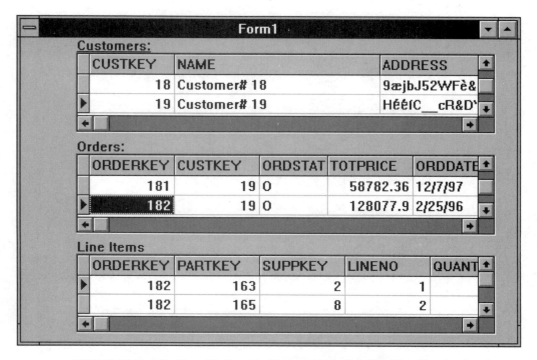

FIGURE 15.15 The Form Displayed in Figure 15.14 in Run-time View Showing Synchronized Records Between Customers-Orders-Order Details

starts, the Edit fields will be black on gray (instead of white), indicating that they are "read-only". We will provide some buttons which all allow the user to enter Edit mode. When in Edit mode, all the navigation buttons will be disabled (so the user can't navigate away from the record that is being edited). There is also a Save and a Cancel button, which are only highlighted when the user is editing the record. Figure 15.16 is a screen shot of the form in "Browse" mode.

This process takes advantage of the fact that all of the actions that you must take with the database table are already provided within the DataSets (Tables and Queries). For example, put the table into Edit mode (Figure 15.17):

```
Table1.Edit;
```

To post the changes that the user has made:

```
Table1.Post;
```

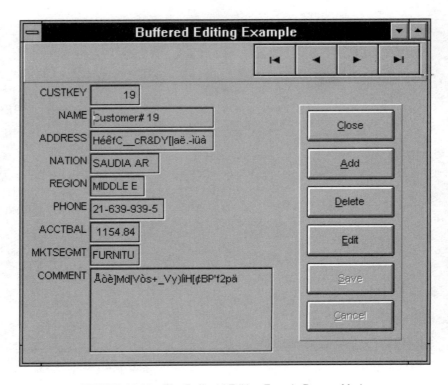

FIGURE 15.16   The Buffered Editing Form in Browse Mode

To cancel the changes that the user has made:

```
Table1.cancel;
```

To add a record:

```
Table1.append;
```

This means that the only code you have to supply is validation code ("Are you sure you want to do this?" dialog boxes, etc.).

The general strategy is simple. In the form's FormCreate method, go through all the editable components on the form and set their ReadOnly property to true and change their color. Then, set the Enabled property for the buttons that shouldn't be active to false. Here is the source code for our form's `FormCreate` method:

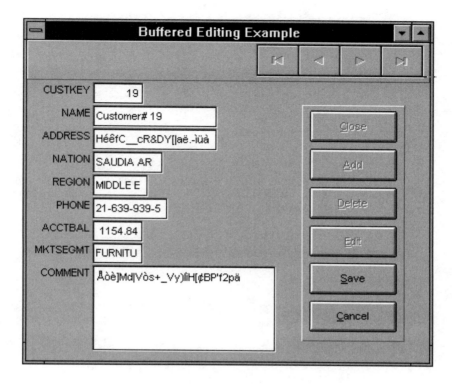

FIGURE 15.17   The Buffered Editing Form in Edit Mode

```
procedure Tform_main.FormCreate(Sender: TObject);
var
   i : integer;
begin
  Table1.Open;
  { loop thru the components and disable the
    relevant ones }
  for i := 0 to ComponentCount - 1 do
  begin
    if components[i] is tDBEdit then
      with components[i] as TDBEdit do
      begin
        readonly := true;
        color := clSilver
      end; {if/with}
    if Components[i] is TDBMemo then
      with components[i] as TDBMemo do
      begin
```

```
            readonly := true;
            color := clSilver
        end {if/with}
    end; {for}
    { disable the buttons that aren't yet relevant }
    savebutton.enabled := false;
    cancelbutton.enabled := false;
end; {procedure}
```

For the Add and Edit buttons, the opposite action has to take place. All the Edit fields and the disabled buttons must be reactivated, and the navigation buttons must be de-activated. Here is the code for the Add button's OnClick (the code for the Edit button is similar, and can be found in the complete listing at the end of this chapter):

```
procedure Tform_main.addbuttonClick(Sender: TObject);
var
  i : integer;
begin
    { save the record we're on in case the user cancels }
    LastRecord := table1.GetBookmark;
    { set the mode }
    CurrentMode := Add;
    { add a new record to the table }
    table1.append;
    { enable the entryfields }
    for i := 0 to ComponentCount -1 do
    begin
      if Components[i] is TDBEdit then
        with components[i] as TDBEdit do
        begin
            readonly := false;
            color := clwhite
        end; {if/with}
      if Components[i] is TDBMemo then
        with components[i] as TDBMemo do
        begin
            readonly := false;
            color := clWhite
        end; {if/with}
    end; {for}
    { enable some buttons . . . }
    savebutton.enabled := true;
    cancelbutton.enabled := true;
    { . . . and disable the others }
    closebutton.enabled := false;
    addbutton.enabled := false;
```

```
      deletebutton.enabled := false;
      editbutton.enabled := false;
      dbnavigator.enabled := false;
  end;
```

The Delete button simply displays a dialog box confirming the deletion, then calls the Delete method for the table:

```
procedure Tform_main.deletebuttonClick(Sender: TObject);
var
  MR : word;
begin
  MR := MessageDlg( 'Are you sure you want to
    delete this record?', mtConfirmation,
    [mbYes, mbNo], 0 );
  if MR = Yes then {user pressed yes}
    table1.delete;
end;
```

The Save button must post the changes to the table and deactivate the fields and buttons that are no longer relevant:

```
procedure Tform_main.savebuttonClick(Sender: TObject);
var
  i : integer;
begin
  { make the changes permanent }
  table1.post;
  { update the mode }
  CurrentMode := neither;
  { disable the entry fields }
  for i := 0 to ComponentCount - 1 do
  begin
    if components[i] is tDBEdit then
      with components[i] as TDBEdit do
      begin
        readonly := true;
        color := clSilver
      end; {if/with}
    if Components[i] is TDBMemo then
      with components[i] as TDBMemo do
      begin
        readonly := true;
        color := clSilver
      end {if/with}
  end; {for}
```

```
{ disable some buttons . . . }
savebutton.enabled := false;
cancelbutton.enabled := false;
{ . . . and enable the others }
closebutton.enabled := true;
addbutton.enabled := true;
deletebutton.enabled := true;
editbutton.enabled := true;
dbnavigator.enabled := true;
end;
```

The Cancel button must do all of the same enabling and disabling of the Save button, but
it must cancel the changes that the user has made by calling the Cancel method for the
table:

```
procedure Tform_main.cancelbuttonClick(Sender:TObject);
var
  i : integer;
  messagereturn : word;
begin
  { make sure the user wants to quit }
  messageReturn := MessageDlg( 'Are you sure you
        want to cancel changes?',
    mtConfirmation, [mbYes, mbNo], 0 );
  if messageReturn = no then
    exit;
  {rollback the changes }
  table1.cancel;
  if CurrentMode = Add then
  begin
    table1.GotoBookmark( LastRecord );
    table1.freebookmark( lastRecord )
  end;
  CurrentMode := neither;
  { disable the buttons }
  for i := 0 to ComponentCount - 1 do
  begin
    if components[i] is tDBEdit then
      with components[i] as TDBEdit do
      begin
        readonly := true;
        color := clSilver
      end; {if/with}
    if Components[i] is TDBMemo then
      with components[i] as TDBMemo do
      begin
```

```
      readonly := true;
      color := clSilver
   end {if/with}
end; {for}
{ disable some buttons . . . }
savebutton.enabled := false;
cancelbutton.enabled := false;
{ . . . and enable the others }
closebutton.enabled := true;
addbutton.enabled := true;
deletebutton.enabled := true;
editbutton.enabled := true;
dbnavigator.enabled := true;
end;
```

Complete Source for the Buffered Editing Main Form

```
unit Fgetest;

interface

uses
   SysUtils, WinTypes, WinProcs, Messages, Classes, Graphics,
Controls,
   StdCtrls, Forms, DBCtrls, DB, Buttons, ExtCtrls, DBTables,
Mask, Dialogs;

type
   Tform_main = class(TForm)
      ScrollBox: TScrollBox;
      Label1: TLabel;
      EditCUSTKEY: TDBEdit;
      Label2: TLabel;
      EditNAME: TDBEdit;
      Label3: TLabel;
      EditADDRESS: TDBEdit;
      Label4: TLabel;
      EditNATION: TDBEdit;
      Label5: TLabel;
      EditREGION: TDBEdit;
      Label6: TLabel;
      EditPHONE: TDBEdit;
      Label7: TLabel;
      EditACCTBAL: TDBEdit;
      Label8: TLabel;
      EditMKTSEGMT: TDBEdit;
      Label9: TLabel;
```

```
    DBMemo1: TDBMemo;
    DBNavigator: TDBNavigator;
    Panel1: TPanel;
    Panel2: TPanel;
    DataSource1: TDataSource;
    Table1: TTable;
    closebutton: TBitBtn;
    addbutton: TBitBtn;
    deletebutton: TBitBtn;
    editbutton: TBitBtn;
    savebutton: TBitBtn;
    cancelbutton: TBitBtn;
    Bevel1: TBevel;
    procedure FormCreate(Sender: TObject);
    procedure closebuttonClick(Sender: TObject);
    procedure addbuttonClick(Sender: TObject);
    procedure deletebuttonClick(Sender: TObject);
    procedure savebuttonClick(Sender: TObject);
    procedure cancelbuttonClick(Sender: TObject);
    procedure editbuttonClick(Sender: TObject);
  private
    { private declarations }
  public
    { public declarations }
  end;

var
  form_main: Tform_main;

implementation

{$R *.DFM}

const
  yes = 6;
  no = 7;

type
  TMode = (Edit, Add, neither);

var
  LastRecord : TBookMark;
  CurrentMode : TMode;

procedure Tform_main.FormCreate(Sender: TObject);
var
  i : integer;
begin
```

```
Table1.Open;
{ loop thru the components and disable the relevant ones }
for i := 0 to ComponentCount - 1 do
begin
  if components[i] is tDBEdit then
    with components[i] as TDBEdit do
    begin
      readonly := true;
      color := clSilver
    end; {if/with}
  if Components[i] is TDBMemo then
    with components[i] as TDBMemo do
    begin
      readonly := true;
      color := clSilver
    end {if/with}
end; {for}
{ disable the buttons that aren't yet relevant }
savebutton.enabled := false;
cancelbutton.enabled := false;
end; {procedure}

procedure Tform_main.closebuttonClick(Sender: TObject);
begin
  close
end;

procedure Tform_main.addbuttonClick(Sender: TObject);
var
  i : integer;
begin
  { save the record we're on in case the user cancels }
  LastRecord := table1.GetBookmark;
  { set the mode }
  CurrentMode := Add;
  { add a new record to the table }
  table1.append;
  { enable the entryfields }
  for i := 0 to ComponentCount -1 do
  begin
    if Components[i] is TDBEdit then
      with components[i] as TDBEdit do
      begin
        readonly := false;
        color := clwhite
      end; {if/with}
    if Components[i] is TDBMemo then
      with components[i] as TDBMemo do
```

```
    begin
       readonly := false;
       color := clWhite
    end; {if/with}
  end; {for}
  { enable some buttons . . . }
  savebutton.enabled := true;
  cancelbutton.enabled := true;
  { . . . and disable the others }
  closebutton.enabled := false;
  addbutton.enabled := false;
  deletebutton.enabled := false;
  editbutton.enabled := false;
  dbnavigator.enabled := false;
end;

procedure Tform_main.deletebuttonClick(Sender: TObject);
var
  MR : word;
begin
  MR := MessageDlg( 'Are you sure you want to delete this
record?', mtConfirmation,
    [mbYes, mbNo], 0 );
  if MR = Yes then {user pressed yes}
    table1.delete;
end;

procedure Tform_main.savebuttonClick(Sender: TObject);
var
  i : integer;
begin
  { make the changes permanent }
  table1.post;
  { update the mode }
  CurrentMode := neither;
  { disable the entry fields }
  for i := 0 to ComponentCount - 1 do
  begin
    if components[i] is tDBEdit then
      with components[i] as TDBEdit do
      begin
        readonly := true;
        color := clSilver
      end; {if/with}
    if Components[i] is TDBMemo then
      with components[i] as TDBMemo do
      begin
```

```
      readonly := true;
      color := clSilver
    end {if/with}
  end; {for}
  { disable some buttons . . . }
  savebutton.enabled := false;
  cancelbutton.enabled := false;
  { . . . and enable the others }
  closebutton.enabled := true;
  addbutton.enabled := true;
  deletebutton.enabled := true;
  editbutton.enabled := true;
  dbnavigator.enabled := true;
end;

procedure Tform_main.cancelbuttonClick(Sender: TObject);
var
  i : integer;
  messagereturn : word;
begin
  { make sure the user wants to quit }
  messageReturn := MessageDlg( 'Are you sure you want to
cancel changes?',
    mtConfirmation, [mbYes, mbNo], 0 );
  if messageReturn = no then
    exit;
  {rollback the changes }
  table1.cancel;
  if CurrentMode = Add then
  begin
    table1.GotoBookmark( LastRecord );
    table1.freebookmark( lastRecord )
  end;

  CurrentMode := neither;
  { disable the buttons }
  for i := 0 to ComponentCount - 1 do
  begin
    if components[i] is tDBEdit then
      with components[i] as TDBEdit do
      begin
        readonly := true;
        color := clSilver
      end; {if/with}
    if Components[i] is TDBMemo then
      with components[i] as TDBMemo do
      begin
        readonly := true;
        color := clSilver
```

```pascal
        end {if/with}
    end; {for}
    { disable some buttons . . . }
    savebutton.enabled := false;
    cancelbutton.enabled := false;
    { . . . and enable the others }
    closebutton.enabled := true;
    addbutton.enabled := true;
    deletebutton.enabled := true;
    editbutton.enabled := true;
    dbnavigator.enabled := true;
end;

procedure Tform_main.editbuttonClick(Sender: TObject);
var
    i : integer;
begin
    { go into edit mode }
    table1.edit;
    { and set the mode status }
    CurrentMode := edit;
    { fix up component appearance }
    for i := 0 to ComponentCount -1 do
    begin
        if Components[i] is TDBEdit then
            with components[i] as TDBEdit do
            begin
                readonly := false;
                color := clWhite
            end; {if/with}
        if Components[i] is TDBMemo then
            with components[i] as TDBMemo do
            begin
                readonly := false;
                color := clWhite
            end; {if/with}
    end; {for}
    { enable some buttons . . . }
    savebutton.enabled := true;
    cancelbutton.enabled := true;
    { . . . and disable the others }
    closebutton.enabled := false;
    addbutton.enabled := false;
    deletebutton.enabled := false;
    editbutton.enabled := false;
    dbnavigator.enabled := false;
end; {procedure}

end.
```

As you can see, buffered editing is a useful technique. In fact, it is so useful that you will probably want to incorporate it into most of your database applications. The easiest way to accomplish this task is to implement a buffered Edit component, which we create for you in the Creating New Components chapter.

We will return to our design discussion in later chapters when we delve into client/server application design.

CHAPTER 16

APPLICATION DEVELOPMENT

MDI vs. SDI APPLICATIONS

MDI Applications

MDI stands for Multiple Document Interface. This is an application design guideline that describes how Windows applications are constructed and how they interact with one another. In particular, MDI addresses how applications that allow you to create multiple documents work.

First, some definitions. In MDI applications, you have a single parent window and one or many child windows. The parent acts as a container for the children, and the children cannot be moved outside the parent. For example, look at the program group windows in Program Manager. Notice that no matter how much you try, you cannot move one of those windows outside the Program Manager window. In this case, Program Manager is the parent window, and all the program group windows are child windows. As another example, consider a word processor that will allow you to have more than one document window open at a time. The main word processor window (which usually has the main menu and the speedbars) is the parent, and all of the individual document windows are children.

With Delphi, you can create MDI applications. In fact, it is one of the options in the Project Template Gallery. To create an MDI application, the main form's FormStyle property must be set to fsMDIForm, and all of the child forms' FormStyle properties must be set to fsMDIChild. Usually, you will create a single MDI child form that will act as a template for which to create all the child forms. However, if you want, you can create different types of MDI child forms.

There are several rules that accompany creating MDI applications:

- The MDI parent form must be the application's main form (set through Project Options).
- There can only be one form whose FormStyle property is set to fsMDIForm (in other words, only one parent form). You application will fail to compile if this is not the case. Also, if you mistakenly set the main form's FormStyle property to fsMDIChild, your project will fail to compile. An MDI application must have a parent form.
- In general, you should not allow Delphi to auto-create the child forms. It is better to do it yourself whenever they are needed. This is especially true if your MDI application is the norm, where all of the child forms are just alike. If you are using several different types of child forms, it is OK to let Delphi auto-create them for you.

MDI child windows.   Typically, the child windows that are contained in an MDI application are all the same. For example, in a word processor, every window that you open to edit a document will have the same characteristics. However, this is not a requirement of MDI applications, only a convention.

In fact, Delphi makes it easy to create child windows that are all basically the same through the CreateChildWindow method that is part of the MDI application template. This routine can be thought of as a template used to create all of the similar child windows. Whenever the user wants to create a new child window, this routine should be called. This means that your MDI applications will typically have a main container form (the MDI parent) and multiple MDI child forms, which are created using this routine as they are needed.

Here is the CreateChildWindow method that is included in our sample application. It creates a new MDI child window based on the file that the user selects from the OpenDialog component. If the text in the file is greater than 32K in size, the exception block is triggered and the child form is closed. The 32K limit arises because Memo components can only contain up to 32K of character information. If you wanted to make this program more robust, you could change to a text object that holds more than 32K.

```
procedure TMainForm.CreateMDIChild(const Name: string);
var
  Child: TMDIChild;
begin
  { create a new MDI child window }
  Child := TMDIChild.Create(Application);
  Child.Caption := Name;
  try
    Child.memoTheFile.lines.LoadFromFile(
        OpenDialog.fileName );
  except
    on EOutOfResources do
```

```
    begin
      MessageDlg( 'Text cannot be greater than 32K!',
            mtError, [mbOK], 0 );
      Child.close
    end {on}
  end; {try}
end;
```

Closing child windows.   The actual guidelines for MDI applications state that the child windows shouldn't close when a close is attempted (either by double-clicking the system menu in the upper left hand corner, choosing Close from the system menu, or hitting Alt-F4), but rather minimize themselves in the parent window. A perfect example of this is Windows Program Manager—notice that you can never actually close the program group windows in Program Manager, they always minimize within the Program Manager parent window. However, almost no real windows applications follow this rule. Most let the user close the child windows.

You can easily accomodate this in Delphi. For the child window, generate an On-Close event for the form by double clicking on the OnClose event in the Object Inspector. Delphi will generate a snippet of code like this:

```
procedure TMDIChild.FormClose(Sender: TObject; var Action:
TCloseAction);
begin
end;
```

Notice that this event handler has a `var` parameter called `Action` in addition to the usual `Sender` parameter. The action parameter allows you to override the standard close for the MDI child. In fact, you can assign the action parameter to any of the pre-defined constants displayed in Table 16.1.

TABLE 16.1   Predefined Action Constants

Action Value	Result
caNone	Prevents the form from closing, essentially ignoring the close request. This is handy to create uncloseable child windows.
caHide	Doesn't close the window, just toggles its Visible property to false. You can still access all the properties and methods for the form, including showing it again.
caFree	Actually closes the child form and releases the memory that it occupies. This is similar to calling the Free method for a form.
caMinimize	This is the default action, which just minimizes the child form within the parent form.

So, if you wanted to actually close the child form instead of minimizing it, you would add the following line to the child form's OnClose event:

```
procedure TMDIChild.FormClose(Sender: TObject; var Action:
TCloseAction);
begin
  Action := caFree
end;
```

MDI window menu.   If you create an MDI application, you should follow the Windows standard and provide a window menu to allow your users to arrange your child windows more easily. In fact, your window menu should at a minimum provide tile, cascade, and arrange icons options. Once you have created the Window menu, create these Onclick events for the menu options using Delphi's predefined menu statements:

```
procedure TMainForm.Tile1Click( Sender : TObject );
begin
   tile
end;

procedure TMainForm.Cascade1Click( Sender : TObject );
begin
   cascade
end;

procedure TMainForm.ArrangeIcons1Click( Sender : TObject );
begin
   ArrangeIcons
end;
```

Of course, if you choose MDI Application from the Project Template Gallery, the window menu, along with these events, are already built-in (along with Open, Save, and Exit speedbar buttons).

SDI Applications

SDI stands for Single Document Interface, which means that you never have windows that are trapped by a main parent window. In fact, the SDI model is simpler and it is going to be the primary type of application for Windows95. Apparently, Microsoft did marketing research that suggested that users are too confused by MDI applications, so they are encouraging new applications to be developed in the SDI model. In fact, Delphi itself is a SDI application. Notice that there is no main window—just a main window bar. When you minimize portions of Delphi (for example, the Object Inspector), it appears on the desktop as if it were a independantly running program, not part of another application. For another good example of a SDI application, look at the MASTAPP sample program that ships with Delphi. It is an SDI customer/orders style application.

The FormStyle fsNormal is used for a SDI form, and generally there is much less work involved in creating an SDI application. You never have to worry about the window menu (SDI applications generally don't have one) and how to tile and cascade child windows.

The MASTAPP sample program has a floating toolbar with a menu attached. Another popular style of SDI application has what is referred to as a "switchboard" or "splash" form. A switchboard form is just a main that has a few buttons on it which take you to the main parts (or most used parts) of an application. Typically, this switchboard also has a menu which allows the user to navigate through the remainder of the application.

As we have stated, you don't have to worry about a window menu for an SDI application. In fact, the only sort of window management that you have to be concerned with is the case where the user opens the SDI main window, then opens some child windows, then tries to close the main form and leave the child windows open. In general, you don't want that to occur, because the child windows would be, in effect, orphaned. Delphi handles this situation for you—when you close the main SDI form, all of the forms that it has opened will close as well, because they are all owned by the same application object. Also, if the main SDI form is minimized, all of the child windows will be minimized "within" the main form's icon. Delphi itself exhibits this same behavior.

Case Study: Lister

The following two examples hightlight the distinction between MDI and SDI applications. It is essentially the same application, but written for the two different application guidelines. The application is a small text file lister which allows the user to view several text files simultaneously. For example, this little utility might be handy to look at VCL source code.

MLister is the MDI version of the application. The SDI version, SLister, uses a small floating speedbar and menu to open several different forms, each with a single file shown.

MDI lister.   Notice that MLister is a standard MDI application with a parent form that contains zero or many child forms. Figure 16.1 shows the MLister main program running, with two open child windows.

Following is the source code listing for the MDI Lister application, including the DPR files, the PAS files, and the DFM files. The form PAS and DFM files for this application aren't shown. The about box is a simple about box form, based on the About box form template that Delphi supplies.

Project file (lister.dpr)

```
program Lister;

uses
  Forms,
```

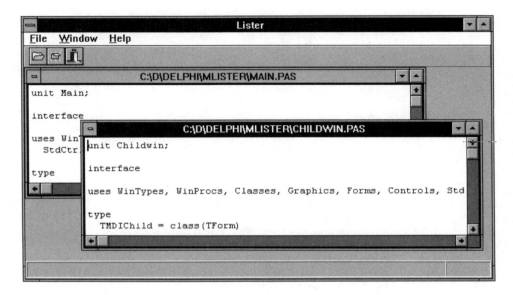

FIGURE 16.1   The MLister Main Form Containing Two MDI Child Forms

```
  Main in 'MAIN.PAS' {MainForm},
  Childwin in 'CHILDWIN.PAS' {MDIChild},
  Fabout in 'FABOUT.PAS' {AboutBox};

{$R *.RES}

begin
  Application.CreateForm(TMainForm, MainForm);
  Application.CreateForm(TAboutBox, AboutBox);
  Application.Run;
end.
```

Main form (main.pas).   This is the code for the main (parent form) of the MDI Lister application:

```
unit Main;

interface

uses WinTypes, WinProcs, SysUtils, Classes, Graphics, Forms,
Controls, Menus,
  StdCtrls, Dialogs, Buttons, Messages, ExtCtrls, fAbout;
```

```
type
  TMainForm = class(TForm)
    MainMenu1: TMainMenu;
    Panel1: TPanel;
    StatusLine: TPanel;
    File1: TMenuItem;
    FileOpenItem: TMenuItem;
    Panel2: TPanel;
    FileCloseItem: TMenuItem;
    Window1: TMenuItem;
    Help1: TMenuItem;
    N1: TMenuItem;
    FileExitItem: TMenuItem;
    WindowCascadeItem: TMenuItem;
    WindowTileItem: TMenuItem;
    WindowArrangeItem: TMenuItem;
    HelpAboutItem: TMenuItem;
    OpenDialog: TOpenDialog;
    WindowMinimizeItem: TMenuItem;
    SpeedPanel: TPanel;
    OpenBtn: TSpeedButton;
    ExitBtn: TSpeedButton;
    SpeedButton_close: TSpeedButton;
    procedure FormCreate(Sender: TObject);
    procedure WindowCascadeItemClick(Sender: TObject);
    procedure UpdateMenuItems(Sender: TObject);
    procedure WindowTileItemClick(Sender: TObject);
    procedure WindowArrangeItemClick(Sender: TObject);
    procedure FileCloseItemClick(Sender: TObject);
    procedure FileOpenItemClick(Sender: TObject);
    procedure FileExitItemClick(Sender: TObject);
    procedure WindowMinimizeItemClick(Sender: TObject);
    procedure FormDestroy(Sender: TObject);
    procedure HelpAboutItemClick(Sender: TObject);
  private
    { Private declarations }
    procedure CreateMDIChild(const Name: string);
    procedure ShowHint(Sender: TObject);
  public
    { Public declarations }
  end;

var
  MainForm: TMainForm;

implementation

{$R *.DFM}
```

```pascal
uses ChildWin;

procedure TMainForm.FormCreate(Sender: TObject);
begin
  Application.OnHint := ShowHint;
  Screen.OnActiveFormChange := UpdateMenuItems;
end;

procedure TMainForm.ShowHint(Sender: TObject);
begin
  StatusLine.Caption := Application.Hint;
end;

procedure TMainForm.CreateMDIChild(const Name: string);
var
  Child: TMDIChild;
begin
  { create a new MDI child window }
  Child := TMDIChild.Create(Application);
  Child.Caption := Name;
  try
    Child.memoTheFile.lines.LoadFromFile(
        OpenDialog.fileName );
  except
    on EOutOfResources do
    begin
      MessageDlg( 'Text cannot be greater than 32K!',
              mtError, [mbOK], 0 );
      Child.close
    end {on}
  end; {try}
end;

procedure TMainForm.FileOpenItemClick(Sender: TObject);
begin
  if OpenDialog.Execute then
    CreateMDIChild(OpenDialog.FileName);
end;

procedure TMainForm.FileCloseItemClick(Sender: TObject);
begin
  if ActiveMDIChild <> nil then
    ActiveMDIChild.Close;
end;

procedure TMainForm.FileExitItemClick(Sender: TObject);
begin
  Close;
end;
```

```
procedure TMainForm.WindowCascadeItemClick(Sender: TObject);
begin
  Cascade;
end;

procedure TMainForm.WindowTileItemClick(Sender: TObject);
begin
  Tile;
end;

procedure TMainForm.WindowArrangeItemClick(Sender: TObject);
begin
  ArrangeIcons;
end;

procedure TMainForm.WindowMinimizeItemClick(Sender:
TObject);
var
  I: Integer;
begin
  { Must be done backwards through the MDIChildren array }
  for I := MDIChildCount - 1 downto 0 do
    MDIChildren[I].WindowState := wsMinimized;
end;

procedure TMainForm.UpdateMenuItems(Sender: TObject);
begin
  FileCloseItem.Enabled := MDIChildCount > 0;
  WindowCascadeItem.Enabled := MDIChildCount > 0;
  WindowTileItem.Enabled := MDIChildCount > 0;
  WindowArrangeItem.Enabled := MDIChildCount > 0;
  WindowMinimizeItem.Enabled := MDIChildCount > 0;
  SpeedButton_close.Enabled := MDIChildCount > 0;
end;

procedure TMainForm.FormDestroy(Sender: TObject);
begin
  Screen.OnActiveFormChange := nil;
end;

procedure TMainForm.HelpAboutItemClick(Sender: TObject);
begin
  AboutBox := TAboutBox.Create( self );
  AboutBox.ShowModal;
  AboutBox.Destroy
end;

end.
```

Virutally all of the .DPR and main form code was generated by utilizing Delphi's MDI Application template, including all of the code that handles child window manipulation (tile, cascade, etc.). Notice the CreateMDIChild method, which takes care of creating new MDI child forms, both for **File | New** and **File | Open.**

Main form DFM File (main.dfm).   Following is the main form's DFM file, with the bitmap information removed. Bitmaps appear in DFM files as a series of hex digits, which are meaningless to most viewers. So, if you were to transcribe this DFM file, the buttons would have images on them—you would have to add new images, yourself.

```
object MainForm: TMainForm
  Left = 232
  Top = 115
  Width = 435
  Height = 300
  ActiveControl = StatusLine
  Caption = 'Lister'
  Font.Color = clWindowText
  Font.Height = -13
  Font.Name = 'System'
  Font.Style = []
  FormStyle = fsMDIForm
  Menu = MainMenu1
  PixelsPerInch = 96
  Position = poDefault
  WindowMenu = Window1
  OnCreate = FormCreate
  OnDestroy = FormDestroy
  TextHeight = 16
  object Panel1: TPanel
    Left = 0
    Top = 228
    Width = 427
    Height = 26
    Align = alBottom
    BorderWidth = 1
    TabOrder = 0
    object StatusLine: TPanel
      Left = 2
      Top = 2
      Width = 362
      Height = 22
      Align = alClient
      Alignment = taLeftJustify
      BevelOuter = bvLowered
      BorderWidth = 1
```

```
        Font.Color = clBlack
        Font.Height = -11
        Font.Name = 'MS Sans Serif'
        Font.Style = []
        ParentFont = False
        TabOrder = 0
      end
      object Panel2: TPanel
        Left = 364
        Top = 2
        Width = 61
        Height = 22
        Align = alRight
        Alignment = taLeftJustify
        BevelOuter = bvLowered
        TabOrder = 1
      end
    end
    object SpeedPanel: TPanel
      Left = 0
      Top = 0
      Width = 427
      Height = 30
      Align = alTop
      ParentShowHint = False
      ShowHint = True
      TabOrder = 1
      object OpenBtn: TSpeedButton
        Left = 7
        Top = 2
        Width = 25
        Height = 25
        Hint = 'Open|'
        Glyph.Data = {}
        NumGlyphs = 2
        OnClick = FileOpenItemClick
      end
      object ExitBtn: TSpeedButton
        Left = 56
        Top = 2
        Width = 25
        Height = 25
        Hint = 'Exit|'
        Glyph.Data = {}
        NumGlyphs = 2
        OnClick = FileExitItemClick
      end
      object SpeedButton_close: TSpeedButton
```

```
              Left = 31
              Top = 2
              Width = 25
              Height = 25
              Hint = 'Close'
              Glyph.Data = {}
              NumGlyphs = 2
              OnClick = FileCloseItemClick
          end
      end
      object MainMenu1: TMainMenu
          Left = 36
          Top = 196
          object File1: TMenuItem
              Caption = '&File'
              Hint = 'File related commands'
              object FileOpenItem: TMenuItem
                  Caption = '&Open'
                  Hint = 'Open an existing file'
                  OnClick = FileOpenItemClick
              end
              object FileCloseItem: TMenuItem
                  Caption = '&Close'
                  Hint = 'Close current file'
                  OnClick = FileCloseItemClick
              end
              object N1: TMenuItem
                  Caption = '-'
              end
              object FileExitItem: TMenuItem
                  Caption = 'E&xit'
                  Hint = 'Exit the application'
                  OnClick = FileExitItemClick
              end
          end
          object Window1: TMenuItem
              Caption = '&Window'
              Hint = 'Window related commands such as Tile and
Cascade'
              object WindowCascadeItem: TMenuItem
                  Caption = '&Cascade'
                  Hint = 'Arrange windows to overlap'
                  OnClick = WindowCascadeItemClick
              end
              object WindowTileItem: TMenuItem
                  Caption = '&Tile'
                  Hint = 'Arrange windows without overlap'
                  OnClick = WindowTileItemClick
```

```
      end
      object WindowArrangeItem: TMenuItem
        Caption = '&Arrange Icons'
        Hint = 'Arrange window icons at bottom of main window'
        OnClick = WindowArrangeItemClick
      end
      object WindowMinimizeItem: TMenuItem
        Caption = '&Minimize All'
        Hint = 'Minimize all windows'
        OnClick = WindowMinimizeItemClick
      end
    end
    object Help1: TMenuItem
      Caption = '&Help'
      Hint = 'Help topics'
      object HelpAboutItem: TMenuItem
        Caption = '&About'
        OnClick = HelpAboutItemClick
      end
    end
  end
  object OpenDialog: TOpenDialog
    DefaultExt = 'pas'
    Filter = 'Units (*.pas) | *.pas | Projects (*.dpr) | *.dpr
| All Files (*.*) | *.*'
    Left = 4
    Top = 196
  end
end
```

Source code for Lister ChildWin (childwin.pas).   Following is the source code for the child form. Remember, the child forms in an MDI application are often just a template, which can produce multiple instances of similar child windows.

```
unit Childwin;

interface

uses WinTypes, WinProcs, Classes, Graphics, Forms, Controls,
StdCtrls;

type
  TMDIChild = class(TForm)
    ScrollBox1: TScrollBox;
    MemoTheFile: TMemo;
    procedure FormClose(Sender: TObject; var Action:
TCloseAction);
```

```
private
  { Private declarations }
public
  { Public declarations }
end;

implementation

{$R *.DFM}

procedure TMDIChild.FormClose(Sender: TObject; var Action:
TCloseAction);
begin
  Action := caFree;
end;

end.
```

DFM file for ChildWin (childwin.dfm).

```
object MDIChild: TMDIChild
  Left = 327
  Top = 200
  Width = 429
  Height = 215
  Caption = 'MDI Child'
  Font.Color = clWindowText
  Font.Height = -13
  Font.Name = 'System'
  Font.Style = []
  FormStyle = fsMDIChild
  PixelsPerInch = 96
  Position = poDefault
  Visible = True
  OnClose = FormClose
  TextHeight = 16
  object ScrollBox1: TScrollBox
    Left = 0
    Top = 0
    Width = 421
    Height = 188
    Align = alClient
    AutoScroll = False
    Font.Color = clBlack
    Font.Height = -13
    Font.Name = 'Courier New'
    Font.Style = []
```

```
      ParentFont = False
      TabOrder = 0
      object MemoTheFile: TMemo
        Left = 0
        Top = 0
        Width = 419
        Height = 186
        Align = alClient
        Lines.Strings = (
          ' MemoTheFile)
        ReadOnly = True
        ScrollBars = ssBoth
        TabOrder = 0
      end
    end
end
```

SDI Lister. Figure 16.2 is a screen shot of the SDI version of the lister application. Notice that this application does not have a main containing window; all of the forms that open are autonomous.

This SDI application starts with a "switchboard" form (shown in the upper left of Figure 16.2) that opens additional listing windows. Notice that each of the listing win-

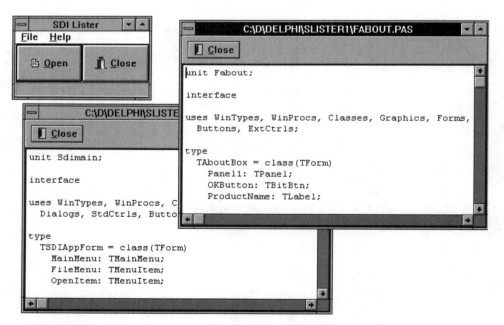

FIGURE 16.2 The SLister Program Running with Two Autonomous Child Windows

dows are independent of the parent, and can be minimized independently. However, like all SDI applications based on the built-in SDI template, when you minimize the main form, all the other forms are minimized "within" the same icon.

This is by no means the only viable SDI design for this application. An alternative would be to have a single tabbed form, where each new file would create a new tab on the form, like the Delphi editor. In fact, notice that the Delphi editor is part of an SDI application (Delphi itself) which needs to be able to show multiple files (the editor files). Borland's solution to this problem is a tabbed form interface which allows them to display mutilple windows which would seem more naturally suited to an MDI application.

You will also notice that the SLister application is simpler and shorter than Mlister—there is no code required to manage the multiple contained child windows. Also notice that, unlike MLister, each child form has a Close button on it, rather than the parent window being responsible for closing the forms.

Source code for the SDI Lister Application. Here are the DPR, PAS, and DFM files for the SDI version of Lister, excluding the about box. Again, the about form is a very simple implementation of the About form template that is supplied with Delphi.

Project source (slister1.dpr)

```
program Slister1;

uses
  Forms,
  Fslster1 in 'FSLSTER1.PAS' {SDIAppForm},
  Fabout in 'FABOUT.PAS' {AboutBox};

{$R *.RES}

begin
  Application.CreateForm(TSDIAppForm, SDIAppForm);
  Application.CreateForm(TAboutBox, AboutBox);
  Application.Run;
end.
```

Source for main SDI Form (fslster1.pas).

This is the source for the main SDI form. In this particular project, the child forms are not explicitly included in the project manager—you will notice that the form FViewer is included in the implementation section of this main file, and all management of this form is handled internally by this form.

```
unit Fslster1;

interface

uses WinTypes, WinProcs, Classes, Graphics, Forms, Controls,
Menus,
   Dialogs, StdCtrls, Buttons, ExtCtrls;

type
  TSDIAppForm = class(TForm)
    MainMenu: TMainMenu;
    FileMenu: TMenuItem;
    OpenItem: TMenuItem;
    ExitItem: TMenuItem;
    N1: TMenuItem;
    OpenDialog: TOpenDialog;
    Help1: TMenuItem;
    About1: TMenuItem;
    StatusBar: TPanel;
    SpeedPanel: TPanel;
    BitBtn1: TBitBtn;
    BitBtn2: TBitBtn;
    procedure ShowHint(Sender: TObject);
    procedure ExitItemClick(Sender: TObject);
    procedure OpenItemClick(Sender: TObject);
    procedure About1Click(Sender: TObject);
    procedure FormCreate(Sender: TObject);
    procedure BitBtn1Click(Sender: TObject);
    procedure BitBtn2Click(Sender: TObject);
  private
    { Private declarations }
  public
    { Public declarations }
  end;

var
  SDIAppForm: TSDIAppForm;

implementation

uses FAbout, FViewer;

{$R *.DFM}

procedure TSDIAppForm.ShowHint(Sender: TObject);
begin
  StatusBar.Caption := Application.Hint;
end;
```

```
procedure TSDIAppForm.ExitItemClick(Sender: TObject);
begin
  Close;
end;

procedure TSDIAppForm.OpenItemClick(Sender: TObject);
begin
  OpenDialog.Execute
end;

procedure TSDIAppForm.About1Click(Sender: TObject);
begin
  AboutBox.ShowModal;
end;

procedure TSDIAppForm.FormCreate(Sender: TObject);
begin
  Application.OnHint := ShowHint;
end;

procedure TSDIAppForm.BitBtn1Click(Sender: TObject);
var
  Viewer : Tform_viewer;
  begin
  if OpenDialog.Execute then
    begin
    Viewer := TForm_Viewer.create( self );
    Viewer.MemoFile.lines.LoadFromFile(
          OpenDialog.FileName );
    Viewer.Caption := OpenDialog.FileName;
    Viewer.Show;
  end; {if}
end; {procedure}

procedure TSDIAppForm.BitBtn2Click(Sender: TObject);
begin
  close
end;

end.
```

DFM file for Main SDI Form (fslster1.dfm).   This is the DFM file for the main SDI form. As before, none of the hex code for the button bitmaps is shown here.

```
object SDIAppForm: TSDIAppForm
  Left = 248
  Top = 74
  Width = 195
  Height = 123
  ActiveControl = SpeedPanel
  Caption = 'SDI Lister'
  Font.Color = clWindowText
  Font.Height = -13
  Font.Name = 'System'
  Font.Style = []
  Menu = MainMenu
  PixelsPerInch = 96
  OnCreate = FormCreate
  TextHeight = 16
  object StatusBar: TPanel
    Left = 0
    Top = 55
    Width = 427
    Height = 22
    Align = alBottom
    Alignment = taLeftJustify
    BevelInner = bvLowered
    Font.Color = clBlack
    Font.Height = -11
    Font.Name = 'MS Sans Serif'
    Font.Style = []
    ParentFont = False
    TabOrder = 0
  end
  object SpeedPanel: TPanel
    Left = 0
    Top = 0
    Width = 187
    Height = 56
    Align = alTop
    ParentShowHint = False
    ShowHint = True
    TabOrder = 1
    object BitBtn1: TBitBtn
      Left = 1
      Top = 0
      Width = 93
      Height = 55
      Caption = '&Open'
      TabOrder = 0
      OnClick = BitBtn1Click
      Glyph.Data = {}
```

```
      NumGlyphs = 2
    end
    object BitBtn2: TBitBtn
      Left = 94
      Top = 0
      Width = 93
      Height = 55
      TabOrder = 1
      OnClick = BitBtn2Click
      Kind = bkClose
    end
  end
  object MainMenu: TMainMenu
    Left = 23
    Top = 46
    object FileMenu: TMenuItem
      Caption = '&File'
      object OpenItem: TMenuItem
        Caption = '&Open . . . '
        Hint = 'Open a file'
        OnClick = BitBtn1Click
      end
      object N1: TMenuItem
        Caption = '-'
      end
      object ExitItem: TMenuItem
        Caption = 'E&xit'
        Hint = 'Exit application'
        OnClick = ExitItemClick
        ShortCutText = 'Alt+X'
      end
    end
    object Help1: TMenuItem
      Caption = '&Help'
      object About1: TMenuItem
        Caption = '&About . . . '
        OnClick = About1Click
      end
    end
  end
  object OpenDialog: TOpenDialog
    DefaultExt = 'pas'
    Filter = 'Unit Files (*.pas) | *.pas | Project Files
(*.dpr) | *.dpr | All Files (*.*) | *.*'
    Title = 'Open File to View'
    Left = 55
    Top = 46
  end
end
```

Source code for the Child SDI Windows (FViewer.pas)

```
unit Fviewer;

interface

uses
  SysUtils, WinTypes, WinProcs, Messages, Classes, Graphics,
Controls,
  Forms, Dialogs, StdCtrls, Buttons, ExtCtrls;

type
  Tform_viewer = class(TForm)
    Panel1: TPanel;
    SpeedButton1: TSpeedButton;
    ScrollBox1: TScrollBox;
    MemoFile: TMemo;
    procedure SpeedButton1Click(Sender: TObject);
  private
    { Private declarations }
  public
    { Public declarations }
  end;

var
  form_viewer: Tform_viewer;

implementation

{$R *.DFM}

procedure Tform_viewer.SpeedButton1Click(Sender: TObject);
begin
  release
end;

end.
```

DFM file for the SDI Child Windows (fviwer.dfm).   This is the DFM file for the SDI child windows. Again, the button bitmap information has been removed.

```
object form_viewer: Tform_viewer
  Left = 200
  Top = 98
  Width = 435
  Height = 300
  Font.Color = clWindowText
```

```
        Font.Height = -13
        Font.Name = 'System'
        Font.Style = []
        PixelsPerInch = 96
        TextHeight = 16
        object Panel1: TPanel
          Left = 0
          Top = 0
          Width = 427
          Height = 41
          Align = alTop
          TabOrder = 0
          object SpeedButton1: TSpeedButton
            Left = 8
            Top = 8
            Width = 73
            Height = 25
            Caption = '&Close'
            Glyph.Data = {}
            NumGlyphs = 2
            OnClick = SpeedButton1Click
          end
        end
        object ScrollBox1: TScrollBox
          Left = 0
          Top = 41
          Width = 427
          Height = 232
          Align = alClient
          TabOrder = 1
          object MemoFile: TMemo
            Left = 0
            Top = 0
            Width = 425
            Height = 230
            Align = alClient
            Font.Color = clBlack
            Font.Height = -13
            Font.Name = 'Courier New'
            Font.Style = []
            Lines.Strings = (
              'MemoFile')
            ParentFont = False
            ScrollBars = ssBoth
            TabOrder = 0
          end
        end
      end
```

INTERFACE DESIGN RULES

This following discussion should by no means be considered an exhaustive treatment of interface design, which is a HUGE area of study in software engineering. Rather, it is meant to bring up a few points about Windows conventions.

Windows is based on a set of user guidelines called CUA (Common User Access) that were originally proposed by IBM. CUA is the guideline that gave us pull-down menus, uniformity among applications, etc. If you are interested in reading these guidelines, they are available from both IBM and Microsoft. But, be forewarned—it is not exciting reading.

If you are interested in the design of things in general, there is an excellent book titled *The Design of Everyday Things* by Don Norman. While this book is ostensibly about general design guidelines, it is good reference material for application designers.

Document Mode vs. Dialog Mode

Generally, most of the interface to a Windows program can be broken down into two modes: Document mode and Dialog mode. Document mode is the general work surface. For example, Document mode for a word processor would be the place where you enter characters, for a spreadsheet; it is the place where you enter numbers and formulas. The main characteristic of Document mode is that you are free to take any available action, whether it is typing, choosing speedbuttons, choosing menu items, etc. In other words, any user event is allowed.

Dialog mode, on the other hand, is usually represented by a dialog box, which stops the normal flow of execution of the user and requires that the user provide some information. Dialog boxes are typically used for configuration, or for setting options, etc.

You should try to emulate this model as much as possible. Try to make the document portion of your application as flexible as possible, and only interrupt the user's normal work flow to get information that is necessary. From the Delphi standpoint, this means that you should open your forms with Show as often as you can (for the Document interface) and open your dialog boxes using ShowModal (for Dialog mode).

Colors

Even though Windows has access to a large number of possible colors, you should restrain yourself. Have you ever noticed that most shrink wrapped Windows applications use the colors (in order of usage) white, black, gray, dark blue, and yellow? As a consequence, most Windows programs aren't very flashy; they commonly use muted colors. If you want your programs to look as much as possible like shrink wrapped programs, you should use muted colors as well. Remember, the big software company's decision to use these muted colors is based on millions of dollars of marketing research, so you can take advantage of this research without having to pay for it by emulating those who did pay for it.

Fonts

There are many types of fonts (fixed pitch vs. proportional, serif vs. sans serif, etc.). Here are some samples:

Proportional font (Times New Roman)

`Non-proportional, fixed pitch font (Courier New)`

Serif font (Times New Roman)

Sans Serif font (Arial)

In general, proportional fonts are easier to read in large bodies of text (like a book). Non-proportional fonts (which is all there was in DOS programs) are good for columnar data, because every character is the same width. Serif fonts are more readable in long passages of text, while sans serif fonts tend to stand out more, making them appropriate for labels and headings.

One other note about fonts. Fonts are usually owned by someone; most are not in the public domain. So, if you have some nifty fonts that were installed by another Windows application and use them in a program written in Delphi, you may owe royalties to the owner of the font. Also, if the user of your program doesn't have that font, you must distribute it with your application. To avoid these hassles, always stick to the fonts that are provided with Windows. You can use them to your heart's content without having to worry about royalties, and it's a good bet that your users already have them installed on their machines.

Also, you should try to use True Type fonts whenever possible. True Type fonts are a newer technology that the older type of fonts, and they tend to look the same on the screen as they do on a printed page. In fact, from the fonts section of the Windows control panel you can instruct Windows to only show you True Type fonts in the standard font picker dialog box.

HELP FILES

One of the marks of a good Windows program is a comprehensive help file. If you are writing Windows programs, you should also be writing help files to go with them. As you have no doubt noticed, there is a definite trend in most Windows software to get away from paper documentation and put more information into help files. In fact, some software ships with no paper documentation at all—it's all in the help file. Another compelling reason to create help files for your applications is to make them as consistent with other Windows applications as much as possible.

One of the most commonly overlooked costs of Windows development is the creation of help files. Creating a good help file is not a trivial undertaking. It takes a fair amount of time, extremely good organization of topics, and thorough knowledge of the application that you are writing help for. However, the help file must be completed before you can distribute the application, so it should get the same priority as other critical pieces of the development process. In fact, some small companies are letting the developers write the help file during beta testing. This way, the people who most intimately know the software can write the documentation while the code is being tested. Hopefully, they can complete the help files even before the testing cycle is over.

This section will serve as an introduction to the topic of creating help files. This is another very large topic, and this material should in no way be considered exhaustive. If you want more information, there are several books available to help you create help files. And, Microsoft also distributes a help file (what else?) called HAG (the **H**elp **A**uthoring **G**uideline) which is available free of charge directly from Microsoft or downloadable from Compuserve.

Creating Help Files

The .HLP file that actually stores the help information is actually made up of several different files that are compiled together from a help project. Help files contain not only the actual help text but bitmaps (including screen shots) and several other types of files as well. The main body of the help text can be created either in a word processor or with a help authoring tool.

From scratch.   Creating a help text file from scratch is a lot of work! You have to create a document in a word processor in **R**ich **T**ext **F**ormat (RTF) which includes not only the text, but also information about jumps to other topics, banners, etc. And you have to manage all this information yourself—there is no built-in support for creating help files. This management problem isn't too bad in small help projects, but grows unwieldy as the help project expands to the size typical for a useful application.

If you are creating a reasonably sized help file, it becomes quite a chore keeping up with all the details involved: making sure that all the hot-links jump to the right place, making sure that the banners are referenced in the correct places, making sure that the correct bitmaps are in their places, etc. Most help writers turn to a help authoring tool to expedite this process.

Using a help authoring tool.   A help authoring tool is a broad category of software that applies to any tool that makes it easier to create help files. These are generally broken down into a couple of categories: those that are collections of macros for a word processor and those that are stand-alone applications.

Some of the help authoring tools are collections of powerful macros for a word processor (usually some version of Word for Windows). These macro packages provide tool bars and automated support for creating the necessary help file elements. These types of tools have advantages and disadvantages. Their advantage is that they can take advantage of the underlying services of the word processor to provide powerful features. Their disadvantage is that you must own the word processor to be able to use the tool (the word processor is not included in the price of the tool). Also, if you upgrade your word processor, your help authoring tool may need to be upgraded to work properly again.

The other category of help authoring tools are stand-alone applications. These are primarily tools that emulate some of the functionality of a word processor but have built-in support for creating the unique elements of a help file. These packages also usually provide some extra tools to help manage help file projects.

There are several of both types of packages on the market, and there is no clear market leader. So, we are going to direct our attention toward one of the available tools (Fore-Help) to give you an idea of what sort of tools are available. ForeHelp is a stand-alone application created by ForeFront, Inc. At the time of this writing, ForeFront was offering a special deal to the recent purchasers of a Borland language product to allow programmers to buy thier product at a fraction of its normal price.

ForeHelp

ForeHelp works very much like a word processor. Figure 16.3 is a screen shot of Fore-Help with a help file loaded.

As you can see, it looks like a regular word processor. However, there are special buttons in the speedbar which allow you to create help topics (which are the highlighted words that are hyperlinks to the subject) and banners (which are small pop-up windows that are typically used to define terms). You can also define your own text styles, including formatting and colors. ForeHelp will also allow you to print out the entire help file. There are also abundant menus to help maintain the help project.

As stated earlier, one of the benefits of using a help authoring tool is the utilities that are provided to ease managing complex interlinking help files. In the case of Fore-Help, there is a utility called Navigator that shows what the relationship between your help topics are.

In Figure 16.4, you can see that the topics on the left lead back to the Customer topic, and the topics on the right are the ones contained in the Customer help screen. The numbers to the left and right indicate how many topics jump into that topic. The eyeglass icon allows you to go to that page in the editor shown in Figure 16.3. You can also double click on any of the topics to "center" it, showing all its relationships.

ForeHelp also allows you to test your help project without compiling it. In other words, ForeHelp will show you the help file just as it will look to your users, and allow you to navigate through it. Building help files can take a long time. It is nice to be able to see the end result without having to compile your project each time.

The help compiler.   The Help Compiler for Windows help files is, ironically enough, a DOS program, HC31.EXE. It is installed in the \delphi\bin directory with all the other Delphi executables. To actually create a .HLP file, you must compile the help project file and all its associated files.

The help project file (HPJ) is a separate text file that describes your help project in a special format. For example, following is the text for the help file shown in Figures 16.3 and 16.4:

```
[OPTIONS]
ERRORLOG=CUSTOMER.ERR
```

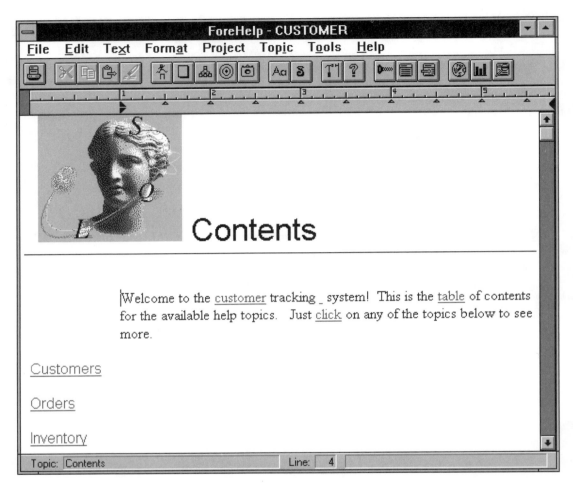

FIGURE 16.3   Forehelp with a Loaded Help File

```
COMPRESS=HIGH
CONTENTS=Contents
TITLE=Customer Sample Program
COPYRIGHT=Copyright 81995, The DSW Group, Ltd.
BMROOT=c:\d\hlp
ROOT=c:\d\hlp

[WINDOWS]
main=,,0,,,0
```

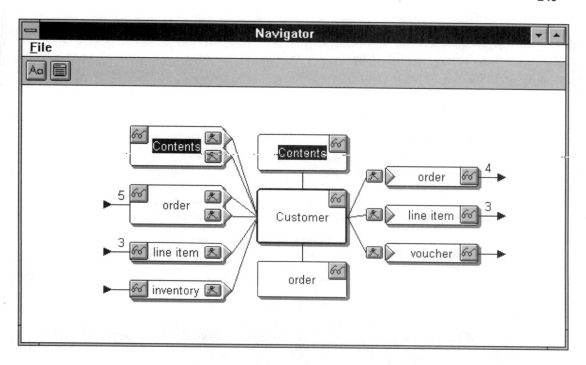

FIGURE 16.4   Forehelp's Navigator Window

```
[FILES]
CUSTOMER.RTF

[MAP]
#define inventory   2
#define voucher     4
#define order       3
#define Customer    1
```

As you can see, help project files are laid out similarly to Windows INI files. We will provide a discussion of the map numbers in the following section.

With some help authoring tools, you can run the help compiler from within the authoring environment. For example, in ForeHelp, you can choose the Build option to compile the help file for you.

One distinct advantage of this compilation process is that the resulting HLP file is completely self-contained. It includes the text and all the bitmaps that you have specified for your help project—there is no need to distribute any other file with the HLP file. It is a stand-alone file that can be run by WinHelp.exe.

ADDING HELP TO YOUR APPLICATION

Once you have created a help file, you must be able to attach it to your Delphi application. Fortunately, it's easy.

Specifying a Help File

There are a couple of ways to specify what help file belongs to a particular application: at design time or at run-time.

To attach a help file to a project, open the Application page of the Project Options dialog box (Figure 16.5).

This is the easiest way to associate a help file with an application. You can also specify a help file at run-time with code placed in the main form's OnActivate event:

```
procedure TForm_main.FormActivate(Sender: TObject);
begin
   Application.HelpFile := 'CUSTOMER.HLP'
end;
```

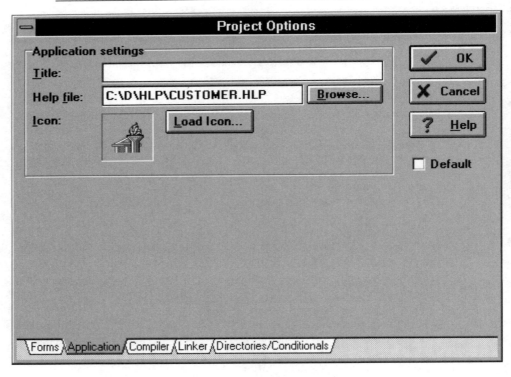

FIGURE 16–5 The Application Page of the Project Options Dialog Box

When this association is made (either in Design mode or at run-time), it indicates in which help file to search for help context numbers.

HelpContext property.   All controls in Delphi have a property named Help-Context. The HelpContext for a component corresponds to which page in the help file the user is taken to if they press the F1 key while that component has focus. In the help file, these context numbers point to a particular topic. In fact, the MAP numbers in our project file listing are the context numbers for our help file. For example, if a particular edit field had a help context of 3, and the orders topic in the help file was associated with 3, then the user would be taken to the orders topic in the help file if they pressed F1 while the edit field had focus. A help context number of 0 takes you to the Contents page of our help file.

```
[MAP]
#define inventory  2
#define voucher    4
#define order      3
#define Customer   1
```

By manipulating the help context numbers, you can control the granularity of your help. For example, you could create context sensitive help for every single edit field and control on your form, so that the user would get a different help screen for every control. However you could just as easily have a single help topic per form, and have all the help context numbers on all the forms components point to the single help page.

Component help.   You can also create custom help screens for the components that you write and merge them into the main Delphi help files. The merge utilities (Keyword Generate and HelpInst) can be found in the Delphi program group. You can create a custom component with its help file and use these merge utilities to *totally* integrate your component into the Delphi environment. You can install it on the component palette, and when the user chooses your component and presses F1, they will get your help file, exactly as if it were a built-in component.

This is yet another way that Delphi promotes true code reuse through components. The programmer who uses your component has no way of knowing whether it was a built-in component or a custom one.

CHAPTER **17**

DELPHI AND THE WINDOWS API

By now, you may have found that Delphi is the most comprehensive programming language you've ever encountered. The developers of the product took great pains to include not only those functions that end-users might expect to find in a general usage and database language, but also any which they found useful when developing the product. However, even with its wealth of predefined components and object properties and methods, you may eventually run into a requirement that it does not directly support.

If Delphi is missing some functional ability you're searching for, it may not really be a flaw in the language. After all, no language can do everything. And you need not give up hope. You can be consoled by the fact that Delphi is an extensible language capable of utilizing (and creating) the numerous DLLs (Dynamic Link Libraries) available from third party vendors as well as those libraries which make up Windows itself—the Windows Application Programming Interface.

STATIC LINKING—EXCESS BAGGAGE

External library functions can be incorporated into an application statically or dynamically. With a *static* incorporation, your language's compiler scans your code to find any references to external functions. When found, these functions are linked from their external libraries to your code and embedded into your code wherever you've used them. This static embedding process, also known as *early binding,* can greatly increase the size of your code. Some compilers embed not only the needed function(s) but the entire source library. More advanced compilers and linkers, like those used by Delphi and C++ developers, embed only the needed functions themselves. Either way, the needed functions become inextricable elements of your final product (Figure 17.1).

Static linking has a major drawback. Every one of your programs that uses a statically linked function carries a copy of that function around with it. The disk space designated to carrying statically linked code within each program can quickly add up. In the Windows environment, a typical commercial software program repeatedly utilizes a host of library calls. Clearly, duplication of code could begin to be a real problem in terms of disk space (Figure 17.2). What's more, in a multitasking environment like Windows, each program that uses the same statically linked routine loads a copy of it into memory. The overhead of juggling repeated instances of the same code in RAM is clearly inefficient and wasteful.

DYNAMIC LINKING—TRAVEL LIGHT

Fortunately, there is a more efficient way of linking your code to external functions. Instead of carrying multiple copies of a routine in each of your programs, you can share the same copy from a Dynamic Link Library created in the New Executable file format. Creators of DLLs encode the ability for their routines to be accessible to running Windows applications. This is known as *exporting* the routines. When Delphi compiles your code, it can track all of the references to external DLL functions and provide *dynamic* links to the containing external libraries (Figure 17.3). This is referred to as *importing* the routines.

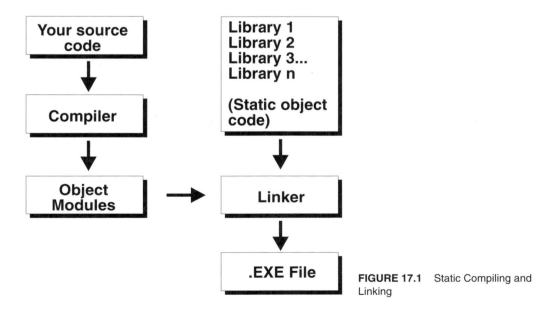

FIGURE 17.1 Static Compiling and Linking

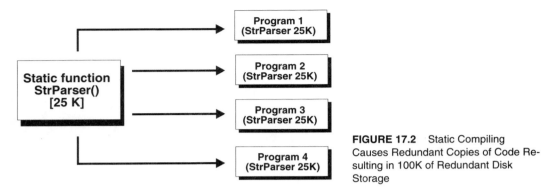

FIGURE 17.2 Static Compiling Causes Redundant Copies of Code Resulting in 100K of Redundant Disk Storage

When your program runs, if it encounters a reference to an external function, Windows dynamically loads the DLL so that your program can have access to all of the library's routines. Your Delphi application then creates a dynamic link, called a *far pointer* to the entry point within the DLL. The entry point can be determined by a named refer-

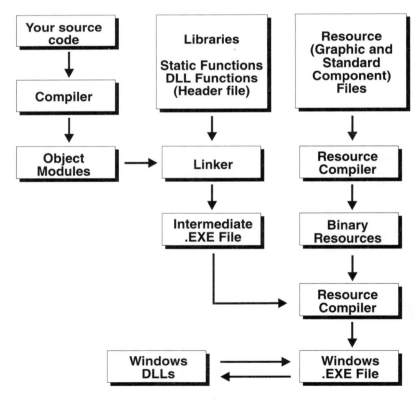

FIGURE 17.3 Dynamic Compiling and Linking

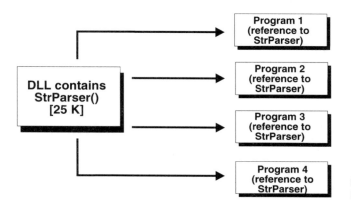

FIGURE 17.4 Dynamic Compiling and Linking Results in 25K of Storage

ence in your code, or by its ordinal position (*ordinal number*) in the DLL. The library address of the needed routine is then resolved dynamically and the appropriate function is linked to your code. Thus, multiple, redundant copies of the same routines are avoided on your disk drive and within RAM. In addition, several Windows applications can simultaneously use the same DLL on your hard drive (Figure 17.4).

THE API—JUST ANOTHER SET OF DLLS

The Windows API is a collection of compiled C language DLLs that help make up Windows itself. The functionality of Windows is completely dependent upon their existence in your Windows directories. Furthermore, these routines are available to anyone writing in a language that allows them to be declared as external library functions, including Delphi. In fact, all Windows applications including Delphi make extensive use of the API in order to participate in the Windows desktop environment. They all share the single copies of the DLLs found in your Window's system directory.

This does not mean, however, that implementing the API is necessarily simple (though as we shall see, the Delphi development team has simplified their use immensely). It does mean that you can extend Delphi to do almost anything that Windows can do by understanding and utilizing these libraries that are part and parcel of your operating environment. One of the first things you'll need to understand is how the API is organized.

Unlike other dynamic link libraries, the Windows API are not always found in files with a .DLL extension. The major libraries have .EXE extensions even though they are nothing more than compiled libraries. Table 17.1 shows just some of Windows API files that you will find on your system.

These and other DLLs provide over 500 functions that constitute Windows 3.1. When Delphi calls on an API function, Windows searches for the required library first in the current directory and then in your \windows and \windows\system directories. If the DLL is not found it then checks the directory for the executable file for the current task.

TABLE 17.1   Common Windows DLLs.

Windows DLL	General Description
GDI.EXE	The Graphics Device Interface library contains routines related to device output including functions for displaying fonts, metafiles, drawing coordinates and vectors, and working within display contexts (forms and printed output).
USER.EXE	This DLL handles all user-interface functions. It contains functions that provide Windows management as well as nondisplay routines for messages, cursors, timers, communications, and carets.
KERNEL	As its name implies, the KERNEL library contains low-level operating functions for memory management, resource handling, and multitask management. Though referenced as the KERNEL library, you won't see KERNEL.EXE but, instead, two files, KRNL286.EXE and KRNL386.EXE.
Printer libraries with .DRV extensions	Every printer manufacturer writes their own DLLs which provide printer setup and control routines.
LZEXPAND.DLL	Windows 3.1 routines provide file compression capabilities.
VER.DLL	Windows 3.1 routines provide software version control.
MMSYSTEM.DLL	The Multimedia library for Windows 3.1 includes extensions for sending control strings to multimedia devices including sound, MIDI music, animation, as well as video components. These are meant to replace the PC speaker functions found in the earlier SOUND.DLL.
KEYBOARD.DLL	Keyboard adaptability functions for converting various keyboard mappings to ASCII codes within Windows.
OLECLI.DLL and OLESVR.DLL	These libraries supply OLE 1.0 client and server functions to OLE 1.0 - compliant products. These two libraries have been replaced by the OLE 2.0 libraries DOCFILE.DLL, OLENLS.DLL, OLE2UTIL.DLL, STORAGE.DLL, COMPOBJ.DLL, OLE2PROX.DLL, OLEDISP.DLL COUNTOLE.DLL OLE2.DLL, and OLE2UI.DLL.

Next it searches the directories specified in your DOS path statements within your AUTOEXEC.BAT file. Lastly, Windows will search the directory map on a networked system. If Windows cannot find the library it will cause a "file not found" error.

DECLARE YOUR INTENTIONS

Your knowledge of Delphi's Object-Pascal already provides you with a good deal of understanding of the API. Delphi object properties often correspond closely to Windows object properties. Basically, you need to shift that knowledge into the API realm to take advantage of these tools.

Before you can utilize a function found in an API DLL, you must declare it. Declaring external functions can be a bit tricky. Basically, you're trying to create a procedure declaration statement in Pascal that can be understood in the host language of the DLL, usually some dialect of C. Most often, the only adjustment you'll have to make is replacing references to a C null-terminated string with a reference variable of the type Pchar. For example, the C language declaration for `GetPrivateProfileInt()` in KERNEL.EXE is:

```
WORD GetPrivateProfileInt(lpApplicationName, lpKeyName,
     nDefault, lpFileName)
```

WORD specifies that GetPrivateProfileInt returns an unsigned 16-bit value. The replaceable arguments with the Hungarian prefix *lp* are long pointers to null-terminated strings. The *n* prefix signifies a signed 16-bit integer. This declaration can be accomodated by Pascal programmers by:

```
function GetPrivateProfileInt(ApplicationName, KeyName:
     Pchar; Default: Integer; FileName: PChar): Word;
```

As we noted, the *lp* C strings have been replaced by Pchar types, and Pascal accomodates the Word return type.

GOOD THINGS COME IN WELL WRAPPED PACKAGES

Luckily, you don't have to declare every API function you need, because Delphi ships with almost all of the Windows API routines already declared. Borland's Delphi development team made extensive use of the API to allow Delphi to perform under Windows. They left their declarations in various Turbo Pascal Run-time Libraries under the \delphi\source\rtl\win directory on your hard drive. (N.B. Before you can look at this file you must have the VCL source code that comes with the Client Server version of Delphi, or you can purchase it separately from Borland).

The importance of these declarations cannot be overly stressed. These run-time libraries relieve you of the very tedious process of declaring and debugging API calls. The run-time library declarations act as "wrappers" for the external API functions which, in turn, relieve you of potential Bad DLL Calling Convention errors, Argument Count Mismatch errors, and possible General Protection Faults. Use the Windows API Help File that comes with Delphi for brief explanations of each declaration, and be sure to examine the various run-time library files.

For instance, WINAPI.PAS contains a host of type, constant, and function declarations. Let's take a look at a sample declaration for the GetVersion function. First, the function is declared in the interface section of the unit:

```
unit WinAPI;

{$S-}
interface

function GetVersion: Longint;
```

Then, the function is defined in the unit's implementation section:

```
implementation

{ KERNEL routines }

function GetVersion;        external 'KERNEL' index 3;
```

Here we see the function definition in the `implementation` section followed by the reserved word `external`. This tells the Delphi compiler that the function will be found in the external DLL whose name follows, that is `'KERNEL'`. Within that DLL `GetVersion` can be found at ordinal position 3 as specified by `index 3`. The specification of the ordinal position makes the creations of the dynamic link at run-time faster, however, the ordinal position may be specific to a specific version of a DLL. Because Microsoft has stabilized the versions of Window's KERNEL, in this instance it is safe to declare the position. For other DLLs that you create, purchase, or receive with parent products, be aware that updated versions of the DLL may differ in regard to the number and position of their internal functions. It is almost always safe to declare the function by its name which can be dynamically referenced in the DLL header's lookup table. Later versions of a DLL will most likely keep the same names within their internal lookup tables, but may not keep the same ordinal numbers.

You can find the ordinal numbers for functions in a DLL in the documentation for the DLL (if any), in the definition file (.DEF) of the DLL if you have access to it, or with a program like EXEHDR.EXE supplied with Microsoft C languages to view the header of the DLL file where the name-to-ordinal-number lookup table is kept.

GetVersion at Work

In the previous code snippets, we noted how the API function `GetVersion` was declared and defined by the Delphi development team. `GetVersion` returns a 32-bit flag containing bits which describe the Windows and DOS version currently running. The flag is returned to Delphi as a long integer whose individual bits must be "decoded" in order to determine the information `GetVersion` supplies. The low 16 bits of the 32-bit long integer contains the Windows version. The low byte contains the major version number (for example, 3 for Windows version 3.10) and the high byte contains the minor version as a two digit resolution decimal number (for example, 10 for Windows 3.10). The high 16 bits of the long integer contain the DOS version currently running. The high byte contains the major version number (for example, 6 for DOS 6.22) and the low byte contains the minor version as a two digit resolution decimal number (for example, 22 for DOS 6.22).

We could place these values into the text of an Edit box on a form by making the following assignments:

```
EditWinVersion.Text := IntToStr(LoByte(LoWord(GetVersion)))
    + '.' + IntToStr(HiByte(LoWord(GetVersion)));
```

```
EditDOSVersion.Text := IntToStr(HiByte(HiWord(GetVersion)))
       + '.' + IntToStr(LoByte(HiWord(GetVersion)));
```

More API from the Development Team

Note the use of the `HiByte`, `LoByte`, `HiWord`, and `LoWord` functions. These too can be found in WINAPI.PAS. The Delphi development team found them so useful that they left them in for our use!:

```
function LoWord(A: Longint): Word;
inline(
  $58/ { POP AX }
  $5A); { POP DX }

function HiWord(A: Longint): Word;
inline(
  $5A/ { POP DX }
  $58); { POP AX }

function LoByte(A: Word): Byte;
inline(
  $58/ { POP AX }
  $32/$E4); { XOR AH,AH }

function HiByte(A: Word): Byte;
inline(
  $58/ { POP AX }
  $8A/$C4/ { MOV AL,AH }
  $32/$E4); { XOR AH,AH }
```

Never mind, for the moment, how these work. (Borland's development team has written these particular DLL calls with Assembler language code so that they can be utilized more efficiently.) Just be thankful that the development team included them for your use. Let's examine how the 32-bit flag they're applied to is formulated.

Windows uses such flags for many of its operations. For instance, Windows retrieves information about your operating system with a 32-bit flag. Each of the bits (positions within the long integer) represent one aspect of your system. Armed with this information, you can make a call to the GetWinFlags API function to retrieve information about Windows configuration and system CPU and coprocessors. GetWinFlags would return a 32-bit flag which might look something like this:

```
10001000 10001010 10101011 01101101
```

Information is derived from the flag by employing bit-wise comparisons of each relevant position with actual values, or better yet, predefined constants that represent those values. When a bit-wise comparison is made, the flag and a mask are overlaid and an AND or an OR operator are applied. For example, if the flag in our example above

```
10001000 10001010 10101011 01101101
```

were overlaid using the AND operator with a mask whose value was

```
11110000 01111111 11111111 11111011
```

the resulting comparison would yield

```
10000000 00001010 10101011 01101001
```

The underlined values represent the conflicting bits whose coupling of TRUE (1) and FALSE (0) with the AND operator result in a FALSE bit value. If the same flag

```
10001000 10001010 10101011 01101101
```

were overlaid using an OR operator with a mask whose value was also

```
11110000 01111111 11111111 11111011
```

the resulting comparison would yield

```
11111000 01111111 11111111 11111111
```

Here, the underlined values represent the conflicting bits whose coupling of TRUE (1) and FALSE (0) with the OR operator result in a TRUE bit value.

WINAPI.PAS already contains many constant declarations for use as bit-wise comparison operators with the Windows API. For the function GetWinFlags, the following constants have been declared:

```
const
WF_PMODE      = $00000001; { Running in protected mode }
WF_CPU286     = $00000002; { System CPU is an 80286 }
WF_CPU386     = $00000004; { System CPU is an 80386 }
WF_CPU486     = $00000008; { System CPU is an 80486 }
WF_STANDARD   = $00000010; { Running in standard mode }
WF_ENHANCED   = $00000020; { Running in enhanced mode }
WF_CPU086     = $00000040; { System CPU is an 8086 }
WF_CPU186     = $00000080; { System CPU is an 80186 }
WF_LARGEFRAME = $00000100; { Windows EMS large-frame
                             configuration }
```

```
WF_SMALLFRAME = $00000200;  { Windows EMS small-frame
                              configuration }
WF_80X87      = $00000400;  { System contains a math
                              coprocessor }
WF_DPMI       = $80000000;  { Running in DOS protected mode }
```

Each constant has been assigned a hexadecimal number that denotes the constant's positional representation for the 32-bit flag returned by GetWinFlags. (Note also that, by tradition, constants for API usage are written in upper case.) Now, we can write code that compares the return flag of GetWinFlags with these constants and retrieves values from various positions within the flag. These comparisons could then be used to represent strings which are output to an Edit box that tells us what CPU our machine employs:

```
if (lngWinFlag and WF_CPU486) <> 0 then
     EditProcessor.Text := '80486 (+)'
else if (lngWinFlag and WF_CPU386) <> 0 then
     EditProcessor.Text := '80386'
else if (lngWinFlag and WF_CPU286) <> 0 then
     EditProcessor.Text := '80286'
else if (lngWinFlag and WF_CPU186) <> 0 then
     EditProcessor.Text := '80186'
else if (lngWinFlag and WF_CPU086) <> 0 then
     EditProcessor.Text := '8086';
```

Note that `WF_CPU486` represents both 486 and 586 processors. We've included API_RPT.DPR and its associated files for your use on the code disk with this book. The project uses just a few of the WINAPI.PAS declarations to generate a form with which you can determine important information about your system (Figure 17.5). You can use the form to display the information directly, or better yet, you could use similar calls to add information to an Errors Log table in a database system you're developing.

All of the procedures for the Windows Environment Report form are called by the Click event of the Report On Environment button:

```
procedure TForm_WindowsEnvironmentReport.ButtonReportClick
   (Sender: TObject);
var
   lngWinFlag : longint;
   strProcessor : string;
begin
   {GetFreeSpace returns the number of bytes free memory}
   Edit_GetFreeSpace.Text := IntToStr(GetFreeSpace(0) DIV
      1024) + ' KBytes';
   {GetFreeSystemResources returns the percentage of free
    GDI, USER and SYSTEM resources}
```

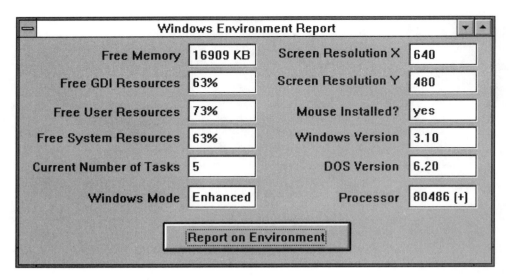

FIGURE 17.5   The Windows System Information Form

```
Edit_FreeGDI.Text := IntToStr(GetFreeSystemResources
   (GFSR_GDIRESOURCES)) + '%';
Edit_FreeUser.Text := IntToStr(GetFreeSystemResources
   (GFSR_USERRESOURCES)) + '%';
Edit_FreeSystem.Text := IntToStr(GetFreeSystemResources
   (GFSR_SYSTEMRESOURCES)) + '%';
{GetNumTasks returns the number of running tasks}
Edit_NumTasks.Text := IntToStr(GetNumTasks);
{GetSystemMetrics returns information about the Windows
 environment depending upon the index passed in}
Edit_ScreenX.Text := IntToStr(GetSystemMetrics
(SM_CXSCREEN));
Edit_ScreenY.Text := IntToStr(GetSystemMetrics
(SM_CYSCREEN));
if GetSystemMetrics(SM_MOUSEPRESENT) = 1 then
   Edit_MouseInstalled.Text := 'yes'
else
   Edit_MouseInstalled.Text := 'no';
{GetWinFlags returns a 32-bit flag containing bits which
 describe your Windows configuration and system CPU and
coprocessors}
lngWinFlag := GetWinFlags;
{if both types of an AND operator are of an integer type,
 the result is the common type of the two operands, thus
 we compare to 0}
if (lngWinFlag and WF_CPU486) <> 0 then
```

```
      Edit_Processor.Text := '80486 (+)'
   else if (lngWinFlag and WF_CPU386) <> 0 then
      Edit_Processor.Text := '80386'
   else if (lngWinFlag and WF_CPU286) <> 0 then
      Edit_Processor.Text := '80286'
   else if (lngWinFlag and WF_CPU186) <> 0 then
      Edit_Processor.Text := '80186'
   else if (lngWinFlag and WF_CPU086) <> 0 then
      Edit_Processor.Text := '8086';
   if (lngWinFlag and WF_STANDARD) <> 0 then
      Edit_WindowsMode.Text := 'Standard'
   else
      Edit_WindowsMode.Text := 'Enhanced';
   {GetVersion returns a 32-bit flag containing bits which
    describe the Windows and DOS version currently running}
   Edit_WindowsVersion.Text :=
      IntToStr(LoByte(LoWord(GetVersion))) + '.' +
      IntToStr(HiByte(LoWord(GetVersion)));
   Edit_DOSVersion.Text :=
      IntToStr(HiByte(HiWord(GetVersion))) + '.' +
      IntToStr(LoByte(HiWord(GetVersion)));
end;
```

I Do Declare . . .

You can write your own declarations for DLL functions that the Delphi development team hasn't already wrapped for you. See the chapter on Dynamic Link Library creation for the steps involved in creating your own DLLs and calling their functions from within your Delphi code.

A FEW LAST WORDS

If you find that you need to declare an external function in any DLL, you need to be very careful about your work habits. If you pass the wrong data type to a Windows DLL, you may receive a Bad DLL Calling Convention message or, worse yet, encounter a General Protection Fault message. Sometimes, Delphi will just ignore the bad call and not let you compile your project into an executable. The screen will flash and nothing will happen. However, in any of these cases, the Windows environment could become incrementally unstable, and repeated attempts to run your project could eventually cause your system to crash. WHENEVER you're working with the API or another DLL, be sure to save your work often, and if possible monitor your system resources with a third party utility.

CHAPTER 18

DYNAMIC LINK LIBRARIES (DLLs)

Dynamic Link Libraries (DLLs) are binary files in the NE (New Executable) format, which was designed by Microsoft (originally as part of the OS/2 project) to supplant the aging EXE file format from DOS. This means that DLLs are executable code, just like EXE files. Because Delphi can create executable files, it can also create DLLs. However, there are several issues surrounding DLLs which we will highlight before we discuss the semantics of DLL creation.

LIBRARY CONSTRUCTION

Programmers, like the practitioners of many fairly new occupations, frequently design the tools that they work with daily. Computer tools are different from simpler tools (like a carpenter's tools) in that a programmer can create an astounding array of complex tools using the same environment that he or she works in.

Why Create Libraries?

Libraries, like the library of code that makes up the VCL library, are created for several reasons, but especially to encapsulate commonly used code and to make it easy to update application features without having to recompile the application.

Commonly used code.   Programmers frequently find that they are writing the same code over and over to perform a particular task. These snippets are candidates for a library, where they can be written once and used as many times as necessary.

In fact, you should strive to create code that solves problems as generically as possible. The goal in software engineering is to create reuseable assets every time you write an application. If you can achieve this, it will take you less time to create subsequent applications, because some of the code will already be written. In fact, you will reach a point eventually where most of all new applications are already written and debugged, sitting in a library.

Dynamic Link Libraries are also useful to share common code between applications. If you have several applications that perform the same task, you can embed that task only once in a DLL and call it from as many different applications as you like. This means that the code will only be generated once, rather than having an additional copy of the same code for multiple applications.

Transparently update features.   Another nice feature of dynamic libraries (like DLLs) is the ability to update application features just by updating the DLL library. Unlike normal library files which are embedded into the application at compile and link time, dynamic libraries are called at run-time. This means that you can create a DLL that will be common to several programs and call the functions in the DLL rather than from within the application. Then, you can later make improvements to your DLL and, as long as the function names and parameters are the same, just replace the DLL. All your applications that use the DLL will immediately benefit. In fact, if you run a Delphi program under Windows95, you will automatically get the Windows95 "look and feel" for dialog boxes and other program elements because the code that implements those features are in an updated DLL.

DLL Limitations

Unfortunately, the Windows architecture was developed before object-oriented programming was widely used, and consequently, the DLL mechanism in Windows was never really designed to encapsulate objects, only functions and procedures.

Functions and procedures in DLLs.   The most common use for DLLs is to embed functions and procedures that might be called from multiple applications. As we stated above, this is one of the most useful features of DLLs. In fact, the entire Windows API is defined in terms of functions and procedures that can be called from a DLL. So, there is no restriction as to which Object-Pascal functions and procedures you can place in a DLL and call from a Delphi application. Because Delphi functions can now return any type (not just a scalar type as was previously the case), you aren't restricted as to which types you can return from a function call that resides in a DLL.

You do, however, have to be careful about memory allocated in a DLL and passed back to an application. The problem lies in how Windows allocates memory for applications. Because DLLs are viewed as a separate application by Windows, you cannot allocate memory inside a DLL and pass that memory back to the application via a pointer. This would cause your application to try to dereference a memory pointer that doesn't belong to the code segment that the application is defined in, and that is the definition of a

General Protection Fault (GPF) in Windows. A GPF occurs when an application tries to access memory that it doesn't own, and that is exactly the case we've just described. You can, however, allocate memory in an application, pass that memory to the DLL to fill with some value, then get it back. There is a "one-way" street in Windows that allows you to pass memory into a DLL and then get it back, but not the other way around.

So, you have to be careful about trying to pass memory that is owned by the DLL back to the application. The only "path" that is safe is to pass memory that has been allocated by the application to the DLL, let the DLL manipulate this memory (through a pointer), and pass the changed values back to the application.

Objects and forms in DLLs.   What you would like to be able to do is to place Object-Pascal classes in DLLs, and instantiate these objects from an application. Unfortunately, because of the architecture of DLLs, you cannot do this easily. If you allocate the memory for the object in the DLL and then try to use that object in a Delphi application, you would be violating the "one-way" rule whereby you cannot reference another application's memory, and you will get a General Protection Fault.

However, there is no restriction on using objects and, by extension, forms (which are after all just objects) in a DLL as long as they are allocated and destroyed within the DLL. So, you can create a DLL that instantiates a form, shows it, gets some information from the user, then destroys it all within the DLL, and then passes the information from the user back to the application that called the DLL. In fact, we will provide an example of this technique at the end of this chapter.

Notice that, because of this architectural limitation, you cannot raise an exception in a DLL and have it handled by your application. As discussed in the chapter on exception handling, exceptions are objects, and when an exception is raised, an object of that exception type is instantiated. This means that if you raise an exception in a DLL that isn't handled in the DLL, you will cause a General Protection Fault! In fact, you never want this to happen, so this is a legitimate use for the else clause of the **try ... except** block—you never want the exception to propagate out of the DLL.

Creating VBX Controls

VBX controls are components that were written (in C or Pascal) to be used in Visual Basic. Delphi can use VBX controls and can create VBX controls as well. A VBX is actually just a DLL with a different extension, and because Delphi can create DLLs, it can create VBXs as well. However, creating VBXs in Delphi is nontrivial and beyond the scope of this book. There have been numerous magazine articles instructing readers how to create VBXs in Borland Pascal 7.0 (the precursor to Delphi), and the same code will work in Delphi.

Actually, the only time you should create VBXs is for use in other products that support them (Visual Basic, dBASE for Windows, etc.). If you want to create reuseable components for Delphi, you should create Delphi components.

CREATING DLLS IN DELPHI

DLL creation in Delphi employs the same basic process as creating an application. Both are compiled as project files (with a DPR extension). However, application project files and DLL project files differ in a few ways.

Project File Changes

There are three changes that you have to make to a basic project file to convert it into a DLL project file. First, substitute the reserved word `program` at the top of the file with `library`. This will cause the compiled executable to be in the DLL format instead of the EXE format.

Secondly, remove the unit `Forms` from the `uses` clause—this unit is not needed in a DLL. This does not affect your ability to create forms in DLLs.

Next, add an `exports` clause before the `begin` at the end of the file. The exports clause specifies what functions this DLL will make visible to other applications. This function is actually implemented in a unit, but you must add the `exports` clause to the DLL project file.

Lastly, you must remove all of the code between the `begin` . . . `end` pair at the end of the file. Because this file will never be directly executed like an application; code at the bottom of the project file would be meaningless.

DLLs *export* a list of functions and procedures that they contain. Other applications don't know any details about the functions and procedures except their name, the parameters they accept, and their return values. This, incidentally, is a good example of the principle of information hiding, discussed in our chapters on software engineering and OOP theory. Because the programmer who uses the DLL can't get to the underlying implementation to take advantage of it, he is forced to use the well-published interface, which makes the code more modular and thus easier to develop and maintain.

To indicate that a function or procedure should be available for the DLL to call, you must add the word `export` to the end of the function definition. Here is an example:

```
Function GetDate(var theDate:TDateTime):boolean; export;
```

When the unit that contains this function is USEd by a DLL project file with this function listed in its export clause, then this function can be called from the DLL.

Here is an example of an application project file:

```
program Cal_app;

uses
  Forms,
  Fcal in 'FCAL.PAS' {Form_calendar};

{$R *.RES}
```

```
begin
  Application.CreateForm(TForm_calendar, Form_calendar);
  Application.Run;
end.
```

Here is an example of the above code as a DLL project file:

```
library Cal_dll; { library instead of program }

uses { no Forms unit in the uses clause }
  Fcal in 'FCAL.PAS' {Form_calendar};

{$R *.RES}
exports { new exports clause }
  GetDate;

begin
  { no code between begin and end }
end.
```

Calling a DLL.   To call a DLL from a Delphi application, you must provide a forward declaration of the function or procedure, providing the parameters and the return values. You must also specify what DLL the function or procedure resides in.

Here is a sample forward declaration:

```
Function GetDate( var theDate : TDateTime ) : boolean; far;
external 'CAL_DLL';
```

In this example, the function `GetDate` takes one var parameter `theDate` and returns a Boolean result. The `far` keyword is required to indicate that the function is not in this application's code segment. The `external` keyword is followed by the name of the DLL in which the function resides. After making this declaration, you can call this function with no further work.

Form Wrapping

If you want to embed a form in a DLL (in other words, call a form in a DLL from an application), you have to take some precautions. We have already discussed the architectural limit of Windows DLLs, which prevents an application from instantiating an object that resides in a DLL. However, this doesn't mean that you can't embed a form in a DLL.

You must "wrap" the form creation and destruction within the DLL, which means that you must create a function or procedure that creates a new instance of a form, instantiates it, and eventually handles its destruction. By taking care of all form access through the internal function or procedure, you never have to worry about violating memory boundaries. In the following case study, we create a function GetDate that creates a form, gets the user's response, and closes the form all from within a DLL. To show the form from another application and get the returned date, you only have to call the GetDate function, which will return the date that the user chose.

Case Study: A Common Date Entry Dialog

The best candidate for a DLL function or procedure is some generic application element that could potentially be used from a variety of different applications. Also, any interfaces that you want to standardize can be encapsulated within a DLL, and called from every program that needs that service.

The example presented here is a common date entry dialog. The need to input a date occurs frequently in applications, so this is a good candidate for DLL wrapping. Figure 18.1 is a screen shot of the calendar form.

However, to invoke this dialog, you must call the GetDate function from the CAL_DLL DLL. The GetDate function opens the form and gets the user's response, which it passes back as a return value.

Before you can call a DLL, you must create it! Here is the project file to create the CAL_DLL DLL:

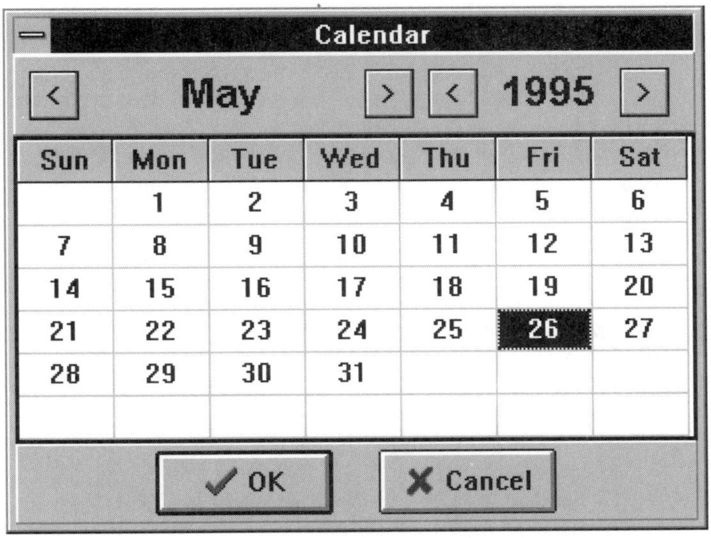

FIGURE 18.1 The Calendar Form

```
library Cal_dll;

uses
  Fcal in 'FCAL.PAS' {Form_calendar};

{$R *.RES}
exports
  GetDate;

begin
end.
```

Notice the changes to the project file syntax. Incidentally, you should name your DLLs something unusual or cryptic. Windows is not very intelligent about how it searches for DLLs, and if your DLL is named the same as another, it might be called by mistake. Or, one could get overwritten during the installation of the other, and the old program will no longer work. So, the more unusual your name, the less likely someone else will come up with the same name and interfere with your application.

Following is the source code for the form that is called. Especially notice the Get-Date function which is declared in the `interface` section as an external function.

```
unit Fcal;

interface

uses
  SysUtils, WinTypes, WinProcs, Messages, Classes, Graphics,
Controls,Forms, Dialogs, Grids, ExtCtrls, Buttons, StdCtrls,
Calendar;

type
  TForm_calendar = class(TForm)
    Panel_SpeedBar: TPanel;
    Label_MonthName: TLabel;
    Label_YearName: TLabel;
    SpeedButton_PrevMonth: TSpeedButton;
    SpeedButton_NextMonth: TSpeedButton;
    SpeedButton_PrevYear: TSpeedButton;
    SpeedButton_NextYear: TSpeedButton;
    ScrollBox_FormBody: TScrollBox;
    Panel_bottomButtons: TPanel;
    Calendar_theCalendar: TCalendar;
    BitBtn_OK: TBitBtn;
    BitBtn_Cancel: TBitBtn;
    procedure FormActivate(Sender: TObject
    procedure SpeedButton_PrevMonthClick(Sender: TObject);
```

```
    procedure SpeedButton_NextMonthClick(Sender: TObject);
    procedure SpeedButton_PrevYearClick(Sender: TObject);
    procedure SpeedButton_NextYearClick(Sender: TObject);
    procedure BitBtn_CancelClick(Sender: TObject);
    procedure BitBtn_OKClick(Sender: TObject);
  private
    { Private declarations }
  public
    { Public declarations }
  end;


function GetDate( var theDate : TDateTime ) : boolean;
export;


implementation

{$R *.DFM}


function NameOfMonth( Month : word ) : string;
const
  Names : array[1..12] of string = ('January', 'Feburary',
'March', 'April', 'May', 'June', 'July', 'August',
'September', 'October', 'November', 'December');
begin
  if (Month > 0) and (Month <= 12) then
    Result := Names[Month]
  else
    Result := '';
end;


procedure TForm_calendar.FormActivate(Sender: TObject);
var
  s : string;
begin
  Label_MonthName.caption := NameOfMonth(
        Calendar_theCalendar.Month );
  str( Calendar_theCalendar.Year:4, s );
  Label_YearName.caption := s
end;


procedure TForm_calendar.SpeedButton_PrevMonthClick(Sender:
TObject);
var
  s : string;
begin
  Calendar_theCalendar.PrevMonth;
  Label_MonthName.caption := NameOfMonth(
        Calendar_theCalendar.Month );
```

```
    if (Calendar_theCalendar.Month = 12) or
       (Calendar_theCalendar.Month = 1 ) then
    begin
      str( Calendar_theCalendar.Year:4, s );
      Label_YearName.Caption := s
    end;
end;

procedure TForm_calendar.SpeedButton_NextMonthClick(Sender:
TObject);
var
  s : string;
begin
  Calendar_theCalendar.NextMonth;
  Label_MonthName.caption := NameOfMonth(
      Calendar_theCalendar.Month );
  if (Calendar_theCalendar.Month = 12) or
     (Calendar_theCalendar.Month = 1 ) then
  begin
    str( Calendar_theCalendar.Year:4, s );
    Label_YearName.Caption := s
  end;
end;

procedure TForm_calendar.SpeedButton_PrevYearClick(Sender:
TObject);
var
  s : string;
begin
  Calendar_theCalendar.PrevYear;
  str( Calendar_theCalendar.Year:4, s );
  Label_YearName.caption := s
end;

procedure TForm_calendar.SpeedButton_NextYearClick(Sender:
TObject);
var
  s : string;
begin
  Calendar_theCalendar.NextYear;
  str( Calendar_theCalendar.Year:4, s );
  Label_YearName.caption := s
end;

procedure TForm_calendar.BitBtn_CancelClick(Sender: TObject);
begin
  ModalResult := mrCancel;
end;
```

```
procedure TForm_calendar.BitBtn_OKClick(Sender: TObject);
begin
  ModalResult := mrOK;
end;


function GetDate( var theDate : TDateTime ) : boolean;
var
  form_Calendar : Tform_Calendar;
begin
  form_Calendar := Tform_Calendar.create( Application );
  try
    if form_Calendar.ShowModal = mrOK then
    begin
      theDate:=
          form_calendar.calendar_theCalendar.calendarDate;
      Result := true
    end
    else
      Result := false;
  finally
    form_calendar.free
  end; {try}
end; {function}


end.
```

The GetDate function is actually implemented at the bottom of the unit. Notice that it creates its own variable of type Tform_Calendar. Then, GetDate creates a new instance of the form and shows it as a modal form. Recall that modal forms prevent the user from switching focus to any other part of the application. Also notice that as soon as we instantiated the form, we started a try . . . finally block. This is important to ensure that even if something happened within this function that raised an exception, the resource allocated to the form object would be released properly, preventing a resource leak.

The rest of the code checks to see if the user terminated the dialog by clicking OK or Cancel by checking the value of ModalResult.

Following is the DFM file for the form:

```
object Form_calendar: TForm_calendar
  Left = 199
  Top = 99
  BorderStyle = bsDialog
  Caption = 'Calendar'
  ClientHeight = 240
  ClientWidth = 342
  Font.Color = clWindowText
```

```
  Font.Height = -13
  Font.Name = 'System'
  Font.Style = []
  PixelsPerInch = 96
  OnActivate = FormActivate
  TextHeight = 16
  object Panel_SpeedBar: TPanel
    Left = 0
    Top = 0
    Width = 342
    Height = 41
    Align = alTop
    TabOrder = 0
    object Label_MonthName: TLabel
      Left = 40
      Top = 8
      Width = 129
      Height = 24
      Alignment = taCenter
      AutoSize = False
      Caption = 'Label_MonthName'
      Font.Color = clBlack
      Font.Height = -21
      Font.Name = 'Arial'
      Font.Style = [fsBold]
      ParentFont = False
    end
    object Label_YearName: TLabel
      Left = 240
      Top = 8
      Width = 57
      Height = 24
      Alignment = taCenter
      AutoSize = False
      Caption = 'Label1'
      Font.Color = clBlack
      Font.Height = -21
      Font.Name = 'Arial'
      Font.Style = [fsBold]
      ParentFont = False
    end
    object SpeedButton_PrevMonth: TSpeedButton
      Left = 8
      Top = 8
      Width = 25
      Height = 25
      Caption = '<'
      OnClick = SpeedButton_PrevMonthClick
```

```
    end
    object SpeedButton_NextMonth: TSpeedButton
      Left = 176
      Top = 8
      Width = 25
      Height = 25
      Caption = '>'
      OnClick = SpeedButton_NextMonthClick
    end
    object SpeedButton_PrevYear: TSpeedButton
      Left = 208
      Top = 8
      Width = 25
      Height = 25
      Caption = '<'
      OnClick = SpeedButton_PrevYearClick
    end
    object SpeedButton_NextYear: TSpeedButton
      Left = 304
      Top = 8
      Width = 25
      Height = 25
      Caption = '>'
      OnClick = SpeedButton_NextYearClick
    end
  end
  object ScrollBox_FormBody: TScrollBox
    Left = 0
    Top = 41
    Width = 342
    Height = 158
    Align = alClient
    TabOrder = 1
    object Calendar_theCalendar: TCalendar
      Left = 0
      Top = 0
      Width = 340
      Height = 156
      Align = alClient
      StartOfWeek = 0
      TabOrder = 0
      UseCurrentDate = False
      OnDblClick = BitBtn_OKClick
    end
  end
  object Panel_bottomButtons: TPanel
    Left = 0
    Top = 199
```

```
    Width = 342
    Height = 41
    Align = alBottom
    TabOrder = 2
    object BitBtn_OK: TBitBtn
      Left = 70
      Top = 4
      Width = 89
      Height = 33
      TabOrder = 0
      OnClick = BitBtn_OKClick
      Kind = bkOK
    end
    object BitBtn_Cancel: TBitBtn
      Left = 182
      Top = 4
      Width = 89
      Height = 33
      TabOrder = 1
      OnClick = BitBtn_CancelClick
      Kind = bkCancel
    end
  end
end
```

Figure 18.2 is an example application that demonstrates calling the DLL.

Next to the prompt for a date, there is a speed button which will show a calendar for data entry. Here is the code for the button's OnClick event:

```
procedure TForm1.SpeedButton1Click(Sender: TObject);
var
  ReturnDate : TDateTime;
begin
  if GetDate( ReturnDate ) then
    Edit_date.text := datetostr( ReturnDate )
  else
    Edit_date.text := ";
end;
```

This event handler calls the GetDate function in the DLL, which passes back the current date in the ReturnDate parameter and returns true if the user clicked OK. However, if the user clicked Cancel, GetDate would return false, and the text value for the entry field would be reset to an empty string.

Here is the application project file for the test program:

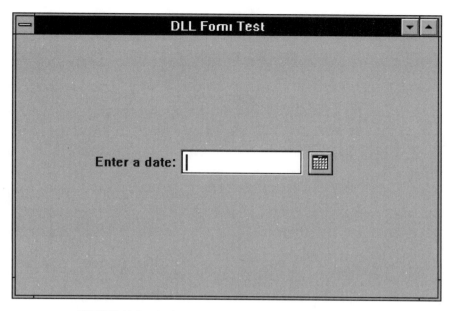

FIGURE 18.2   An Application Calling our DLL in Design View

```pascal
program Dll_test;

uses
  Forms,
  Fcaltest in 'FCALTEST.PAS' {Form1};

{$R *.RES}

begin
  Application.CreateForm(TForm1, Form1);
  Application.Run;
end.
```

Here is the Object-Pascal source for the project's form:

```pascal
unit Fcaltest;

interface

uses
  SysUtils, WinTypes, WinProcs, Messages, Classes, Graphics,
  Controls,Forms, Dialogs, Buttons, StdCtrls;
```

```
type
  TForm1 = class(TForm)
    Label_prompt: TLabel;
    Label3: TLabel;
    Label_theResult: TLabel;
    SpeedButton1: TSpeedButton;
    Edit_Date: TEdit;
    procedure SpeedButton1Click(Sender: TObject);
  private
    { Private declarations }
  public
    { Public declarations }
  end;

var
  Form1: TForm1;

implementation

{$R *.DFM}
Function GetDate(var theDate : TDateTime) : boolean; far;
external 'CAL_DLL';

procedure TForm1.SpeedButton1Click(Sender: TObject);
var
  ReturnDate : TDateTime;
begin
  if GetDate( ReturnDate ) then
    Edit_date.text := datetostr( ReturnDate )
  else
    Edit_date.text := ";
end;

end.
```

Notice in particular the forward declaration of the function name and type, as well as the DLL name in which it resides. The function is then called as a normal function. Here is the DFM file for the above project:

```
object Form1: TForm1
  Left = 200
  Top = 99
  Width = 435
  Height = 300
  Caption = 'DLL Form Test'
```

```
        Font.Color = clWindowText
        Font.Height = -13
        Font.Name = 'System'
        Font.Style = []
        PixelsPerInch = 96
        TextHeight = 16
        object Label_prompt: TLabel
          Left = 80
          Top = 124
          Width = 82
          Height = 16
          Caption = 'Enter a date:'
        end
        object Label3: TLabel
          Left = 216
          Top = 160
          Width = 4
          Height = 16
        end
        object Label_theResult: TLabel
          Left = 224
          Top = 160
          Width = 4
          Height = 16
        end
        object SpeedButton1: TSpeedButton
          Left = 296
          Top = 120
          Width = 25
          Height = 25
          Glyph.Data = {}
          NumGlyphs = 2
          OnClick = SpeedButton1Click
        end
        object Edit_Date: TEdit
          Left = 168
          Top = 120
          Width = 121
          Height = 24
          TabOrder = 0
        end
      end
end
```

As you can see, it is very easy to create DLLs in Delphi. It would be nice if DLLs were robust enough to allow classes to be embedded in them, but they are still quite useful in some situations. For example, the sample DLL above could potentially be used by many applications, any time a date was required. This means that the code to get dates from the user only resides in one location (the DLL) instead of being duplicated in every application. It also means that your applications' interfaces will all be more similar, because all the applications are using the same interface elements. However, be wary of the constraints that the Windows architecture places on the functionality of DLLs as object-oriented components.

CHAPTER 19

SIMPLE COMPONENT CREATION

One of the huge advantages that Delphi enjoys over competing products is the ability to create components using Object-Pascal. VBX controls are a step in the right direction for users of Visual Basic and dBASE for Windows (and many other products that now support VBX controls), but their primary disadvantage is that they must be written in another language (usually C or Pascal). Delphi is the first environment that makes it easy to write custom controls without going elsewhere.

Delphi consists of what is known as a Component Based Architecture, meaning that almost every nontrivial action is accomplished through components. For example, all database manipulation is performed through components rather than form properties. This architecture along with the ease with which programmers can create new components is revolutionary. Delphi is a big step toward what has been talked about for years but never seems to become a reality: truly reuseable code. The marriage of objects and components means that you can treat components as completely encapsulated "black boxes" that do some useful work, which is one of the great advantages of object-oriented programming. Because components have such a well-published interface to the Delphi design environment, it is easy for someone who knows nothing about creating components to still use them very productively.

In fact, there are really two classes of users of Delphi: component users and component writers. Component users are those programmers who are mostly concerned with rapid application development, or those who would rather not delve into the intricacies of component creation. The other class of users are those who can see truly generic solutions to problems, and can abstract these solutions into reusable components.

Fortunately, Delphi will allow you to get your feet wet before you plunge in over your head. This chapter deals with creating a simple component, and provides the steps needed for you to immediately create your own simple components. But first, let's discuss the types of components that you can create in Delphi.

TYPES OF CUSTOM COMPONENTS

There are roughly three types of custom components in Delphi. The first is a component that is basically one of the built-in components with some default property values set. This is the type of component that we are going to create in this chapter. The second type is a component that adds new properties that weren't in the parent component. The third is a component that adds properties and events to a built-in component or creates a component from scratch by inheriting directly from the TComponent class. There are a lot of issues involved in writing the two more advanced types of components. However, creating the first type is very easy.

Components as Units and Classes

Components are really just objects which are created from a component class. For example, you may be accustomed to dealing with DBNavigator1, which is an instance of the TDBNavigator class. Thus, to create a new component class, we can inherit from an existing one. Remember, whenever you inherit from another class you automatically receive all the properties and methods that that parent class has. To create a simple component you have to inherit from an existing class and set some default values for the properties.

Of course, in Delphi, classes are generally kept in units, and component classes are no different. When you create new components, you should put them in their own unit file and, when an application needs to use your component, include the unit name in the project's uses clause.

Let's enumerate the steps required to create one.

STEPS TO CREATE A SIMPLE COMPONENT

These steps walk you through the creation of a simple component. Even if you don't completely understand the code that is generated, you can follow these general guidelines to make components of your own. The more often you do it, the more sense it will make.

Make a Skeleton with the Component Expert

The first step to create a simple component is to actually generate the unit file that the component will reside in. Fortunately, Delphi handles this chore with the Component Expert (Figure 19.1), which is available under the file menu.

The Component Expert allows you to specify the new component's name (which should start with a "T", because you are creating a new type). You then specify what component you want to inherit from. In the case of simple components, you want to in-

FIGURE 19.1   Delphi's Component Expert Dialog

herit from the component whose properties you want to provide default values for. Lastly, you can specify what tab to put the component under within the Delphi environment. If the tab doesn't exist, Delphi will automatically create it for you.

After you have filled in the appropriate values, Delphi generates a unit file:

```
unit Unit2;

interface

uses
   SysUtils, WinTypes, WinProcs, Messages, Classes,Graphics,
   Controls,Forms, Dialogs;

type
   TTestComponent = class(TComponent)
   private
     { Private declarations }
   protected
     { Protected declarations }
   public
     { Public declarations }
   published
     { Published declarations }
   end;

procedure Register;

implementation
```

```
procedure Register;
begin
  RegisterComponents('Custom', [TTestComponent]);
end;

end.
```

Notice that the Component Expert has created a class skeleton for you, based on the component that you are inheriting from (in this case, TComponent). The Component Expert also takes care of installing your new component on the component palette with the `Register` procedure. In this example, it will place the component named TTestComponent on the Custom page of the component palette.

Change the Unit Name

The first step after creating the skeleton with the Component Expert is to give the component a useful name. Notice that the default name of the component in this case is Unit2, which is not very descriptive. Go to the top of the unit and change the unit name to something that makes sense for your component. Also, save the unit under its new name using the **File | Save As** command.

As an aside, you should come up with a naming scheme for all the files that Delphi produces so that it is easier to maintain and catalog them. We suggest that you preface all component unit files with a "c", all form unit files with an "f", all nonform units with a "u", and all projects with no special first letter. This way, you can look at the name of the file and tell what it is. This is especially handy in Delphi because all the files except the project files are .PAS files.

Override the Constructor

If you were going to set the default values programmatically for a component, you could do so in the constructor for the component. In other words, as soon as the component is constructed, set the values that you want. So, to set the default values for your custom component, you should override its constructor. By overriding the constructor you are writing the constructor code for the component yourself. Syntactically, go to the class definition and place the following code under the `public` keyword:

```
constructor Create( AOwner : TComponent ); override;
```

The entire class for your custom component definition should now look like this (assuming that your new component is named TCustomClass and you are inheriting from TComponent):

```
type
  TCustomClass = class(TComponent)
  private
    { Private declarations }
```

```
protected
  { Protected declarations }
public
  { Public declarations }
  constructor Create(AOwner : TComponent ); override;
published
  { Published declarations }
end;
```

Placing the constructor under `public` ensures that everyone who uses this class can properly call it. All constructors look the same—the `constructor` keyword, followed by the name `Create` (which takes one parameter of type TComponent), followed by `override`. You **MUST** follow the constructor definition with override to alert Delphi that you are overriding the built-in constructor.

Implement Your Constructor

Now that you have told Delphi that you are going to override the constructor, you have to actually write the new constructor! Don't worry, it's very simple for these types of components. You essentially have to handle two things: Make sure you call the inherited constructor and set your default values.

To create your constructor, go to the implementation section of the unit file and declare a new procedure:

```
constructor Create( AOwner : TComponent );
begin
end;
```

This creates the shell of the new constructor. We will add to it shortly. Notice that you cannot place the override directive here in the implementation section—it only belongs in the class definition.

Call the inherited constructor.   All the components in Delphi have some constructor code that already exists. It does things like allocate storage for the component, set some values, etc. It is the constructor that sets up the component's eventual behavior, both in Design mode and at run-time. The point is that you have no way of knowing what code the constructor of the component that you are inheriting from does, and fortunately you don't have to know. Delphi has a mechanism that allows you to call the parent's constructor from within one of the components that inherits from it. The syntax is:

```
inherited Create( AOwner );
```

This is the only code that you have to place in your constructor to call the parent's constructor, which will take care of all those hidden details of setting the component up. This is what your constructor implementation should look like now:

```
constructor Create( AOwner : TComponent );
begin
    inherited Create( AOwner );
end;
```

It is extremely important that you call the inherited constructor as the first thing you do in your new constructor! If you don't, you are almost guaranteed to generate a General Protection Fault. This must always be the first line of code in the constructor of your custom components.

Specify your customizations.   Once you have called the inherited constructor, you are free to make assignments to the properties of your new component to customize it. For example, for your new component, suppose you wanted to set a default Caption of "MY component" and set its visible property to default to false:

```
constructor Create( AOwner : TComponent );
begin
    inherited Create( AOwner );
    caption := "MY component";
    visible := false
end;
```

Once you have called the inherited constructor, you are free to manipulate the component with the same code that you would use at run-time.

All you are really doing is providing some code for Delphi to execute as it creates the component. As you can see, by using the Component Expert and following these guidelines, it is fairly straightforward to create components that have some default properties.

Install Your Component

Once you have your component done, you need to install it into the component palette with all the other components. To install a new component, go to **Options | Install Components . . .** , which will lead to the dialog shown in Figure 19.2.

The default library name is COMPLIB.DCL, and the default path is specified. However, when you add a component, it will add the path to your component to the Search path automatically. Once you click on the Add button, you get a dialog which asks for the module name. Enter the name of your unit file and click OK. Delphi will determine what component classes are in the unit (if it is already compiled) and add it to the list on the right. Now, just click OK. You will see Delphi recompile and relink the library, and shortly you will see the new component appear on whatever page of the component palette you've specified. You can now use your Custom component exactly as you use the other components in the palette.

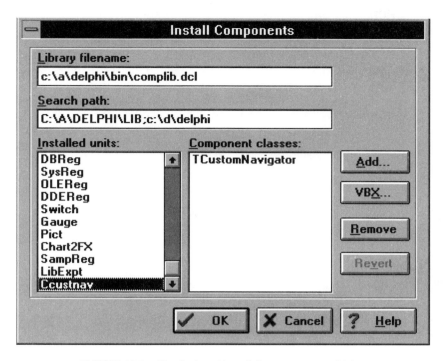

FIGURE 19.2 The Options | Install Components . . . Dialog

Incidentally, you can also create help for your components and merge your help files with the Delphi help files (using some supplied utilities) so that whenever a user has your component selected and presses F1, your help for that component will appear.

CASE STUDY: COMPONENT CREATION

You saw the steps necessary in the last section to create your own component. In this section, we are actually going to build a small sample component, following those guidelines.

The DBNavigator is a very nice control, and you will find that you use it a lot. However, the current defaults for the DBNavigator have it appear with all the buttons visible and with ShowHints off. If you have users that don't want to deal with the extra buttons (or don't need to do anything except browse through the data), you have to drop the DBNavigator on the form and change the VisibleButtons property every time you use it. Also, you will frequently want to have the hints (tool tips) turned on to make it easier for your users. Both of these processes can be accomplished easily enough in the Form designer, but you are likely to find yourself setting the same properties again and again. If that is the case, you have a perfect candidate for a simple custom component.

Below is the complete source code for a DBNavigator component whose properties mentioned above are defaulted to the new requirements. It was created by the Component Expert, so most of the code was placed in the file for us by Delphi. Notice that we specified in the Component Expert that it be placed on the "Custom" page of the component palette. You can see in the `Register` procedure below that this unit registers one component named `TCustomNavigator` and places it on the Custom page. If the custom page doesn't exist yet, Delphi will add it automatically.

```
unit ccustnav;

interface

uses
  SysUtils, WinTypes, WinProcs, Messages, Classes,
  Graphics, Controls, Forms, Dialogs, ExtCtrls,
  DBCtrls;

type
  TCustomNavigator = class(TDBNavigator)
  private
    { Private declarations }
  protected
    { Protected declarations }
  public
    { Public declarations }
    constructor Create( AOwner : TComponent ); override;
  published
    { Published declarations }
  end;

procedure Register;

implementation

procedure Register;
begin
  RegisterComponents('Custom', [TCustomNavigator]);
end;

constructor TCustomNavigator.Create( AOwner : TComponent );
begin
  inherited create( AOwner );
  VisibleButtons := [nbFirst, nbPrior, nbNext, nbLast];
  ShowHint := true
end;
end.
```

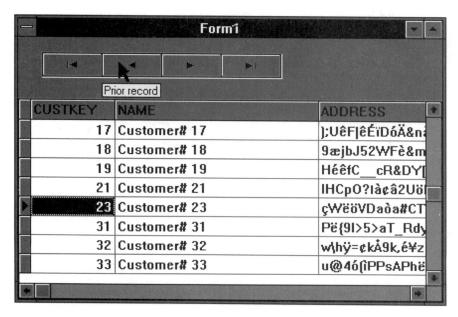

FIGURE 19.3 TCustomNavigator on a Running Form

First, notice that we changed the unit name to CCUSTNAV, which follows our naming scheme of placing a "c" as the first letter of the component name. Next, we created our new class TCustomNavigator by inheriting from TDBNavigator, which means that our new class now has every property and method that the TDBNavigator class has.

We then placed the constructor override statement in the class definition under public, and we specified the override directive. Next, we defined the new constructor and inserted it in the implementation section. Of course, the first thing we did in the constructor code was to call the inherited constructor. Then, we specified values for the VisibleButtons set (it is a set which determines which buttons will appear; in this case we filled the set with just the values we wanted) and we set the ShowHint property to true.

Figure 19.3 is a screen shot of our TCustomNavigator on a running form. We didn't have to specify that only these buttons show—it was like that when it was dropped on the form. Also, in the figure you will see one of the ToolTips for the Prior button. The ShowHints property defaulted to ON because of our Custom component specifications.

Component creation can be as simple and useful as our example. Whenever you find yourself setting the same property values or repeating the same coding processes from application to application, think component creation and save yourself hours of work.

CHAPTER 20

CREATING NEW COMPONENTS

One of the great advantages that Delphi has over competing visual design environments is the ability to extend the Component Library in a seamless and consistent way by allowing the user to create his or her own components. Because the VCL takes advantage of OOP principles, it is easy to create very powerful components by basing them on existing components. Delphi allows you to change some of the functions of a component while leaving the remainder encapsulated (that is, good information hiding).

This chapter is an overview of component creation. However, this is a large topic (there is an entire Delphi manual devoted to it—the *Component Writer's Guide*), and this material shouldn't be considered a substitute for it. Instead, we will highlight some important issues that revolve around component creation as it pertains to OOP theory and practice.

As you will see, the hardest part of creating a component is not writing the code to implement it, but rather understanding how it should be designed. The Delphi environment makes it very easy to create your component once you have decided what it will do and how it should do it.

ESTABLISH THE ABSTRACTION

The first step in component creation, as in all design based on OOP theory, is to *establish the abstraction*. Something is always being in a computer program, and OOP makes it easier to make realistic models. So, the first step is to determine how you are going to create your classes to most closely model the abstraction you have in mind.

Toolset Abstraction Revisited

We discussed toolset abstraction in the chapter on OOP Design. This type of class creation creates tools that aid in the construction of applications, such as form classes and button classes.

The main emphasis in Delphi is on toolset abstraction. The VCL is entirely a toolset abstraction. This is the type of modeling that is easiest to accomplish when creating components. Because of the nature of VCL, whenever you create a new component that extends a current VCL component, you are writing at the toolset abstraction level.

Domain Abstraction Revisited

We also discussed domain abstraction in the chapter on OOP Design. Domain abstraction involves building classes that model real world objects. For example, domain abstraction would govern the creation of a Customer object and an Orders object.

Most of the emphasis in Delphi is on toolset abstraction. However, this shouldn't deter you from still using domain abstraction whenever possible. For example, if you keep customer data in a local database file, you want whatever rules you have determined (that is, picture clauses and validations) to be enforced in every form that accesses the data. You could place a Table component representing the Customer table on all the forms that access customer data and set all the Table and Field properties by hand. However, the better way to handle this is to inherit from the Table component and create a CustomerTable component. Within the CustomerTable component, create your own Field objects, and attach the appropriate code to them. Then, on every form that needs access to the Customer table, use the CustomerTable component instead. All your business rules are encapsulated within the Table component, and you only have to write and maintain that code in one place.

Identifying Needed Components

The major work in component creation is determining what components to create. You should think of all functionality in a Delphi application as being encapsulated within components, and all the generic code that you write should be componentized, if possible.

Anytime you discover yourself using the same components and setting the same properties again and again you should realize that you have found a good candidate for a component. An example of that dilemma is in the chapter on simple component creation. You can also create components that extend an existing component to add some functionality; for example, a DateEdit component, which only receives date values. Another example is at the end of this chapter and creates a Table component that gives the user a visual indication of what mode he or she is in.

COMPONENT CREATION STEPS

Components are new object classes derived, at minimum, from the TComponent class. The TComponent class encapsulates the ability for the component to be placed on the component palette, and to have its properties available for the Object Inspector at design time. This is one of the advantages of encapsulation and information hiding—you never have to worry about how that code works to create components. Those abilities are in the base class, and invisible to the writer of the component.

New Properties

Properties are the values that you can set through the object inspector. Remember, when you define classes, the published scoping designation allows the items that are in the published group to be visible (and modifiable) at design time. To create a new property, you have to declare it within the published section of the class. However, the value that the property sets should be a private variable. Here is the syntax for declaring a property:

```
property DisabledColor : TColor read FDisabledColor write
FDisabledColor;
```

The `property` keyword indicates that it is a property, and it is followed by the property's name. This is the name that will appear in the Object Inspector. Following the name is the type of the property, which can be any valid Object-Pascal type. In fact, the Object Inspector is smart enough to recognize property types, and will show them in the most appropriate manner. For example, for a TColor property (or any enumerated type), the Object Inspector will show the possible values in a list and allow double clicking to toggle between all the available values.

Next, the reserved word `read` is followed by either a variable name or a routine name, and the reserved word `write` is followed by either a variable name or a routine name. Whenever the user changes the value of a property or needs to read the value of a property, the read and write indicators determine how the information is handled. If there is only a variable name following `read` or `write`, then the value of the variable is passed on. However, if there is a routine following the `read` or `write`, that routine will execute. This follows the object-oriented design principle of Get/Set routines. We have suggested that you should never directly access object attributes by reading or writing. Rather, you should use a routine to Get the value when you need it and another to Set the value when you want to change it. This technique offers good information hiding, because you would be free to change the underlying implementation of the class without changing the Get/Set routines, and thereby improve the underlying class.

Delphi has this Get/Set functionality built into it. For Read (Get) routines, you can write a function that returns the type of the property (note that Pascal functions can now return any type). For Write (Set) routines, you can write a procedure that takes a single var parameter of the same type as the property. You don't have to provide both—you can provide a routine for one and a variable name for the other. You can also leave one or both of these modifiers out, creating read-only or write-only components. Typically, you will provide the variable name for the read operation and a procedure name for the write operation. The write procedure takes a single parameter (usually called Value) of the same type as the property, and assigns the internal variable to Value.

Notice that Delphi automatically handles the firing of these routines for you. When you change the value of a property in code, you are just making an assignment. Delphi is handling actually firing the Set procedure, making it look like a simple assignment. This is where the real power of component creation occurs, because it means that you can write code that will execute *just because an assignment has taken place.* This allows the programmer to create "side effects" that occur whenever this assignment occurs. So, for example, just setting the Align property of a panel component in the Object Inspector (or in a program) looks like a simple assignment. However, Delphi is actually running the code that is attached to the Write portion of the property, which actually moves the panel into the new position.

You should always make the actual value that is being set a private member of the class. This hides the true value from every other class (even direct descendants), so that you can be sure that it is hidden. This means that all other classes must access your internal variables through the Read/Write routines, which form a well-published interface to your component's functionality.

Default Properties

When you define properties, you can also define default values for them. The default values determine which items are streamed out into the form's DFM file. All properties that are different from the default are streamed into the DFM. This allows the DFM file to be relatively small because it doesn't have to hold all the values of all the properties on the form.

Here is an example of a property with a default value:

```
property DisabledColor : TColor read FDisabledColor write
SetDisabledColor default clSilver;
```

However, defining a default property will not set the property to that value. You must do this yourself in the inherited Create constructor. The default only determines what is streamed into the DFM file—it does not change the value.

Here is an example of the overridden Create constructor, where the value of the default is actually set:

```
constructor TVisTable.Create( AOwner : TComponent );
begin
  inherited Create( AOwner );
  {set default values}
  DisabledColor := clSilver;
end; {constructor}
```

For a complete example of a new component class with default properties and Read/Write routines, look at the example at the end of this chapter.

New Events

It is also possible in Delphi to add any standard Windows event awareness to any component and also to create your own events. Creating your own events is very rare, and is beyond the scope of this book. After all, Windows defines the number of events that the operating system can send to your application. The standard events that Delphi defines are listed in Figure 20.1.

There are two ways you might wish to modify components to take advantage of events. First, you can create a control that recognizes new standard events. All components that are descended from TControl can recognize the events listed in Figure 20.1, and likewise for descendants of TWinControl. However, you may not see these events when you instantiate one of their descendants. This is because some of these events (the ones that didn't seem useful for the particular component) were included as protected members of the class. This means that you can inherit from the existing component and redeclare the event handler within the published part of the new class. When you redefine a method by moving it to a different class scope, but don't include the override keyword or any actual implementation code, you have effectively just changed the class scoping of the method.

The other modification that you might want to make to events is to embellish how they are handled. If you were dealing with the event during the design of an application, you could just write code for the event handler. However, when you are creating components, you don't want your code in a place where the user could either modify it or wipe it

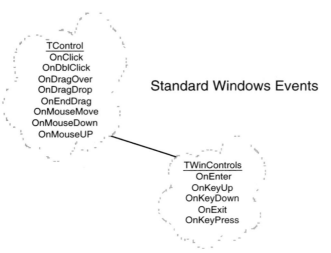

FIGURE 20.1 Windows Events that Delphi Provides for Components

out. What you should do instead is create a descendant of the component and override the event handler that you want to embellish. In the overridden event handler, call the inherited event handler when you want it to execute. This will handle executing any code that must be executed for the component to function, and it will also execute any code that the user has added to the event handler. So, you can embellish what an event handler does, and still leave the user of the component a slot in which he can place his own code. The code added to the event handler that you have created is invisible to the user. Again, for an example, see the case study at the end of the chapter. Our VisTable component uses this technique to perform an action during an event while allowing the user to also provide event handling code for that event.

COMPONENT WRITERS' RULES TO LIVE BY

If you look at the source code for the VCL (which is available for purchase from Borland, and is included in the Client/Server version), you will see numerous naming conventions and other rules that the Borland development team programmers followed. None of these conventions are enforced by the compiler or the environment, yet they are good guidelines to follow. This section reveals some of these conventions, which will make writing components easier and at the same time more consistent with the supplied components.

Internal Data Storage

Property values should be stored in a private member of the class. Identifiers for the private member should start with the letter "F", followed by the name of the property. For example, if you had a Color property, the actual private name would be FColor. This ensures good encapsulation and data hiding, and means that the side effects that determine how the component works will continue to work in descendants, no matter how many times it has been inherited from.

Also, Read functions should be named Get plus the property name, and Write procedures should be named Set plus the property name. So, if you have a Color property whose value is stored internally as FColor, the Read function would be GetColor and the Write procedure would be SetColor.

Verify Value Change before Assignment

Within your Write procedures, always check to see if the value that is passed as a parameter has changed. Remember, the Write procedure takes a single parameter, of the same type as the property, and assigns the internal value to what was passed. The Set routine can also cause other actions to occur. This is why you should always check to see if the value has changed. If the value hasn't changed (that is, the passed parameter and the internal member have the same value), you shouldn't assign it again. Because Delphi depends on side effects to occur in response to property assignments, it potentially takes much longer to assign property values than simple variables. There is no way for the end programmer to know how much code will be executed as a result of the assignment! So, it is best to only make assignments to properties when you must.

Here is an example of verifying the change before the assignment:

```
procedure TVisTable.SetEnabledColor(Value: TColor);
begin
  if FEnabledColor <> Value then
    FEnabledColor := Value;
end;
```

Don't Use the Private Value Lightly

You should only access the private data storage for your property within the Get/Set routines for that property. You can use it anywhere in the class, but it will be more consistent with how your users will access it if all access is done through the routines. There are some situations where you must refer to it directly, but it should be the exception rather than the rule.

Don't Forget to Set the Defaults

Even when you specify that a property has a default value, you must still make the assignment of that value in the constructor for the component. For example, if you specify a value with the `default` keyword you must still manually assign the property to that value within the component's constructor.

Event Handlers Are Always Procedures

You have the ability to declare new event handlers as either procedures or functions, but you should always declare them as procedures. If the event handler is a procedure, it won't matter if the user doesn't attach any code to an event handler during an application. An empty procedure just returns. However, if it were defined as a function, and the empty function is undefined, a run-time error would occur.

Event Handlers Are Optional

You should always keep in mind that the user isn't required to provide any code for an event handler. In fact, if your component depends on the user providing event handler code, you should probably redesign your component. Components should place no restrictions whatsoever on the user, and there shouldn't be any hidden knowledge required to use them.

As a corollary to this, you should allow the user to write any code they like within an event handler. In other words, don't design your component in such a way that legitimate code written by the user to handle an event will cause an exception.

Method Guidelines

When you make new methods for components, you should adhere to the following guidelines:

- Always minimize the interdependencies between methods in your component. Don't create methods that only work before or after other methods have run. Try to make your methods as encapsulated as possible. Particularly avoid methods that put the component in an indeterminate state. Your component should act as much as possible like the built-in components.
- Make your method name very descriptive. Remember that code is read three times as often as it's written, and the first 64 characters of variable names are significant, so don't be shy about long, descriptive variable names!
- Limit the class scoping of methods as much as possible. In other words, if the method will only be called internally, make it private instead of public. In general, you should try to limit the scope of all program elements as much as possible.

CASE STUDY: VISTABLE COMPONENT

As an example, we are going to create a new component, derived from one of the built-in components. But first, a statement of the problem and the solution is required.

As you may have noticed, Delphi provides an easy way for users to lock the current record the form is displaying (by going into Edit mode) and then either Posting the changes or Canceling them, returning the record back to its previous state. You can also set a property on a DataSource which enables AutoEdit which automatically puts the table in Edit mode as soon as the user starts typing. However, when AutoEdit is false, the user must explicitly go into Edit mode (usually by clicking on the Edit button on the DBNavigator).

The problem is that there is no visible cue that indicates which mode the table is in. If AutoEdit is on, you can start editing a record by just typing in the field, and then post the changes by moving off the record. However, what if the user places the record in Edit mode and doesn't realize it, and leaves it in Edit mode for a very long time? The record is locked for the entire time it is in Edit mode, possibly locking out other users. Also, a person who is accustomed to the AutoEdit behavior might not realize that you can cancel changes to correct mistakes.

The solution is to provide the user with a clear and visible cue to indicate which mode the table is in. That is what the VisTable component does. The TVisTable component is inherited from a TTable, which means that it has all the functionality of a Table component. We added several properties to TTable: EnabledColor, DisabledColor, and Navigator. EnabledColor is the color that the field backgrounds will be when the table is in Edit mode, DisabledColor is the color when they are disabled. Navigator can optionally point to a DBNavigator on the form. If this property is set to a Navigator, the Navigator visible buttons will change to only Post and Cancel. This indicates to the user that those are the only two options available. If you don't want VisTable to affect the Navigator, just don't assign it to the property. If this is the case, and AutoEdit is true, the VisTable will automatically go into Edit mode when the user types in the fields thereby changing the field backgrounds, and changing the colors back when either Post or Cancel occur, or when the user navigates to a different record (which causes an automatic Post). The VisTable component also automatically disables all the edits and memos on the form when the form opens, so that they start in the nonedit state.

Figure 20.2 shows an example of a form that is not in Edit mode and has a VisTable component instead of a Table component. Note the disabled buttons on the navigator.

Figure 20.3 shows the same form after the Edit button has been pressed.

Notice that the entry fields are now black on white, and the navigator has changed into Post and Cancel buttons only. This gives a clear indication to the user that the mode has changed.

Following is the source code for the TVisTable class:

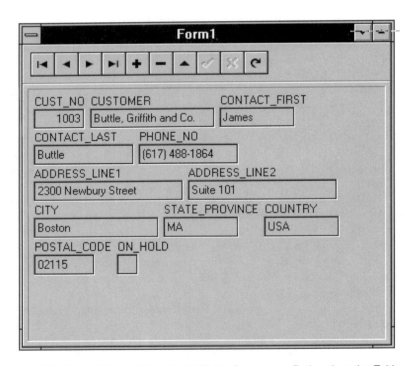

FIGURE 20.2   A Form Using the VisTable Component Rather than the Table Component

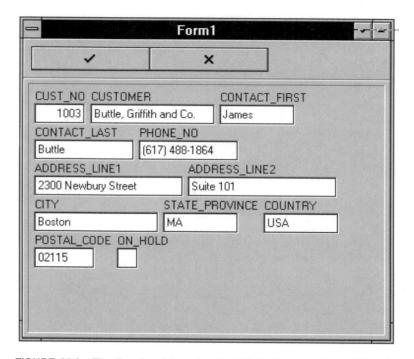

FIGURE 20.3 The Results of Pressing the Edit Button on a Form Using the VisTable Component

```
unit Tvistabl;

interface

uses
   SysUtils, WinTypes, WinProcs, Messages, Classes, Graphics,
   Controls, Forms, Dialogs, DB, DBTables, DBCtrls;
```

Notice that a new type is needed to indicate whether to enable or disable the controls. The UpdateControls method uses this type to determine which action to take.

```
type
   TVisTableAction = (acVTEnable, acVTDisable);
```

In the declaration of the TVisTable class below, notice that the actual values of the new properties have private variables that begin with "F". Also, the Set functions are declared as private methods. There is no need for any descendant classes to directly call these methods—if they need to call them, they can do so by assigning a property value. We also define a new private variable to hold the initialization status of the Navigator. The first time we encounter the Navigator, we need to be able to save its button configuration. This variable allows us to check for this condition.

```
TVisTable = class(TTable)
private
  { Private declarations }
  FDisabledColor : TColor;
  FEnabledColor : TColor;
  FNavigator : TDBNavigator;
  NavigatorButtons : TButtonSet;
  NavigatorInitialized : Boolean;
  procedure SetDisabledColor( Value: TColor );
  procedure SetEnabledColor( Value: TColor );
  procedure SetNavigator( Value : TDBNavigator );
```

The method UpdateControls in the code snippet below, which is an internal routine, is declared in the protected section as a virtual method. There might eventually be a need to a descendant class to override this method to add to its functionality; that is why it is in the protected section, not the private section.

```
protected
  { Protected declarations }
  procedure UpdateControls( Action : TVisTableAction );
virtual;
  public
    { Public declarations }
    constructor Create( AOwner : TComponent ); override;
```

Next, we have the overridden published events that we are going to modify. Because these events were declared virtual in the parent class, we can override them here and add functionality to them. Then, we declare the new properties, setting the Read value to directly reference the private variable, and setting the Write value to the Set routine. We also set default values for the two colors.

```
published
  { Published declarations }
  procedure DoAfterOpen; override;
  procedure DoAfterEdit; override;
  procedure DoAfterInsert; override;
  procedure DoAfterPost; override;
  procedure DoAfterCancel; override;
```

```
   property DisabledColor : TColor read
      FDisabledColor write SetDisabledColor
      default clSilver;
   property EnabledColor : TColor read
      FEnabledColor write SetEnabledColor default clWhite;
   property Navigator : TDBNavigator read FNavigator
      write SetNavigator;
end;
```

Following is the `Register` procedure, which enables components to be installed on the component palette. Delphi provides this code for you, so you don't have to worry about writing it.

```
procedure Register;

implementation

procedure Register;
begin
   RegisterComponents('Custom', [TVisTable]);
end;
```

The `constructor` follows. Notice that the first thing we do is call the inherited `constructor`. That takes care of any initialization code that the parent usually performed when it was instantiated. Next, we set the `default value` of the default properties.

```
constructor TVisTable.Create( AOwner : TComponent );
begin
   inherited Create( AOwner );
   {set default values}
   EnabledColor := clWhite;
   DisabledColor := clSilver;
   NavigatorButtons := [];
   NavigatorInitialized := false;
end; {constructor}
```

Next are the Set routines for the two color properties and the Navigator property. Notice that we check the existing value before we make the assignment.

```
procedure TVisTable.SetEnabledColor(Value: TColor);
begin
   if FEnabledColor <> Value then
      FEnabledColor := Value;
end;
```

```
procedure TVisTable.SetDisabledColor(Value: TColor);
begin
  if FDisabledColor <> Value then
    FDisabledColor := Value;
end;

procedure TVisTable.SetNavigator(Value: TDBNavigator);
begin
  if FNavigator <> Value then
    FNavigator := Value;
end;
```

TVisTable.UpdateControls is the real workhorse method. It is an internal method that handles the chore of enabling or disabling all the Edit and Memo fields on the form that are attached to this VisTable. First, we loop through all the components on the form, which are kept within the Table component as the Owner property. For each component on the form, we check to see if it is a DBEdit, DBMemo, or a DBNavigator. If it is, then the appropriate action is taken. Notice that we are checking both the type and the DataSource's DataSet for each component, and we're only taking action if both tests are true. This enables the user to place as many VisTable components on the form as desired, which means that this component acts like a regular Table to the user.

Also notice that we save the Navigator's button configuration the first time we encounter the Navigator. Because the first action we take on the controls is to disable them, we must know what the button configuration is before we can set it.

```
procedure TVisTable.UpdateControls( Action :
      TVisTableAction );
var
  i : integer;
begin
  { loop thru the components and disable the relevant ones }
  with owner do
    for i := 0 to ComponentCount - 1 do
    begin
      if (components[i] is tDBEdit) and
        ((components[i] as TDBEdit).datasource.dataset =
          self) then
        with components[i] as TDBEdit do
          if Action = acVTDisable then
            color := DisabledColor
          else
            color := EnabledColor;
      if (Components[i] is TDBMemo) and
        ((components[i] as TDBMemo).datasource.dataset =
          self) then
        with components[i] as TDBMemo do
```

```
        if Action = acVTDisable then
          color := FDisabledColor
        else
          color := FEnabledColor;
    if (Components[i] is TDBNavigator) and
       ((components[i] as TDBNavigator)= Navigator) then
      with Navigator do
      begin
        if not NavigatorInitialized then
        begin
          NavigatorButtons := VisibleButtons;
          NavigatorInitialized := true
        end; {if}
        if Action = acVTEnable then
        begin
          NavigatorButtons := VisibleButtons;
          VisibleButtons := [nbPost, nbCancel]
        end {if}
        else
          VisibleButtons := NavigatorButtons;
      end; {with}
  end; {for}
end; {procedure}
```

The rest of the component's source code contains the overridden events. Notice that in every case we called the `inherited` event first. It is not a requirement that it be first (as in a constructor), and indeed you may need it to be in the middle of some of your code. The important point is that is should be called sometime within the event. It is this inherited event handler that is attached to the user's code, and if you don't call the inherited event, the user's code inexplicably won't work.

```
procedure TVisTable.DoAfterOpen;
begin
  inherited DoAfterOpen;
  UpdateControls( acVTDisable );
end; {procedure}

procedure TVisTable.DoAfterEdit;
begin
  inherited DoAfterEdit;
  UpdateControls( acVTEnable )
end; {procedure}

procedure TVisTable.DoAfterInsert;
begin
  inherited DoAfterInsert;
```

```
    UpdateControls( acVTEnable );
end; {procedure}

procedure TVisTable.DoAfterPost;
begin
  inherited DoAfterPost;
  UpdateControls( acVTDisable );
end; {procedure}

procedure TVisTable.DoAfterCancel;
begin
  inherited DoAfterCancel;
  UpdateControls( acVTDisable );
end; {procedure}

end.
```

As you can see, we tried to design this component to behave as much as possible like the built-in components. We took special pains to make sure that it wouldn't affect components that were not attached via the datasource to the table, which means that there can be multiple VisTables on a form that don't interfere with one another. We also made the color of the enabled and disabled fields a property, to allow the user as much flexibility as possible in color choices.

This also shows the great power of a well-designed application framework. Notice that we didn't have to know any details about how the database retrieval was taking place for this component. That functionality stayed safely hidden in one of the ancestor classes. And because this component is based on a TTable, this component works equally well with local tables or client/server tables. In fact, the screen shot demonstration shown in Figure 20.3 was a VisTable component connected to an InterBase database. To create something so useful with so little code speaks well for object-oriented programming in general (and especially the toolset abstraction that is embodied in this product).

CHAPTER 21

DELPHI'S DDE CONNECTION

DYNAMIC DATA EXCHANGE

DDE is an interprocess commmunication (IPC) protocol for synchronizing data exchange between Windows programs. This protocol is a set of common rules that all DDE applications follow. DDE applications utilizing this protocol fall into four broad categories:

- *Client applications* request data from or send data into a server application.
- *Server applications* respond to a client's demands or receive a clients data.
- *Client-Server applications* can both request/send data and provide services to another client application.
- *Monitor applications* intercept DDE messages from other applications but do not act upon them.

We should note that ocassionally, DDE clients are referred to as *destination* applications, and servers are referred to as *source* applicatons. We will maintain the client/ server terminology that has carried over to OLE.

Dynamic Data Exchange takes place when a client application *initiates* a conversation (*link*) with a server application over a communication *channel*. Windows provides an integer value as a unique identifier (*handle*) for the channel. After establishing the link, the client can then request information (*peek*) from the server, send (*poke*) data to the server, initiate actions within the server (*execute* macros), and close its conversation (*terminate* the channel) and release the handle.

The link describes how the data is exchanged. A *cold link* allows a client to request data which is immediately provided by the server. When a server advises a client that a data item has changed but does not provide its value, a *warm link* occurs. Through a *hot link,* a server provides a data item to a client dynamically whenever the value of the item changes.

Each type of link is established by the client by stating both the *service name* and a legitimate *topic* of the server. The service name (known in versions of Windows prior to 3.1 as the *application name*) is the name by which the Windows Task Manager recognizes the server applicaton. The topic is generally a document recognized by the server.

For example, in a conversation with Microsoft Word 6.0, the service would be "Winword" (the executable file name without the .EXE extension) and the topic might be "c:\word6\my_files\year_end.doc". For Novel Quattro Pro 6.0, the service would be "QPW", and the topic might be a notebook "c:\my_qpw\my_book.wb2". If the server is a Delphi application, the server is the project name without the .DPR extension. The topic is the caption of the form containing the data, or the name of a DDEServerConv component on the form.

Data exchanged accross the DDE channel is always the value of an *item* recognized by the server. In the Word example, this could be the name of a bookmark. In the Quattro Pro notebook, it might be an individual cell on a page such as "$C:$C$23..$C$23". For a Delphi application, the item is the name of a linked DDEServerItem component on the server form.

COMPONENT DRIVEN DDE

In other languages, such as Visual Basic for Applications, DDE is controlled solely through code. The Borland development team decided to apply OOP techniques to DDE in Delphi and have provided a suite of four DDE components on the System page of the standard component palette. These four components are the simple basis for all DDE between Delphi and other applications (Figure 21.1).

DDE Clients

The client conversation and Client Item components work together as a team for Delphi client applications. The Conversation component has DDEService and DDETopic properties that you set to establish conversations with DDE servers. The Client Item component is used to specify items of conversation.

For example, you can set a Delphi DDEClientConv component's DDEService property to "Excel" and its DDETopic property to "c:\excel\myfiles\dde_expl.xls" to prepare to initiate a conversation with an Excel spreadsheet named "dde_expl.xls". At run-time you then use the SetLink (or OpenLink) method of the DDEClientConv component to set the link by hard coding the reference:

```
DDEClientConv1.SetLink('excel',
        'c:\excel\myfiles\dde_expl.xls');
```

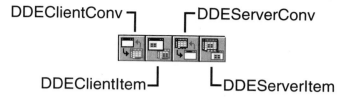

DDEClientConv ── ──DDEServerConv

DDEClientItem ── ──DDEServerItem

FIGURE 21.1 The Delphi DDE Components from the System Page

or by referring to its preset properties:

```
DDEClientConv1.SetLink(DDEClientConv1.DDEService,
    DDEClientConv1.DDETopic);
```

Additionally, all DDE servers are required to support the *System* topic that returns infomation about the server including identifiers to other valid topics. Using it, you could, for instance, send a macro to open a new workbook:

```
DDEClientConv1.SetLink('excel', 'system');
DDEClientConv1.ExecuteMacro(AnExcelMacro, True);
```

It is very important to terminate your DDE conversations when you are finished. Not terminating your conversation is analogous to you and a friend not hanging up your telephones after a long-distance conversation. You will tie up your line and lose precious resources (incoming calls as well as money). The Windows channel assigned to your DDE conversation uses precious Windows resources. Always terminate your conversation properly: Simply use the `CloseLink` method of the DDEClientConv component:

```
DDEClientConv1.CloseLink;
```

A DDEClientItem component has a `DDEConv` property whose setting assigns the Item component to work through a DDEClientConv component. It also has a `DDEItem` property that can be set at run-time to an item for which the server can supply or accept data. For example, to poke data into a column of cells in our Excel spreadsheet, we might set the DDEClientITem component in a loop:

```
DDEClientItem1.DDEConv := 'DDEClientConv1';
for I := 1 to 100 do
begin
  Randomize;
  StrPCopy(PCharStuff, IntToStr(Random(100)));
  DDEClientItem1.DDEItem := 'R' + IntToStr(i) + 'C1';
  DDEClientConv1.PokeData(DDEClientItem.DDEItem,
      PCharStuff);
end;
```

Here, we have associated the Client Item component with our DDEClientConv component. We then utilized a PChar variable for the transfer of data through our DDE channel and assigned random numbers to it within the loop. The values are poked into Excel by the conversation component to the cell address specified by the Client Item component.

DDE Servers

Delphi also provides a DDEServerConv component and a DDEServerItem component for the creation of server applications. Like the Client Item component, a DDEServerItem must be associated with a Server Conversation component. Data requests and macro strings are processed by the DDEServerConv component. It is the DDEServerItem which actually receives the data into its Lines property which, like other Lines properties (that is, in ListBoxes), is a TStringList. If the poke involves a macro string, the server Conversation components must have code associated with its ExecuteMacro event to process the string. For example:

```
procedure TForm1.DDEServerConv1ExecuteMacro(Sender: TObject;
    Msg: Tstrings);
begin
  if Msg.Strings[0] = 'turn red' then
    self.Color := clRed;
end;
```

If the Server component receives a data string, it is sent into the Lines property of the associated Server Item component. Because the Lines property can also be used through a text control (for example, a Memo component) to send data to the client, it is necessary to control the flow of the data to the DDE Item component through the text control's OnChange event:

```
var
  PokeInProgress : Boolean;
  .
  .
procedure TForm1.Memo1Change(Sender: TObject);
begin
  if not PokeInProgress then
    DDEServerItem1.Lines := Memo1.Lines;
end;

procedure TDDEServerItem1PokeData(Sender: TObject);
begin
  PokeInProgress := True;
  Memo1.Lines := DDEServerItem1.Lines;
  PokeInProgress := False;
end;
```

DDE and Null-terminated Strings

DDE servers always send and receive data as strings. Additionally, all DDE statements are transmitted as *null-terminated strings,* which are different from the Object-Pascal string type. A null-terminated string is actually a pointer to a series of characters, whose length is indeterminate. An ASCII character 0 (null) is used to mark the end of the string (thus the name). Windows uses null-terminated strings natively because Windows is written in C, and null-terminated strings are the only option in C. Thus, to send or receive data, you must consistently translate your strings of data into the null-terminated PChar datatype. This is easily accomplished with the StrPCopy and StrPas functions. But first, you must allocate memory to a PChar transmission variable. Use the Getmem function to allocate the memory, and the Freemem function to retrieve it when you are finished. For example:

```
var
  PCharStuff : PChar;
  strData : string;

begin
  {allocate memory for the variable}
  getmem(PCharStuff, 255);
  try {start a resource protection block }
    {prepare the data to be sent}
    StrPCopy(PCharStuff, '=AVG(R1C1:R25C1)');
    {here send the data to the server}
    . . .
    {after receiving some data into PCharStuff}
    strData := StrPas(PCharStuff);
    {here output it to an Edit component, etc.}
  finally
    freemem(PCharStuff);
  end; {try}
end;
```

A WORKING EXAMPLE

For this chapter, we have implemented a DDE conversation between a Delphi client and an Excel notebook acting as the server. Numeric data is generated and analyzed using Excel's built-in statistical functions. This is a perfect example of why you might use DDE: to take advantage of the Windows hyper-environment and utilize the capabilities of a server application. Exceldde.dpr sends data into and requests statistical data back from a predefined Excel worksheet. This relieves us of the burden of writing the same statistical functions found in Excel.

We've used the Windows API call WinExec to start Excel and open a spreadsheet titled dde_expl.xls found in our c:\excel directory. The WinExec API call has been implemented to allow us to set the ConnectMode property of our DDEClientConv component to `ddeManual`. This way, Excel does not automatically startup while working in Delphi's Design mode, and furthermore prevents multiple copies of Excel attempting to open dde_expl.xls.

The OpenLink and SetLink methods of the Client Conversation component are then both used because the ConnectMode property of our DDEClientConv component has been set to `ddeManual`. If the link is successful, random number data is poked into rows 1 through 25 of the first column of the spreadsheet. Calls to Excel statistical functions are then poked into the first rows of columns 2 through 7 as shown in Figure 21.2.

Excel processes these functions on the fly, (provided the R_iC_j referencing system is set properly) and their results are requested by our client application and output to a series of text boxes on our form shown in Figure 21.3.

In order to run this applet, be sure that Excel is pathed on your system, and that you've created a notebook entitled dde_expl.xls and placed it in your c:\excel directory. If you've installed Excel elsewhere, make appropriate changes in the path statement within the code as well as in the DDETopic property of the Client Conversation component. Also, be sure that the spreadsheet is not already open when you begin the DDE process. Lastly, be sure that your copy of Excel uses the R_iC_j cell referencing system used in the code. If not, you'll either have to change the cell referencing in Excel, or change all the references in the code to the A_i system used on your machine.

When you run the applet, you will have to press three buttons for the entire process to take place. Be sure each process is complete before pressing the next enabled button

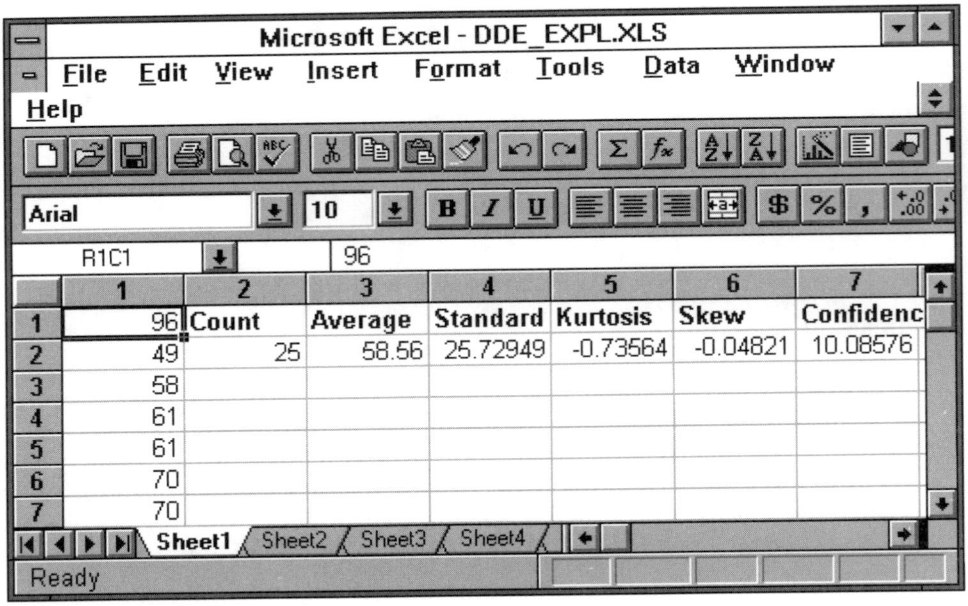

FIGURE 21.2   The Excel Spreadsheet Populated through a Delphi DDE Link

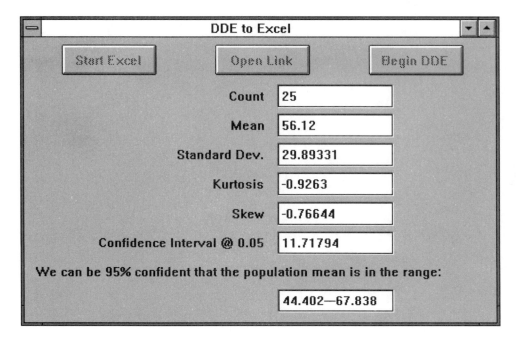

FIGURE 21.3 The Exceldde Form After a Successful DDE Conversation

(see the limitations of DDE section within this chapter). The complete, commented code for the applet follows:

```
unit Ddeexcel;

interface

uses
  SysUtils, WinTypes, WinProcs, Messages, Classes, Graphics,
Controls,
  Forms, Dialogs, StdCtrls, DdeMan, ExtCtrls;

type
  TFormDDEExcel = class(TForm)
    DdeClientConv1: TDdeClientConv;
    DdeClientItem1: TDdeClientItem;
    ButtonBegin: TButton;
    EditCount: TEdit;
    LabelCount: TLabel;
    EditMean: TEdit;
    LabelAverage: TLabel;
```

```
    EditStdDev: TEdit;
    LabelStdDev: TLabel;
    EditKurtosis: TEdit;
    LabelKurtosis: TLabel;
    EditSkew: TEdit;
    LabelSkew: TLabel;
    EditConfInt: TEdit;
    LabelConfidenceInterval: TLabel;
    EditMeanRange: TEdit;
    LabelResults: TLabel;
    ButtonStartExcel: TButton;
    ButtonOpenLink: TButton;
    TimerWait: TTimer;
    procedure ButtonBeginClick(Sender: TObject);
    procedure ButtonStartExcelClick(Sender: TObject);
    procedure ButtonOpenLinkClick(Sender: TObject);

  private
    { Private declarations }
  public
    { Public declarations }
  end;

var
  FormDDEExcel: TFormDDEExcel;

implementation

{$R *.DFM}

procedure TFormDDEExcel.ButtonBeginClick(Sender: TObject);
var
  PCharStuff : PChar;
  i : integer;
  j : longint;
  strData, S : string;
  v, x, y, z : single;

begin
    {allocate memory for the null terminated string}
  getmem(PCharStuff, 255);
  try
  if DDEClientConv1.OpenLink then
  begin
      {disable repeated attempts}
    ButtonBegin.Enabled := False;
    MessageDlg('Link established', mtInformation, [mbOK], 0);
    for i := 0 to 25 do
```

```
begin
    {load the notebook sheet with a random data set}
    Randomize;
    StrPCopy(PCharStuff, IntToStr(Random(100)));
    DDEClientItem1.DDEItem := 'R' + IntToStr(i) + 'C1';
    DDEClientConv1.PokeData(DDEClientItem1.DDEItem,
      PCharStuff);
end;
    {find the count}
DDEClientItem1.DDEItem := 'R1C2';
StrPCopy(PCharStuff, 'Count');
DDEClientConv1.PokeData(DDEClientItem1.DDEItem,
  PCharStuff);
DDEClientItem1.DDEItem := 'R2C2';
StrPCopy(PCharStuff, '=COUNT(R1C1:R25C1)');
DDEClientConv1.PokeData(DDEClientItem1.DDEItem,
  PCharStuff);
    {find the average}
DDEClientItem1.DDEItem := 'R1C3';
StrPCopy(PCharStuff, 'Average');
DDEClientConv1.PokeData(DDEClientItem1.DDEItem,
  PCharStuff);
DDEClientItem1.DDEItem := 'R2C3';
StrPCopy(PCharStuff, '=AVERAGE(R1C1:R25C1)');
DDEClientConv1.PokeData(DDEClientItem1.DDEItem,
  PCharStuff);
    {find the sample standard deviation}
DDEClientItem1.DDEItem := 'R1C4';
StrPCopy(PCharStuff, 'Standard Deviation');
DDEClientConv1.PokeData(DDEClientItem1.DDEItem,
  PCharStuff);
DDEClientItem1.DDEItem := 'R2C4';
StrPCopy(PCharStuff, '=STDEV(R1C1:R25C1)');
DDEClientConv1.PokeData(DDEClientItem1.DDEItem,
  PCharStuff);
    {find the kurtosis}
DDEClientItem1.DDEItem := 'R1C5';
StrPCopy(PCharStuff, 'Kurtosis');
DDEClientConv1.PokeData(DDEClientItem1.DDEItem,
  PCharStuff);
DDEClientItem1.DDEItem := 'R2C5';
StrPCopy(PCharStuff, '=KURT(R1C1:R25C1)');
DDEClientConv1.PokeData(DDEClientItem1.DDEItem,
  PCharStuff);
    {find the skew}
DDEClientItem1.DDEItem := 'R1C6';
StrPCopy(PCharStuff, 'Skew');
DDEClientConv1.PokeData(DDEClientItem1.DDEItem,
```

```
   PCharStuff);
DDEClientItem1.DDEItem := 'R2C6';
StrPCopy(PCharStuff, '=SKEW(R1C1:R25C1)');
DDEClientConv1.PokeData(DDEClientItem1.DDEItem,
   PCharStuff);
   {find the confidence interval}
DDEClientItem1.DDEItem := 'R1C7';
StrPCopy(PCharStuff, 'Confidence Interval');
DDEClientConv1.PokeData(DDEClientItem1.DDEItem,
   PCharStuff);
DDEClientItem1.DDEItem := 'R2C7';
StrPCopy(PCharStuff, '=CONFIDENCE(0.05,R2C4,R2C2)');
DDEClientConv1.PokeData(DDEClientItem1.DDEItem,
   PCharStuff);
   {output the count}
PCharStuff := DDEClientConv1.RequestData('R2C2');
strData := StrPas(PCharStuff);
EditCount.Enabled := True;
EditCount.Text := Copy(strData, 1, Length(strData) - 2);
   {output the mean}
PCharStuff := DDEClientConv1.RequestData('R2C3');
strData := StrPas(PCharStuff);
EditMean.Enabled := True;
EditMean.Text := Copy(strData, 1, Length(strData) - 2);
   {output the standard deviation}
PCharStuff := DDEClientConv1.RequestData('R2C4');
strData := StrPas(PCharStuff);
EditStdDev.Enabled := True;
EditStdDev.Text := Copy(strData, 1, Length(strData)-2);
   {output the kurtosis}
PCharStuff := DDEClientConv1.RequestData('R2C5');
strData := StrPas(PCharStuff);
EditKurtosis.Enabled := True;
EditKurtosis.Text := Copy(strData, 1, Length(strData)-2);
   {output the skew}
PCharStuff := DDEClientConv1.RequestData('R2C6');
strData := StrPas(PCharStuff);
EditSkew.Enabled := True;
EditSkew.Text := Copy(strData, 1, Length(strData)-2);
   {output the confidence interval}
PCharStuff := DDEClientConv1.RequestData('R2C7');
strData := StrPas(PCharStuff);
EditConfInt.Enabled := True;
EditConfInt.Text := Copy(strData, 1, Length(strData)-2);
   {output the results}
Val(EditConfInt.Text, v, i);
Val(EditMean.Text, x, i);
   {the lower range}
```

```
      y := x - v;
        {and the upper range of the population mean}
      z := x + v;
      Str(y:6:3, strData);
      Str(z:6:3, S);
      EditMeanRange.Enabled := True;
      EditMeanRange.Text := strData + '---' + S;
        {to prevent a loss of Windows resources}
      DDEClientConv1.CloseLink;
    end
    else
    begin
      i := MessageDlg('DDE error . . . Unable to link to Excel',
        mtError, [mbOK], 0);
        {disable repeated attempts}
      ButtonBegin.Enabled := False;
    end;
    finally
        {deallolocate the PChar memory}
      StrDispose(PCharStuff);
    end;
end;


procedure TFormDDEExcel.ButtonStartExcelClick(Sender:
      TObject);
var
  PCharStuff : PChar;
  i : integer;
begin
    {disable repeated attempts}
  ButtonStartExcel.Enabled := False;
    {allocate memory for the null terminated string}
  getmem(PCharStuff, 255);
    {presuming that Excel is pathed, create the command
     line}
  StrPCopy(PCharStuff, 'Excel c:\excel\dde_expl.xls');
    {use the API to start Excel minimized without focus}
  i := WinExec(PCharStuff, 2);
    {enable the next step}
  ButtonOpenLink.Enabled := True;
    {deallolocate the PChar memory}
  freemem(PCharStuff, 255);
end;


procedure TFormDDEExcel.ButtonOpenLinkClick(Sender:
TObject);
begin
    {disable repeated attempts}
```

```
    ButtonOpenLink.Enabled := False;
       {activate the link}
    DDEClientConv1.OpenLink;
    DDEClientConv1.SetLink(DDEClientConv1.DDEService,
        DDEClientConv1.DDETopic);
       {enable the next step}
    ButtonBegin.Enabled := True;
  end;
  end.
```

LIMITATIONS OF DINOSAUR DATA EXCHANGE

DDE conversations must take place on a single computer because the exchange of data takes place through the Windows Clipboard. (This restriction does not apply if you are using the Network DDE features of Windows for Workgroups.) Because the data transfer occurs through the Clipboard, DDE is a relatively risky business. If your user decides to utilize the Clipboard during a conversation, the flow of data can be totally interrupted resulting in cascading errors or a complete breakdown of the conversation.

Additionally, with DDE, you may never know whether your code executed properly. For this reason it may be unwise to depend on DDE for unmonitored critical tasks. Delphi is so fast that continuous lines of code performing DDE may be executed before the associated client or server can respond. Note that, in our example, the initialization of the server, the setting of the link, and the exchange of data are controlled by three separate user controlled buttons. This is to ensure, through user feedback, that the DDE takes place properly. The first button delays the enabling of the second button, and likewise, the second delays the third. In practice, the user should wait for the server application to surface, set the link, wait a few moments, and then exchange data. If the timing of the conversation takes place too quickly, it can fail completely. Keep your DDE tasks simple and under user control.

Unterminated links can devour your Windows system memory. In fact, some older DDE servers have memory leaks which may occur regardless of whether you've terminated your link properly. Keep an eye on Windows system resources when performing DDE.

Lastly, numeric data sent to the server is received according to the server's numeric format. Because you are changing data types repeatedly in order to pass null-terminated strings, you may experience inaccuracies in precision and/or rounding errors through data type inconsistencies between Delphi and your server application.

Hopefully, Borland will institute a fully OLE 2.x compliant component in its Windows95 release so that developers in need of interprocess communication can turn to OLE Automation instead of DDE. Meanwhile, except for third party add-ons (see our chapter on OLE 2.0), Delphi developers are stuck with, albeit a robust implementation of, **Di**nosaur **D**ata **E**xchange.

CHAPTER **22**

¡OLE !

Early versions of Microsoft Windows used a method of interprocess communication (IPC) called Dynamic Data Exchange, or DDE for short (see our chapter on Delphi and DDE for an up-to-date coverage of this topic). With the release of Windows 3.1 Microsoft made a shift in its IPC protocol and standardized on Object Linking and Embedding or OLE (pronounced just like the Spanish ¡ OLE!).

In this chapter, we will describe what OLE is, and how to use OLE to embed and link graphics, word processing documents, spreadsheets, and a host of other information formats directly into your Delphi applications. We'll also differentiate between OLE 1.0 and OLE 2.0 formats and show you how to make direct communication between your Delphi application and your OLE server applications.

OUT WITH THE OLD AND IN WITH THE NEW

Like DDE, OLE is a client/server architecture for interapplication information sharing. However there are significant differences that will make you think of DDE as *dinosaur data exchange*. In DDE, your client application pokes commands into a server application and requests resulting data from the server application in a format that your client understands. With OLE, your server application supplies an OLE object which contains the desired information to your client application.

When you implant data in this manner you are creating a *compound document*, an application document that combines data created by different applications within the same document. These compound documents can be word processing documents, spreadsheets, slide shows, multimedia presentations, or database applications, to name a few. Only OLE compliant applications can create compound documents. The client application's document (the compound document) that contains the OLE object data is also referred to as the *destination document,* while a server application supplies the *source document* for the OLE object.

OLE, however, continues to go far beyond DDE by encapsulating its shared information into objects that have *properties* and *methods.* The properties describe the object's data, while the methods consist of all the capabilities appropriate to the information object being passed. For example, an OLE word processing document's properties would describe the text therein as well as any formatting information. The document's methods might include the ability to print, italicize, etc. Ultimately, you can manipulate the object's properties and methods in situ or remotely to build highly flexible applications with seemingly complex interprocess communications (multitasking without all the tasks). Let's take a look at the history of OLE.

OLE 1.0x

The first version of OLE (OLE 1.0) was a great success. It gave users the ability to directly implant data from other applications within their client applications. In fact, many common server applications remain OLE 1.0 type servers. Windows Paintbrush, and all the other "free" software that comes with Windows are OLE 1.0x servers. Microsoft has not invested the time and money to upgrade these products to OLE 2.0 status in anticipation of possible 32-bit versions for Windows95. Hopefully some OLE 2.0 version of these familiar products will be included with Windows95 or Win*Ever.*

If you use an OLE 1.0x server application, you can implant your data in one of two ways. Your data can be contained and displayed within a special OLE object frame within your destination document, or it can remain in its original file and merely be represented by an icon or thumbnail image (Figure 22.1). For example, an OLE object representing a Microsoft Word document could display the first page of the source document, or just a Microsoft Word icon. Some source documents, such as sound files, can only be displayed as an icon.

Embedding

Implanting the data within your client application's destination document is called *embedding.* You usually copy data from your server application into the Windows Clipboard and paste it directly into your client application. You can also embed an entire file, such as a Windows bitmap (.BMP file) or a word processing document.

Once your OLE 1.0x data is embedded, you can then edit it by activating the object, usually by double clicking on it, which then launches the server application in its own window displaying your data as an editable source document. When you save your edits and return to your destination document in your client application, the OLE 1.0x object reflects any changes you made during your editing session. With embedding, the data in your destination document is a copy of the original data that you copied from your server application's source document. Thus, any edits to the object are *not* reflected in your original source document but merely to the copy embedded in your client's destination document.

If you use an OLE 1.0x server application, you can implant your data in one of two ways. Your data can be contained and displayed within a special OLE object frame within your destination document,

or it can remain in its original file and merely be represented by an icon or thumbnail image.

delphi.bmp

FIGURE 22.1   OLE 1.0x Objects Embedded in a MS Word Document

Linking

Linking is another OLE 1.0x method for implanting source document data in your destination document. Linking requires that the data for the OLE object originate as an entire file. When you link rather than embed data, you insert a reference to the source document's file name and its drive path into an OLE object within your destination document. If you activate an OLE 1.0x linked object, the server application for the source document is launched in its own window displaying your OLE data as the original source file. Any edits you make and save to the source document are actually saved in the source file. When you return to your destination document you must then update the display of your OLE object to reflect the changes in the underlying source document file.

Linking vs. Embedding

Linking and embedding each have advantages and disadvantages. Embedding OLE objects has the distinct advantage of ensuring that the OLE data displayed in your destination document reflects any changes made by your users through the destination document, and is always an up-to-date representation of your embedded data. Any edits made to a linked OLE 1.0x source document will not be reflected in your destination document until you update the OLE object's link. Also, if a linked object is moved from one directory to another, its file name/path will no longer be valid and the destination document will lose the ability to activate the object and make edits through the server application. You can, however, update the linked objects path and restore the ability to edit directly from your destination document.

Linking has its advantages. Perhaps you are tracking legal documents and maintain references to those documents as linked OLE objects in a database. You could store the documents on a server which would allow the editors of the documents ready access to them. Each time you peruse a document from within the database you could automatically update the link to view the version with the latest edits.

Linking graphics can have an unfortunate side effect. For some destination documents, a linked graphic is represented as a metafile image of the original source document. Because the metagraphic is just as large in terms of storage as the original source document, you won't save any space by keeping the source document out on your hard drive and linking to it. In fact, you can more than double the necessary storage by maintaining not only the original source document but also the metafile representation and its link within your destination document.

Linking does have the advantage of being forward looking in regard to the upcoming hyper-environments that our software operates in. In an ideal world, updates to linked objects should be automatically reflected in any compliant destination documents. Multiple users should be able to access and edit the same source document for linked OLE objects, and all users should see those edits in near real-time. This is just one of the capabilities promised by OLE 2.0x, though not yet delivered.

INTRODUCING OLE 2.0X

OLE is really not just about embedding or linking objects within compound documents. Object linking and embedding just happens to be the first successful implementation of Microsoft's OLE standard. What OLE is really about is Bill Gate's strategy for a *Common Object Model* with which you can build customized applications composed of components derived from mega-applications such as Delphi, Microsoft Word, Excel, Shapeware's Visio, and a host of other applications to arrive in the near future. OLE 1.0x was the first generation of software implementations in support of this strategy. As its name implies, OLE 2.0x is the second generation.

OLE 2.0x can be summarized by four principal characteristics:

1. A binary standard and structured storage for objects
2. Drag-and-drop embedding and in-place editing
3. OLE Automation and OLE Custom Controls
4. The Common Object Model and distributed objects

We shall discuss each of these individually and then see how they apply to Delphi.

A Binary Standard and Structured Storage for Objects

The OLE 2.0x generation defines the OLE Component Object Model standard for creating objects and achieving communication between objects. With it, objects can be embedded within other objects with no (theoretical) limit on the number of nested levels. Thus, your Delphi project might nest an Excel spreadsheet, which could nest a Word document, which could nest a CorelDRAW! graphic, which could nest a Sound Recorder .WAV file. This object nesting is possible because the OLE 2.0x standard has simplified the way objects interact with each other resulting in reduced overhead. Furthermore, OLE 2.0x is backward compatible with OLE 1.0x, so you can store either type of object in your OLE-Container components.

In-place Editing and Drag-and-drop Embedding

OLE 2.0x compatible products allow you to drag-and-drop objects from one document into another. The destination document in OLE 2.0x is now referred to as the *OLE container* (not to be confused with Delphi's OLEContainer component). For example, if you embed a Delphi executable into a MS Word 6.0x document, you'll see the Delphi icon and the name of your .EXE file, as shown in Figure 22.2.

Word 6.0x, being OLE 2.0x compatible, can act as an OLE container, and it supports drag-and-drop embedding. You could move this Delphi executable to another Word 6.0x document by simply dragging it between document windows. As with any executable OLE embedded object, if you double click on the Delphi icon within the Word document, it will run the executable. Thus, if you e-mail the document to a friend, and they double click the icon, they too can run your Delphi application.

The 2.0x generation of OLE software also supports *in-place activation*. This means that if the embedded object is OLE 2.0x compatible *and* is an editable object, when you

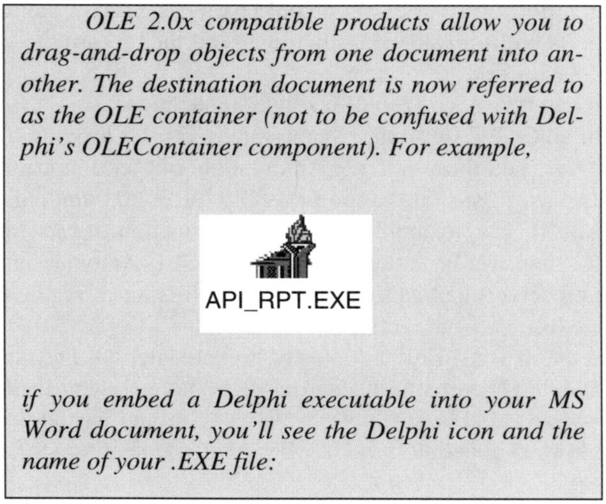

OLE 2.0x compatible products allow you to drag-and-drop objects from one document into another. The destination document is now referred to as the OLE container (not to be confused with Delphi's OLEContainer component). For example,

API_RPT.EXE

if you embed a Delphi executable into your MS Word document, you'll see the Delphi icon and the name of your .EXE file:

FIGURE 22.2 A Delphi Executable Embedded in a MS Word 6.0x Document

double click on it, the embedded object will replace the menus of the container document with its own menus so that you can begin editing it. The common elements of the OLE container application and the embedded object's server application are merged in a fashion similar to the way multiple products can share Windows API Dynamic Link Libraries (see our chapter on Delphi and the Windows API). This kind of window sharing reduces the consumption of Windows resources and thus, your Windows environment is more flexible and responsive.

You may find this kind of editing disconcerting, especially if you accidentally click outside of the object you are in-place editing. Your editing session will end and you will be thrown back into the client application. This can be especially annoying if you are working on an object embedded within a memory intensive application.

In-place activation *may* also mean that you can run the embedded object within a host window (component) of the client application. Note however, that for all products, linked OLE 2.0x documents do not support in-place activation.

OLE Automation and OLE Custom Controls

OLE Automation is intended to replace DDE (Dynamic Data Exchange) as the principal method of interprocess communication (IPC) between Windows applications. DDE is like shooting off a distress flare and then waiting blindly in the dark to find out if anyone will answer it. You never know if your DDE conversation was a success until you examine your target application's data.

OLE Automation allows you to assign object variables in your client application to *exposed* objects in an OLE 2.0x server application. You can then manipulate the server object through your code variable which assumes all of the properties and methods of the server object. In fact, depending on the server application, it need not become an instance of a running application within your Windows Task Manager. The ultimate strategy of OLE Automation is that you will have interapplication functionality without the overhead of multiple application tasks. For example, you might expose a spreadsheet object from another application within your application's code. You could then pass it data, call upon it to do some data analysis with its built-in statistical functions, and then return the value to your application—all behind the scenes.

An OLE 2.0x application can be categorized as a server application, a client application, both server and client, or an OLE 2.0x applet. Shapeware's Visio is an example of a server application. It can provide data through OLE Automation, but it cannot initiate interprocess communication. (In fact, it was one of the first fully OLE 2.0 compliant applications in 1993.) MS Access "2.0" is an example of a client application. It can initiate IPC with other applications but cannot yet be called upon through OLE Automation. MS Excel "5.0" is both a client and a server application. MS Graph 5.0 is an example of an OLE 2.0x applet. It can only be executed from within an OLE client.

Unfortunately, for Delphi enthusiasts, Borland has not implemented OLE Automation in the current version of Delphi. There is no OLE Automation component included with the product nor an OLE object variable available in Pascal. Borland has adopted a strategy of waiting for the Windows95 generation of OLE before implementing OLE Automation in Delphi. Remember, Win*Ever* had been promised for quite some time, and Borland needed to get Delphi out into the marketplace without building in soon-to-be-obsolete 16-bit OLE adaptations.

There is a third party OLE automation control that has appeared on the Delphi forum on Compuserve. We have tinkered with it a bit and find that, if you absolutely must have OLE automation, it can do the job. However, it is nothing like the simple declaration of an object variable in VBA; each method of the component's server application must be defined for every implementation of the component.

For now, we may have to put up with DDE. Luckily, Delphi's implementation is quite robust. See our chapter on Dynamic Data Exchange.

OLE custom controls.   Another type of OLE applet is the current generation of OLE Custom Controls. OLE Custom Controls (.OCX controls) are OLE Automation server applets that have their own *fire events;* events to which you can attach code. These OLE 2.0x generation controls are designed to replace the .VBX controls familiar to Visual Basic programmers. They are currently implemented as 16-bit applets, and as a result, have not proliferated in the Windows application development market. Developers have no desire to invest their time in producing 16-bit technologies with a new 32-bit version of Windows promised for the autumn of 1995. Again, Borland has omitted this component type from Delphi in favor of waiting for the new environment.

The strategy behind .OCX controls is that the inclusion of these applets in your application will allow you to create component based products without the overhead of elements from full-blown applications.

You can embed an .OCX control on a Delphi form (see Figure 22.3), but it behaves erratically and is not yet of any use in application development. You cannot get at its properties or methods. Besides, the few that are available, except for Microsoft's Data Outline Control, are already supplanted by the components in the default VCL.

The Common Object Model and Distributed Objects

OLE 2.02 (the current version at the time of this writing) only supports interprocess communication on a single computer. As a result, DDE remains alive for developers who need IPC in a network environment. In the future, OLE will provide network IPC via Microsoft's Remote Procedure Call (RPC) mechanism. Microsoft has teamed up with Digital Equipment Corporation to create an IPC new standard that will utilize a Common Object Model to provide interapplication and cross network transportation of program objects.

This technology will ultimately change the way in which many of our applications are modeled. OLE superclasses representing engines, front-ends, and programmable object applets will be combined by users to perform everyday tasks that are now tackled by multitasking. You could conceivably work in the front end of a database package, use OLE Automation to analyze data with a spreadsheet engine, and then display your data through embedded applets.

The advantage to this object-oriented division of tasks is part and parcel of good

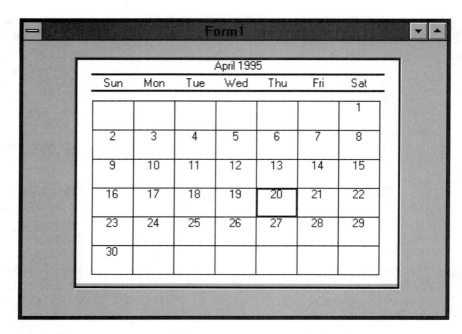

FIGURE 22.3 A Delphi OLEContainer Component with an Embedded .OCX Control

programming methodology. Each superclass can share common functions from within Dynamic Link Libraries which, in turn, minimizes the storage necessary for superclasses. IPC will be achieved by an adoption of an *Esperanto* scripting language, or perhaps a common syntax understood by a user's favorite language. Bill Gates is pressing for the adoption of Visual Basic for Applications (VBA) as the underlying *lingua franca* of application programming, despite the fact that it remains an interpreted (noncompiled) language. Perhaps he knows something we don't about the speed of near-future computing platforms.

Meanwhile, you're probably reading this book not because you can't work in VBA—after all, it looks quite like Pascal—but instead because of your desire to attain a satisfactory computing speed now. Let's take a look at what Delphi can do in the OLE realm.

DELPHI'S OLECONTAINER COMPONENT

The OLEContainer component (on the System page) is a form area that can accept an OLE object. It can hold either embedded or linked objects.

Inserting an OLE Object

To insert an OLE object, you need to call the `InsertOleObjectDlg` function, which brings up a dialog box on the screen and allows you to either create a new OLE document or open an existing document to insert. The syntax for the InsertOleObjectDlg function follows:

```
function InsertOleObjectDlg(Form: Tform; HelpContext:
   THelpContext; var PInitInfo: Pointer): Boolean;
```

Table 22.1 defines the parameters for the function. If the function returns true, you can initialize your OLE component:

```
var
   Info : Pointer;
begin
if InsertOLEObjectDlg(Form1, 0, Info) then
   begin
      OLEContainer1.PInitInfo := Info;
      ReleaseOLEInitInfo(Info)
end;
```

It is always important to release the memory occupied by the Info variable, otherwise your application will have "leaked" that memory (that is, it will not have been reclaimed). The built-in `ReleaseOLEInitInfo` procedure releases the memory. It is also possible to paste an OLE object from one application into another, but it is considerably more complex than inserting an object.

Once you have created an OLE object, you can save it in a special binary file. Note

TABLE 22–1   InsertOleObjectD1g Function Parameters

Parameter Name	Parameter Type	Description
Form	TForm	The form that the OLE container belongs to.
HelpContext	THelpContext	The help context number for the OLE container. See the chapter on adding help to Delphi applications for more details.
PInitInfo	Pointer	A pointer to a special operating system construct that initializes an OLE object.
Return value	Boolean	If the function returns true, initialize the OLE component's PInitInfo property with the information returned in the PInitInfo structure.

that this file is not a regular document file from the OLE server application, but a propri-etary binary format specific to Delphi. Therefore, you cannot open this file from the appli-cation that created the OLE document.

The `LoadFromFile` method of the OLE component will load an OLE file and in-sert it into the OLEContainer:

```
OLEContainer1.LoadFromFile( 'c:\oletest\word6.ole' );
```

To save a reference to an OLE object, use the `SaveToFile` method:

```
OleContainer1.SaveToFile( 'c:\oletest\pntbrsh3.ole' );
```

OLE SAMPLE PROGRAM

Our sample application demonstrates both of these methods. It also demonstrates how to manipulate OLE objects and containers. It is an MDI application which can contain as many OLE containers as you like. In fact, each of the MDI child windows are OLE con-tainers. You can either specify a new OLE object, or insert an existing OLE object. You can save the current object under a different name using the Save As button. Figure 22.4 is a screen shot of the application, with an open child window.

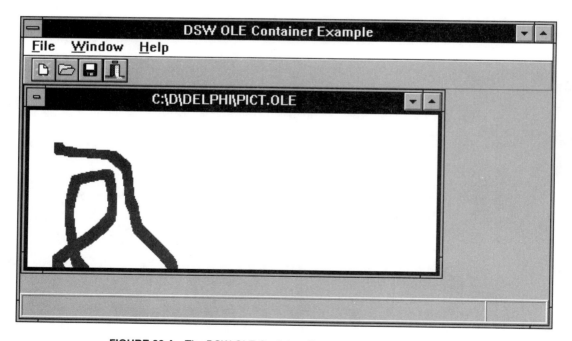

FIGURE 22.4   The DSW OLE Container Example with a Single OLE Child Window

When this program runs, you can use either OLE version 1.0 or version 2.0 linking or OLE embedding. For OLE 2.0 compliant applications, you will see in-place activation occur because this Delphi application has a main menu and speedbar. For example, if you embed a Word document into the Window, Word's menus and speedbars will replace those of the application.

This application uses all standard Delphi components, including component dialog boxes to handle the opening and saving chores. The MDI application was created from the MDI application template, so no work was required to implement the MDI features (tiling and cascading child windows, minimizing them all, etc.). This example also demonstrates how quickly Delphi applications that perform sophisticated actions can be put together.

The complete source code for this program follows, including the code for the DFM files. In the DFM files, the glyph data has been left out, because it appears in text files as long streams of binary digits. This means that if you transcribe this DFM file into Delphi, your speed buttons won't have bitmaps on them.

This is the application project file, which defines the units and forms that the application will use, along with the code to start the application running:

```
program Mdiapp;

uses
    Forms,
    Main in 'MAIN.PAS' {MainForm},
    Childwin in 'CHILDWIN.PAS' {OLE_form},
    Fabout in '\FABOUT.PAS' {AboutBox};

{$R *.RES}

begin
    Application.CreateForm(TMainForm, MainForm);
    Application.CreateForm(TAboutBox, AboutBox);
    Application.Run;
end.
```

Following is the code for the unit which contatains the main application form (that is, the MDI parent form). You should realize that most of the code shown below was generated as part of the MDI application template. In particular, look at the code for the `Create-OLE_form` method. This routine creates the child windows, which are defined to hold just an OLE container component. This routine is called from both the `Open` child window and `Create` child window routines. It determines which called it by the caption for the form: If the caption contains the string `'OLE Container'`, that means that this is a new OLE object. Otherwise, we are opening an existing OLE object (which was saved earlier) using the `Save` routine. The `Save` routine prompts the user for a file name, then saves the file and changes the caption of the form to reflect the name of the file. Most of the remainder of the code was generated by utilizing the MDI application template.

```pascal
unit Main;

interface

uses WinTypes, WinProcs, SysUtils, Classes, Graphics, Forms,
Controls, Menus,
  StdCtrls, Dialogs, Buttons, Messages, ExtCtrls, ToCtrl;

type
  TMainForm = class(TForm)
    MainMenu1: TMainMenu;
    Panel1: TPanel;
    StatusLine: TPanel;
    File1: TMenuItem;
    FileNewItem: TMenuItem;
    FileOpenItem: TMenuItem;
    Panel2: TPanel;
    FileCloseItem: TMenuItem;
    Window1: TMenuItem;
    Help1: TMenuItem;
    N1: TMenuItem;
    FileExitItem: TMenuItem;
    WindowCascadeItem: TMenuItem;
    WindowTileItem: TMenuItem;
    WindowArrangeItem: TMenuItem;
    HelpAboutItem: TMenuItem;
    OpenDialog1: TOpenDialog;
    FileSaveItem: TMenuItem;
    WindowMinimizeItem: TMenuItem;
    SpeedPanel: TPanel;
    OpenBtn: TSpeedButton;
    SaveBtn: TSpeedButton;
    ExitBtn: TSpeedButton;
    SpeedButton1: TSpeedButton;
    SaveDialog1: TSaveDialog;
    procedure FormCreate(Sender: TObject);
    procedure FileNewItemClick(Sender: TObject);
    procedure WindowCascadeItemClick(Sender: TObject);
    procedure UpdateMenuItems(Sender: TObject);
    procedure WindowTileItemClick(Sender: TObject);
    procedure WindowArrangeItemClick(Sender: TObject);
    procedure FileCloseItemClick(Sender: TObject);
    procedure FileOpenItemClick(Sender: TObject);
    procedure FileExitItemClick(Sender: TObject);
```

```
    procedure FileSaveItemClick(Sender: TObject);
    procedure WindowMinimizeItemClick(Sender: TObject);
    procedure FormDestroy(Sender: TObject);
    procedure HelpAboutItemClick(Sender: TObject);
  private
    { Private declarations }
    procedure CreateOLE_form(const Name: string);
    procedure ShowHint(Sender: TObject);
  public
    { Public declarations }
  end;

var
  MainForm: TMainForm;

implementation

{$R *.DFM}

uses ChildWin, FAbout;

procedure TMainForm.FormCreate(Sender: TObject);
begin
  Application.OnHint := ShowHint;
  Screen.OnActiveFormChange := UpdateMenuItems;
end;


procedure TMainForm.ShowHint(Sender: TObject);
begin
  StatusLine.Caption := Application.Hint;
end;


procedure TMainForm.CreateOLE_form(const Name: string);
var
  Child: TOLE_form;
begin
  { create a new MDI child window }
  Child := TOLE_form.Create(Application);
  Child.Caption := Name;
  if pos( 'OLE Container', Name ) = 0 then
    child.OLEContainer1.LoadFromFile( Name );
end;

procedure TMainForm.FileNewItemClick(Sender: TObject);
var
  Info: Pointer;
  ActiveForm : TOLE_form;
begin
```

```
  CreateOLE_form('OLE Container ' + IntToStr(MDIChildCount +
1));
  ActiveForm := ActiveMDIChild as TOLE_form;
  if InsertOLEObjectDlg(ActiveForm, 0, Info) then
  begin
    ActiveForm.OLEContainer1.PInitInfo := Info;
    ReleaseOLEInitInfo(Info)
  end
  else
    ActiveForm.close;
end;

procedure TMainForm.FileOpenItemClick(Sender: TObject);
begin
  if OpenDialog1.Execute then
    CreateOLE_form(OpenDialog1.FileName);
end;

procedure TMainForm.FileCloseItemClick(Sender: TObject);
begin
  if ActiveMDIChild <> nil then
    ActiveMDIChild.Close;
end;

procedure TMainForm.FileSaveItemClick(Sender: TObject);
var
  ActiveForm : TOLE_form;
begin
  { save current file (ActiveMDIChild points to the window) }
  if SaveDialog1.execute then
  begin
    ActiveForm := ActiveMDIChild as TOle_form;
    ActiveForm.OleContainer1.SaveToFile(
SaveDialog1.FileName );
    if ActiveForm.caption  SaveDialog1.FileName then
      ActiveForm.caption := SaveDialog1.FileName
  end
end;

procedure TMainForm.FileExitItemClick(Sender: TObject);
begin
  Close;
end;

procedure TMainForm.WindowCascadeItemClick(Sender: TObject);
begin
  Cascade;
end;
```

```
procedure TMainForm.WindowTileItemClick(Sender: TObject);
begin
  Tile;
end;


procedure TMainForm.WindowArrangeItemClick(Sender: TObject);
begin
  ArrangeIcons;
end;


procedure TMainForm.WindowMinimizeItemClick(Sender:
TObject);
var
  I: Integer;
begin
  { Must be done backwards through the MDIChildren array }
  for I := MDIChildCount - 1 downto 0 do
  MDIChildren[I].WindowState := wsMinimized;
end;


procedure TMainForm.UpdateMenuItems(Sender: TObject);
begin
  FileCloseItem.Enabled := MDIChildCount > 0;
  FileSaveItem.Enabled := MDIChildCount > 0;
  SaveBtn.Enabled := MDIChildCount > 0;
  WindowCascadeItem.Enabled := MDIChildCount > 0;
  WindowTileItem.Enabled := MDIChildCount > 0;
  WindowArrangeItem.Enabled := MDIChildCount > 0;
  WindowMinimizeItem.Enabled := MDIChildCount > 0;
end;


procedure TMainForm.FormDestroy(Sender: TObject);
begin
  Screen.OnActiveFormChange := nil;
end;


procedure TMainForm.HelpAboutItemClick(Sender: TObject);
begin
  AboutBox.ShowModal;
end;

end.
```

DFM File for Main

We saved our DFM file as text and pasted it into this chapter and then read it into Delphi to convert it back to a binary file. It shows all of the components and how their properties deviate from the defaults for those properties.

```
object MainForm: TMainForm
  Left = 232
  Top = 115
  Width = 435
  Height = 300
  ActiveControl = StatusLine
  Caption = 'DSW OLE Container Example'
  Font.Color = clWindowText
  Font.Height = -13
  Font.Name = 'System'
  Font.Style = []
  FormStyle = fsMDIForm
  Menu = MainMenu1
  PixelsPerInch = 96
  Position = poDefault
  WindowMenu = Window1
  OnCreate = FormCreate
  OnDestroy = FormDestroy
  TextHeight = 16
  object Panel1: TPanel
    Left = 0
    Top = 228
    Width = 427
    Height = 26
    Align = alBottom
    BorderWidth = 1
    TabOrder = 0
    object StatusLine: TPanel
      Left = 2
      Top = 2
      Width = 362
      Height = 22
      Align = alClient
      Alignment = taLeftJustify
      BevelOuter = bvLowered
      BorderWidth = 1
      Font.Color = clBlack
      Font.Height = -11
      Font.Name = 'MS Sans Serif'
      Font.Style = []
      ParentFont = False
```

```
      TabOrder = 0
    end
    object Panel2: TPanel
      Left = 364
      Top = 2
      Width = 61
      Height = 22
      Align = alRight
      Alignment = taLeftJustify
      BevelOuter = bvLowered
      TabOrder = 1
    end
  end
  object SpeedPanel: TPanel
    Left = 0
    Top = 0
    Width = 427
    Height = 30
    Align = alTop
    ParentShowHint = False
    ShowHint = True
    TabOrder = 1
    object OpenBtn: TSpeedButton
      Left = 31
      Top = 2
      Width = 25
      Height = 25
      Hint = 'Open|'
      Glyph.Data = {}
      NumGlyphs = 2
      OnClick = FileOpenItemClick
    end
    object SaveBtn: TSpeedButton
      Left = 55
      Top = 2
      Width = 25
      Height = 25
      Hint = 'Save As'
      Glyph.Data = {}
      NumGlyphs = 2
      OnClick = FileSaveItemClick
    end
    object ExitBtn: TSpeedButton
      Left = 80
      Top = 2
      Width = 25
      Height = 25
      Hint = 'Exit|'
```

```
      Glyph.Data = {}
      NumGlyphs = 2
      OnClick = FileExitItemClick
    end
  object SpeedButton1: TSpeedButton
    Left = 8
    Top = 2
    Width = 25
    Height = 25
    Hint = 'New|'
    Glyph.Data = {}
    NumGlyphs = 2
    OnClick = FileNewItemClick
  end
end
object MainMenu1: TMainMenu
  Left = 36
  Top = 200
  object File1: TMenuItem
    Caption = '&File'
    Hint = 'File related commands'
    object FileNewItem: TMenuItem
      Caption = '&New'
      Hint = 'Create a new file'
      OnClick = FileNewItemClick
    end
    object FileOpenItem: TMenuItem
      Caption = '&Open'
      Hint = 'Open an existing file'
      OnClick = FileOpenItemClick
    end
    object FileCloseItem: TMenuItem
      Caption = '&Close'
      Hint = 'Close current file'
      OnClick = FileCloseItemClick
    end
    object FileSaveItem: TMenuItem
      Caption = '&Save'
      Hint = 'Save current file'
      OnClick = FileSaveItemClick
    end
    object N1: TMenuItem
      Caption = '-'
    end
    object FileExitItem: TMenuItem
      Caption = 'E&xit'
      Hint = 'Exit the application'
      OnClick = FileExitItemClick
    end
```

```
        end
      object Window1: TMenuItem
        Caption = '&Window'
        Hint = 'Window related commands such as Tile and
  Cascade'
          object WindowCascadeItem: TMenuItem
            Caption = '&Cascade'
            Hint = 'Arrange windows to overlap'
            OnClick = WindowCascadeItemClick
          end
          object WindowTileItem: TMenuItem
            Caption = '&Tile'
            Hint = 'Arrange windows without overlap'
            OnClick = WindowTileItemClick
          end
          object WindowArrangeItem: TMenuItem
            Caption = '&Arrange Icons'
            Hint = 'Arrange window icons at bottom of main window'
            OnClick = WindowArrangeItemClick
          end
          object WindowMinimizeItem: TMenuItem
            Caption = '&Minimize All'
            Hint = 'Minimize all windows'
            OnClick = WindowMinimizeItemClick
          end
        end
      object Help1: TMenuItem
        Caption = '&Help'
        Hint = 'Help topics'
          object HelpAboutItem: TMenuItem
            Caption = '&About'
            OnClick = HelpAboutItemClick
          end
        end
    end
  object OpenDialog1: TOpenDialog
    DefaultExt = 'OLE'
    Filter = 'OLE Files|*.OLE'
    Left = 4
    Top = 200
  end
  object SaveDialog1: TSaveDialog
    DefaultExt = 'OLE'
    Filter = 'OLE Files|*.OLE'
    Title = 'Save OLE File As . . . '
    Left = 72
    Top = 200
  end
end
```

Unit FAbout

The following code is the source code for the about box. This is a very simple form, created from the About box form template.

```
unit fabout;

interface

uses WinTypes, WinProcs, Classes, Graphics, Forms, Controls,
StdCtrls,
   Buttons, ExtCtrls;

type
  TAboutBox = class(TForm)
    Panel1: TPanel;
    OKButton: TBitBtn;
    ProductName: TLabel;
    Version: TLabel;
    Copyright: TLabel;
    Comments: TLabel;
    Image1: TImage;
    procedure OKButtonClick(Sender: TObject);
  private
    { Private declarations }
  public
    { Public declarations }
  end;

var
  AboutBox: TAboutBox;

implementation

{$R *.DFM}

procedure TAboutBox.OKButtonClick(Sender: TObject);
begin
  ModalResult := mrOK;
end;

end.
```

DFM File for FAbout

What follows is the DFM file for the About box form.

```
object AboutBox: TAboutBox
  Left = 238
  Top = 104
  ActiveControl = OKButton
  BorderStyle = bsDialog
  Caption = 'About'
  ClientHeight = 213
  ClientWidth = 298
  Font.Color = clWindowText
  Font.Height = -13
  Font.Name = 'System'
  Font.Style = []
  PixelsPerInch = 96
  Position = poScreenCenter
  TextHeight = 16
  object Panel1: TPanel
    Left = 8
    Top = 8
    Width = 281
    Height = 161
    BevelInner = bvRaised
    BevelOuter = bvLowered
    TabOrder = 0
    object ProductName: TLabel
      Left = 88
      Top = 16
      Width = 109
      Height = 13
      Caption = 'OLE Example'
      Font.Color = clBlack
      Font.Height = -11
      Font.Name = 'MS Sans Serif'
      Font.Style = [fsBold]
      ParentFont = False
      IsControl = True
    end
    object Version: TLabel
      Left = 88
      Top = 40
      Width = 65
      Height = 13
      Caption = 'Version 1.0'
      Font.Color = clBlack
      Font.Height = -11
      Font.Name = 'MS Sans Serif'
      Font.Style = [fsBold]
      ParentFont = False
```

```
      IsControl = True
    end
  object Copyright: TLabel
    Left = 8
    Top = 80
    Width = 225
    Height = 33
    Caption = 'Copyright (c) 1995. All rights reserved.'
    Font.Color = clBlack
    Font.Height = -11
    Font.Name = 'MS Sans Serif'
    Font.Style = [fsBold]
    ParentFont = False
    WordWrap = True
    IsControl = True
  end
  object Comments: TLabel
    Left = 8
    Top = 120
    Width = 265
    Height = 17
    Caption = 'Very simple example of the OLE containter.'
    Font.Color = clBlack
    Font.Height = -11
    Font.Name = 'MS Sans Serif'
    Font.Style = [fsBold]
    ParentFont = False
    WordWrap = True
    IsControl = True
  end
  object Image1: TImage
    Left = 8
    Top = 8
    Width = 73
    Height = 65
  end
end
object OKButton: TBitBtn
  Left = 111
  Top = 178
  Width = 77
  Height = 27
  Font.Color = clBlack
  Font.Height = -11
  Font.Name = 'MS Sans Serif'
  Font.Style = [fsBold]
  ParentFont = False
  TabOrder = 1
```

```
      OnClick = OKButtonClick
      Kind = bkOK
      Margin = 2
      Spacing = -1
      IsControl = True
   end
end
```

Our example program demonstrates OLEContainer components in an MDI application which allows the user to create an OLE link in each of the child windows. The user can also save and restore OLE files. This application also allows in-place activation for OLE 2.0 compliant servers.

CHAPTER 23

CLIENT/SERVER BASICS

WHAT IS CLIENT/SERVER?

The term "client/server" is used to describe many things within the programming community. The functionality of a DLL call can be considered a client/server relationship. In this case, the DLL function is acting as the server with the application acting as the client. OLE and DDE are examples of client/server relationships in that the calling application is once again the client and the called application is the server. For the purposes of this chapter, we will be discussing client/server with respect to database storage and manipulation.

Generally, the *client* part of client/server refers to a program that runs on a computer attached to a network. It is the "front end," where all the data input and output occurs. For example, a Delphi program could be the client application that performs data input and output for a database server that resides on the network.

The *server* portion of client/server refers to a specialized database server. This is a software application (or group of applications) that accepts requests to enter and retrieve data. You can think of the database server as a "black box" that provides database services. Multiple users can access the database simultaneously with requests, and servers are designed to withstand very high network transaction rates.

The server database registers itself with the network, so that it appears to users of the network as another network service (just like the print server). Using special software drivers, the client application(s) can send data to and receive data from the server.

CLIENT/SERVER ARCHITECTURE

It is important to understand the underlying structure of network and client/server architecture in order to take full advantages of the facilities available using a database server.
By realizing the work that goes into an application's request for information, you can better optimize and configure your server and application.

OSI Layers

The underlying structure of most networks in use today is based on the design set forth by
the International Standards Organization (ISO) in the early 1970s. They identified seven
layers of communication and hardware that can be used to identify the working components of a network. These are known as the Open Systems Interconnect (OSI) Model. The
OSI Model identifies the different aspects of a network architecture that lay between the
physical transmission media (coax cable, fiber-optics, twisted-pair, etc.) and the applications running on an individual workstation. Figure 23.1 is a schematic of the different OSI
layers.

The *physical layer* identifies the actual media being used to transport messages
across the local area network (LAN). This might be coaxial cable or other media. The
datalink layer allows for the formatting of data messages, identifying nodes for the messages and determining the message passing scheme to use. This layer will identify the

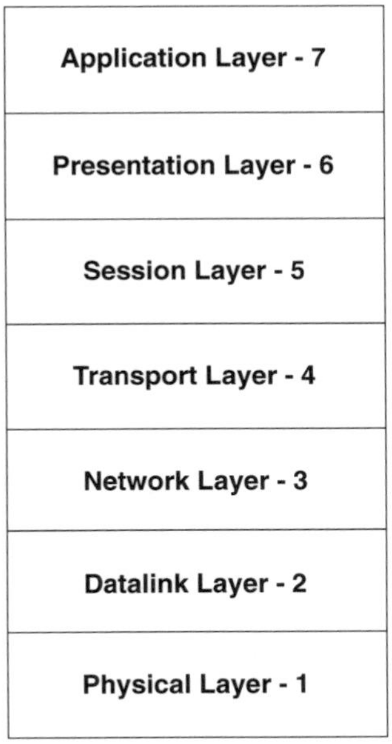

Application Layer - 7
Presentation Layer - 6
Session Layer - 5
Transport Layer - 4
Network Layer - 3
Datalink Layer - 2
Physical Layer - 1

FIGURE 23.1   OSI Network Layers
Model

message protocol such as Token Ring, Arcnet, and Ethernet. The *network layer* is designed to resolve messages and address conflicts when transporting messages.

The *transport layer* handles the disassembling and assembling of messages. It is used to guarantee a complete message transmission. It is at this layer such protocols as Transmission Control Protocol/Internet Protocol (TCP/IP) exist. They are designed to manage network traffic and ensure completeness.

The *session layer* is designed to establish specific communications between computers on the LAN. This layer allows applications to communicate with one another. Network logging and security are implemented at this layer. The commonly used NetBIOS Extended User Interface (NetBEUI) resides at this layer.

The *presentation* and *application layers* are where front end software resides and provides the interface between the user and the network. The application layer is where a Delphi application resides. Recognizing the location of different software communication layers will allow you to better troubleshoot any database server implementation.

Server Software Configuration

There are numerous SQL server packages that can be used to create a client/server environment. Using the SQL Links native drivers that ship with the client/server version of Delphi, you can connect to Informix, SQL Server, Oracle, and Interbase. Each of these server platforms have different capabilities and run on a variety of operating system platforms. Each understands a different dialect of SQL as well. In addition, developers can also use one of the many ODBC drivers that exist for the various server platforms to attain the connectivity required.

In order to connect to a specific server on the network, the BDE configuration utility must be used to set up an "alias" to the server database. The screen shot shown in Figure 23.2 shows the configuration utility displaying a sample of installed drivers. When you purchase the client/server version of Delphi you automatically receive the drivers for the servers mentioned above.

As you can see, you have the option of adding new ODBC drivers to the list. Once a driver has been installed, you need to create an alias to the database you wish to connect to using the proper driver. The simplest aliases are those that use the standard driver (for DBF and DB data files). These aliases just point to a simple directory on either a local or network drive. The Figure 23.3 shows a standard alias configuration.

This example shows an alias called dsw_dbs which references a local drive and directory (c:\dsw_dbs). In order to connect to a database server, more than just a drive and directory must be specified. The alias in Figure 23.4 demonstrates the options that will need to be set in order to connect to a local Interbase SQL Server database through the local Interbase engine.

First, you must select the New Alias button which will prompt you to enter an alias name and a driver. Figure 23.4 shows this dialog with the Interbase driver and name assigned as IBLOCAL.

Once the alias is added, you must assign some of the different configuration options to it. Figure 23.5 shows the new IBLOCAL alias with the different options set. The only

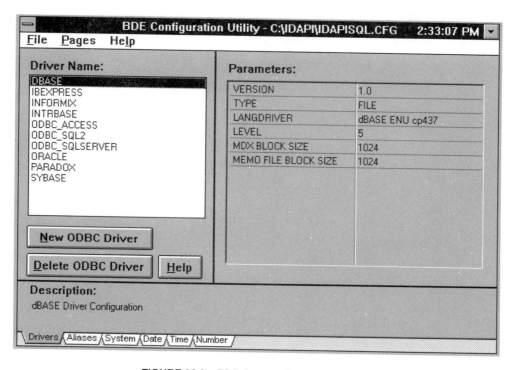

FIGURE 23.2 BDE Configuration Drivers Tab

option that has been changed from its default value is the Server Name parameter. This has been changed to point to the database desired for this alias. Other options can be changed and will affect the performance and capabilities of the connection.

Following is a list of the different parameters that can be set for an alias and their meanings:

- The **TYPE** indication determines which driver will be used for the connection.
- The **PATH** parameter is not used for Interbase connections but is reserved for future use.
- The **SERVER NAME** determines which Interbase database is to be used. For other drivers, this name refers to the server name on the network.
- The **USE NAME** parameter determines the default user ID to use when a connection is made to the server.
- The **OPEN MODE** determines whether the connection will be READ WRITE or READ ONLY.
- The **SCHEMA CACHE SIZE** sets the number of tables that will be cached when a connection is achieved.
- The **LANGDRIVER** defaults to using US language defaults for the server but can

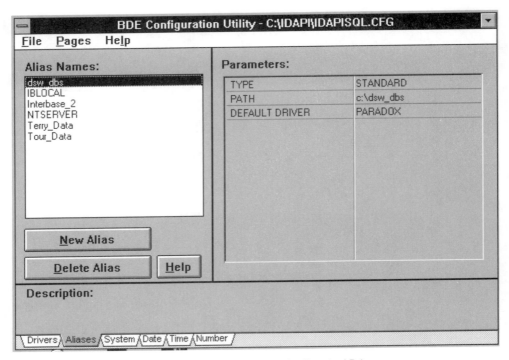

FIGURE 23.3   BDE Alias Using the Standard Driver

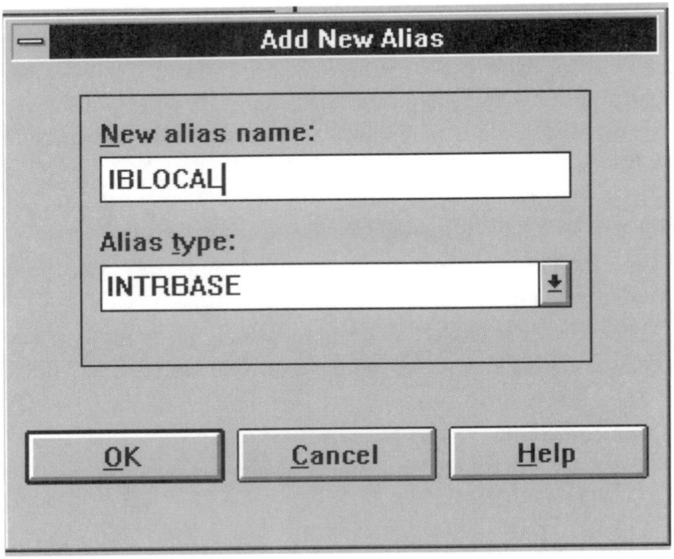

FIGURE 23.4   New Alias with Interbase Driver

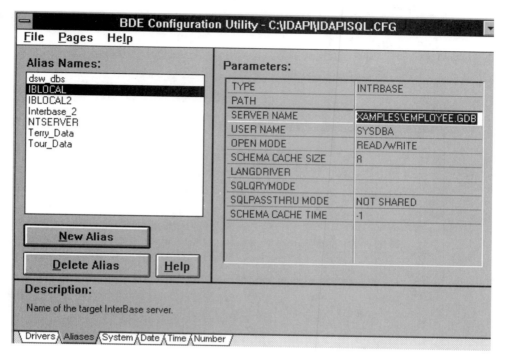

FIGURE 23.5   Interbase BDE Alias Configuration

be set for other language character sets. This setting must match the setting already configured for your server.

- **SQLQRYMODE** determines whether or not the local BDE engine will attempt to perform any queries if they fail on the server. No setting defaults to an attempt at the server first and then an attempt by the local engine should the server fail. Options for this parameter include SERVER and LOCAL. These settings will force performance of any SQL code to either local or server only.

- **SQLPASSTHRUMODE** determines whether BDE and pass-through queries will share the same connection to the server. Options for this parameter include NOT SHARED (blank setting), SHARED AUTOCOMMIT (default), and SHARED NO AUTOCOMMIT. We will discuss this option in more detail later.

- **SCHEMA CACHE TIME** specifies how long cached table information will be stored in seconds. The default setting is -1, indicating information should be cached until the table is closed. This setting can be used to fine-tune server performance.

Some server drivers add additional parameters due to the specific features found in the server software. For example, the SYBASE SQL Server driver adds a BLOB EDIT LOGGING and DATE MODE parameters to help configure the storage of these data

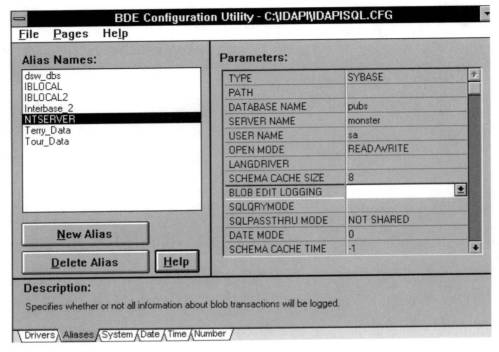

FIGURE 23.6   BDE Alias Configuration for MS-SQL Server

types on the server. The ORACLE driver uses still other parameters. This variation in parameter settings is provided for to enable the developer to better control the back end server. Since the drivers of SQL Links were written for each specific platform, this should be expected. Figure 23.6 shows a BDE alias configured using the SYBASE driver connecting to a Microsoft SQL Server (both servers use the same driver).

ODBC Configuration

There are many more database servers than SQL Links for them. Developers may have a need to connect to a DB2 database server, BTreive data, or Access .MDB files. For these connectivity situations, Borland has included with the BDE the ability to use Open Database Connectivity (ODBC) drivers. ODBC, like the BDE, is a middle-ware product specification designed to allow for the standardization of front end application development tools. Front ends conforming to the ODBC standard have the ability to use these drivers to connect to a variety of server back ends. ODBC throughput tends to be slower than native drivers like SQL Links and are not preferred when the native links are available.

In order to use an ODBC driver you must first install it on your Windows platform (normally placed in the \WINDOWS\SYSTEM directory). Once installed you can use the ODBC Administrator utility located within the control panel application. The ODBC Ad-

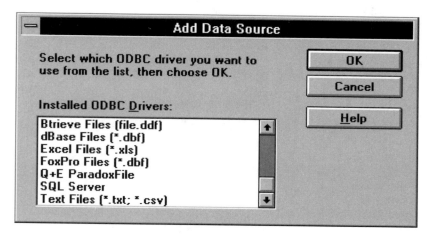

FIGURE 23.7   ODBC Administrator Add Driver Dialog

ministrator allows you to create data sources which use ODBC driver DLL files to access the proper back end. Once you run the ODBC Administrator, you will have the option to Add a new driver from the drivers you have installed. The ODBC Administrator uses the term "Driver" to indicate a connection. The BDE uses the term "Alias". Selecting Add from the button list will give you the dialog in Figure 23.7.

Once you select a driver you will be able to set up the driver by adding a Datasource Name and set the Database option. Figure 23.8 shows the set-up dialog with the values filled in for accessing a set of dBASE files via ODBC.

Each ODBC set-up screen will differ depending on the driver used. Once the driver is set up, you will be able to add the driver to the BDE using the New ODBC Driver button on the drivers page. You will be required to enter a BDE name for the driver and point it to the newly created ODBC DatabaseSource Name. Figure 23.9 below shows the set-up for the dBASE driver installed in our example.

After the driver is installed and named in the BDE you will be able to create a link to the tables by simply adding a new Alias. Be aware that many drivers that claim to be ODBC compliant may not be. Manufacturers may create drivers that will work as ODBC connections in some products but do not conform to the standards as set out by Microsoft. Just because a driver works in one product does not guarantee it will work in another. Figure 23.10 shows the Alias created in the BDE for the dBASE ODBC driver.

SERVER FEATURES

There are distinct advantages in using a database server to store your data. Most server implementations support many features that can isolate your application from the underlying data it acts upon. This level of isolation makes it easier to develop consistent data access methodologies across a range of applications and development platforms. The fol-

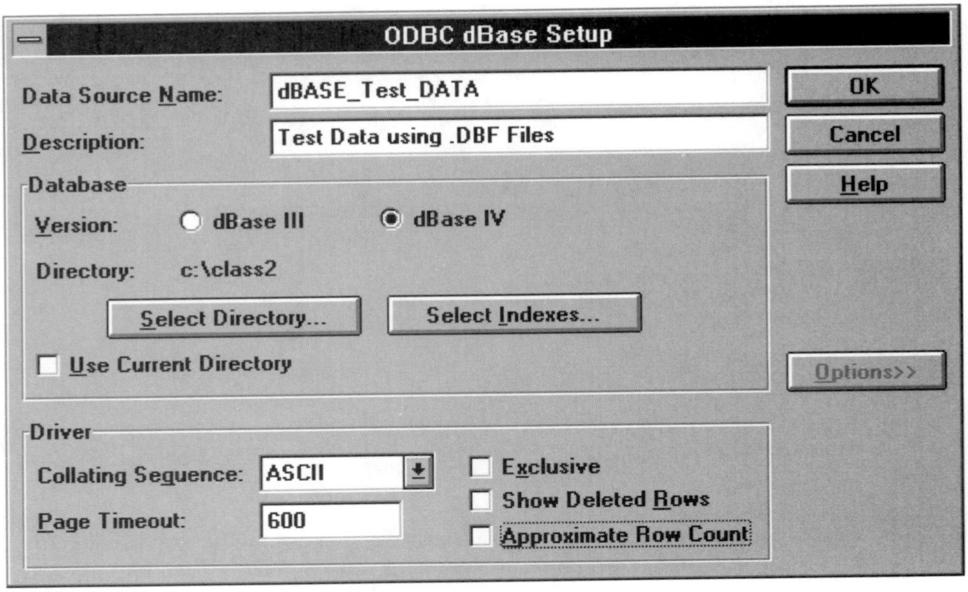

FIGURE 23.8   ODBC Setup for dBase IV Tables

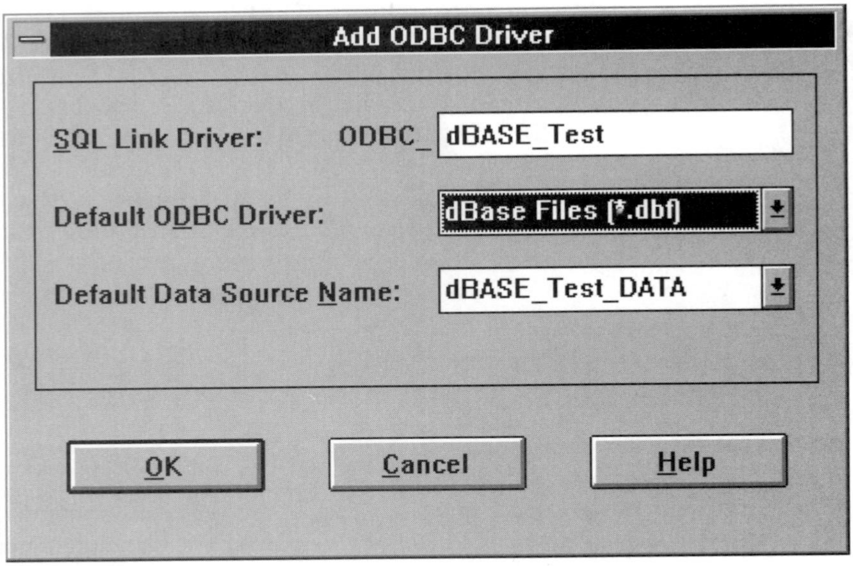

FIGURE 23.9   New ODBC Driver Dialog in BDE

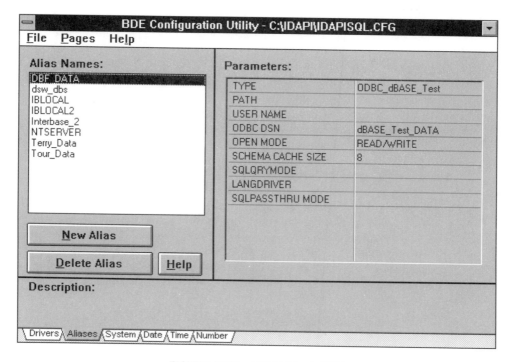

FIGURE 23.10   ODBC Alias in BDE

lowing sections describe some basic features found in database server software that can aid you in this effort.

Stored Procedures

All database servers speak some dialect of SQL. However, SQL is strictly a data access language, so each vendor has added extensions to their version of SQL to handle other chores. All of these SQL languages have enough flexibility so that you can write all your data intensive operations on the server instead of having the client application do it. These procedures that are written in the server's SQL dialect are called stored procedures because they are stored with the data in the server and executed by the server. (See the chapter entitled Client Server Applications for a look at some examples of writing stored procedures and calling them from applications.)

Stored procedures serve to isolate your application from the server data and give a standard interface to several applications at the same time. Consider the idea of writing three applications that all access the same database on a server. Each of these applications might access the data through the use of some SQL language code in order to create a set of records to act upon. If the database structure changes then each of the applications would need to be modified in order to take into account this change. If a stored procedure is used instead, only the procedure would need to be changed. This technique follows along with the principles discussed in the chapter on modular programming.

Triggers

Triggers are specialized stored procedures that "fire" whenever a value is changed within the database. Triggers can serve many purposes within a database. Most tables have a unique value that differentiates records, referred to as the primary key. This key value can be generated by the server using a trigger that fires whenever a new record is inserted into the table. This would prove to be a much more difficult task if each application using the data was responsible for supplying it.

Triggers can also be used to validate data in some server environments. Triggers can be used to help enforce referential integrity as well. Suppose an application attempts to delete a customer record for which orders exist in the Orders table. A trigger can be used to automatically cascade the delete, and remove all of the orders. The trigger could also be used to prevent the deletion until all of the orders are removed or transferred to a "dead customer" account. Triggers can be used in a wide variety of ways to maintain consistent data and enforce certain rules on applications using the data.

Security

A server database is more secure than a shared table on a network because the database format is highly proprietary. For example, if you have DBF tables that reside in a network directory, anyone with a copy of dBASE can open the tables and copy or manipulate your data. So even if you've spent a lot of time implementing validation rules and formats, someone can easily bypass all your safeguards. Servers, on the other hand, are much more secure and have strict controls on how data access is accomplished.

Most servers have enhanced security which allows the database administrator to set specific database rights for each user, so that each user can only access the data that he or she should be able to access. Using different security schemes, administrators can assign database owners, available columns, and the operations a user can perform. Most server security systems provide a range of options to make the job of securing data easier.

Views

Since it is often cumbersome for users of server data to be intimately familiar with the data storage details of a database, Views were created. Views are selections of data that are stored on the server. Users no longer need to know the exact relationships between tables on the server. They can access a predefined view of the data that has the relationship or set of records already set for viewing. Views are very powerful in that they provide an abstraction of the data that doesn't require any knowledge of the actual stored data formats. Some server platforms even allow tables stored in separate databases to be coupled together within a View without the user's knowledge. This gives database administrators much more flexibility in the mechanisms they use to arrange a database structure.

For example, a customer table might exist in a database along with an orders table.

Users may require the need to see both the customer and the order information related together. The user of the data has no need to know about the fact that there are two tables, particularly if the user is only interested in looking at the data. Rather than forcing the user to learn the nuances of table relations, the database administrator can set up the View to be used. The user can access the View and see a nonnormalized perspective of the data, never knowing about the underlying data structure.

Transaction Processing

Most database applications have a need to write data as well as read it. The BDE provides a record-based transaction processing capability. Unfortunately, most applications need more than a simple record-oriented approach. Suppose a user needed to access and change data about an order in an order entry system. The order might be made up of information from various tables. For the purposes of this example, let us say that there are two tables that track information about orders, ORDERS and LINEITEMS. Changing an order might require the need to modify both a record in the ORDERS table and several records in the LINEITEMS table.

Single, record-based transactions would not suffice in this situation. Once the user saved changes to one record, there would be no way to rollback the changes later should the need arise. For this reason, most database servers support some form of complex transaction tracking. These facilities allow programmers to write applications that change multiple records and still give the user the ability to "back out" of the transaction. Each server platform provides a slightly different method of accomplishing this task. Developers would need to learn the capabilities of each server to take full advantage of these features. Fortunately, the BDE has facilities for accessing each of these different server transaction systems through the SQL Links or ODBC drivers.

SQL Basics

The underlying language used by most database servers is some dialect of SQL. The SQL language standard provides a methodology for accessing data in a consistent way across applications and servers. Unfortunately, the current SQL-92 standard implementation does not go far enough to satisfy the needs of most data processing professionals. Most server vendors have extended the SQL language in order to offer the tools needed to develop enterprise wide database solutions. This section will discuss some of the basics of SQL and its role in application development. This is not intended as an exhaustive treatment of the material needed to develop truly complete applications or databases on any SQL server platform.

DDL

In order to create databases on a server, you must first learn something about its Data Definition Language (DDL). The DDL is a set of SQL commands that provide developers a way to create databases and tables on their servers. Each server's DDL implementation is slightly different and offers different features. For the purposes of this discussion, we will stick to the most common of DDL statements.

The SQL statement used to create tables within a database is the CREATE DATA-BASE command. The syntax in the following code snippet shows the CREATE TABLE command as defined for an Interbase server. As you can see, using the CREATE TABLE command you define a table's name and fields along with each field's type and length. You also have the option of defining whether or not a specific field can contain null values. Unlike many desktop data file formats, database servers provide a way to store a null value in a field if no value is provided. This differs from file formats like .DBF files which force a zero or blank character string value in for undefined field values.

```
CREATE TABLE <tablename>
      (<Fld1) <Type>(<Length>)    [NOT NULL],
      [<FldN> <Type> (<Length>) [NOT NULL]])
```

While this is not the full syntax for creating a table, it gives you an idea of the types of information that must be provided. Additionally, the Interbase CREATE TABLE statement will allow you to set primary keys, force column data to be unique, set integrity constraints and other functionality.

Some DDLs allow you to create column types of your own, or domains. Column typing can provide for consistent table creation specifications. For example, you may wish to create a column type called phone_number. This type could then be used by several tables within a database or server and force consistency within your table definitions. Some servers also allow for the creation of validation rules for columns.

Stored procedures and triggers are also part of the DDL. As we have discussed, using these features in creating a database will promote data consistency and referential integrity. Additionally, procedures and triggers will allow different applications to access and modify data within your server without having to write SQL statements for each.

DML

SQL commands like SELECT, INSERT, DELETE, and UPDATE are part of the SQL Data Manipulation Language (DML). Using these statements, developers can view, add, remove, and modify records within server tables. Entire books are written on the subject of DML. Each server has a specific dialect of SQL DML and developers can benefit from learning their specific platform before setting out to write an application for a server.

Local SQL in Delphi

Delphi provides access to a SQL language dialect called Local SQL. This can be used to assign SQL strings to TQuery components that act on local tables such as DB or DBF files. This is a subset of ANSI standard SQL and has some limitations. Since Local SQL does not act in conjunction with a server, many statements that result in datasets provide nonmodifiable result sets.

The DDL for Local SQL provides the following statements:

- CREATE TABLE
- ALTER TABLE
- DROP TABLE
- CREATE INDEX
- DROP INDEX

The DML provides the ability to modify and view data on local tables as you would with a server. The following is a list of supported SQL statements in Local SQL:

- SELECT
- INSERT
- UPDATE
- DELETE

As mentioned above, these are a subset of the ANSI SQL and have limitations associated with them. For example, datasets created with the SELECT statement in Local SQL that use the ORDER BY clause are read-only. SELECTs that cross multiple tables are also read-only. See your Delphi help file under Syntax Requirements for a Live Result Set for more information on these limitations.

Heterogeneous Joins

One advantage to conforming to Local SQL statements is the ability to perform heterogeneous joins across server platforms. Using a TQuery object on a form, you can specify a table from a local drive and a table from a server database within a SELECT statement. This facility allows for the viewing of related data only. As mentioned above, tables joined with Local SQL are not modifiable.

We have seem many of the features that are associated with a client/server implementation. In the following chapter we will look at how these features are implemented in Interbase. Local Interbase ships with each copy of Delphi and has many of the features we have discussed in this chapter. Most of the techniques demonstrated in the next chapter can be performed with any robust database server software.

CHAPTER **24**

LOCAL INTERBASE

INTERBASE AND LOCAL INTERBASE

InterBase is Borland's database server. It is a full featured database server that supports all of the features highlighted in the last chapter and more. The full-blown, multi-user Local InterBase server is included in the client/server version of Delphi.

Local InterBase, which is included in the desktop version, is a single user version of the server. Local InterBase is designed to

- provide server quality features for a single user database application
- build full-scale client/server systems

Local InterBase allows you, as the programmer, to work on a server based project without the necessity of being logged onto a network. Then, when it's time to distribute the application, you can just transfer the alias to the network InterBase server and your application should run without any need for alterations.

Local InterBase is a good alternative to .DBF and .DB tables because it allows you to store the data integrity rules at the database level rather than at the client level. This is a good idea because the database will look at every attempt to submit data, whereas if you forget to add the integrity rules into one of your input screens at the client level then you might have invalid data entered by accident.

There is an interactive tool that you can use to access local InterBase called Windows ISQL (Interactive Structured Query Language).

354

Windows ISQL

Windows ISQL allows you to submit SQL commands one at a time to the InterBase server. This is handy if you need to do database administration or to set up tables, add triggers, etc.

When you run Windows ISQL, you're presented with the work area shown in Figure 24.1.

As you can see, you enter commands in the upper window, and the results of the commands appear in the lower window. However, before you can access the data on the server, you first must log on to it. This is part of the enhanced security that InterBase provides over DBF and DB tables.

To log on to the database, go to **File | Connect to Database . . . ,** which will bring up the dialog shown in Figure 24.2.

At the top, you can specify whether you want the local version or the remote version. The database used here is the sample employee database that ships with Delphi.

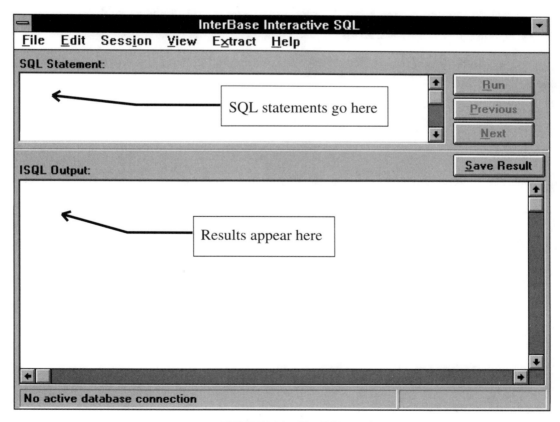

FIGURE 24.1   The ISQL Interface

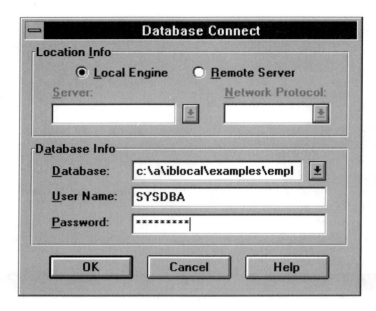

FIGURE 24.2   ISQL Log-in Dialog

"SYSDBA" is the built-in name for the database administrator, which can be modified. The password (unless you or someone else has changed it) is "masterkey" (and it IS case sensitive, so you must type "masterkey" in all lower case). When you click on OK, you will experience a slight pause and then a cursor will appear in the input window. You can now submit SQL commands to InterBase.

For example, to show all the columns and all the rows of the Employee table, enter the following command in the input pane:

```
select * from employee
```

Select the Run button to process the SQL request. Because SQL commands can be multilined, you must click Run for the SQL command to be executed. The result of this query is shown in Figure 24.3. Notice that the results pane echoes the command and then displays the results.

CREATING DATABASES

The first step in using any client/server environment is to create databases. Using the DDL of the language product effectively can greatly increase the integrity of the data stored on the server. This section deals with the basics of creating databases in InterBase.

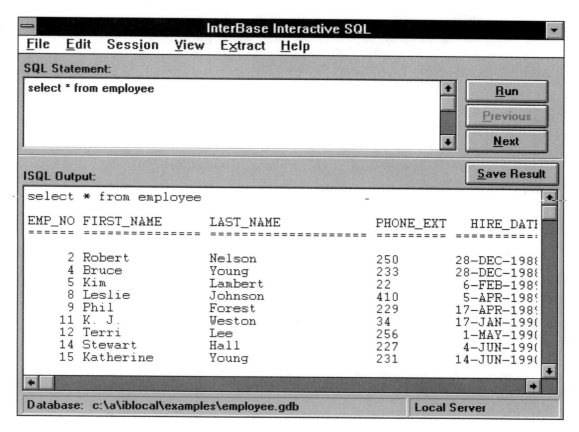

FIGURE 24.3   SQL Results in ISQL Windows

Most database server environments will accept substantially similar SQL commands as the ones presented here.

Create Database

The CREATE DATABASE command is used by most database server products. Inter-Base is no exception. You can use this command in ISQL to define your database along with its page size, character set, and secondary files. A simpler method is to use the ISQL **File | Create Database** menu option which presents you with the following dialog shown in Figure 24.4.

You will notice that you are required to use a log-in and password that has the rights to create a database with your server. The database entry should include a full path and optional file extension. In the example above, our database is called TOURDATA. The Database Options box can be used to specify other creation options supported by the In-

FIGURE 24.4   InterBase Create
Database Dialog

terBase CREATE DATABASE SQL statement. For more information on this, consult
your SQL language guide.

Dropping Databases

Once a database has been created, you have the option of dropping it with all of its tables
and other metadata. This can be easily done using the **File | Drop Database** menu option
or the **DROP DATABASE** SQL statement. You must be connected to the database in
order to drop it. Dropping a database deletes the database file from the hard disk.

Saving an ISQL Session

Windows ISQL keeps track of all of the work you have done in each session. Should you
desire to keep a permanent record of your executed statements you can save your session
to a text file. Select the **File | Save Session to File** option from the menu. You will be pre-
sented with a Save File dialog. You can save your file with any extension but the default
is .SQL.

Saved sessions can be executed again using the **File | Run an ISQL Script** menu option. This save and run mechanism is extremely useful when creating and manipulating database information over a period of days. Because Script files are just saved as ASCII text, you can create them using any editor or modify existing scripts that will be run later.

Metadata

Each database created contains **metadata.** Metadata is general information about the database which includes all of the information used to create the database and any tables within it. You can view this metadata using the **View | Metadata Information** option from the menu. You will be prompted with the diagram shown in Figure 24.5. Select the aspect of the database you would like to see information about. The pull-down list allows you to choose between the different items available. The dialog allows for the entry of an object name should you choose an information category that might apply to several objects in the database.

If you were to choose the Table option, you could enter a specific database table name if you only wanted its metadata. Leaving this item blank will result in seeing all of the objects of that type. The listing below is the result of selecting the Database option from the metadata information dialog. This listing shows the results of the database created in the earlier example.

```
SHOW DB
Database: c:\tourdata\tourdata.gdb
        Owner: SYSDBA
PAGE_SIZE 1024
Number of DB pages allocated = 202
Sweep interval = 20000
```

In addition to showing the basic creation options for this database, the output displays the owner, page size, pages allocated, and sweep interval. The page information tells us how much space the database takes up and how large a block of space will be allocated for data storage. The sweep interval gives us information on how often the database tables

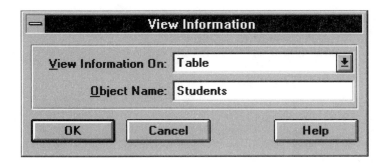

FIGURE 24.5 View Metadata Information Dialog

will have deleted information permanently removed. Consult your *InterBase Database Administrator's Guide* for information on how to optimize these settings.

CREATING TABLES

A database is of little use without the presence of tables. Creating tables within Windows ISQL is fairly straightforward. Using the SQL CREATE TABLE command, you can generate table structures for new tables. This command can be very simple and can include basic field information. It can also take on a very complex nature if creating complicated structures with validation checks and key information.

Simple Table Creation

For the purposes of this discussion, we will be creating a database that contains tables designed to track attendees in a seminar. The first table to be created will contain information about zip codes. This table will have three fields that are all character information: ZIPCODE, STATE, and CITY. The source code listing below shows the creation of a simple zip code table.

```
CREATE TABLE ZipCode (ZIPCODE char(5), STATE char(2), CITY
varchar(25))
```

Notice that the first two fields in the table used the `char` type and the city was created as `varchar`. Since ZIPCODE and STATE will always take up the same amount of space. The `varchar` type only uses the amount of space needed to contain the actual data. `Char` types are more efficient if you have columns that will be a fixed size. Consult your Windows ISQL help system for a list of available types.

There are some limitations we would like to have on our new table. First, it is important that no two zip codes are the same. While many applications would require us to code this at the client level, server technology can help us enforce this rule. The following code listing will create a table that only allows unique zip codes within the table. The UNIQUE keyword is now used in the CREATE TABLE statement.

```
CREATE TABLE ZipCode (ZIPCODE char(5) NOT NULL UNIQUE, STATE
char(2), CITY varchar(25))
```

Notice that the NOT NULL modifier was also added to the statement. This is required due to the possibility that new records inserted into the table may not have zip code values. InterBase prevents this from happening by requiring all UNIQUE columns be defined as NOT NULL. Any column can be NOT NULL in order to prevent "empty" values in the table. We may want to add this constraint to the CITY and STATE columns as well. This will ensure that the table contains no zip codes without cities and states.

Adding Key References

One of the basic elements to database table relationships is *primary* and *foreign keys*. Keys tie the information between tables together and cause the database server to force proper entry of records that are to be related to records in other tables. The PRIMARY KEY option allows you to define a field within a table as being the primary key in the table. This will prevent nonunique values from being written to the table and provide a linking value through which records from other tables can be tied. Here is the table definition for our Zipcode table using a PRIMARY KEY.

```
CREATE TABLE ZipCode (ZIPCODE char(5) NOT NULL PRIMARY KEY,
STATE char(2), CITY varchar(25))
```

Now that we have created a single table, we can use the same techniques for creating the remaining tables we need for our seminar tracking system. The listing below shows the creation of a `seminar` table which will contain information about the different seminars that will be offered.

```
CREATE TABLE Seminar (SEMINAR_ID smallint NOT NULL PRIMARY
KEY, SEMINAR_CITY varchar(30), INSTRUCTOR varchar(3),
SEMINAR_DATE date)
```

This table uses an integer value for its key field. Later, we will look at a way to generate values that are unique from the server. Finally, we need to create a `Students` table that references the key values within our other two tables. In addition to defining a primary key for the table, we will also be adding a FOREIGN KEY keyword to the fields that reference columns within the Zipcode and Seminar tables. Below is the listing for the `Students` table SQL creation.

```
CREATE TABLE Students
(STUDENT_ID smallint NOT NULL,
LAST_NAME varchar(20),
FIRST_NAME varchar(15),
TITLE varchar(20),
COMPANY varchar(30),
STREET_ADDRESS varchar(25),
STREET_ADDRESS2 varchar(25),
ZIPCODE char(5) NOT NULL,
PHONE_NUMBER char(13),
EXTENSION char(4),
FAX_NUMBER char(13),
REGISTERED char(1),
SEMINAR_ID smallint NOT NULL,
INVOICE_NUMBER char(4),
PAYMENT_METHOD char(1),
```

```
        SOURCE_ID smallint NOT NULL,
        CONFIRMATION_LETTER char(1),
        CREDIT_CARD_NUMBER char(19),
        EXPIRATION_DATE date,
        PO_NUMBER char(20),
        INVOICE_ATTN char(25),
        INVOICE_STREET_ADDRESS varchar(25),
        INVOICE_STREET_ADDRESS2 varchar(25),
        INVOICE_ZIPCODE char(5) NOT NULL,
        DISCOUNT char(1),
        OPERATOR_ID char(3),
        COMMENTS varchar(100),
        PRIMARY KEY (STUDENT_ID),
        FOREIGN KEY (ZIPCODE) REFERENCES ZIPCODE (ZIPCODE),
        FOREIGN KEY (INVOICE_ZIPCODE) REFERENCES ZIPCODE (ZIPCODE),
        FOREIGN KEY (SEMINAR_ID) REFERENCES SEMINAR (SEMINAR_ID),
        FOREIGN KEY (SOURCE_ID) REFERENCES SOURCE (SOURCE_ID))
```

You can see from this example that it is possible to have several fields within a table reference a primary key within other tables. In this example we even have two fields (ZIPCODE and INVOICE_ZIPCODE) referencing the same foreign key. This example also demonstrates that the PRIMARY KEY identification can be placed at the end of the CREATE TABLE statement. You may find the creation of tables as complex as this to be troublesome when using ISQL. We strongly recommend that you create script files that you run in order to debug your SQL code.

DATA MANIPULATION

In addition to standard data definition, InterBase supports a superset of SQL-92 in its data manipulation language. Your applications will have a need to add, edit, and delete records from within the tables that are created. The following discussion will give you and overview of these statements and their syntax.

Inserting Records

Before being able to do anything else with your tables, you will need to add records to them. This is accomplished using the insert statement. The insert statement has two basic syntax. The first is very simple and requires you to place a value for every field in the proper order when adding a record to a table. The example below demonstrates the addition of a zip code to our table.

```
INSERT INTO ZipCode values ("30339","GA","Georgia")
```

This syntax can become cumbersome, particularly if you are not sure of the field order in the table or only want to set the value of certain fields. The more robust syntax allows for the naming of fields and subsequent new values. Since our Zipcode table con-strains us from adding the same zip code again, the following statement will add a new one.

```
INSERT INTO ZipCode (ZIPCODE, CITY, STATE) values
("30067","Marietta","GA")
```

Notice that in this example the field list was not in the same order as that in the table. You also have the option with InterBase (and most other server platforms) to move data from a text file or other source rather than having to issue several thousand INSERT statements when upsizing an existing application.

Updating Records

The UPDATE statement is used to modify the values stored to records already in the table. It requires a WHERE clause in order to identify which record should be modified. Suppose we had entered in the wrong state value for a particular zip code. Rather than deleting the record and reinserting it, we can issue the following UPDATE statement.

```
UPDATE ZIPCODE SET STATE = "GA" WHERE ZIPCODE = "30303"
```

You have the option of modifying multiple fields or several records at once using the UP-DATE statement. More detailed information on this command can be found in your SQL reference.

Deleting Records

Deleting records from an InterBase table is very simple using SQL. The DELETE state-ment will remove all records from the table that match the condition specified in the WHERE clause. The example below shows a way to delete all of the zip code records in Georgia.

```
DELETE FROM ZIPCODE WHERE STATE = "GA"
```

All modifications made during an ISQL session are not permanent until you commit your changes. This can be accomplished by selecting the **File | Commit Work** menu op-tion. Alternatively, you have the option of undoing all of the work you have done modify-ing records by selecting the **File | Rollback Work** option.

Selecting Records

The SQL SELECT statement gives you a wide variety of ways to see the data stored within the tables in your database. Most SQL language books spend the majority of their time showing the many facets of the SELECT statement. This book is not intended as a SQL reference and as a result, we will not be taking any pains to show you different ways of selecting records to view. However, many of the examples in later discussions may use SELECT statements to accomplish their tasks. We refer you to your SQL reference if there is any confusion.

DOMAINS

The need to constantly recreate a field definition has led to the creation of user-defined data types within most database server environments. InterBase refers to this capability as *domain* creation. Domains allow you to create a column definition and apply it to many different fields across tables within your database. We saw in the Students table that there was a need to define a phone number field twice (PHONE_NUMBER and FAX_NUM-BER). By creating a domain, we could eliminate the need to define this column twice and have the ability to change the definition of both columns at once by modifying the domain. Additionally, domains allow you to provide default values and check constraints on the values inserted and updated in your tables.

Creating a Domain

The CREATE DOMAIN statement is used in InterBase to define a new column type. In the last table creation example, we could have used a domain to define a data type that would be used for the definition of the phone number columns in our table. The following domain definition defines a type to use for this purpose.

```
CREATE DOMAIN PHONE_NUMBER_TYPE char(13)
```

We can now drop our existing table and create it anew with the new type. Rather than re-typing all of this information over and over, we will use an ISQL script file. As we mentioned earlier, these are simple text files that can be created with any ASCII Editor. The listing below shows the new script file using the PHONE_NUMBER_TYPE domain.

```
Connect c:\tourdata\tourdata.gdb USER SYSDBA PASSWORD
"masterkey" ;
DROP TABLE STUDENTS;
CREATE TABLE Students
(STUDENT_ID smallint NOT NULL,
LAST_NAME varchar(20),
FIRST_NAME varchar(15),
TITLE varchar(20),
COMPANY varchar(30),
STREET_ADDRESS varchar(25),
STREET_ADDRESS2 varchar(25),
ZIPCODE char(5) NOT NULL,
PHONE_NUMBER PHONE_NUMBER_TYPE,
EXTENSION char(4),
```

```
         FAX_NUMBER PHONE_NUMBER_TYPE,
         REGISTERED char(1),
         SEMINAR_ID smallint NOT NULL,
         INVOICE_NUMBER char(4),
         PAYMENT_METHOD char(1),
         SOURCE_ID smallint NOT NULL,
         CONFIRMATION_LETTER char(1),
         CREDIT_CARD_NUMBER char(19),
         EXPIRATION_DATE date,
         PO_NUMBER char(20),
         INVOICE_ATTN char(25),
         INVOICE_STREET_ADDRESS varchar(25),
         INVOICE_STREET_ADDRESS2 varchar(25),
         INVOICE_ZIPCODE char(5) NOT NULL,
         DISCOUNT char(1),
         OPERATOR_ID char(3),
         COMMENTS varchar(100),
         PRIMARY KEY (STUDENT_ID),
         FOREIGN KEY (ZIPCODE)          REFERENCES ZIPCODE (ZIPCODE),
         FOREIGN KEY (INVOICE_ZIPCODE)  REFERENCES ZIPCODE (ZIPCODE),
         FOREIGN KEY (SEMINAR_ID)       REFERENCES SEMINAR
         (SEMINAR_ID),
         FOREIGN KEY (SOURCE_ID) REFERENCES SOURCE (SOURCE_ID));
         EXIT;
```

You will notice the CONNECT statement at the top of the script. Before any operation can be performed on the database a connection must be made. This line executes the connection. You may also notice that a script can contain multiple statements. The semicolon is used to separate statements within a script. Finally, our script ends with an EXIT statement. This tells the server to commit all of the changes made by the script.

Altering a Domain

Once a domain is established, you will run into the need to alter the domain. Your first thought might be to drop the existing domain and recreate it. Should you attempt this after assigning a column using that domain, you will get an error. The dialog in Figure 24.6 shows the details of the error generated when we attempt to drop the PHONE_NUM-BER_TYPE domain from our database.

The ALTER DOMAIN statement must be issued in order to change an existing domain. The syntax below shows how the domain we created can be changed to have a default value of "( ) - ".

```
     ALTER DOMAIN PHONE_NUMBER_TYPE SET DEFAULT "( ) - "
```

This example shows the capability of setting default values within a domain. It is impor-

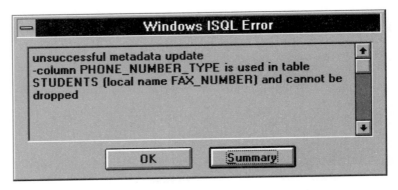

FIGURE 24.6   Error Details when Attempting DROP DOMAIN

tant to note that once a domain is created, its type and size cannot be altered. This would require a substantial change to any table that uses the domain.

Check Constraints

Check constraints provide you with a rudimentary ability to validate data within a table as it is inserted or updated. Using the CHECK clause in a domain statement, you can assign a Boolean phrase which will be evaluated any time the columns associated with the domain change. The example below demonstrates creating a domain that can be used for "yes" or "no" values in a column and defaults to "yes".

```
CREATE DOMAIN NO_YES char(1) DEFAULT "N" CHECK (VALUE IN
("N","Y"))
```

Check constraints can be fairly complicated if you want them to be.

Advanced DDL

InterBase's data definition language has several features that we have yet to discuss. As with most database servers, the language has extensions to SQL-92 that improve the server. In this section we will discuss a few of the other DDL features of InterBase's SQL implementation and show a few examples of using them.

The DEFAULT Clause

In addition to being able to set default values for domains, you can also set them for simple columns. The syntax is the same as with a domain and eliminates the need for creating a domain for a column type that will only be used once. Here is a CREATE DATABASE statement that used default values for one of the fields.

```
CREATE TABLE OPERATORS
(OPERATOR_ID smallint NOT NULL PRIMARY KEY,
COMPANY varchar(20) DEFAULT "The DSW Group",
NAME varchar(15))
```

This technique can eliminate the need for users to always enter in an initial value that typically has only one value. Fields also have the ability to have checks. These are entered in the CREATE DATABASE statement the same as when creating a domain.

Creating Computed Columns

Another requirement of many database server users is the ability to create computed values within tables. These are columns that are calculated and not actually stored to the table. The OPERATORS table defined earlier could have a calculated field that shows the complete name of the individual based on first and last names.

```
CREATE TABLE OPERATORS
(OPERATOR_ID smallint NOT NULL PRIMARY KEY,
COMPANY varchar(20) DEFAULT "The DSW Goup",
FIRST_NAME varchar(10),
LAST_NAME varchar(15),
FULL_NAME COMPUTED BY (FIRST_NAME || " " || LAST_NAME))
```

Other computed fields are also possible using more elaborate syntax. Be aware that this type of column can tax the server by requiring it to constantly maintain data that could always be calculated on the fly by the application once it has retrieved the records it needs.

Creating Views

Another level of encapsulation supported by servers is that of Views. InterBase provides a way to create a view of a table or set of tables that can be accessed just like any other table in the database. This capability gives database administrators and developers a way to store information in a format that is never really seen by the user of the data. This can also help give the developer the ability to use a View instead of the actual table. By doing so, the application can be protected from minor changes in the fields within the table. Should the table need to be changed, only the Views using that table will need updating. Applications using the Views could remain unchanged.

The CREATE VIEW command is used to accomplish this task. The following example uses a single table but strips off many of the fields that are not needed for the application at hand. The view can then be used to write the application without concerns about missing fields. From the Views perspective, there are no more fields.

```
CREATE VIEW STU_NAMES AS SELECT FIRST_NAME, LAST_NAME,
TITLE, COMPANY FROM STUDENTS
```

This view would limit the application to only the fields specified. Obviously, more advanced views are possible. Views can come from multiple tables as well. There are some limitations associated with multitable views. Under some situations, the View cannot be updated by the user. Consult your ISQL reference for these conditions.

TRIGGERS

Triggers provide a way for developers to have the database server perform activities any time certain information within a table changes. These activities can include many things including generating unique values on inserts, cascading deletes to child tables, keeping track of transactions beyond the normal capabilities of the server, and many more. Any time you would like an activity performed when data changes, use a trigger.

Generators

One of the key elements in using triggers with InterBase concerns generators. Generators are a built-in functionality that InterBase provides to give new unique values each time they are invoked. In the tables we have created there are several key fields that could benefit from the use of generators. By using generators we can avoid the need to have the applications using the data from having to create these values.

To create a generator you use the CREATE GENERATOR statement. This allows you to set a new database object to automatically increment when combined with the GEN_ID procedure. The example below demonstrates the use of the CREATE GENERATOR statement and the related SET GENERATOR statement.

```
CREATE GENERATOR Seminar_Gen;
SET GENERATOR Seminar_Gen TO 0;
```

These statements are taken from an ISQL script file (note the use of the semicolon statement separator). Now that a generator is created we can associate it with a trigger. We would like our Seminar table to use the generator to assign new values to the SEMINAR_ID field. This can be accomplished by using the CREATE TRIGGER statement to handle this process. The trigger routine defined below will accomplish our goal.

```
Connect c:\tourdata\tourdata.gdb USER SYSDBA PASSWORD
"masterkey" ;

/* create a trigger for adding seminars with unique IDs */
SET TERM !! ;
CREATE TRIGGER SET_SEMINAR_ID FOR SEMINAR
BEFORE INSERT AS
BEGIN
   NEW.SEMINAR_ID = GEN_ID(SEMINAR_GEN,1);
```

```
END !!
SET TERM ; !!
EXIT;
```

There are a few new items in this example that require explanation. The /*..*/ characters indicate comments in a script file. The SET TERM statement identifies a new termination character for SQL statements for the trigger definition. This is required as the CREATE TRIGGER must be a single statement. Since our trigger has a semicolon within it, we have to redefine the termination character while the trigger is being defined. Notice that once the definition is complete, we put the termination character back to its default.

The GEN_ID procedure accepts two parameters. The first is the generator defined earlier. The second value is the increment value. We want our SEMINAR_IDs to be consecutive so the value 1 is appropriate. This trigger is specified to fire whenever an INSERT is executed on the SEMINAR table. Other choices for triggers include AFTER INSERT, BEFORE or AFTER, either UPDATE or DELETE.

Cascading and Nullifying Changes

We would like the ability to have our database cascade or disallow deleted from tables from which a foreign key is taken. For example, should the user of the SEMINAR table decide to delete a seminar, we would want to make sure that there are no students attending that seminar. This can be accomplished using triggers. Here is a trigger that will fire before a deletion on the SEMINAR table. It removes all of the students along with the seminar.

```
Connect c:\tourdata\tourdata.gdb USER SYSDBA PASSWORD
"masterkey" ;

/* create a trigger for adding seminars with unique IDs */
SET TERM !! ;
CREATE TRIGGER DEL_SEMINAR_ID FOR SEMINAR
BEFORE DELETE AS
BEGIN
    DELETE FROM STUDENTS WHERE
        STUDENTS.SEMINAR_ID = OLD.SEMINAR_ID;
END !!
SET TERM ; !!
EXIT;
```

By default users would not be able to delete a seminar if there were students registered for it. This would violate the integrity constants of the database. This trigger allows them the powerful ability to remove the students along with the seminar. Using a trigger in this case allows applications written for this database to not have to concern themselves with deleting students first. This is known as a cascading deletion.

These two examples only scratch the surface when it comes to the useability of triggers. Most server platforms support the creation of triggers and you should utilize them as much as possible. They lend consistency of data access and modification and reduce the traffic on the network by handling activities automatically at the server.

STORED PROCEDURES

Another feature of database servers that can cut down on application development work and network traffic is the ability to create stored procedures. Stored procedures are a lot like triggers except that the application gets to fire them when it wants. The same syntax and statements that are allowed in triggers are permitted in stored procedures. Stored procedures can be placed in two categories: those that result in a set of records and those that return values. We will look at examples of these in the following examples.

Returning a Set of Records

Rather than issuing commonly used SELECT statements from multiple applications, you have the option of creating stored procedures that contain them. Suppose we have a need in our seminar tracking system to get a listing of all of the students within a particular seminar. The following script file defines a stored procedure that can be used in this effort.

```
Connect c:\tourdata\tourdata.gdb USER SYSDBA PASSWORD
"masterkey" ;

/* create a procedure for getting students in a seminar */ SET
TERM !!;
CREATE PROCEDURE GET_SEMINAR_NAMES (ID smallint)
RETURNS (LastName varchar(20), FirstName varchar(15),
        Title varchar(20), Company varchar(30))
AS
BEGIN
    FOR SELECT LAST_NAME, FIRST_NAME, TITLE, COMPANY
        FROM STUDENTS
        WHERE SEMINAR_ID = :ID
        INTO :LastName,:FirstName,:Title,:Company
    DO
        SUSPEND;
END !!
EXIT;
```

The first item you will notice in the CREATE PROCEDURE statement is the parameter (ID) that is accepted. Without parameters stored procedures would not be very flexible. The RETURNS clause defines the variables that will be sent back to the calling routine or

SQL statement. These are also defined with their intended type. Like triggers, stored procedures have a BEGIN . . . END construct.

In this example, the FOR SELECT . . . DO construct was used to make iterations through the list of selected names. Each CREATE PROCEDURE statement must contain a list of return values and their types. The do not have to have the same names as the fields they represent. The SUSPEND statement halts the procedure upon each iteration and returns the current values. The INTO clause on the select determines where the information selected is placed. This procedure can be utilized as shown below.

```
SELECT * FROM GET_SEMINAR_NAMES(3)
```

In this example we are retrieving all of the names of students in the seminar with the SEMINAR_ID equal to 3. This is a simple, yet powerful example of using stored procedures.

Returning a Value

Stored procedures can also be used to return individual values. The following stored procedure tells us the total number of students registered in a seminar.

```
Connect c:\tourdata\tourdata.gdb USER SYSDBA PASSWORD
   "masterkey" ;

/* create a procedure for counting students in a seminar */
SET TERM !!;
CREATE PROCEDURE SEMINAR_COUNT (ID smallint)
RETURNS (Total smallint)
AS
BEGIN
   SELECT count(*) FROM STUDENTS
      WHERE SEMINAR_ID = :ID
      INTO :Total;
   SUSPEND;
END !!
EXIT;
```

Using the EXECUTE PROCEDURE statement you can run any procedure and see the results. Figure 24.7 shows the ISQL interface results when running the procedure defined above.

Other Uses

Beyond the few examples we have shown, stored procedures can become the mainstay of your client/server application development process. By storing routines at the server and executing the remotely, you can reduce network traffic, speed response time and standard-

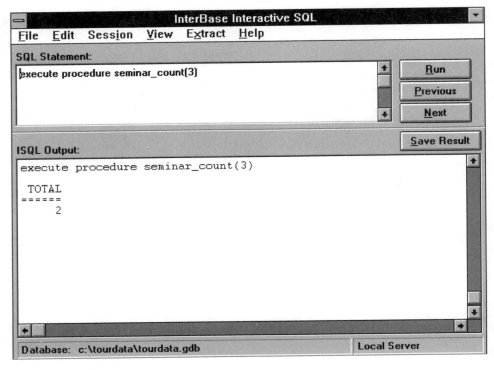

FIGURE 24.7   ISQL Results of Calling Stored Procedure

ize your access to data. Unlike normal SQL requests, servers generally precompile stored procedures and keep them in server memory after they are executed. This allows applications much greater speed of data access than passing SQL strings to the server on the fly.

InterBase provides a fully functional language with control structures and variable declarations to make stored procedures more valuable. Using the TStoredProcedure object class on your forms will give you access to the results of stored procedure calls and remove the need for application developers working with the Delphi interface from having to learn SQL. This will also make your applications more portable in that all of the data access specifics will be isolated on the server.

CREATING FORMS IN CLIENT/SERVER

You can specify an InterBase database as the DatabaseName property of a Table or Query component (even in the Form designer) and use the InterBase table exactly as you would a DB or DBF table. Figure 24.8 shows a form that was created by the Form Expert that allows browsing and editing the sample Employee table (and the programmer wrote no code whatsoever—this functionality was provided by the Form Expert).

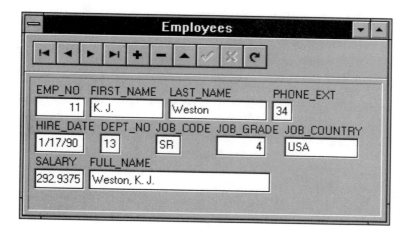

FIGURE 24.8   InterBase Based Table Access Form

Beyond the ability to create simple table forms, using the TDataBase component, you can access your servers transaction processing and security. Adding the use of TStoredProcedure components will give you the full access to the server database information without the need to write any SQL.

CONCLUSION

We have seen with InterBase (and other servers) that the need to isolate your application from the underlying database is important. Doing so increases the flexibility of the application and allows it to access the data on the back-end server with a minimum of information. This follows the precepts we mentioned in earlier chapters regarding encapsulation and information hiding. Client/server development should always be viewed in context with the rest of your application development priorities and should follow the same principles.

MIGRATING TO CLIENT/SERVER

MIGRATING YOUR DATABASE

Creating a client/server application by converting an existing desktop application is a fairly common activity these days. Delphi makes this process a painless one by giving us the tools we need to accomplish the task. There are several potential avenues that you can take when considering the move from the desktop to a client/server environment. The first step should always start by determining where you are. Setting off in a direction without getting your bearings is always going to cause you problems.

Suppose you are currently developing applications using local InterBase. Converting these applications will be a very painless process because your database storage format and application code will not need to change at all. The only change you will need to make will be to install your new server software and change the connection information within the BDE configuration utility to have your alias point to the new server. What could be easier?

A more common starting point is the current use of local tables such as DB or DBF files. These database file formats support different features and conventions than do most true client/server environments. You will have to concern yourself with the transfer of data to the new format and the creation of server-based activities like triggers and rules. Additionally, server platforms are more restrictive on the use of names for fields within tables, and as a result, you may need to change your applications to use the new names.

For the purposes of creating an understandable example, we will show how to move a desktop table-based application to an InterBase client/server application. The first step is to create a new database structure on the server. Use the Windows ISQL utility to accomplish this task. Beyond creating simple rows and columns, you can use ISQL to create relationships between the tables and rules that govern the addition of data to the tables. Rather than starting off by creating the tables directly through SQL code, using an existing database design and the Database Desktop, you can more easily create tables and see any naming conflicts that exist between the local file format and the server.

Using the **New|Table** option within the Database Desktop application, specify the type of table you wish to create. In our case, we will be creating an InterBase table (Figure 25.1). Once presented with the table design dialog, you can use the *Borrow* button to use an existing table structure for your new table. Creating tables in this way has a few advantages. First, it guarantees that you will not forget to place a field in the table. It also is much easier than typing the information in directly or using a complicated SQL script. Finally, this technique will show you where column-naming convention conflicts exist between the old file format and the new one. The screen shot shown in Figure 25.1 demonstrates this. Be sure to create the database within Windows ISQL and an alias in your BDE configuration before attempting to save a table design to it.

The **seminar_id** field in the new InterBase table uses an underscore to separate words in the field's name. Using DB files, we could have multiword names. InterBase tables (or most other server platforms) do not support this feature. The Database Desktop automatically added the underscore character. You can see from Figure 25.1 that the same holds true for the new **seminar_city** field. Our DATE field was modified to prevent a conflict since InterBase reserves the token "date." In this case, the field name is changed to **dat_**. This is not a very descriptive name and we should probably change it to something new. *Be sure to change any field names before saving the new table.* Once you create a table, it can be a difficult task to change its structure when it is full of data.

When working with client/server databases you are typically required to specify certain fields as "NOT NULL" to use them for primary and foreign keys. You should mark these fields as required fields within your initial table creation dialog. You cannot change these settings after data is entered into the table.

After you create the table, you can easily migrate your data to the new platform using one of the utilities within the Database Desktop. The **Utilities|Add** option can provide a simple interface for adding records to your new server-based table. You will need to supply a TO and FROM table name. Using existing BDE aliases and tables, you can accomplish this task quickly. Be forewarned, if you are migrating a large amount of data from a local format to your server platform, this step can take a fairly large amount of time. As another alternative, you can convert your data to an ASCII file format. Your server can then easily read in from this text file. Some server environments will operate much faster this way rather than using the Database Desktop.

If you decide to add triggers, rules, or stored procedures to your server database, you can do this after you create tables using an SQL interface tool like Windows ISQL. You may wish to add your existing data after rules are put in place on the server. Data that does not conform to the integrity or domain rules in place on the database will not be added by the Database Desktop. Instead, these records are placed in a key violation table in your work directory. You can then correct them and re-add them to the database if needed.

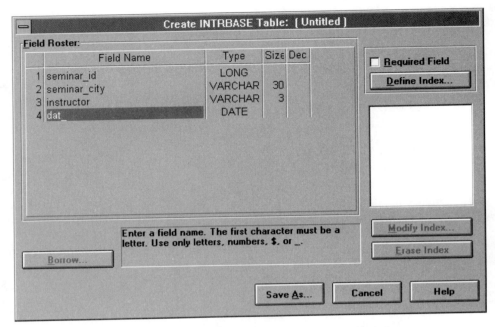

FIGURE 25.1   Creating InterBase Tables with Borrow Technique

MODIFYING APPLICATIONS

The changes we have needed to make to migrate our application's database will definitely affect the way the application operates. Strewn throughout any application will be references to field names. These can be in the form of direct references through objects on a form or in source code. Even with the tools found in Delphi, there is no simple way to perform a mass change, like changing a field's name in all the places it occurs.

Any application will probably make use of a field name several times within a unit. Using the tools will require manipulating each object on a form and changing the coded events or changing properties. This is very cumbersome and leads to a much more difficult task that it needs to be. Fortunately, there is an alternative to using the tools.

Because of Delphi's use of two-way tools, developers have the option of modifying source code directly. While this is usually not the most optimal way of setting a particular property or writing an event, the use of the unit source code directly can greatly reduce the modification work to change an existing application's operation.

Simple modifications such as changing a field's name can be accomplished using the editor within Delphi directly. A simple search and replace can be done to find all occurrences of a field's name within a unit and change it to a new value. This will not only change properties of the field object itself. It also serves to change any references to the field's name within event code and other object's properties. Consider the simple form in Figure 25.2.

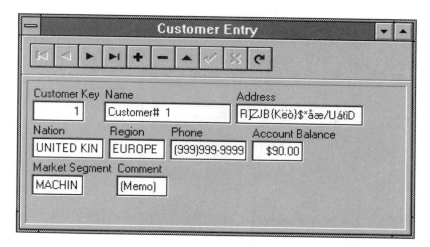

FIGURE 25.2   Typical Table-based Form

The Account Balance field may need to be modified to match up with a new field name within the table. If we change the table's structure we will soon run into difficulties opening the form in the designer. This is particularly true if we went through the trouble of creating field objects for each of the columns within our table. This adds multiple references to the field's name within the form code. It is also possible that we created some type of validation code for our Account Balance field as well. This will also need to be changed when we change the field name. If we change the table's structure and modify the field's name (let's say we put in an underscore in anticipation of moving the data to a client/server platform later), we will encounter the following error message (Figure 25.3) the next time we open the form in the designer.

You can correct this error using the tools within Delphi. First, to remove this error message we must know the cause. In this case, our creation of field objects for our table causes the error. Each of these references one of the fields in the table by name. When we opened the form again, the resulting error informs us that a field name has changed or is in some other way missing. To correct this error we must open the field editor and remove the offending field and replace it with the newly named field. Figure 25.4 shows the new field name using the underscore within the list of field objects defined for the table.

FIGURE 25.3   Open Form Error Dialog

FIGURE 25.4 Fields Editor Dialog

Now, with the field changed, we can attempt to compile our application again. Unfortunately, another error will occur. This time the problem results from the fact that the form designer automatically names the field objects using the table object's name concatenated with the field's name. When fields have a space character within their names, the space is ignored in naming the field object. In our case, the old field object was named "Table1AccountBalance" and the new name is "Table1Account_Balance".

There are several options we can choose from to fix our application. The source code below shows the offending routine that used the old name of the field.

```
procedure TForm_Customer.EditAccountBalanceExit(Sender:
TObject);
begin
  if Table1AccountBalance.AsFloat <= 0.00 then
  begin
    showmessage('Must be greater than 0');
    EditAccountBalance.setfocus
  end;
end;
```

Our first option is to change the field name reference within the source code. In this case it is a very simple matter to change the **if** statement to use the new name. This is a fairly simple task in this application. Unfortunately, most applications use field objects in more than one place. An alternative is to change the field object's name within the object inspector to match up with the old name. This will allow all existing code to be compiled without any errors. Once this change is made, our application compiles correctly. We run into trouble again when trying to run the application. One of our TDBEdit objects on the form still references the field under the previous name.

The TDBEdit object will need to be changed within the object inspector to reference the correct field. Once this is accomplished, our form will then work again.

We still have one problem to solve. The new form uses a new field object. This means that any properties we set on the old field object will be lost. These can include things like validations, edit masks, and currency settings. In this case, our new field does not have the Currency property set as it was using the old field object. We can set it again using the object inspector.

Finally, our form works again. We were required to make the following changes to make this happen.

1. Delete the old field object and add a new one
2. Modify existing source code that uses the old field object's name
3. Change the TDBEdit component that referenced the old field name
4. Change the properties on the new field object to match up with the previous object's settings.

This is typical, but not the limit, of the steps needed to change a simple table column name. There could have been several places where the field object was referenced within the events on the form. Also, several components on the form might have referenced the old field name. Finally, while this field object only had one property that needed resetting, many fields might have event code that would need to be rewritten if the field was eliminated. All of these changes lead us to the conclusion that there must be a better way. And there is!

PAS AND DFM FILES

All the changes we have made to our form were stored in the unit PAS file or the DFM file associated with it. Most Delphi developers are perfectly comfortable spelunking within their PAS files but take great pause at ever looking at or modifying their form's DFM file. This trepidation is not without cause. Any time you modify a DFM file, you risk leaving the file out of sync with its corresponding PAS file.

There are times when changing your application purely in source code can save you time and frustration. Delphi forms are merely stored in a binary format within the DFM file. The file can be edited directly using the **Open|File** dialog and specifying DFM files. If you attempt to open a DFM with its form already open and unsaved, you will get the dialog shown in Figure 25.5.

As you can see from this dialog, the form's graphical representation and its DFM file are tied together. They, in fact, are the same file. The form designer is just a graphical representation of the DFM. You cannot have the file open in both views at the same time. After responding yes to this dialog, you will be able to view the DFM file. The DFM file

FIGURE 25.5   DFM File Open Confirmation Dialog

is not a text-based file like the PAS files. It is a binary file that can be edited in a textual way using the Delphi editor. Delphi converts the file to a text format for you to view or edit. The listing below shows a DFM file.

```
object SeminarForm: TSeminarForm
  Left = 192
  Top = 108
  Width = 425
  Height = 341
  ActiveControl = Panel1
  Caption = 'Seminars'
  Font.Color = clBlack
  Font.Height = -11
  Font.Name = 'MS Sans Serif'
  Font.Style = []
  FormStyle = fsMDIChild
  PixelsPerInch = 96
  Position = poScreenCenter
  Visible = True
  OnClose = FormClose
  OnCreate = FormCreate
  TextHeight = 13
  object Panel1: TPanel
    Left = 0
    Top = 0
    Width = 417
    Height = 41
    Align = alTop
    TabOrder = 0
    object DBNavigator: TDBNavigator
      Left = 8
      Top = 8
      Width = 241
      Height = 25
```

```
        DataSource = DataSource1
        Ctl3D = False
        ParentCtl3D = False
        ParentShowHint = False
        ShowHint = True
        TabOrder = 0
      end
    end
    object Panel2: TPanel
      Left = 0
      Top = 41
      Width = 417
      Height = 273
      Align = alClient
      BevelInner = bvLowered
      BorderWidth = 4
      Caption = 'Panel2'
      TabOrder = 1
      object DBGrid1: TDBGrid
        Left = 6
        Top = 6
        Width = 405
        Height = 261
        Align = alClient
        BorderStyle = bsNone
        DataSource = DataSource1
        TabOrder = 0
        TitleFont.Color = clBlack
        TitleFont.Height = -11
        TitleFont.Name = 'MS Sans Serif'
        TitleFont.Style = []
      end
    end
    object DataSource1: TDataSource
      DataSet = Table1
      Left = 287
      Top = 5
    end
    object Table1: TTable
      Active = True
      DatabaseName = 'Tour_Data'
      TableName = 'seminar.db'
      Left = 260
      Top = 5
      object Table1SeminarID: TIntegerField
        FieldName = 'Seminar ID'
      end
      object Table1SeminarCity: TStringField
```

```
      FieldName = 'Seminar City'
      Size = 30
    end
    object Table1Instructor: TStringField
      FieldName = 'Instructor'
      Size = 3
    end
    object Table1Date: TDateField
      FieldName = 'Date'
      EditMask = '!99/99/00;1;_'
    end
  end
end
```

The DFM file is not written in Pascal source code. It is a structured look at the objects and properties that you have set using the form designer. You can modify this file using the editor and see the changes within the form when you open it in the designer. You will notice that not all the object's properties are shown in this file. Only those properties set that are different from the class's default will appear in this file. *This means that changes made to the class definition that might affect the default values of object properties can affect existing forms.*

It is a simple exercise to use the find and replace dialog within the source code editor to change every instance of a field's name with the new name. It is just as simple to make mass changes to the field references within the DFM file. If you decide to make your changes to both files in order, you will not even have to type the find/replace tokens in more than once. In the case of our **seminar_id** field change, the dialog to replace the field name will look like that shown in Figure 25.6.

Field names with spaces within them cause us to do extra work when changing the DFM file in this way. Because the spaces cannot be used by the form designer when creating method names, the designer merely omits the space. This requires us to perform two searches for every field that needs to be updated. These searches can be performed on all the fields within PAS file as well. One other difficulty that you might come across involves the changing of field types from one platform to another. This is not usually necessary but is sometimes forced upon you. In the case of our new **seminar_date** field, we were forced to use a DATE type within InterBase. This column type also contains a time element and requires that our field object created within the PAS and DFM files be a **TDateTimeField** type. Once we make this change, our form works perfectly within a client/server environment.

There are some lessons to learn from this migration. If create a desktop databased application and you intend to take it to a client/server environment in the future, you should select your field names so that they are compatible with your server environment. Taking this extra precaution can save you hours of work in the migration of your application.

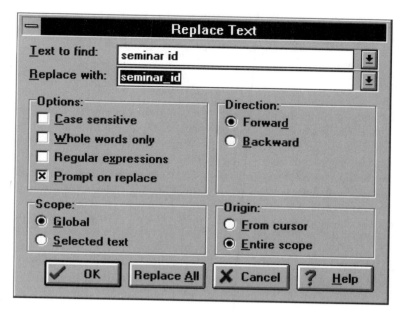

FIGURE 25.6   Replace Text Dialog Used in Migrating to C/S

CLIENT/SERVER OPTIONS

Server environments give you extra services not found within most desktop-based data file formats. InterBase supports the creation of triggers and stored procedures to minimize network traffic and the workload on applications. It also can manage referential integrity for your data. This feature may not all be present in your desktop database environment. Merely changing from using desktop data to client/server will not incorporate these features into the application.

Additional work and understanding of your server environment and its features can improve your application's performance and reliability. For example, using a stored procedure as a dataset within a form will reduce network traffic as opposed to using **TTable** objects to manage your data access. Setting up triggers within your new database may eliminate some code from your application by moving this functionality to the server. This also will enforce the rules associated with the trigger on all applications that use the data.

Servers also support a robust security system. You can use this to your advantage and eliminate application specific security for your data access. Applications written to use a server will automatically require the user to log in to access the database.

Domain-based validation is also a key element to most server environments. Using domains within your server database forces a consistent validation of data entered into the tables. This enforcement does not necessarily preclude the need to perform this type of operation at the application level. Using the event model present within Delphi forms you can prevalidate the data before it is saved to the underlying table. This will help reduce the number of exceptions generated when invalid data is saved to the database.

CONCLUSION

Moving applications to a client/server environment can be an easy process with Delphi. This is especially true if you had a specific server platform in mind before you began the development process. Carefully choosing your field names can reduce the code changes needed to move to your server. While this process results in a simple migration, it may not be sufficient for most server-based environments. Taking advantage of your server's features will make your application more maintainable and efficient.

CHAPTER 26

CLIENT/SERVER AND NETWORK APPLICATIONS

Once you have completed the data and application migration to your server environment, you will want to begin to modify your application to operate more efficiently with your server. There are several techniques that you can use to improve your application performance and data integrity. In this chapter we will show some of the different object classes that exist within Delphi and how to use them to improve your applications.

TDATABASE COMPONENTS

The TDatabase component serves as an excellent conduit for connecting to a database. Creating a TDatabase component allows you to more readily control the connection to your application's underlying data. Use these components with both desktop and client/server databases. Once you place a TDatabase component on a form, double-clicking on the component will launch the dialog shown in Figure 26.1.

Use this **Database Properties Editor** to configure your TDatabase object so that it can be used by TDataset components (that is, TTables or TQueries) within your application. Your TDatabase component can be accessed by multiple TDataset components and should be created only once in an application. If you want your application to reference an existing BDE alias, use the *Alias Name* combobox to select one. All you need to do is set the **Name** option that your application will use to reference this BDE alias. TDatabase components used in this way will allow an application to be written for an application specific alias. This gives you the flexibility to change which BDE alias your application uses without the need to modify all the TDataset objects in your application. After you create the application specific alias, all the TTable (or other TDataset) objects will be able

385

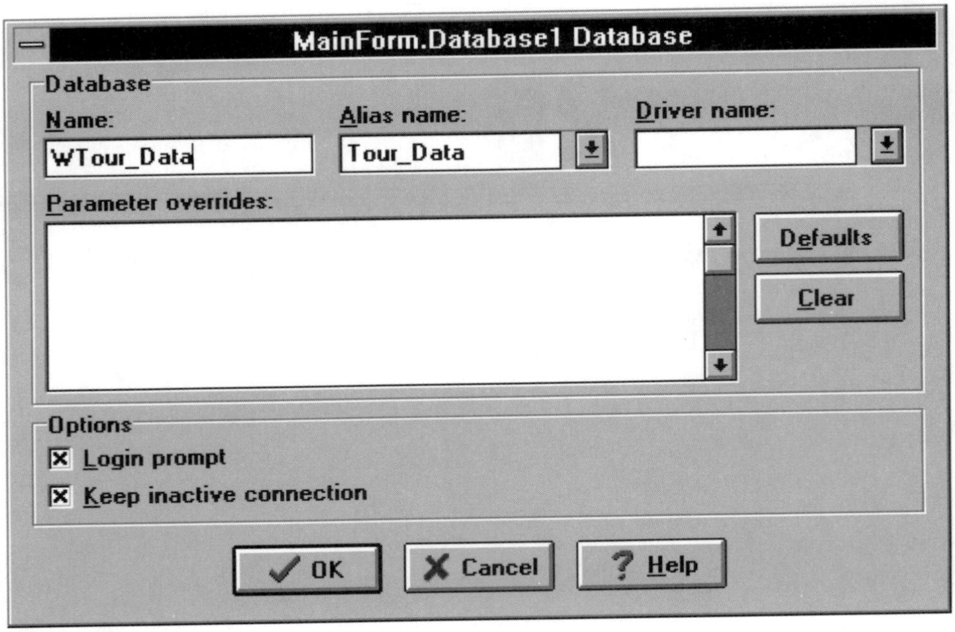

FIGURE 26.1   Database Properties Editor

to select it within their Database property pulldown list. This feature alone is a compelling reason to use TDatabase components within your application, but it is by no means the only reason.

You also have the ability to create aliases for your application that do not require the use of an existing alias within the BDE configuration. This allows you the freedom to create aliases solely within your application without regard for the existing configuration on your user's machine. This is not to say that your users will not need the BDE installed or that they will not need the appropriate drivers. It only means that you can create a usable alias "on the fly" from within your application.

Setting the *Driver* in the **Database Properties Editor** option allows you to configure an alias not found within your users BDE configuration. If you set this option you will not be able to use an existing BDE alias for your TDatabase. Instead, you will need to set the required parameters using the parameter overrides section within the **Database Properties Editor** dialog. You can easily see the available parameters for the selected driver by pressing the *Defaults* button. Figure 26.2 shows the use of the driver for pointing to a directory containing Paradox DB tables.

The **Parameter overrides** edit window allows you to set the path to use for this new alias. These parameters are not only assignable at design time. They can also be changed at run-time. This allows your applications to change which database is used while it is active. You may have a need to use separate databases to track information.

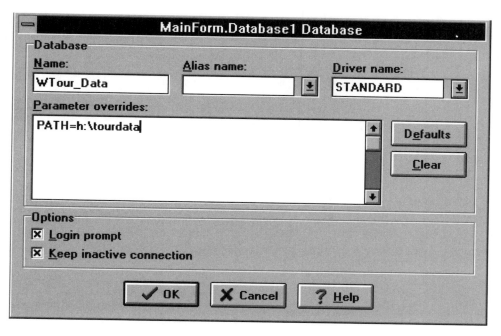

FIGURE 26.2   Using Drivers to Create Aliases

While this is normally considered poor database design, at times the business rules that are being applied make this an unfortunate necessity.

The TDatabase component shown in Figure 26.1 uses a network path to point to a set of tables used on our application. We would like to have a set of data that is not live so that we can test changes to the application. This allows us the ability to modify data in the testing phase without worrying about affecting live data. The **Params** property on the TDatabase component is a zero based array of TStrings. We set these using code as shown below.

```
Database1.Params[0] = 'PATH=H:\TOURDATA';
```

It is difficult to memorize the ordinal positions of the parameters within the TString array. For that reason, we suggest an alternate approach to assigning these values. The source code listing below shows how the to use the values property to assign parameters by name as opposed to their ordinal positions.

```
Database1.Params.Values['PATH'] := 'C:\TOURDATA'
```

This methodology is much more easily read and debugged. The standard driver used in the previous example only uses one parameter. Client/server-based drivers can have many parameters. Before discussing the use of server-based drivers, let us look at an example of using the capability of detaching from one database to connect to another. The source code listing below was placed as the onclick event for a menu option on the main form of an MDI application. The code checks to make sure that all child windows are closed before disconnecting the database. This is important. Disconnecting a database with active TTable objects will result in those tables being placed in the inactive state. By ensuring that no child windows are present, this example removes the necessity of checking for open tables and having to reactivate them.

```
procedure TMainForm.UseLocalData1Click(Sender: TObject);
begin
  { make sure no forms with active tables are open in the
app }
  if MDIChildCount > 0 then
    showmessage('Must close active forms to select this
option')
  else
    begin
      { reverse the check mark on the menu option }
      UseLocalData1.Checked := NOT UseLocalData1.Checked;
      { be sure to disconnect before changing path }
      Database1.Connected := FALSE;
      { if using local data now }
      if UseLocalData1.Checked then
        { Use local data }
        Database1.Params.Values['PATH'] := 'c:\tourdata'
      else
        { use network data }
        Database1.Params.Values['PATH'] := 'h:\tourdata';
      { reconnect to database after path change }
      Database1.Connected := TRUE
    end { begin }
end;
```

The menu option used in this example will appear checked if the local tables are in use. The connected property of a TDatabase object must be set to FALSE before any changes are made to the parameter values. Once the parameter is changed, reconnect the TDatabase object to the new database.

Using INI Files

A common convention in Windows applications is to keep configuration information (including paths to data files) in .INI files. For local tables (DBF or DB tables), the TDatabase component's path parameter is used to allow the user to place the path information into an INI file. This is handy for users who do not know or do not want to know anything about the BDECFG program or database aliases. When they move their data files, they can just change the path in the INI file to update where the application looks for its data. Of course, this also makes it easy for the programmer to provide an option (on a menu or button) to allow the user to change the data file location.

Like so many aspects of Delphi, dealing with INI files has been largely taken care of. Delphi includes an INIFile class that gives easy access to a INI file, including reading and writing sections and values in sections for a particular setting. All the programmer is required to do is to instantiate the INIFile class into an object (passing the name of the INI file to the constructor) and read and write the values.

The following code is from a form's **OnCreate** event handler. It takes the name of the application, snips off the "EXE" part of the name and adds "INI" to it (which assumes that the INI file has the same name as the application, standard in Windows programs), then reads the data path from the INI file and passes it to the Database component. This example uses exception handling to handle the case of an invalid path or missing INI file. In the case of either error, the application displays an error dialog then terminates. The INI file for this example only has one section and one value—here is a copy of the entire INI file:

```
[DB File Location]
path=c:\tour\data
```

Here is the code for the form's **OnCreate** event:

```
procedure TForm1.FormCreate(Sender: TObject);
var
  INIFile : TINIFile;
begin
  try
    database1.connected := false;
    INIFile := TINIFile.create(
      ChangeFileExt(application.exename, '.INI'));
    Database1.Params.Values['PATH'] :=
      INIFile.ReadString( 'DB File Location', 'path', " );
  try
    database1.connected := true;
    Table1.Open;
  except
    on EDBEngineError do
    begin
      MessageDlg( 'Could not locate the data files. '+
        'Check the path in the application"s INI file.',
        mtError, [mbOK], 0 );
      application.terminate
    end {on}
  end; {try}
```

```
finally
   INIFile.free
end {try}
end;
```

This example could be improved to automatically create the INI file if it does not exist (which is again standard behavior for Windows applications).

By using the above technique, you can allow your users to provide the path for your application's data files in a single location (the application's INI file), which makes this job both easier and more compliant with Windows' standards.

TSessions and Local Tables

Before leaving the discussion surrounding the use of DB tables, we think it is necessary to point out some of the potential pitfalls associated with using these tables in a network environment. The Paradox driver installed within the BDE configuration contains a setting called *Net Dir* that specifies the location of the PDOXUSR.NET file needed to manage multiple applications accessing the same tables. This setting is used by all Delphi applications that operate against DB files. Since many environments may use multiple databases and many applications, the existence of this setting is somewhat limiting. This is especially true for developers who wish to install applications on machines for which this setting is already assigned.

To avoid the problem of having to set this value on each installed machine, you can utilize the **TSession** object created automatically in your application. The **TSession** object contains several properties that control the overall behavior of your application. One of the important properties within a **TSession** object is the *NetFileDir* property. You set which directory's PDOXUSR.NET file is used by your application by setting this property on your application's **TSession** object. The variable Session is used by every Delphi application to contain the **TSession** object. You should not destroy this object. It is automatically released when your application terminates. Setting the NetFileDir property as the Session object will cause your application to ignore the setting found in the BDE configuration in favor of this local setting. We suggest you assign this value within your applications if you are using DB tables.

You can also use the TSession class properties to determine the number of TDatabase components that exist within the application and to act on them in a global way. For example, suppose you wish to disconnect all the TDatabase objects within your application. Using your TSession object's **Databases** array and **DatabaseCount** properties you can identify and modify all the databases within the application.

Finally, the **TSession** object contains a **KeepConnections** property that overrides the setting found within the application's virtual TDatabase components. If you do not explicitly create TDatabase components, Delphi creates virtual ones. These components will connect and disconnect to the underlying database each time tables are opened and closed within it if this property is set to FALSE. The default value for this is true.

TDatabase and Client/Server

You may notice when first upsizing an application that each form launched that accesses a server table requires the user to login. This is a cumbersome task for the user to perform. Each form will require a login. The creation of an explicit TDatabase component will remove this problem. Just place a TDatabase component on your application's main form for each server database you need to connect to. The user will be required to login only once for each TDatabase component. Since most applications use only one database, this makes it easy for the user.

As with DB tables, you can configure TDatabase components that use server drivers. There are several parameters contained within the default settings for TDatabase components that use server drivers. All parameters that exist within a BDE alias are available within a TDatabase's parameter settings. The listing below shows the default settings for an TDatabase component using the InterBase driver.

```
SERVER NAME=IB_SERVER:/PATH/DATABASE.GDB
USER NAME=MYNAME
OPEN MODE=READ/WRITE
SCHEMA CACHE SIZE=8
LANGDRIVER=
SQLQRYMODE=
SQLPASSTHRU MODE=NOT SHARED
SCHEMA CACHE TIME=-1
PASSWORD=
```

You can configure each of these settings to customize the interface between your application and the server. For example, if you are using local InterBase, you will need to change the **SERVER NAME** parameter to point to a drive, directory and the database file you want to access. You will also need to remove the **IB_SERVER** preface from the setting. This only applies to the use of client/server InterBase. You may also need to change the **USER NAME** parameter unless you want *MYNAME* to be the default login ID. You even have the option of setting the **PASSWORD** for the component. If you enter this setting into the parameters list and change the **LoginPrompt** property to FALSE, your application will not prompt the user to login. It will login automatically provided the USER NAME and PASSWORD are valid. We do not recommend this technique for most client/server applications since this effectively bypasses server security. If you wish to use local InterBase for its transaction processing and greater data integrity only, this is an option. Figure 26.3 shows a TDatabase component configured to reference a local InterBase database with the USER NAME and PASSWORD set. Notice that the **Login prompt** option has been unchecked. Parameter settings that you remove from the overrides assume their default values.

In the same way we changed the PATH setting in the earlier TDatabase component

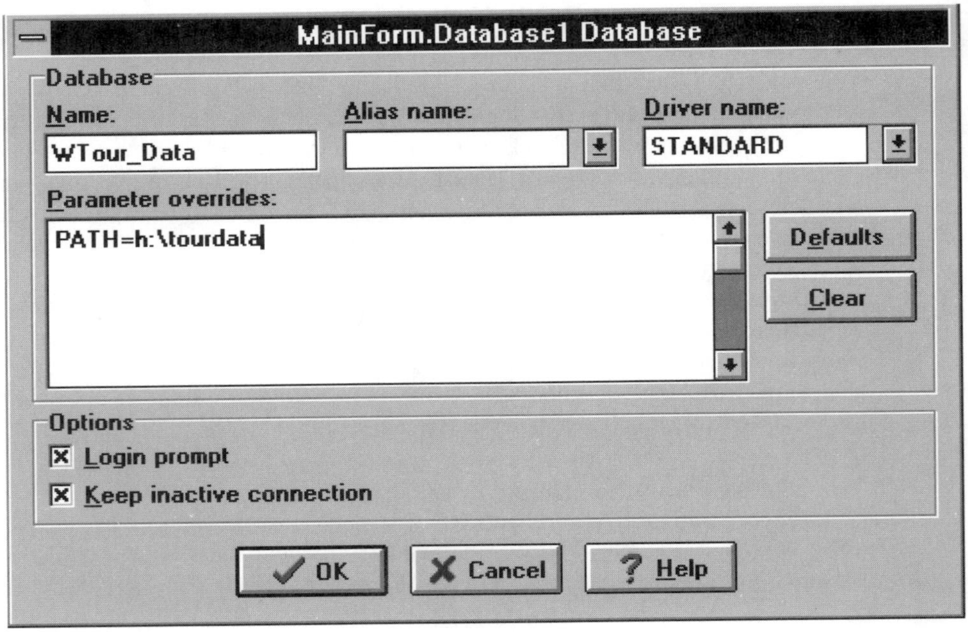

FIGURE 26.3   TDatabase Component Configured for Local InterBase

example, you can change the SERVER NAME parameter with local InterBase to utilize
an alternate database at run-time.

SQLPassThruMode

In addition to the settings we have already discussed, TDatabase components that use
server-based drivers contain an **SQLPassThruMode** parameter. This parameter controls
how transactions are handled within a database. The value of this parameter defaults to
NOT SHARED when using the InterBase driver. Other settings for this parameter are
SHARED AUTOCOMMIT and **SHARED NOAUTOCOMMIT.** Using **NOT
SHARED** will cause your application **TQuery** objects to use a different connection to the
database than other Delphi components that have methods to access data (e.g., TTable
components). Should these two types of connections mix, your application could get un-
reliable results when viewing and updating data. A **SHARED AUTOCOMMIT** setting
indicates that SQL and method-based updates will be committed to the server as each row
of data is updated. This can be inefficient on most server platforms. A **SHARED NOAU-
TOCOMMIT** setting will result in SQL and method-based updates using the same connection but all transactions must be manually controlled by the application (see Transaction Processing later in this chapter). We recommend using the **NOT SHARED** setting to
ensure SQL and method-based updates do not conflict.

TRANSACTION PROCESSING

One of the key advantages to using a server-based database is the use of transactions. Delphi automatically uses transactions anytime a record is edited within a form using TTable objects. When the table is placed in an **Edit** mode the transaction begins. The transaction is either committed or rolled back based on the user's desire to save or cancel the edit process. We handled this through the **Post** and **Cancel** methods. You can easily write forms that allow users to add, edit, and delete records from a table using a TDBNavigator component. The database expert uses this component when it lays out the new form.

Suppose your application needed to be able to have a one-to-many interface that contained two related tables. A typical interface would contain the top half of the form showing the parent table's record and the bottom half with a browse view of the child records. The form shown in Figure 26.4 demonstrates a one-to-many interface created with the form expert. We have added a TDatabase component to the form to control the BDE access.

To modify the parent and children records the user would merely place the tables in an edit mode. Unfortunately, if your user wanted to edit multiple child records as part of the edit transaction he or she would be unable to revert a record to its original state once the new record was moved. This is due to the inherent *implied* transactions that are imple-

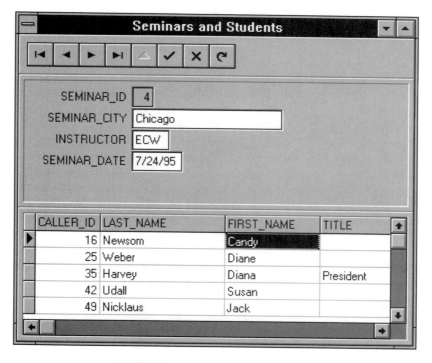

FIGURE 26.4   Typical One-to-many Form

mented as a part of Delphi TDatasets. To have an application that controls the transactions manually and provides the user the ability to revert several records across different tables, the user must *explicitly* control the transactions.

To control transactions manually within your applications, you must utilize the methods available within the TDatabase component. *Local tables (DB and DBF) do not have explicit transaction control capabilities.* You can use three methods within the TDatabase component class to start, commit, or rollback transactions. Figure 26.5 shows the object inspector with the different events we used to implement the transaction processing scheme.

We placed the following code in the **BeforeEdit** event.

```
procedure TForm_SemStud.Table_SeminarBeforeEdit(DataSet:
TDataset);
begin
  Database_IBTour.StartTransaction;
  DBGrid1.ReadOnly := FALSE
end;
```

The TDatabase object accepts the **StartTransaction** message that tells the server to begin the transaction. We also set the DBGrid's **ReadOnly** property to TRUE so that the user can access the child records. We set this property to a false value within the designer. The

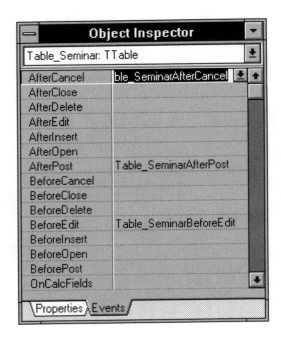

FIGURE 26.5 Methods Used for Transactions

following code listings show the **AfterCancel** and **AfterPost** events designed to handle transaction completion and rollback.

```
procedure TForm_SemStud.Table_SeminarAfterPost(DataSet:
TDataset);
begin
  DBGrid1.ReadOnly := TRUE;
  Database_IBTour.Commit
end;

procedure TForm_SemStud.Table_SeminarAfterCancel(DataSet:
TDataset);
begin
  DBGrid1.ReadOnly := TRUE;
  Database_IBTour.Rollback;
  Table_Students.Refresh;
end;
```

Along with issuing a rollback, we needed to refresh the data within the child record grid. Without the refresh, the user would still see the modified values when canceling the transaction. The DBGrid component uses a buffer to show the data from the child table and needs to be told to update the buffered records if they are not current. This represents only the simplest of transaction examples. Using the TDatabase components you can write very sophisticated transactions without using any SQL code.

You have the option to use SQL code to control your transactions if you wish to incorporate TQuery components into your applications. This will require you to have a complete knowledge of your server platform and commit your application to only working with that type of server. TTable and TDatabase components allow you to ignore specific server implementation issues while still retaining the features you want. This is not without a cost. Using SQL code can improve the performance of your Delphi application and allow you to take advantage of server specific features.

Other Transaction Processing Strategies

The strategy discussed above can cause problems on some server platforms. Most database servers don't perform multiuser locks at the record level as DBF and DB tables do. When using local tables, you can lock a single record by putting the table in edit mode while sitting on the record. That is one of the duties of the edit method for local tables. However, on some servers (for example, Microsoft SQL Server and Sybase), locking occurs at the *page* level instead of the record level.

Database servers typically allocate space for records in pages, which are areas of disk space of a specified size. The size of the pages is one of the parameters you can change through the server's administration application, and there is usually some reasonable default value. A page usually holds several records. These server platforms cannot lock a single record as part of a transaction. Instead, the server locks the entire page on which the record resides. Therein is the problem with the above strategy.

When you are doing transaction processing as described above, every time you change one of the student records, the server is performing a page lock on it, which it doesn't release until you have either committed or rolled back the transaction. This means that you are locking not only the records that you are actually editing, but all the other records on that page in the database as well. This is obviously a problem in a situation where many users might need to access the data concurrently.

Several solutions exist for this problem. First, you could change the way you do transaction processing by using local tables to actually edit the data. The scenario is as follows: Whenever the user wants to edit the parent and child records, copy the seminar and student information to local tables (DB or DBF tables) and change the DataSource for all the visible controls to point to the local tables instead of the server tables. You can modify to what table the visible controls are pointing by changing the DataSet property of the DataSource. This will allow the user to edit the records in the local tables. If the user decides to post the changes, update the records on the server based on the values in the local tables. If the user decides to roll back the changes, just delete the changes in the local tables. In either case, you should then set the DataSource for the visible controls to point back to the server tables.

This strategy can be accomplished in several ways. Probably the easiest way to perform the copies from the server and the update back to the server uses a BatchMove component. You can **batCopy** the records to the local tables, then perform a **batAppend-Update** from the local tables back to the server tables. Another way to perform this same action involves creating stored procedures on the server to handle the copying and updating. Of the two, the stored procedure method is preferred because it places the burden of data manipulation on the server, not on the client application. However, because it entails writing a nontrivial amount of server-specific SQL code, it is not as easy to implement as the former method.

This strategy also has a problem with multiuser access. You will no longer get many conflicts because of page locks (because the pages are only being locked during the update from local table phase, not during the entire editing of the record), but another problem may occur. What if a user (User A) makes a change to a record by using the copy to local tables method? While User A is editing the record, another user (User B) also starts editing the same record. Whichever user finishes editing the record last will win! In other words, both sets of changes will not be kept—only the changes made by the user who saved the record last will be kept. In our example, if User A finishes editing before User B, only User B's changes will be reflected in the database. All the changes that User A made will be overwritten when User B saves the record. This is essentially the same situation that would occur if there were no locking scheme.

Ultimately, the only way to completely control transaction processing is to write your own record-locking scheme. For example, you could add a field to the table that could act as a flag, indicating that the current record is being edited by someone. Whenever your application wants to edit a record, it first checks the flag. If the flag is not set, then set it, and allow the transfer and edit in local tables. If the flag is set, inform the user that another user is currently editing the record.

Transisolation Levels

When writing transactions within your applications you consider how the database writes of other users will affect your transactions. Suppose your application is in the middle of a transaction and needs the value stored in a field on which to base a calculation. Should your application get the most recent changes to the field or should it use the value stored in the field when the transaction started? The answer to this questions is application specific. Sometimes, getting the most recent data is best. Sometimes your application needs to rely only on what it saw when its transaction began.

Use the TDatabase **Transisolation** property to force your application transactions to read the data in a particular way. This property has three potential values: **tiDirtyRead, tiReadCommitted, tiRepeatableRead.** If you decide that your application needs to see the most current data within the database, regardless of whether it has even been committed to the database, use the **tiDirtyRead** setting. This will cause your application transaction to continually poll the database for changes made to the data by other users, even if the changes have not been committed. This is a dangerous setting to use since it allows your transactions to rely on uncommitted data. Should another user roll back a transaction, the information used by another transaction is no longer valid. Few database servers support dirty reads.

The **tiReadCommitted** setting only updates transactions to data that have been already committed by other users. This level still keeps transactions abreast of the latest changes to the database but only does so once the changes are committed. This is generally a better setting than using dirty reads and is supported by most servers.

Finally, the **tiRepeatableRead** setting completely isolates any transactions from other user's data changes. This setting forces a transaction to use the same values throughout a transaction. This level keeps transactions completely isolated from one another but can cause problems in highly transaction-intensive environments. Consider an inventory/sales application. If two users wanted to sell the same part (a likely occurrence) they might both read the inventory level at the same time. Once each user was ready to complete the sale, both would decrement the inventory value from its original setting. If the inventory setting started off at 10 and each user sold 5 parts, the final value written by each transaction would be 5. This means that even though both users sold 5 parts the final inventory value would not be zero. Because of situations like this, you should rarely use **tiRepeatableRead** for your **transisolation** property. Again, only a few server platforms even support this type of data access.

USING TQUERY COMPONENTS

In all the examples we have encountered until this point we have used TTable components for our datasets. We will now look at using TQuery components to get sets of records. Unlike TTables, TQueries require that you have some knowledge of SQL to use them. TQuery components are designed to allow for better access to server-specific features than those contained within TTables. Using SQL you can sometimes write a significantly smaller amount of code that would be required with TTables. Also, TQuery objects allow the server back end to process the data request. This allows developers to reduce the network traffic that results from accessing and processing large sets of data or large numbers of transactions.

TQuery components contain properties that hold a query SQL string and parameters. Let's look at how to assign an SQL string to a TQuery. Like other components, you must place a query component on a form to utilize it. Using the object inspector, select the SQL property editor. This allows you to use the string list editor to enter an SQL string for the component. The diagram in Figure 26.6 shows this dialog with a sample SQL statement.

This dialog allows you to use previously created SQL statements that were saved to text files by using the **Load** button. You can also save statements using **Save**. The statement shown in Figure 26.6 will create a result set. Some SQL statements do not create a result set. These include the use of the **UPDATE, DELETE,** or **INSERT** statements. If a query string will result in a set of records, use the **Open** method to execute the query. The source-code listing below shows how the statement in this example can be executed.

```
with Query_StuCount do
  begin
    if not Prepared then
      Prepare;
    Open;
```

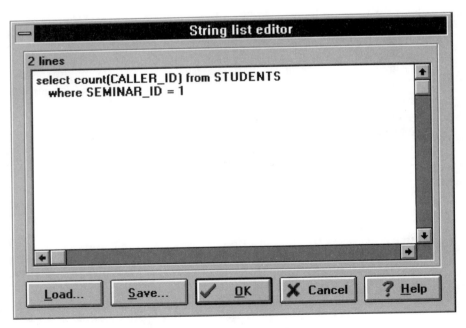

FIGURE 26.6 String List Editor with SQL Code

We use the **Prepared** property to determine if the query has been sent to the server for optimization. Any SQL statement must be optimized by the server to determine the most efficient way to handle the SQL request. Delphi automatically performs this operation each time the query is executed if you do not prepare the query manually. Since it is not very efficient to have your server optimize the same statement repeatedly, you should use the **Prepared** method before you first execute the query. Once this operation has been performed, you use the **Prepared** method to avoid doing it again.

TQUERY PARAMETERS

The example above used an SQL statement that selected a set of records from a table. The statement created a result set of one record that contained a count of those STUDENT records whose **SEMINAR_ID** was equal to one. This query would not be useful for any seminar that had number other than one. To make this query more useful, we can introduce a query parameter that can be changed to different values depending on the seminar we want. The new SQL statement will be the listing shown below.

```
select count(CALLER_ID) from STUDENTS
   where SEMINAR_ID = :ID
```

The last keyword in the select statement indicates that a parameter will be passed to the query and placed in the ID variable. To set parameter values at design time, select the **Params** property in the object inspector and launch the property editor. The dialog shown in Figure 26.7 allows you to set values for the parameters referenced within the SQL statement.

We have selected an Integer type for the parameter. We did not place a value for the

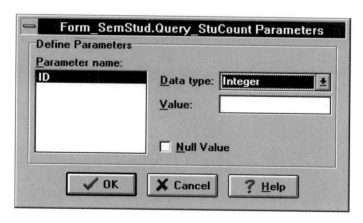

FIGURE 26.7 Query Parameters Dialog

parameter. We plan to do this at run-time. The **Params** property is a zero-based array of values that correspond with the parameter's position within the SQL statement. If you use three parameters within your SQL statement, the first parameter encountered within the string is referenced in the zero position in the array. The second and third parameters referenced will be stored in the first and second elements respectively. If you are unsure of the positions of your parameters within the **Params** array, just open the property inspector.

After assigning the parameter type, we must determine where within our application code we will assign the parameters and open the query. There are two ways to assign query parameters within code. You can use the ordinal position of the parameters within the **Params** property to assign them as shown below.

```
Query_StuCount.Params[0] := 1;
```

This method of assigning parameters is difficult to read and maintain. Should the parameter positions change, all code that references them by position will need modification. Also, using the ordinal positions makes it difficult for others to understand which parameter is being assigned without memorizing the parameter positions. A better alternative is to use the **ParamByName** method available within the **TParam** object class. Using this method, you assign parameters based on their names and not their positions. This makes code easier to read and maintain. The source-code listing below demonstrates the assignment of our ID parameter.

```
Query_StuCount.ParamByName('ID').AsInteger := 1;
```

We would like our SQL statement to always total the number of students in the seminar we are currently viewing within the form. We accomplish this by using the **OnData-Change** event contained within the TDataSource class. We utilize the seminar table's datasource to have the SQL statement re-execute each time the record changes within the seminar table. The event code for this is shown below. Notice that we used a TField object's value to assign the ID parameter.

```
procedure TForm_SemStud.DataSource1DataChange(Sender:
 TObject; Field: TField);
begin
  with Query_StuCount do
  begin
    if not Prepared then
      Prepare;
    Close;
    ParamByName('ID').AsInteger :=
        Table_SeminarSeminar_ID.Value;
    Open;
  end; { with }
end;
```

We invoke the **Close** method to allow the parameter value to change. After we change the value, we reopen the query. Displaying the resulting count on a form is simple. We create a TDBLabel component and assign its DataField property to the COUNT field in the query's resulting dataset. Like TTable components, you must use a TDataSource component to pass data through to your other data controls. Figure 26.8 displays the new form with the DBLabel component and its resulting value.

Since this query does not rely on record by record movement to count the students it results in less network traffic than methods using TTable objects. Once the user closes a form that uses a TQuery component, you should inform the server that the optimized query is no longer needed. You accomplish this using the **UnPrepare** method. Place the call to the **UnPrepare** method in the **OnClose** event for your form. The source-code listing below demonstrates this technique.

```
procedure TForm_SemStud.FormClose(Sender: TObject;
  var Action: TCloseAction);
begin
  { close and unprepare the query }
  Query_StuCount.Close;
  Query_StuCount.UnPrepare;
end;
```

If you are unfamiliar with the syntax of SQL code, you can use the Query designer that comes with the client/server version of Delphi. Use the right mouse button after selecting the query component on your form. The speedmenu will have a *Query Builder* option. Selecting this option will launch a driver/alias selection dialog. Select the alias for

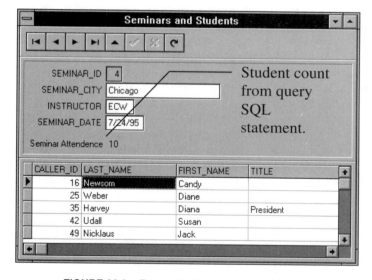

FIGURE 26.8   Form with SQL Query Result Shown

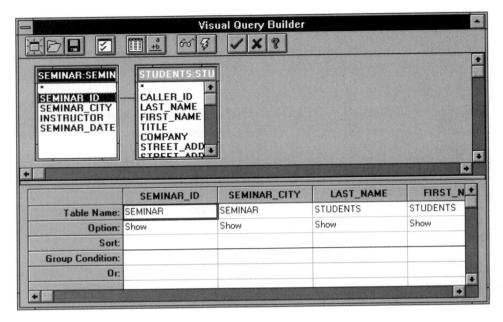

FIGURE 26.9   Visual Query Designer

the data for which you would like to create a query. For server-based tables you will have to also enter a password. Once you have completed this dialog, the query designer is presented. You must first select the table you want to base your query on from the *Add Table* dialog.

After you select the tables, you are presented with the dialog shown in Figure 26.9. From here you select fields from the tables by clicking on the appropriate name in the upper half of the designer. The browse window in the lower half shows the resulting data. By clicking and dragging the mouse from one table to another, you set relations between the tables. A line between the fields indicates a relationship. Other controls within the designer allow you to set query conditions and even see the resulting SQL code. Unfortunately, the designer does not allow you to see the current SQL code placed in a query component. *Do not use the designer if you have already created an SQL statement for your query.* It will eliminate any previous SQL code entered. The best way to store and retrieve SQL code using the query designer is to save the code to a file and restore from that file the next time you open the designer. Once you become comfortable with SQL code, you will more than likely shun the designer.

USING STORED PROCEDURES

The use of stored procedures is one of the advantages of using a database server. Stored procedures allow you to isolate data manipulation activity entirely within the server platform. This allows multiple applications to use the same code and forces consistency across the applications. Delphi provides an easy mechanism, the TStoredProcedure class, to access and execute stored procedures. We start by placing a stored procedure component on a form. The component, like TTables and TQueries, is a dataset subclass. We use it in the same fashion as we did the TQuery component. The only difference between them is that the SQL code for a stored procedure resides on the server. The application does not need to know how the code is written, only how to invoke it.

Once you place the stored procedure component on the form, assign the **Database-Name** property in the object inspector. If the database assigned references a server database that contains stored procedures, you can assign the component's Name property from the dropdown list to one of the available procedures. In our example, we assign the component to the SEMINAR_COUNT procedure created within our database. The listing below shows the SQL code needed to implement this procedure on an InterBase server.

```
Connect c:\tourdata\tourdata.gdb USER SYSDBA PASSWORD
"masterkey" ;

/* create a procedure for counting students in a seminar */
SET TERM !!;
CREATE PROCEDURE SEMINAR_COUNT (ID smallint)
RETURNS (Total smallint)
AS
BEGIN
   SELECT count(*) FROM STUDENTS
      WHERE SEMINAR_ID = :ID
      INTO :Total;
   SUSPEND;
END !!
EXIT;
```

An ISQL script file contains this code. Notice that the procedure accepts a single parameter called ID and returns a value called Total. Each of these is defined as a small integer type within the procedure. Unlike our query example, the stored procedure is designed to return a single value and not a result set. This requires us to use the component's **ExecProc** method to execute the procedure. Once the procedure is referenced by the component, you can assign and examine the required parameters by launching the editor for the **Params** property. This dialog is shown in Figure 26.10 with the **Total** parameter highlighted. While this is a return value, it is represented as an *Output* parameter within the designer.

Like the query components, we will want to assign the parameter values at runtime. This will allow the parameters to take on values corresponding to the current record. We use the same **Datasource** event to execute the stored procedure as we did with the query component. The listing below shows the use of the stored procedure within the **On-DataChange** event for the seminar table's datasource.

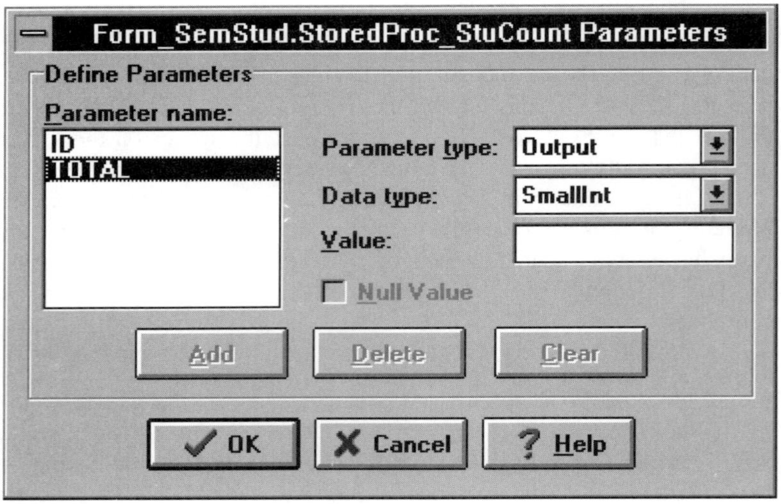

```
┌────────────────────────────────────────────────────────┐
│ ─  │   Form_SemStud.StoredProc_StuCount Parameters       │
├────────────────────────────────────────────────────────┤
│ ┌─Define Parameters──────────────────────────────────┐  │
│ │  Parameter name:                                    │  │
│ │  ┌──────────────┐   Parameter type:  ┌─────────┬──┐ │  │
│ │  │ ID           │                    │ Output  │ ± │ │  │
│ │  │ TOTAL        │   Data type:       ┌─────────┬──┐ │  │
│ │  │              │                    │ SmallInt │ ± │ │  │
│ │  │              │   Value:           ┌──────────── │  │
│ │  │              │                    │             │  │
│ │  │              │      ☐ Null Value               │  │
│ │  └──────────────┘                                   │  │
│ │      ┌────────┐   ┌────────┐   ┌────────┐          │  │
│ │      │  Add   │   │ Delete │   │ Clear  │          │  │
│ │      └────────┘   └────────┘   └────────┘          │  │
│ └────────────────────────────────────────────────────┘  │
│        ┌──────────┐  ┌───────────┐  ┌──────────┐         │
│        │ ✓  OK    │  │ ✗ Cancel  │  │ ? Help   │         │
│        └──────────┘  └───────────┘  └──────────┘         │
└────────────────────────────────────────────────────────┘
```

FIGURE 26.10   Stored Procedure Parameters Dialog

```
procedure TForm_SemStud.DataSource1DataChange(Sender:
TObject;
  Field: TField);
begin
{ Stored Procedure way }
  with StoredProc_StuCount do
  begin
    if not Prepared then
      Prepare;
    ParamByName('ID').AsInteger :=
Table_SeminarSeminar_ID.Value;
    ExecProc;
    Label_SPCount.Caption := ParamByName('TOTAL').AsString;
  end; { with }
end;
```

We optimized the stored procedure on the server in the same way as we did the query component. Because the stored procedure does not create a result set, we must use a TLabel component to display the resulting count. Once the procedure is executed, we merely assign the **Caption** property of the label to the resulting value.

Stored procedures must also be unprepared when they are no longer needed. As with the TQuery component, we use the form's **OnClose** event to handle this activity. The source-code listing below shows this simple task.

```
procedure TForm_SemStud.FormClose(Sender: TObject;
  var Action: TCloseAction);
begin
{ unprepare the Stored Procedure to free server resources }
  StoredProc_StuCount.UnPrepare;
end;
```

Stored Procedures versus Queries

Almost anything you can do with a TQuery can be accomplished with a stored procedure. Which is best? The answer depends on what you are trying to accomplish with your application. If you plan to create a server independent application that can run against most back-end servers, you should use queries. This makes your application portable and does not require the installation of your application to create procedures in the specific dialect of SQL that the user's server needs. For example, the procedure shown above would not work on a Microsoft SQL server because that server platform uses Transact SQL to implement procedures. Since this SQL version is different from ISQL, the procedure would have to be rewritten. Even using TQuery components, you will have to be careful to not use server specific SQL dialect features if you want your application to be portable.

If you know your application will be running against a specific server, stored procedures offer a speed and data consistency advantage. Using a procedure does not require the SQL string to be passed across the network since it already resides on the server. Also, having the procedure on the server allows other applications use them without duplicating effort. This also means that data definition changes will need to take place mostly at the server and be isolated from applications.

BATCHMOVE COMPONENTS

Another component that can be useful in the movement of data from one platform or database to another is the BatchMove component. Applications that require data replication can make use of this component to move data across platforms simply and easily. The BatchMove component is useful for backing up data from one disk to another. To use the component, you need to have two dataset components to use as source and destination for records. Set the **Source** and **Destination** properties on the BatchMove component to these component names.

In our sample application, we would like to back up our students table on a regular basis. We have added three new components to our main form (two TTable and one BatchMove component). The TTable components are each set to the live and backup tables for the student data. The BatchMove component will use these tables for its source and destination properties. Along with setting these properties we must also set the **Mode** property on the component. The BatchMove component can transfer data in a variety of ways. It can be used to append, update, copy, and delete records between the tables. In this case, we want to both update existing records and append new records that were added since the last backup.

The **Mode** property can be set to any of the following values: **batAppend, batUpdate, batAppendUpdate, batCopy** and **batDelete.** Since we want to both append and update, we set the **Mode** property to **batAppendUpdate**. To use either of the update settings, the destination table must contain an index on which to update records. You will always want to update based on the primary key in your source table. The source code to perform the backup is very simple and in shown in the listing below.

```
procedure TMainForm.BackupData1Click(Sender: TObject);
begin
  if MessageDlg('Want to backup Student Records?',
               mtConfirmation,
               [mbYes,mbNo],0) = mrYes then
    BatchMove_Stu.Execute
end;
```

We have added a menu option that prompts the user using the MessageDlg() routine. We call the **Execute** method if the user answers "Yes" to the question. You can test your BatchMove component in the design mode by double-clicking on it or using its speed-menu. That's all there is to it. The component has been designed to be as simple as possible to move and update records across tables. The tables used do not even have to be of the same type. You can move tables from a server platform to local tables and back again.

If your tables do not have the same field names, use the **Mappings** property to assign "to" and "from" field relationships. Use the **Mappings** property to update only certain fields as well. The **Mappings** property editor shown in Figure 26.11 demonstrates this use. Here we have only included a few fields from our source table to be mapped into the destination table. You must include any fields that are required in the destination table. In our case, all the fields listed in addition to the LAST_NAME and FIRST_NAME fields fall into this category.

Besides the properties already mentioned, there are a few that we must note. The **ChangedCount** property will contain the number of records processed in the **Execute** method. This will include the table's record count for update operations. You use the **RecordCount** property to specify a limit to the number of records processed during execution. If any records might cause data write errors or key violations in the destination table, you should use the **ProblemTableName** and **KeyViolTableName** properties.

The **ProblemTableName** property indicates the name of a local DB table that is created and contains the records that caused data write errors. These errors result from field length mismatches between the source and destination tables. A more common error is a key violation. Should the record being added or updated in the destination table cause a key violation, the **KeyViolTableName** indicates the name of the local DB table to contain these records. If either the **AbortOnProblem** or **AbortOnKeyViol** properties are TRUE, these tables will contain at most a single record because problems and violations will stop the execution of the data transfer.

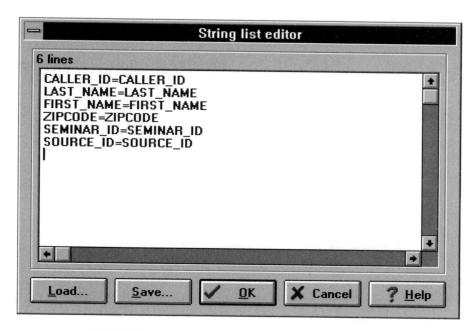

FIGURE 26.11   Mappings Values for TBatchMove Component

Using ODBC Drivers

Delphi allows you to use third party ODBC drivers to access data for your application. The open architecture of the BDE makes it simple to add new ODBC drivers so that applications can access and manipulate data from platforms beyond those supported with SQL Links. ODBC drivers are readily available for many database environments, including those already supported by SQL Links. Be careful in choosing an ODBC driver. They do not all support the same functionality and have varying performance specifications. We suggest using Borland's SQL Link drivers in most cases. They support all the back-end database features and can be distributed with your applications for no additional fees. The SQL Link drivers come with the client/server version of Delphi.

To use an ODBC driver you must install it under Windows and configure it using the ODBC Configuration Utility. This utility is located within the Windows Control Panel application. Figure 26.12 shows the utility.

The **Data Sources** dialog shows all the ODBC connections that you have created within your Windows environment. Each **Data Source** has an associated driver name listed with it. To create a data source, click on the **Add** button. You will be presented with the **Add Data Source** dialog from which you must select an installed driver type. The configuration utility presents you with the driver setup dialog once you have selected a driver. This dialog will vary depending on the driver type you have chosen. Figure 26.13 shows this dialog when a Microsoft SQL Server ODBC driver was selected from the driver list.

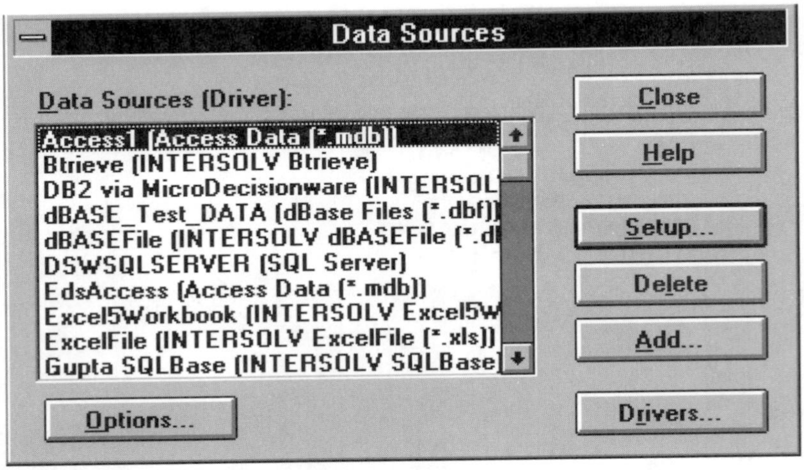

FIGURE 26.12   ODBC Configuration Utility

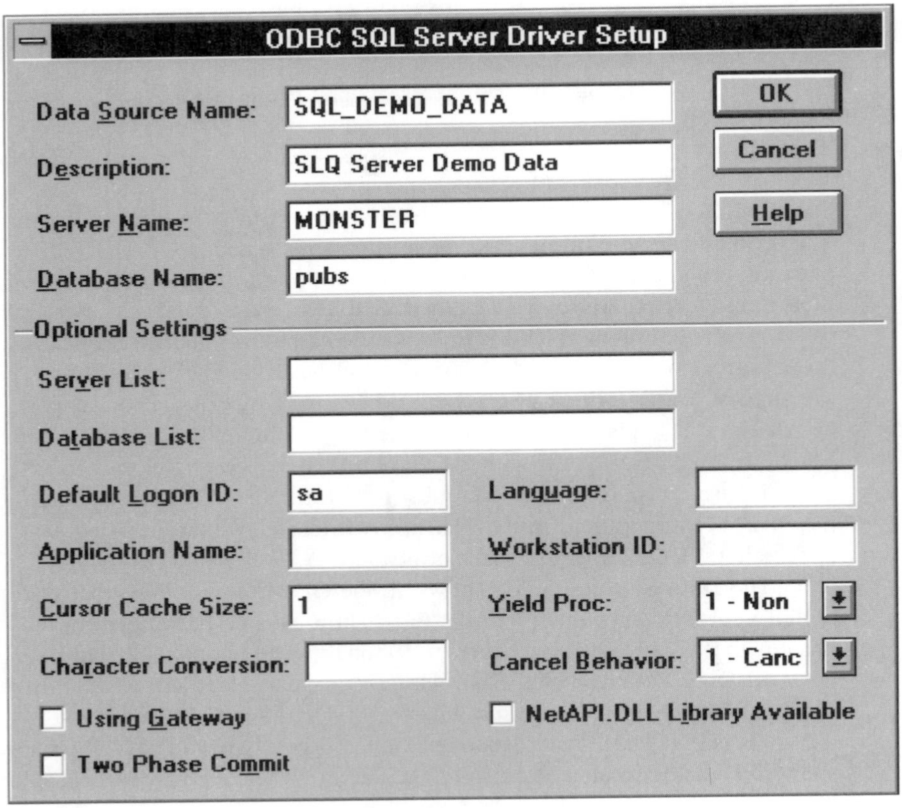

FIGURE 26.13   Microsoft SQL Server ODBC Driver Setup

You will need to enter whatever settings your server requires into this dialog. In Figure 26.13 we have set up the new data source to point to the pubs sample database that comes with Microsoft SQL Server. Some settings are optional and we left them blank in this example. You will always need to give your source a name. In this case we called our source SQL_DEMO_DATA. Your source settings can be changed later by using the Setup button on the main dialog.

After creating a data source, you must add the source as a new driver in your BDE configuration utility. The New ODBC Driver button allows you to perform this task. This step is a little confusing. You are not actually adding an ODBC driver. You are adding an ODBC data source. Each ODBC driver can be used to create several data sources. You must give the source a BDE name that always starts with ODBC_. Figure 26.14 shows the dialog you will use to add the new source.

You will need to identify the actual driver name and then select one of the sources for that driver. In this example, we are using an Intersolv SQLServer driver and have selected the SQL_DEMO_DATA source we created earlier. Once you click OK, the new source will show up in the driver list in the configuration utility. You will then need to create an alias for the driver under the alias page in the configuration utility.

The **Add New Alias** button launches a dialog that allows you to create an alias name and select the new ODBC BDE driver name you specified. Select the driver from the list and give the alias a name. Once you complete this step, you can use the new alias just like any other alias within your Delphi applications.

Be aware when using ODBC drivers that you may need to pay fees for each machine on which you install the driver. Also, since drivers are often not compatible, make sure that your ODBC driver allows for the maximum level of data type transfers for your

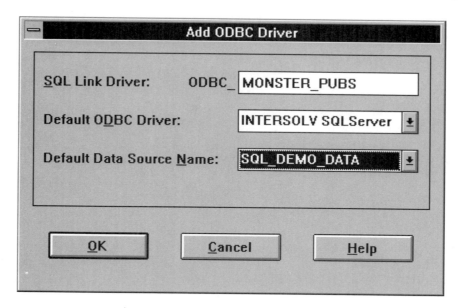

FIGURE 26.14   Add ODBC Driver BDE Dialog

server. For example, some drivers do not support the ability to pass BLOB data to the application or do not support the ability to call stored procedures. Generally, it is cost efficient to purchase the client/server version of Delphi and use the SQL Links drivers. They tend to be faster than most ODBC drivers and support the full range of communications between application and server.

INDEX

THERE ARE MANY BENEFITS WE CAN BRING TO YOUR ORGANIZATION

EXPERIENCE. The DSW Group, a SOFTWARE DESIGN AND DEVELOPMENT FIRM, founded in February, 1987, has extensive experience in meeting the customized software design, development and training needs of hundreds of organizations. We bring a total team of full-time employees to every design and development project and to every developer training project.

RAPID APPLICATION DEVELOPMENT. Because we use Object-Oriented development techniques for application development, we create custom Delphi applications which are produced faster and more error-free than applications created with conventional methods.

SIGNIFICANT LONG-TERM MONEY SAVINGS. Most organizations will spend more on maintenance than on the initial application development. We create custom Delphi applications that will reduce your total long-term costs by designing your software application from the ground up with easier maintainability and system extensibility.

YOUR DEVELOPERS CAN BENEFIT FROM OUR EXPERIENCE. Since our custom software developers ARE ALSO TRAINERS, and our trainers ARE ALSO DEVELOPERS, whether you have us do a project or have us train your developers, either way we can increase the effectiveness and efficiency of YOUR developers by bringing to your staff our greater expert knowledge and better understanding of how to use the Delphi development tool in which we specialize.

DELPHI CLIENT/SERVER PRODUCT COMPLETE WITH RAMP-UP TRAINING. As experts in Delphi, we can provide you Delphi Client/Server Product complete with the training and support that ensures fast-track start-up and usage of this new development tool, thereby leading to faster productivity in your organization.

OUR PHILOSOPHY IN SOFTWARE DESIGN AND DEVELOPMENT RELATED TO BOTH THE ORGANIZATION AND THE USER. Designing effective software applications that meet the needs of the client organization as well as the users is a creative intellectual art, which we excel at because of our focused specialization as a design firm. And every month, every year, that depth and breadth of focused expertise grows as we continue to design and develop more custom applications for a wide diversity of client organizations. Whether we do a complete design and development project for you or train your staff, your organization benefits from application work that reflects a high-level of craftsmanship and user-friendliness, meeting both the needs of the organization as well as the end-user.

The DSW Group, Ltd.
Toll-Free (800)-356-9644 * TEL (770)-953-0393 * FAX (770)-955-7238
1775 The Exchange, Suite 220
Atlanta, Georgia 30339-2016

The
DSW
Group, Ltd.

The authors are consultants and instructors for The DSW Group, Ltd. To reach the authors for questions or comments:

Ed Weber: 71620.3105@compuserve.com
Neal Ford: 72674.237@compuserve.com

About The DSW Group...

The DSW Group, founded in 1987, is a custom software design and development firm. We specialize in client or client/server Windows-based application projects, utilizing Borland's Delphi.

For the following services, telephone Sharon Sherman, Marketing Coordinator, at 1-800-356-9644

- Custom Delphi Client/Server Product Solutions
- Custom "Off-Site" Developer Training Seminars
- Custom "Our-Site" Hands-On Developer Training
- Custom "Your-Site" Hands-On Developer Training

For the following services, telephone David Carnell, Business Development Manager at 1-800-356-9644

- Custom Software Design
- Custom Software Prototyping
- Custom Application Programming
- Custom Software Tool Development
- Custom Developer Mentoring Services